Civil Society and Gl

C000056590

"Important and timely . . . thoughtful and constructive."
Andrew Crockett, *General Manager, Bank for International Settlements*

Davos, Genoa, Prague, Porto Alegre, Quebec, Washington: recent years have seen civil society take centre stage in the politics of global finance. NGOs, churches, trade unions, business associations, student groups and more have demanded their say in the way that global finance is governed. Enthusiasts have applauded this trend, while sceptics have deplored it. *Civil Society and Global Finance* brings together twenty leading activists, officials and researchers from five continents to provide rare authoritative assessments of the issue.

This collection shows that civil society plays an important and growing role in global finance: as a purveyor of information, as a source of moral energy, and as a spur to democracy. On the other hand, the competence and democratic credentials of civil society activism on global finance are not always secure. We are at an early stage of a development that will significantly shape future global governance. *Civil Society and Global Finance* suggests how this development can move forward in positive directions.

Jan Aart Scholte is Professor in the Department of Politics and International Studies and Associate of the Centre for the Study of Globalisation and Regionalisation at the University of Warwick. He is the author of *Globalization: A Critical Introduction, International Relations of Social Change*, and co-author of *Contesting Global Governance*.

Albrecht Schnabel is Academic Programme Officer in the Peace and Governance Programme of the United Nations University. He is the co-editor of *Conflict Prevention: Path to Peace or Grand Illusion?, Kosovo and the Challenge of Humanitarian Intervention, United Nations Peacekeeping Operations*, and editor of *Southeast European Security*.

Routledge/Warwick studies in globalisation

Edited by Richard Higgott and published in association with the Centre for the Study of Globalisation and Regionalisation, University of Warwick

What is globalisation and does it matter? How can we measure it? What are its policy implications? The Centre for the Study of Globalisation and Regionalisation at the University of Warwick is an international site for the study of key questions such as these in the theory and practice of globalisation and regionalisation. Its agenda is avowedly inter-disciplinary. The work of the Centre will be showcased in this new series.

This series comprises two strands:

Warwick Studies in Globalisation addresses the needs of students and teachers, and the titles will be published in hardback and paperback. Titles include:

Globalisation and the Asia-Pacific
Contested territories
Edited by Kris Olds, Peter Dicken, Philip F. Kelly, Lily Kong and Henry Wai-chung Yeung

Regulating the Global Information Society
Edited by Christopher Marsden

Banking on Knowledge
The genesis of the global development network
Edited by Diane Stone

Historical Materialism and Globalisation
Essays on continuity and change
Edited by Hazel Smith and Mark Rupert

Civil Society and Global Finance
Edited by Jan Aart Scholte with Albrecht Schnabel

Routledge/Warwick Studies in Globalisation is a forum for innovative new research intended for a high-level specialist readership, and the titles will be available in hardback only. Titles include:

Non-State Actors and Authority in the Global System
Edited by Richard Higgott, Geoffrey Underhill and Andreas Bieler

Globalisation and Enlargement of the European Union
Austrian and Swedish social forces in the struggle over membership
Edited by Andreas Bieler

Civil Society and Global Finance

Edited by
Jan Aart Scholte with
Albrecht Schnabel

First published 2002
by Routledge
11 New Fetter Lane, London EC4P 4EE

Simultaneously published in the USA and Canada
by Routledge
29 West 35th Street, New York, NY 10001

Routledge is an imprint of the Taylor & Francis Group

© 2002 Jan Aart Scholte with Albrecht Schnabel, editorial material and
the collection as a whole; the contributors, relevant chapters

Typeset in Baskerville by M Rules
Printed and bound in Great Britain by
Biddles Ltd, Guildford and King's Lynn

British Library Cataloguing in Publication Data
A catalogue record for this book is available from the British Library

Library of Congress Cataloging in Publication Data
Scholte, Jan Aart
    Civil society and global finance / Jan Aart Scholte with Albrecht
    Schnabel.
        p.   cm. – (Warwick studies in globalisation)
    Includes bibliographical references and index.
    1. International finance. 2. Civil society. 3. Globalization.
    I. Schnabel, Albrecht. II. Title. III. Series.

    HG3881 S3744 2002
    332′.042 – dc21   2001048815

ISBN 0–415–27935–6 (hbk)
ISBN 0–415–27936–4 (pbk)

Contents

Tables

Figures

Contributors

Gemma Adaba is the Representative of the International Confederation of Free Trade Unions (ICFTU) to the United Nations in New York. Previously, she was Director of the ICFTU/ITS (International Trade Secretariats) Washington Office, where she supported trade union policy and advocacy work *vis-à-vis* the Bretton Woods institutions. Before that, she held positions as Research Officer in the Economic and Social Policy Department of the Brussels-based ICFTU and as Assistant Secretary of the ICFTU/ITS Working Party on Multinational Companies. She has developed several policy papers for the ICFTU, including most recently *Globalizing Social Justice – the Challenge for the UN Millennium Summit* (September 2000) and *Harnessing Financial Resources for Shared Prosperity – ICFTU Statement to the Preparatory Committees for the Financing for Development UN High Level Event* (February 2001).

Gita Bhatt was with the IMF's External Relations Department as the NGO liaison official when her chapter was written. She now works with the IMF's Policy Development and Review Department. She has an MSc in Economics from the London School of Economics and a BA in Economics and Philosophy from George Washington University. She has also worked in India for a financial institution.

Nancy Birdsall is Senior Associate and Director of Economics Programs at the Carnegie Endowment for International Peace in Washington, DC. She was the Executive Vice President of the Inter-American Development Bank from 1993 until 1998. She holds a doctorate in Economics from Yale University and was previously Director of the Policy Research Department of the World Bank. Dr Birdsall has been a senior advisor to the Rockefeller Foundation and a member of various study committees of the National Academy of Sciences. She has written extensively about development issues, most recently on the causes and effects of inequality in a globalizing world.

Sandra Cesilini, a citizen of Argentina, holds a degree in Political Science. She joined the World Bank in 1995, and since 1998 has served as Social Development Specialist for Argentina, Chile and Uruguay. Based in Buenos Aires, her work involves the coordination and implementation of various activities, including the World Bank's liaison with civil society organizations, the development of poverty alleviation partnerships, evaluation of the possible social impacts of Bank-financed projects in the region, and indigenous peoples' programmes. Before joining the World Bank she was a Director in the Mother and Infant Nutrition Programme of the Argentine Ministry of Health.

Manuel Chiriboga, a citizen of Ecuador, studied Sociology at the Catholic University of Louvain, Belgium, and holds a diploma in Development Studies. He teaches at the Universidad Central del Ecuador. Currently he is the Executive Secretary of the Latin American Association of Advocacy Organizations (ALOP), a region-wide NGO network with forty-five members. He is also Chair of the International Forum on Capacity Building of Southern NGOs, former Chair of the NGO Working Group on the World Bank, and former Co-Chair of the World Bank NGO Committee. He is also a Steering Committee member of the Coalition against Hunger and Rural Poverty and a convener for the coordination of National and Regional NGO associations of Latin America.

John D. Clark has worked for the World Bank since 1992 as manager of the NGO and Civil Society Unit and as Lead Social Development Specialist for East Asia. Prior to joining the Bank, he worked for eighteen years for NGOs, mostly at Oxfam UK. During 2000–2 he is on sabbatical leave based at the Centre for Civil Society, London School of Economics, writing a book and serving on a Task Force advising the UK Prime Minister on Africa. He is the author of three books, including *Democratizing Development: The Role of Voluntary Agencies* (London: Earthscan and Kumarian, 1991).

Thomas C. Dawson II, a national of the United States, has been Director of the International Monetary Fund's External Relations Department since 1999. Previously he was a Director in the Financial Institutions Group of Merrill Lynch in New York. In 1989–93 he served as the Executive Director for the United States at the IMF. He was named Deputy Assistant Secretary for Developing Nations at the US Department of Treasury in 1981 and Assistant Secretary for Business and Consumer Affairs in 1984. Between 1985 and 1987 he served in the White House Chief of Staff's office. From 1971 until 1976 he was a US Foreign Service Officer, and from 1978 to 1981 he was a consultant with McKinsey and Co. A native of Washington, DC, he holds a bachelor's degree in Economics and an MBA from Stanford University.

Andrea Durbin is currently the National Campaigns Director for Greenpeace USA. Previously she was the International Program Director with Friends of the Earth for twelve years, based in the United States. In this position she led efforts to reform the international financial institutions, which included spearheading an NGO coalition to monitor private-sector lending of the World Bank Group. She has authored articles on globalization, finance and trade issues as they relate to the environment, testified before the US Congress, and served as an NGO Representative on the US delegation to the Organization for

Economic Cooperation and Development. She graduated with a degree in International Studies from the University of Washington in Seattle.

Zie Gariyo is Coordinator of the Uganda Debt Network, a leading civil society advocacy organization based in Kampala, Uganda. He holds a master's degree in Development Studies from the Institute of Social Studies, The Hague, and a Diploma in Development Studies from Cambridge University in the UK. He is also a Research Fellow of the Centre for Basic Research in Kampala. He has published on the NGO sector in East Africa and on the impact of structural adjustment programmes on low-income urban households. He is currently conducting research on the role of the Poverty Action Fund in poverty eradication in Uganda.

Barry Herman is Chief of the Finance and Development Branch in the United Nations Department of Economic and Social Affairs. His primary assignment is to support preparations for the "Financing for Development" conference in 2002. From 1995 to 1999, he had primary responsibility for the UN's annual *World Economic and Social Survey*. Before joining the UN Secretariat in 1976, he taught development and international economics. He holds a PhD from the University of Michigan and an MBA from the University of Chicago. He recently edited two books, *Global Financial Turmoil and Reform* and *International Finance and Developing Countries in a Year of Crisis* (with Krishnan Sharma), both published by UNU Press.

Kamal Malhotra has been Senior Civil Society Adviser at UNDP in New York since August 1999. He was Co-Founder and Co-Director (1995–99) of Focus on the Global South in Bangkok, known for its progressive policy work on democratizing global finance during and after the Asian crisis. In 1988–95 he was Director, Overseas and Aboriginal Program, Community Aid Abroad (OXFAM Australia). Before that, from 1982–88, he worked and lived in the Philippines. He has degrees in Development Economics, Business Management and International Affairs. He has published over fifty papers and articles and is the co-author or co-editor of a number of books, including *Reimagining the Future: Towards Democratic Governance* (Melbourne: La Trobe University, 2000) and *Global Finance: New Thinking on Regulating Speculative Capital Markets* (London: Zed, 2000).

James C. Orr is the president of James Orr Associates, a Washington-based management consulting and government relations company, which advises a group of international clients in the financial services industry, as well as foreign governments and international agencies. He also serves as Executive Director of the Bretton Woods Committee, a group of 600 corporate chief executives, former cabinet officials and other prominent Americans dedicated to increasing understanding of the international financial institutions. Previously he served as legislative counsel to the International Trade and International Development Subcommittees in the US House of Representatives. He holds an undergraduate degree in Economics from Wesleyan University and a master's degree in

International Economics from the School of Advanced International Studies, The Johns Hopkins University.

Albrecht Schnabel is an Academic Programme Officer in the Peace and Governance Programme of the United Nations University, Tokyo, Japan. He was educated at the University of Munich, the University of Nevada, and Queen's University, Canada, where he received his PhD in Political Studies in 1995. He has taught at Queen's University, the American University in Bulgaria and the Central European University. Recent edited books include *The Southeast European Challenge: Ethnic Conflict and the International Response* (with Hans-Georg Ehrhart, Baden-Baden: Nomos, 1999), *Kosovo and the Challenge of Humanitarian Intervention: Selective Indignation, Collective Action, and International Citizenship* (with Ramesh Thakur, Tokyo: UNU Press, 2000), *Conflict Prevention: Path to Peace or Grand Illusion?* (with David Carment, Tokyo: UNU Press, 2001) and *Southeast European Security: Threats, Responses, Challenges* (Huntingdon, NY: Novo Science Publishers, 2001).

Jan Aart Scholte is Professor in the Department of Politics and International Studies and Associate of the Centre for the Study of Globalisation and Regionalisation at the University of Warwick. Previously he held positions at the Institute of Social Studies, The Hague, and the University of Sussex, Brighton. He is author of *Globalization: A Critical Introduction* (Basingstoke: Palgrave, 2000) and *International Relations of Social Change* (Buckingham: Open University Press, 1993), as well as co-author of *Contesting Global Governance: Multilateral Economic Institutions and Global Social Movements* (Cambridge: Cambridge University Press, 2000). His current research explores the relationship between civil society and democracy in global economic governance.

Roberto Senderowitsch is a Regional Civil Society Consultant to the Latin America and Caribbean Region of the World Bank. He is also a Professor of Human Resource Management and Volunteers Development at the Universities of San Andrés and Di Tella, both in Buenos Aires. Previously he worked for the independent sector in Washington, DC, coordinating a programme for CIVICUS North America. He has extensive experience working in civil society organizations, both in Argentina and internationally, including a two-year assignment in Cuba. He holds a Master's in Policy Studies from the Johns Hopkins University and an equivalent degree in Educational Sciences from the University of Buenos Aires.

Nodari Alexandrovich Simonia is Director of the Institute of World Economy and International Relations (IMEMO) and Member of the Presidium of the Russian Academy of Sciences. He is the author of seventeen books and more than 200 articles, including *Civil Society and State* (Sapporo, 1997), *Development of Russia's Statehood* (Sapporo, 1997), *Bureaucratic Capitalism instead of Democracy* (Moscow, 1999), *Corruption and State* (Moscow, 2000) and *Economic Interests and Political Power in Post-Soviet Russia* (Oxford: Oxford University Press, 2001). His current research explores the formation of bureaucratic capitalism in contemporary Russia.

Irene van Staveren is Lecturer in Labour Economics of Developing Countries at the Institute of Social Studies, The Hague, where she works on gender and economics, labour economics, and ethics and economics. She has also worked for five years as an activist-researcher for the Dutch NGO, Oikos. She is a founding member of the Feminist Economics Network in the Netherlands (FENN) and a member of Women in Development Europe (WIDE). For WIDE, she is currently involved in teaching economic literacy courses and in developing indicators to assess the gender effects of bilateral trade agreements of the European Union. In 2000 her doctoral dissertation won the Gunnar Myrdal Prize, subsequently published as *The Values of Economics: An Aristotelian Perspective* (London: Routledge, 2001).

Alison Van Rooy is a Research Associate with the Ottawa-based North–South Institute, where she has written on the politics and advocacy of nongovernmental organizations and on the idea of civil society in development thinking. Building on doctoral research at Oxford, her publications include *Civil Society and the Aid Industry: The Politics and the Promise* (London: Earthscan, 1998) and the *Canadian Development Report: Civil Society and Global Change* (Ottawa: North–South Institute, 1999), as well as dozens of articles and studies that examine the future directions of civil society activism.

Carol Welch is Deputy Director of International Programs for Friends of the Earth–US. Previously she served as an international policy analyst for Friends of the Earth. She is responsible for FoE's advocacy campaigns on the international financial institutions and served on the Executive Committee of Jubilee 2000/USA. She has a bachelor's degree in Foreign Service from Georgetown University and a master's degree from the Fletcher School of Law and Diplomacy.

Yu Yongding is Professor of Economics and Director of the Institute of World Economics and Politics, Chinese Academy of Social Sciences. He has held various research positions at the Institute since joining it in 1979. He obtained a DPhil in Economics from Nuffield College, Oxford University, in 1994. He has published many papers on macroeconomics, international finance, regional economic cooperation and other economic issues. He is also author or co-author of six books on various economic issues.

Foreword

It gives me great pleasure to contribute the Foreword to this important and timely book, a result of collaboration between the Centre for the Study of Globalisation and Regionalisation at the University of Warwick and the Peace and Governance Programme of the United Nations University.

The functioning of the financial system has always had an important impact on economic welfare and has thus been a legitimate focus of political debate. In recent years, however, several factors have come together to further tighten the linkage between financial developments and social well-being: hence the growing relevance of the dialogue between civil society and those responsible for managing the financial system.

The financial system is, in a sense, the central nervous system of the economy. It directs real resources to end-users. If it does the job well, growth and employment are optimized. If it does it badly, the result is, at best, output forgone and, at worst, a costly crisis.

For several decades after the Second World War, financial systems were constrained by regulations imposed in the wake of the turmoil of the 1930s. Gradually, however, forces of deregulation and innovation led to much greater freedom for financial transactions, both within and between countries. This yielded enormous benefits in the form of more efficient services at lower cost. It facilitated greater savings mobilization and a better allocation of investment. As a result, living standards rose more rapidly than would otherwise have been the case, and whole regions (I think in particular of South-East Asia) have been moving out of poverty.

But there is also a darker side. Greater freedom in finance has been associated with greater excesses. Booms have been followed by busts. The financial cycle has arguably intensified the economic cycle.

Globalization in finance has broadened the benefits of a liberalized financial system but also sharpened the costs. We now need to find a better balance, to seek ways of dampening disruptive financial cycles without throwing away the benefits of efficient financial intermediation.

It is here that an intensified dialogue between civil society and those responsible for the operation of the financial system comes in. Civil society can sensitize the official sector to the practical hardships to which a malfunctioning financial system gives rise. And financial officials can explain the dilemmas they face in trying to reconcile efficiency and equity, growth and stability. Together, civil society and official circles can explore new ways of managing the financial system in ways that foster efficiency, while heading off damaging episodes of instability.

Hence the importance and timeliness of this volume. In my capacity as Chairman of the Financial Stability Forum, I have found considerable benefit in meeting representatives of civil society in a constructive search for improved balance in the functioning of the financial system. The development of standards and codes for the promotion of best practice in financial systems is one example of this cooperation. Standards and codes are at the centre of current efforts to strengthen the international financial system. But they have been developed by a variety of different bodies in ways that are not always fully transparent. The standards have drawn on expert professional input but have so far given less attention to building understanding in a wider constituency.

All this, to my mind, places a premium on developing channels of communication with a broad range of interested parties, including civil society. Where standards and codes are produced by restricted groupings, which may be unavoidable in highly technical subjects, it is important that genuine consultation and an open dialogue be established with those affected by their implementation. This includes official entities outside the "core" standard-setting membership, parliamentarians and civil society.

Doubtless, such consultation will be perceived as inadequate by some. But only by engaging in the process can we expect to improve over time. It is for that reason, among others, that I welcome this book and the thoughtful and constructive ideas set forth in its various contributions.

Andrew Crockett
General Manager, Bank for International Settlements

Acknowledgements

This book is the work of the Civil Society and Global Finance Project, a collaborative effort of the Centre for the Study of Globalisation and Regionalisation (CSGR) at the University of Warwick and the Peace and Governance Programme of the United Nations University (UNU). We are grateful to these institutions for their joint funding of the project and to Richard Higgott, Director of CSGR, and Ramesh Thakur, Vice-Rector of UNU, for their personal support of this initiative.

Next, our thanks go to the eighteen authors who have written for this volume. All of them are heavily engaged in advocacy, policy and research on questions of global finance. It is our privilege that they have taken time from their busy schedules to present richly detailed and critically reflective accounts of their fields of work. All the authors write in a personal capacity, with views that do not necessarily reflect the positions of the organizations that employ them.

The project first convened in a workshop at the University of Warwick in March 2000. In addition to contributions from most of the authors whose analyses are published here, this meeting obtained much-appreciated inputs from Ralph C. Bryant of the Brookings Institution, Pierre Cailleteau of the Financial Stability Forum Secretariat, Hidenori I of the Japan Center for International Finance, Inge Kaul of the United Nations Development Programme, Malcolm McIntosh of the Warwick Business School, Keith Muhakanizi of the Uganda Ministry of Finance, Sir Shridath Ramphal of the Commission on Global Governance, Ajay Sharma of the UK Department for International Development, and Karen Shepherd of the European Bank for Reconstruction and Development.

In April 2001 project results were presented in public forums at the United Nations in New York and the International Monetary Fund in Washington. We thank Jacques Fomerand, Mary Esther Leung and Ramon Ray of the UNU Office in North America for their help with the UN event. We thank Thomas Dawson, Gita Bhatt and Simon Willson for their help with the IMF forum. Terry Collins assisted us greatly with press contacts.

Throughout we have had indispensable support from CSGR and UNU staff. Denise Hewlett, Jill Pavey and Domenica Scinaldi have kept things in order from the Warwick side, while Yoshie Sawada has given organizational support at the Tokyo end. We further thank Monica Blagescu and Liliana Pop for their editorial assistance.

As ever, our families have borne many inconveniences that global research places on home life. We therefore thank Masha, Polly, Kathleen, Joseph, Rafael and Daniel as our foremost unofficial project participants.

Jan Aart Scholte
Albrecht Schnabel
Coventry and Tokyo, October 2001

Introduction

Jan Aart Scholte and Albrecht Schnabel

Recent decades have witnessed an unprecedented globalization of finance. Along with the traditional world money, gold, various national currencies, the euro, and the Special Drawing Right (SDR) have also become mediums of exchange, units of account, and stores of value across the planet. Moreover, most foreign exchange transactions now take place through telephone and computer networks in a round-the-world, round-the-clock market. In other financial transactions, too, most major banks, investment houses, pension funds, insurance companies, and hedge funds today operate in a global market. Concurrently a number of multilateral agencies have either newly emerged (like the International Organization of Securities Commissions, IOSCO) or expanded (like the International Monetary Fund, IMF) in order to monitor and regulate transworld financial flows.

Although the contemporary globalization of finance has yielded various efficiency gains, it has also brought problems. For example, large, frequent, and rapid swings in foreign exchange values have regularly destabilized the so-called 'real' economy. Meanwhile, transborder lending has saddled many poor countries with debilitating debt burdens. In addition, enormous and swift withdrawals of transborder portfolio investments have contributed to a succession of financial crises: in Latin America 1994–5, Asia 1997–8, Russia 1998, and Brazil 1999. A series of debacles in derivatives markets (e.g. Barings 1995, Long Term Capital Management 1998) have raised the spectre – albeit perhaps exaggerated – of a systemic financial collapse. Meanwhile, burgeoning offshore finance has greatly complicated efforts to achieve an equitable distribution of tax burdens.

The growth of global finance and its associated problems have attracted considerable and increasing attention in civil society over the past decade. Business associations, nongovernmental organizations (NGOs), research institutes, and trade unions have advanced countless proposals for adjustment or overhaul of the so-called 'global financial architecture'. NGOs, churches, and local community groups have mounted large and sustained pressure for debt relief in respect of poor countries, most prominently in the global Jubilee 2000 campaign pursued in 1996–2000. Mass street demonstrations have become a regular fixture at the Annual and Spring Meetings of the IMF and the World Bank, as well as successive summits of the Group of Eight (G8).

What are we to make of these new politics? How can and/or should civil society become involved in global finance? How may inputs from civil society contribute to and/or detract from efficient, stable, just and democratic operations of global finance?

This volume aims to shed light on these questions. It offers the first full-length examination of civil society and global finance. The role of civil society in contemporary global politics has attracted substantial research and comment, but the involvement of civil society in global finance more particularly has been largely neglected. True, several works have considered relations between NGOs and the multilateral development banks (MDBs),[1] and one of the directors of this project has explored relations between civil society and the IMF.[2] However, no previous work has assessed the actual and potential role of civil society in the wider problematic of global finance.

This study is therefore important. Global finance has become a key element in today's economy, and civil society has become a key element in today's polity. However, it remains far from clear how we can best govern global finance; nor do we yet have much idea what role civil society can and ought to play in this regard. This publication by no means pronounces the final word on these matters, but it is the first volume to lay out a breadth and depth of arguments and evidence on the subject.

The book is an outcome of the Civil Society and Global Finance Project, jointly sponsored by the Centre for the Study of Globalisation and Regionalisation at the University of Warwick and the Peace and Governance Programme of the United Nations University. This project has brought together two dozen leading thinkers and practitioners on the subject, representing a very broad range of experiences and views. Regionally, the contributors are drawn from Africa, Asia (East and South), Europe (East and West), Latin America, and North America. Sectorally, the participants come from academic, business, labour, NGO, and official circles. In terms of intellectual training, the authors include economists, political scientists, and sociologists. As for perspectives on civil society involvement in the governance of global finance, the group includes enthusiasts, sceptics, and agnostics.

The project participants met at the University of Warwick in March 2000 to discuss draft papers. They subsequently revised these writings to become the chapters that are published here. The rest of this introduction summarizes the main points that are raised in the various contributions to the book. First, however, we should consider our core terms.

Definitions

A project on 'civil society' and 'global finance' confronts major problems of definition. 'Civil society' and 'globalization' rank among the most contested concepts in contemporary political discussions. This is not the place to review those debates.[3] Moreover, it would be folly to impose precise and purportedly definitive conceptions of either term, particularly on a group as diverse as the contributors to this volume. Hence we have opted for broader and looser notions that individual authors can elaborate and specify as they see fit.

'Civil society' is understood in the present context as *a political space where voluntary associations seek deliberately to shape policies, norms, and deeper social structures.* In other words, civic groups (the individual elements of civil society) are nonofficial and nonprofit bodies that share an interest to reinforce, reform, or radically transform the rules that govern one or the other aspect of social life. The 'aspect of social life' in question here is global finance; hence the present book is concerned with voluntary groups that aim to affect the regulations, institutional arrangements, and values that reign in this realm.

Of course no definition is airtight. The lines between civil society, the market, and the public sector often blur in practice. However, on the whole, civic associations pursue neither public office nor commercial gain.

From the wide perspective adopted here, then, civil society encompasses efforts to shape rules through academic institutions, business forums, clan and kinship circles, consumer advocates, development cooperation initiatives, environmental movements, ethnic lobbies, faith-based circles, farmers groups, human rights promoters, labour unions, local community groups, peace movements, philanthropic foundations, professional bodies, relief organizations, think tanks, women's networks, youth associations and more. Clearly this notion of civil society stretches much wider than NGOs and other professional nonprofit organizations, although some of the contributors to this volume adopt a narrower conception.

Next, what is 'global' about global finance? Again, this is not the place to rehearse heated debates concerning the definition, measurement, chronology, causes, consequences, and policies of globalization. For present purposes it suffices to say that 'global' relations are those which connect people across the planet. At its most elementary, then, 'global' finance refers to the distribution and circulation of money, savings, and credits on a world scale.

The globalization of finance has several related attributes. For one thing it involves internationalization, with a major expansion of financial flows between countries. In addition, globalization involves liberalization, as states increasingly remove legal barriers to cross-border financial movements (like foreign-exchange restrictions and capital controls). Concurrently, globalization involves universalization, as certain instruments, rules, and procedures of modern finance spread to all corners of the earth. Finally, contemporary globalization involves deterritorialization, inasmuch as electronic financial flows through telecommunications and computer networks substantially transcend the geography of territorial places, territorial distances, and territorial borders.

Among other things, globalization has important implications for governance: that is, the ways that society manages collective issues. Prior to the contemporary upsurge of global relations, governance took a mainly statist form: that is, the management of collective affairs was invested overwhelmingly in territorial states. Globalization has upset that system. Now that many social relations – including a substantial proportion of financial transactions – operate within a world realm, governance mechanisms based on the state – rooted as it is in a limited territorial space – cannot by themselves be effective. Not surprisingly, then, recent decades have witnessed a proliferation and growth of interstate, trans-state, suprastate, and market-based governance mechanisms for finance alongside older, unilateral state arrangements. Chapter 1 of this volume reviews these developments in greater detail.

In turn, civil society organizations have since the 1980s increasingly questioned the adequacy of these post-statist governance arrangements for global finance and put forward proposals for improvement. Some civic groups have suggested only modest fine-tuning of the existing system, whereas others have advocated a complete overhaul. The contributors to this book consider a host of these civic initiatives, coming from different parts of the world, different parts of civil society, and different political persuasions.

General project findings

Drawing on their diverse experiences, participants in the Civil Society and Global Finance Project have had the common concerns to:

* *describe* the kinds of civil society activities that have transpired so far in respect of global finance;
* *assess* the fruits, unfulfilled potentials, and/or negative repercussions of civil society engagement with global finance to date; and
* *prescribe* what steps could help to maximize the benefits and minimize the shortcomings of civil society inputs with regard to global finance.

As might be expected given the diversity of their backgrounds and viewpoints, the twenty contributors to this book have not arrived at a consensus position: that is, beyond a general agreement that civil society involvement in global finance is an important question worthy of study. On the other hand, the chapters collectively do develop five general themes that recur throughout and integrate the book as a whole.

First, the contributors show that the 'civil society' which pursues questions of global finance is highly heterogeneous. For one thing, the features and depth of civil society vary considerably between, say, Argentina, China, the European Union, North America, Russia, and Uganda. In addition, civil society engages global finance through multiple and overlapping local, national, regional, and transworld networks. Moreover, different issues of global finance attract different assemblages of civil society actors (for example, the Third World debt crisis as against the supervision of derivatives markets). In short, we cannot speak of a single and uniform civil society in respect of global finance.

Second, the chapters collectively indicate that civil society actors differ considerably in the forms and extents of access that they obtain to market players and governance bodies in the area of global finance. On the whole, business forums and think tanks have enjoyed the easiest and closest contacts with corporate and official decision takers. In contrast, trade unions, church groups, and professional NGOs have usually needed to press hard to gain even limited entry into policy circles. Meanwhile, grassroots groups have tended to be shut out altogether. Across all sectors of civil society, associations based in the North have generally had greater access to influential actors in global finance than those based in the South and the so-called 'countries in transition'.

Third, in terms of civil society's impacts on global finance, the contributors to this volume repeatedly cite the significance of these voluntary associations both as a *source of information* and as a *spur to democracy*. By feeding in data, analysis, and opinion from society at large, civil society groups can offer an important 'reality check' for market bodies and governance institutions in global finance. In addition, civil society organizations can play an important role of public education about global finance and its governance. As a force for democracy in global finance, civil society can offer a platform to stakeholders who tend not to be heard through market and official channels. Civil society groups can also help to fill shortfalls of public transparency and accountability in global finance. These benefits of civil society engagement of global finance do not flow automatically, nor has practice always lived up to promise, but the proven and potential contributions are noteworthy.

Fourth, the chapters in this collection continually raise key issues of strategy and tactics that civil society actors confront as they deal with global finance. On the matter of objectives, for instance, civic groups face a critical choice between supporting the status quo, seeking incremental reform, or pursuing radical transformation of global finance. As for targets, civil society associations must determine whether they best focus their efforts on multilateral organizations, on national governments (particularly of the G8), or on leading financial corporations. Various strategic choices in regard to coalitions must also be made. For example, in what ways and how far can academic, business, labour, NGO, and religious elements of civil society collaborate? On what terms can South-based and North-based groups work together? As for campaigning style, civil society associations need to choose between – or in some way combine – public manifestations through the streets and the mass media on the one hand and quiet lobbying behind the scenes on the other.

Finally, a fifth recurrent theme in this group study concerns the legitimacy of civil society involvement in global finance. On what grounds, if any, could civil society have a recognized right to exert authoritative influence in the governance of global finance? Three broad bases might be distinguished: performance legitimacy, democratic legitimacy, and moral legitimacy.[4]

Performance legitimacy rests on technocratic criteria. In this case, civil society initiatives in respect of global finance might be deemed legitimate (or illegitimate) insofar as the actors in question hold (or lack) technical expertise regarding the workings of the sector. Civil society organizations derive performance legitimacy from their information, knowledge, competence, cost effectiveness, and so on.

Alternatively – or additionally – civil society's legitimacy can be assessed against democratic criteria. Civil society involvement might enhance public participation and public accountability in global financial governance. At the same time, to be democratically legitimate civil society actors would need to be suitably representative of the affected public. They would also require adequate mechanisms of participation, transparency and accountability in their own operations. Several of our authors raise the further intriguing question of whether direct civil society engagement of global governance agencies complements or undermines legitimate democratic authority through the state.

Finally, civil society actors can establish their legitimacy on moral grounds. They can pursue noble objectives and fulfil the role of a (global) social conscience. They can promote the public interest and the common good, especially against arbitrary privilege and abusive power. Arguably, civil society campaigns on social protection, ecological integrity, cultural pluralism, equitable distribution, and democracy in global finance have often met this criterion.

The chapters of this book develop the general themes just surveyed in various combinations and in different directions. In taking contrasting positions on the issues, the contributors aptly reflect the current state of the wider debate on civil society and global finance. We hope that the Civil Society and Global Finance Project will advance that debate, contributing not only academic knowledge, but also ideas for more effective and meaningful collaboration between civil society actors, market organizations, and governance bodies.

As such, this volume has a pronounced policy orientation. Indeed, most of the authors are practitioners who bring a rich insider's perspective on the challenges at hand. Although each chapter is carefully conceived, the book does not claim – and has not aimed – to offer the particular kind of academic rigour and finesse that characterizes professional research monographs. The distinctive and valuable contribution of *Civil Society and Global Finance* is the presentation of reflective assessments by experienced practitioners themselves.

Chapter overview

The sixteen chapters in the volume are grouped into five parts. The first part, on General Issues, comprises a chapter by Jan Aart Scholte that reviews the historical evolution and broad policy concerns of civil society's engagement of global finance. The chapter surveys the globalization of finance, its governance, and the rise of civil society interest in these problems. Following this general overview, other chapters show how different parts of civil society in different parts of the world have taken different kinds of initiatives to address different aspects of global finance.

In part two of the book, five chapters examine civil society engagement of global finance in different regions. In Chapter 2, Manuel Chiriboga, Executive Secretary of the Latin American Association of Advocacy Organizations (ALOP), based in Quito, discusses the evolution of advocacy efforts of Latin American NGOs in respect of multilateral financial institutions and the challenges that these groups face in constructing their own regional and national agendas. In Chapter 3, Zie Gariyo, Coordinator of the Uganda Debt Network, considers how civil society organizations in Africa have mobilized on global financial issues, with the particular example of the Poverty Reduction Strategy Paper consultations in Uganda. In Chapter 4, Kamal Malhotra, Senior Civil Society Adviser at the United Nations Development Programme, draws on his earlier experience as co-director of Focus on the Global South in Bangkok to discuss civil society activities in the Asian financial crisis of the late 1990s. In Chapter 5, Nodari Simonia, Director of the Institute of World Economy and International Relations of the Russian Academy of Sciences in Moscow, assesses the role of 'uncivil society' in Russia's unhappy experiences with global finance after the dissolution of the Soviet Union. In Chapter 6, Yu Yongding, Director of the Institute of World Economics and Politics at the Chinese Academy of Social Sciences in Beijing, considers the so far limited responses of civil society in China to global finance.

In part three of the book the microphone passes to official circles, with four contributions from multilateral institutions. In Chapter 7, John Clark, Lead Social Development Specialist at the World Bank, examines how civil society has come to play an influential role in shaping Bank policies and programmes, and the dilemmas and challenges that this trend presents to both parties. In Chapter 8, Roberto Senderowitsch and Sandra Cesilini, World Bank staff working on Argentina, complement Clark's general overview of Bank practices regarding civil society with a field perspective, looking in particular at the consultative processes undertaken when formulating the latest Country Assistance Strategy for Argentina. In Chapter 9, Thomas Dawson and Gita Bhatt of the External Relations Department at the International Monetary Fund look at the evolution of the IMF–civil society dialogue and its likely future intensification. In Chapter 10, Barry Herman, Chief of the Finance and Development Branch at the United Nations Secretariat, explores the involvement of civil society organizations in the current UN initiative on Financing for Development.

The fourth part of the book offers four views from different sectors of civil society: organized labour, business forums, environmental movements, and women's associations. (Academic institutes and development NGOs have a hearing in parts one and two.) In Chapter 11, Gemma Adaba of the International Confederation of Free Trade Unions examines the labour movement's engagement of global financial institutions on a range of economic and social issues. In Chapter 12, James C. Orr, Executive Director of the Washington-based Bretton Woods Committee, considers the experiences of business associations that have attempted to influence global financial governance. In Chapter 13, Andrea Durbin and Carol Welch of the International Program of Friends of the Earth–US analyse the efforts of the environmental movement to influence multilateral economic institutions and global financial flows to promote ecological sustainability. In Chapter 14, Irene van Staveren of the Institute of Social Studies, The Hague, and Women in Development Europe, Brussels, assesses the gender dimensions of global finance and the initiatives of women's movements in respect of these issues.

The fifth and final part of the book contains two contributions that explore ways forward for civil society engagement of global finance. In Chapter 15 Alison Van Rooy, Associate of the Ottawa-based North–South Institute, outlines key questions and presents several future scenarios, anticipating in particular that civic associations could obtain a more formal and direct role in policymaking around global finance. In the concluding chapter Nancy Birdsall, Director of Economics

Programmes at the Carnegie Endowment for International Peace in Washington, assesses the possible contributions of civil society with regard to improving democratic representation in global financial governance.

N.B. All $ figures in this book refer to United States dollars.

Notes

1 Paul J. Nelson, *The World Bank and Non-Governmental Organizations: The Limits of Apolitical Development*, London: Macmillan, 1995; Jonathan A. Fox and L. David Brown (eds), *The Struggle for Accountability: The World Bank, NGOs, and Grassroots Movements*, Cambridge, MA: MIT Press, 1998; Gabriel Casaburi, María Pia Riggirozzi, María Fernanda Tuozzo and Diana Tussie, 'MDBs, Governments and Civil Society: Chiaroscuros in a Triangular Relationship', *Global Governance*, Vol. 6, No. 4 (October–December 2000), pp. 493–517.

2 Jan Aart Scholte, '"In the Foothills": Relations between the IMF and Civil Society', in Richard A. Higgott, Geoffrey R.D. Underhill and Andreas Bieler (eds), *Non-State Actors and Authority in the Global System*, London: Routledge, 2000, pp. 256–73.

3 On concepts of civil society see, e.g., Jean L. Cohen and Andrew Arato, *Civil Society and Political Theory*, Cambridge, MA: MIT Press, 1992. On globalization debates see, e.g., David Held and Anthony McGrew (eds), *The Global Transformations Reader: An Introduction to the Globalization Debate*, Cambridge: Polity Press, 2000; and Frank J. Lechner and John Boli (eds), *The Globalization Reader*, Oxford: Blackwell, 2000.

4 See further L. David Brown *et al.*, 'Civil Society Legitimacy: A Discussion Guide', in Brown (ed.), *Practice-Research Engagement and Civil Society in a Globalizing World*, Cambridge, MA: Hauser Center for Nonprofit Organizations, Harvard University, 2001, pp. 63–79.

Part I

General issues

1 Civil society and the governance of global finance

Jan Aart Scholte[1]

Summary	
• Introduction	11
• Globalization and governance	12
• Financial globalization	15
• Governance of global finance	17
• Key issues for the governance of global finance	20
• Civil society initiatives on global finance	22
• Civil society and global finance: potential benefits	24
• Civil society and global finance: possible problems	26
• Conclusion	29

Introduction

Civil society has figured with increasing prominence in the recent history of global governance. The Secretary-General of the United Nations, Kofi Annan, has declared that "there are few limits to what civil society can achieve," while the President of the World Bank, James Wolfensohn, has affirmed that "civil society is probably the largest single factor in development."[2] The recently retired Managing Director of the International Monetary Fund, Michel Camdessus, has similarly applauded "the valiant efforts of NGOs" in the area of social development.[3]

Such public pronouncements are perhaps tinged with hyperbole, but it is clear that civil society matters in contemporary world politics. Countless civil society organizations (CSOs) have taken initiatives to shape global rules and institutions.[4] Most major transworld governance agencies have established special mechanisms for interaction with civil society bodies.[5] Various theorists of world politics have in this regard described the emergence of an "enlarged" or "complex" multilateralism marked by intricate networks of relationships between state, substate, suprastate, and nonstate actors.[6]

Yet, as the Introduction to this book notes, very little research to date has considered the role of civil society in one of the principal areas of contemporary globalization, namely finance. Various previous studies have assessed the involvement of civil society associations in other issues of global governance, including the HIV/AIDS challenge, humanitarian relief, the status of women, and trade.[7] However, the nexus of civil society and global finance has been left largely unexplored.

The task of this opening chapter is to outline some general parameters for an investigation of civil society engagement of global finance. The first section below describes certain changes in governance, consequent upon contemporary globalization, that have encouraged the rise of civil society activity in world politics. The second and third sections review, respectively, globalization in the realm of finance and the arrangements that have emerged to govern it. The fourth section identifies the main policy challenges that currently face the governance of global finance, while the fifth section surveys the initiatives taken by civil society actors to meet these challenges. The final two sections outline potential benefits as well as possible problems of civil society activity in the area of global finance.

In short, this general chapter sets the scene for more specific investigations of civil society and global finance. Subsequent parts of the book offer accounts of concrete experiences from different regions of the world, different governance institutions, different sectors of civil society, different disciplinary perspectives, and different political persuasions. Collectively, these analyses offer rich evidence for determining to what extent the promises and perils of civil society involvement in global finance have been realized in practice thus far and how maximum benefits might be achieved in the future.

Globalization and governance

Globalization means many things to many people, but most will agree that, broadly speaking, the trend involves a growth of social connections on a planetary scale. As noted in the Introduction to the present volume, this greater interconnectedness has several aspects. For one thing, globalization brings increased interaction and interdependence between countries: there is more international communication, investment, trade, and travel. In addition, globalization involves reductions in statutory barriers to cross-border flows: fewer tariffs, fewer foreign-exchange restrictions, fewer capital controls, and (at least for citizens of some states and certain classes of workers) fewer visa requirements. Furthermore, globalization increases the numbers of objects and experiences that spread to most, if not all, corners of the inhabited earth: the Gregorian calendar, McDonald's restaurants, etc. And, with globalization, people acquire various social connections that largely transcend territorial geography, for example, in regard to telecommunications and global ecological changes.

Thus globalization has several interrelated facets: internationalization, liberalization, universalization, and deterritorialization. Different commentators give one or the other of these aspects more attention. My own emphasis goes to the fourth: that is, globalization as the proliferation and expansion of relatively deterritorialized spaces. Global relations can on these lines be characterized as "supraterritorial", "transworld", or "transborder" relations.[8]

This is not to discount the reality and importance of present-day international-ization, liberalization, and universalization. However, these three tendencies have appeared in substantial measure in earlier history, long before talk of "globaliza-tion" became popular in the late twentieth century. Concepts of globality give new, distinctive and important insights into the contemporary world when they are for-mulated in terms of supraterritorial connectivity. In global relations of this kind, terrestrial distances can be covered in effectively no time, and territorial frontiers present no particular impediment. Thus supraterritorial connections unfold in the world as a single place.

Supraterritoriality has become commonplace for hundreds of millions of people in recent decades. For example, humanity is today interconnected through over a billion telephone lines, a billion television sets, two billion radio receivers, and 250 million Internet users.[9] At the same time the contemporary world is marked by per-vasive transborder production processes, global marketing of thousands of goods and services, unprecedented levels of anthropogenic transworld ecological changes, a substantial rise of global consciousness among people, and (as elaborated below) an immense globalization of finance.

To be sure, global relations have spread unevenly. They have concentrated more in countries of the North, in professional and wealthier classes, and in urban cen-tres relative to rural areas. However, globalization has left few inhabitants of today's world completely untouched.

Nor does this globalization thesis maintain that territorial spaces no longer matter. On the contrary, territorial economies, territorial governments, and terri-torial identities continue to exert very significant influences on contemporary society. However, social geography is today no longer *wholly* territorial. We have moved from a territorial*ist* world to one where territorial realms co-exist with (rapidly expanding) global spaces.

This reconfiguration of geography has far-reaching implications for governance, that is, the ways that people manage their collective affairs. Global flows defy effective management through the statist mode of governance that prevailed during most of the twentieth century. The old model of sovereign statehood – where a centralized national government holds singular, comprehensive, supreme, and absolute authority over a given territory – is plainly not suitable for the man-agement of transborder air traffic, transworld disease, and many other policy matters, including supraterritorial finance. Contemporary governance has to entail more than government as traditionally understood.

This is not to suggest that states are on the verge of demise. On the contrary, most states across the world are today as large and active as ever. However, it is equally clear that territorially discrete states cannot by themselves effectively handle the many and large global flows that impact upon their jurisdictions. Major inno-vations are necessary in the ways that we manage many problems of collective concern. Indeed, globalization has already prompted some shifts in the contours of governance, trends that seem likely to unfold further in the future.

For instance, states in the contemporary globalizing world have increasingly turned from unilateral to multilateral approaches to many policy issues. This trend has been apparent in, among other things, the expansion of interstate consultations at ministerial level, including special conferences of the United Nations (UN) since the 1960s and meetings of the Group of Seven (G7) since the 1970s. The rise of multilateral governance has also occurred through the growth of transstate networks, where civil servants from parallel agencies in multiple states develop close regulatory collaboration in a particular policy area.[10]

In addition, multilateral governance has seen considerable transfers of regulatory competence to permanent suprastate institutions. Some of these agencies, like the European Union (EU), have a regional scope. Others, like the International Monetary Fund (IMF), operate on a transworld scale. "Suprastate" does not mean "nonstate", in the sense that these agencies have gained full independence from and control over their state members. However, like most organizations, suprastate bureaucracies have acquired some initiative and power of their own, particularly in respect of weaker states.

Globalization has encouraged not only a shift of many regulatory competences "upwards" to suprastate bodies, but also various moves "downwards" to substate agencies. In recent decades most states have pursued some degree of devolution from national to provincial and local authorities. Sometimes these transfers have been specifically prompted by a judgement that certain global problems (for example, transborder crime or transworld ecological degradation) can in some respects be tackled more effectively at a substate level.

Along with the dispersion of authority "upwards" and "downwards" from the state, globalization has also promoted "lateral" shifts of governance from the public sector to nonofficial quarters.[11] This privatization of governance has transpired, for example, in increased reliance on nongovernmental organizations (NGOs) to implement development cooperation projects and several multilateral environmental agreements. As detailed below, considerable private governance has also arisen in respect of global finance.

Together, the developments just described have brought an end to the statist governance that accompanied the territorialist geography of old. Theorists have variously dubbed emergent circumstances as "multilayered", "post-sovereign", "post-Westphalian", "neo-medieval", or "networked" regulation. Whatever label one applies to it, governance in the context of contemporary globalization is different from the territorialist-statist mode that predominated for some 300 years from seventeenth-century Europe to the mid-twentieth-century world.

Much post-statist governance of global relations remains ad hoc, experimental, and problematic. On the technical side, the new conditions of more dispersed authority have raised major challenges of efficiency and coordination. On the normative side, globalization has raised substantial challenges to human security, social justice, and democracy. Indeed, it is widely felt that currently prevailing approaches to the regulation of global spaces are wanting on both efficiency and normative grounds.

These circumstances have spurred a notable growth of civil society involvement in the governance of global relations. As already indicated, in certain cases civil society associations have even acquired the role of direct policy executors.

More often, civil society organizations like business forums, local community associations, NGOs, religious groups, think tanks, and trade unions have pursued advocacy campaigns to improve the capacities of governance to deliver efficiency, stability, equity and/or democracy in respect of global flows. Frustration with these governance deficits has in recent years drawn substantial numbers of civil society critics into a so-called "anti-globalisation movement" that has attracted much media attention.[12]

This rise of civil society activism has had a mixed reception. Enthusiasts have placed high hopes on the contributions of civil society to enhance management of global issues with invaluable information and expertise as well as greater democratic credentials and more equitable policy outcomes. Other commentators have been less sanguine. For the sceptics, civil society interventions in global governance tend to be disruptive, ill-informed, unrepresentative, self-serving, and unaccountable. These potential positive and negative effects are elaborated in the final sections of this chapter.

Financial globalization

Before proceeding to that step, however, we should relate the general themes just outlined concerning globalization and governance to the specific area of finance. Indeed, the financial sector has shown some of the most far-reaching globalization in recent history.[13]

For one thing, globalization has given certain monies a substantially supraterritorial character. Several national denominations like the US dollar and the Japanese yen have become global currencies. They circulate just about everywhere on earth and move instantly by electronic transfer anywhere in the world. In addition, the euro and – on a much more limited scale – the Special Drawing Right (SDR) have emerged through the EU and the IMF, respectively, as suprastate monies with transworld use. Many bankcards (such as those connected to the Cirrus network) can extract cash in local currency from over 400,000 automated teller machines across the planet. Meanwhile, global credit cards like Visa and MasterCard are used to make payments at millions of establishments spread over 200 jurisdictions.

Financial globalization has also transpired in the ways that money circulates. For instance, foreign-exchange trading today occurs through a round-the-world, round-the-clock market that connects dealing rooms in London, New York, Tokyo, Zürich, Frankfurt, Hong Kong, Singapore, Paris, and Sydney. The average daily volume of foreign exchange transactions reached $1,500 billion in 1998, up from $100 billion in 1979.

In global banking, the world total of bank deposits owned by nonresidents of a given country rose from $20 billion in 1964 to $7,900 billion in 1995, including several trillion dollars' worth in offshore accounts. Electronic payments through the Society for Worldwide Interbank Financial Telecommunications (SWIFT), founded in 1977, averaged more than $5,000 billion per day in 1999. Outstanding balances on syndicated transborder bank loans rose from under $200 billion in the early 1970s to almost $10,400 billion in 1990, and new facilities of this kind reached $1,100 billion in 1997.[14]

Other global lending has occurred on a notable scale through official financial institutions. For example, the IMF has provided balance of payments support to its member governments, occasionally (as in the cases of Korea in 1997 and Russia in 1998) to the tune of tens of billions of dollars. A number of multilateral development banks (MDBs) have emerged since the 1940s, including the World Bank Group, the Islamic Development Bank, and regional development banks for Africa, the Americas, Asia, the Caribbean, and Europe. With the huge growth of private global finance, MDB loans amount to but a tiny proportion of the total of transborder credit flows. However, the MDBs remain the principal source of global finance for many poor countries.

Contemporary securities markets have also acquired substantial supraterritorial attributes. For example, bonds, medium-term notes, and short-term credit instruments have a global character when they are denominated in a transworld money and involve borrowers, investors, managers and/or exchanges that are spread across multiple countries. The largely supraterritorial eurobond market grew from its inception in 1963 to a level of $371 billion in new borrowings in 1995. The net issuance of all cross-border bonds and notes reached $1,157 billion in 1999.[15] In stock markets, various companies have developed global share listings, that is, on several exchanges spread across the world. Meanwhile, electronic communications have enabled investors and brokers instantly to transmit and execute orders to buy and sell securities anywhere in the world. The two main clearing houses for transborder securities trading, Euroclear and Clearstream (formerly Cedel), together accumulated an annual turnover of nearly $60,000 billion in 1999.

Additional globalization has occurred in respect of financial derivatives, an industry that has burgeoned since the early 1970s. Traditionally, instruments like forwards, futures, and options mainly "derived" from agricultural and mineral commodities, but more recently huge global markets have developed in derivative contracts related to foreign-exchange rates, interest levels, securities prices, stock market indices, and other financial indicators. Several derivatives exchanges (for example, London–Singapore and Chicago–Sydney) have established direct links to enable round-the-world, round-the-clock dealing in certain futures and options. The notional amount of outstanding over-the-counter financial derivatives contracts alone (thus excluding exchange-based derivatives) reached $88,200 billion at the end of 1999.[16]

Finally, much contemporary insurance business has gone global. Countless insurance policies have global coverage, are denominated in a global currency and/or are handled by global companies in global financial centres. Meanwhile, insurance brokers have developed networks that allow them to transact business across the planet from their office computers.

In sum, much contemporary finance has a supraterritorial character that was barely, if at all, evident before 1960. Territorial places, distances, and borders are not irrelevant in today's banking, securities, derivatives and insurance industries, but many of these activities also substantially transcend territorial geography.

Moreover, the sums of business in global finance are staggering, dwarfing the numbers associated with sales turnover in other sectors of the global economy. It is understandable in this light that many worries regarding "globalization out of control" have concerned finance.

Governance of global finance

Global finance is obviously not "controlled", in the sense of being ruled by a sovereign world government; nevertheless, these activities are subject to considerable, if imperfect, governance. Recent developments in the regulation of global finance largely conform to the general trends in contemporary governance noted earlier. In other words, states remain key, but they have increasingly adopted strategies of multilateral (both interstate and suprastate) management of transworld finance. In addition, substate actors have begun to figure in this realm, albeit still marginally. Also, regulatory mechanisms based in private-sector agencies have gained substantial significance in the governance of global finance. The following paragraphs elaborate these points in turn.

States are still, on the whole, the primary actors in the governance of finance under conditions of contemporary globalization. Any examination of the management of global finance must therefore consider the activities of national central banks, national treasuries, national securities and exchange commissions, and national insurance supervisors. Of course, some states (like France and the USA) have figured more prominently and powerfully in the governance of global finance than others (like Uzbekistan and Zambia). Indeed, limited capacity for financial regulation at national level has left many states in a very weak position *vis-à-vis* global finance.

Yet even the strongest states have not tackled the governance of global finance alone. Multiple networks of intergovernmental consultation and cooperation have developed in tandem with the accelerated globalization of finance during recent decades. For example, central bank governors of the so-called "Group of Ten" (G10)[17] advanced industrial countries have met regularly at Basle since 1962 to discuss monetary and financial matters of mutual concern. An Intergovernmental Group of Twenty-Four on International Monetary Affairs (G24) was established in the early 1970s as a South-based counterpart to the G10, though it has held far less influence.[18] The G7 summits, held annually since 1975, have also frequently discussed issues related to global finance.[19] A separate G7 finance ministers' group was established in 1986 and normally meets three to four times per year. In September 1999 the G7 finance ministers created the Group of Twenty (G20) in order to include governments of so-called "emerging markets" in structured discussions concerning global financial stability.[20]

Both the G10 and the G7 have from time to time set up working parties to explore specific issues related to global finance. The best-known example is the Basle Committee on Banking Supervision (BCBS), formed as a standing group of the G10 in 1975.[21] Most significantly, the BCBS has formulated the Basle Capital Accord, a framework first issued in 1988 for assessing the capital position of transborder banks, and Core Principles for Effective Banking Supervision, published in 1997. On a more specific problem, the G7 created the Financial Action Task Force (FATF) in 1989 to combat drug-related money laundering.[22] More recently, the G7 has promoted the establishment of a Financial Stability Forum (FSF), first convened in April 1999. The FSF is meant to enhance information exchange and cooperation among states in the supervision and surveillance of commercial financial institutions.[23]

As the existence of such working groups indicates, much intergovernmental collaboration on policy regarding global finance has occurred among civil servants rather than at a ministerial level. Other significant transgovernmental links among financial technocrats have developed through the so-called Paris Club (with a secretariat in the French Treasury since 1974) that convenes from time to time to reschedule the bilateral debts of Southern states. Other transgovernmental groups have met under the auspices of the Organization for Economic Cooperation and Development (OECD), for example, to formulate measures in respect of financial liberalization, offshore finance centres, taxation of transborder portfolio investments, and development assistance. The OECD has also housed the secretariat of the FATF. In respect of bond and stock markets more particularly, the International Organization of Securities Commissions (IOSCO) was created as an inter-American body in 1974, went global in 1983, and now involves nearly 100 national securities authorities.[24] In addition, the International Association of Insurance Supervisors (IAIS) was formed in 1994 and has quickly grown to link authorities in over 100 countries.[25] Since 1996 the BCBS, IAIS, and IOSCO have convened a Joint Forum on Financial Conglomerates to promote cooperation between banking, securities, and insurance supervisors, given that global financial corporations increasingly operate across the three sectors.

As the work of the OECD, IOSCO, and IAIS illustrates, intergovernmental collaboration in respect of global finance is being increasingly institutionalized in permanent suprastate bodies. The oldest such agency, the Bank for International Settlements (BIS), dates back to 1930, but it has become especially active in recent decades. The voting membership of the BIS has increased to 45 national central banks, and the institution has other dealings with several score more. The BIS convenes several influential working groups, including the Committee on the Global Financial System and the Committee on Payment and Settlement Systems. The organization also houses secretariats for the BCBS, the IAIS, and the FSF. The BIS staff has grown to total nearly 500.[26]

The IMF has undergone even more striking expansion in conjunction with the globalization of finance. Its membership has risen from 62 states in 1960 to 183 states today. Its quota subscriptions have multiplied tenfold, from the equivalent of 21 billion SDRs in 1965 to 212 billion SDRs in 1999. Its staff numbers have quadrupled from 750 in 1966 to 3,082 in 1999.[27] The Fund took a leading role in the management (some say mismanagement) of the Third World debt crisis in the 1980s and the emerging market financial crises of the 1990s. More generally, IMF surveillance of its members' macroeconomic situation has expanded since 1997 to include assessments of the financial sector.[28] In several countries the Fund has taken a substantial role in restructuring the finance industry after a crisis. Since 1996 the IMF has promoted data standards that aim to make information on and for financial markets more reliable and accessible.[29] IMF management and senior staff have contributed extensively to recent discussions on the global financial architecture. The Fund's International Monetary and Financial Committee (IMFC, formerly Interim Committee) has served as an important forum for inter-governmental consultations regarding this architecture, drawing upon discussions in the FSF and the G20.

The IMF's Bretton Woods twin, the World Bank, has played a less prominent role in the governance of global finance (as opposed to lending activity itself). The Bank's main intervention in respect of regulatory frameworks has involved loans and technical assistance for financial sector development in various countries of the South and the East. In recent years the Bank's policies in this area have focused on sector restructuring with programmes of privatization and legal reform.

Several other suprastate agencies have also served as forums for intergovern-mental discussion of global financial issues. The OECD has done so through its Economic Policy Committee and Working Party Three of that body, which between them meet six times per year. Within the United Nations system the General Assembly, the Economic and Social Council, the regional economic and social commissions, the Department of Economic Affairs, UNCTAD, UNDP, and UNICEF have all addressed issues of global financial governance. However, UN intergovernmental forums have adopted mainly hortatory resolutions in this area, as opposed to formulating and implementing specific regulatory measures. The Financing for Development Initiative at the United Nations, launched in late 1997, represents an attempt to integrate wider economic and social concerns into the governance of global finance (see Herman in this volume).

Some further suprastate governance of global finance has emerged in recent years through the World Trade Organization (WTO). The Uruguay Round (1986–94) produced a General Agreement on Trade in Services (GATS) that extended multilateral liberalization of international commerce *inter alia* to finance.[30] Since 1995 a WTO Committee on Financial Services has overseen the operation of GATS in respect of finance. In 2000 the WTO launched further mul-tilateral negotiations on trade in services.

While contemporary globalization has often encouraged a rise of substate as well as suprastate competences in governance, devolution has been less apparent in respect of finance than in other areas of regulation. True, various provincial and municipal governments have turned to global sources like the eurobond market for credits. However, these substate authorities have rarely participated in regulatory activities *vis-à-vis* transworld finance. A few exceptions might be noted, such as the inclusion of agencies from two Canadian provinces as Associate Members of IOSCO and the membership of bureaux from Hong Kong, Labuan, New South Wales, and Ontario in the IAIS. However, for the moment official governance of global finance remains almost entirely at state and suprastate levels.

On the other hand, the financial sector presents an outstanding example of another major trend in contemporary governance: namely, the turn to nonofficial mechanisms of regulation. A number of national securities and exchange commissions have lain in the private sector for some time, of course, and IOSCO also includes over 50 securities exchanges and dealers associations as Affiliate Members. Meanwhile, several industry associations have promoted the transworld harmonization of standards and devised a number of self-regulatory instruments for bond and equity business in global financial markets. These bodies include the International Council of Securities Associations (ICSA), the International Federation of Stock Exchanges (FIBV), the International Primary Market Association (IPMA), and the International Securities Market Association (ISMA). In addition, bond-rating agencies like Moody's Investors Service and Standard & Poor's – and the financial markets whose sentiments they reflect – have come to exercise considerable disciplining authority over many national governments.[31]

Private-sector inputs to the governance of global finance have figured also outside the securities area. For example, nongovernmental groups like the Group of Thirty (composed of economists and businesspeople) and the Derivatives Policy Group (drawn from major investment banks) have taken a lead in developing rules for derivatives markets.[32] Two other private-sector bodies, the International Accounting Standards Committee (IASC) and the International Federation of Accountants (IFAC), have devised the main accountancy and auditing norms currently in use for global business.

In sum, then, governance of global finance is both multilayered and dispersed. It involves complex networks of state, suprastate, substate, and private-sector actors. As such, developments in respect of global finance conform to the broad patterns discerned earlier regarding post-statist governance in the context of large-scale globalization.

Key issues for the governance of global finance

Not only is the governance of global finance complex, but it is also particularly challenged in meeting the demands of efficiency, stability, social justice, and democracy. Almost no one argues that current regulatory arrangements for transborder finance are satisfactory, although the diagnoses of problems and the prescriptions of solutions vary widely.

In respect of efficiency, many observers have worried that global finance currently operates with substantial data deficits. Indeed, transborder financial markets are often distorted owing to missing data, rumour, and harmful manipulations of information. Limited competition has been a further efficiency concern. Market concentration in global finance has seen a progressively smaller number of corporate conglomerates come to dominate the banking, securities, and insurance industries. Some critics have also charged that global finance in its current form tends to divert investment from the "real" economy, where it would better serve general public welfare. The multifaceted character of governance arrangements for global finance raises additional efficiency concerns, as multiple forums address the same problems in an often ad hoc and loosely coordinated fashion.

In respect of stability, many commentators have argued that current global financial markets are inordinately volatile, creating insecurities that range well beyond normal investor risk to touch the basic livelihood of the public at large. Some of these harmful instabilities have arisen from large and rapid speculative swings in foreign-exchange values (as occurred, for example, in the European exchange-rate mechanism in 1992). Other excessive volatility has come from enormous and swift withdrawals of transborder finance capital, especially short-term credits (as in the Asia, Latin America, and Russia crises of the late 1990s). In addition, many stock and bond markets have since the late 1980s experienced wildly unstable courses of steep climbs and precipitous downturns. Derivatives markets, too, have suffered a series of debacles: the Metall Gesellschaft and Orange County affairs in 1994; Barings in 1995; Sumitomo in 1996; and Long Term Capital Management in 1998.

In respect of social justice, critics have worried that contemporary global finance sustains or even widens arbitrary inequalities of opportunity in the world economy. For example, people living in the North have on the whole enjoyed far better access to and far more benefits from global financial markets than people resident in the South. Meanwhile, onerous transborder debt burdens have – it is now generally agreed – hampered the development efforts of poor countries. Other injustice has arisen between income groups, as the gains of transworld finance (including the "tax efficiency" of offshore centres) have flowed largely to a wealthy minority of the world's people. As for gender equity, feminist critiques have highlighted limited access for women to global credit markets, a low representation of women in the management of global finance, and disproportionate hardships suffered by women in economic crises induced (at least partly) by global finance (see van Staveren in this volume).

In respect of democracy, considerable unease has developed that current arrangements of global financial governance are insufficiently participatory, consultative, representative, transparent, and publicly accountable. For one thing, most states have been excluded from the G7, the G10, the G20, and the OECD, while weighted votes have given a handful of states predominance in the Bretton Woods institutions. At the level of citizens, the vast majority of people across the world have scarce, if any, awareness of the rules and regulatory institutions that govern one of the most important areas of the global economy. Few governments have taken initiatives of public education to improve this sorry situation. Apart from a poll in 1992 on Switzerland's membership of the IMF and the World Bank, states have never conducted popular referenda on questions of global finance. In all countries, popularly elected bodies have had little direct involvement in, or exercised much supervision over, the trans-state networks, suprastate institutions, and private regimes that have largely governed global finance. Nor have suprastate and private regulatory bodies included any representative organs of their own.

Mounting concerns about these various policy challenges have generated much discussion in recent years about change in the so-called "global financial architecture". Innumerable suggestions have circulated to establish new principles, new policies, and new institutional mechanisms to govern global finance. Some of these proposals have promoted modest rewiring of the system (e.g. increased flexibility regarding the use of capital controls). In contrast, other recommendations have envisioned large-scale reconstruction (e.g. the creation of a fully-fledged world central bank). It is likely that the coming years will bring change in the global financial architecture, although the extent, speed, and direction of reconstruction remain to be determined.

Civil society initiatives on global finance

Many of the calls for change in the governance of global finance have emanated from civil society. The main sectors of civil society that have engaged with questions of global finance are business forums, development NGOs, environmental NGOs, organized labour, policy research institutes, and religious bodies (principally Protestant and Roman Catholic churches). These civil society associations have addressed five main concerns: transborder debt problems of the South; project loans by the MDBs; structural adjustment loans, mainly from the IMF and the World Bank; global commercial finance; and the shape of the overall global financial architecture. The following paragraphs review these five subjects of activism in turn.

Some of the most notable civil society involvement in global finance has come in respect of the transborder debt burdens of poor countries. Indeed, two major industry associations, the Institute of International Finance (IIF) and the Japan Center for International Finance (JCIF), were established in 1983 largely in response to the debt crisis of that day. While business forums have focused their concerns with debt on the financial interests of the creditors, other civil society bodies have highlighted the economic and social plights of the borrowers. Several think tanks, like the Washington-based Overseas Development Council (ODC), have given extensive attention to mechanisms for debt relief. In addition, the social costs of debt burdens in the South have occupied many Christian groups, including the Roman Catholic and Anglican churches. Numerous development NGOs have also pursued campaigns for debt relief in the South. Leading players in this regard have included the US Debt Crisis Network (which operated in 1985–90), the Freedom from Debt Coalition in the Philippines, the European Network on Debt and Development (EURODAD), and national debt networks in several African countries like Mozambique and Uganda. The transborder Jubilee 2000 Campaign, with its demand for "the cancellation of the unpayable debt of the world's poorest countries", attracted affiliates in over 65 countries by its close at the start of the new millennium.[33] Several successor initiatives now carry forward the Jubilee project.

Other NGO-led campaigns have highlighted social and environmental questions connected to the project loans of the multilateral development banks, especially the World Bank. Environmental NGOs have pursued some of the most highly publicized campaigns, sometimes in coalition with indigenous peoples and other local associations.[34] Women's NGOs have called attention to possible adverse gender consequences of various MDB (particularly World Bank) projects.[35] In addition, many development NGOs have criticized both the general paradigms and the specific conditions of MDB loans.[36]

Various civil society groups have also since the early 1980s given attention to structural adjustment lending, especially by the IMF and the World Bank. For example, certain business associations have intervened in respect of macroeconomic reform programmes when proposed policy changes have touched on their members' commercial interests. In addition, a number of think tanks, trade unions, development NGOs, and environmental NGOs have argued that IMF/World Bank-sponsored structural adjustment brings unacceptable social and environmental impacts, or indeed can harm a country's overall position in the world economy. Prominent actors in these debates have included the London-based Overseas Development Institute (ODI), the former Harvard Institute for International Development (HIID), the International Confederation of Free Trade Unions (ICFTU), the global network of Oxfams, the Washington-based Development GAP, Friends of the Earth–US, and the World Wide Fund for Nature (WWF). Since 1995 the World Bank has pursued a Structural Adjustment Participatory Review Initiative (SAPRI) that has come to involve over 1,200 civil society associations in the South and North.[37] In September 1999 the IMF and the World Bank redefined their approach to lending for low-income countries with the launch of Poverty Reduction Strategy Papers (PRSPs), the formulation of which is meant to involve broad participation from civil society.[38]

In comparison with MDB and IMF lending, the governance of commercial global finance has received much less attention in civil society, apart from academic studies (mainly in the field of political economy) and self-interested initiatives by business groups. Some CSOs have in recent years supported revived proposals for a redistributive global tax on foreign exchange trading, as first advocated by James Tobin in 1971 (and hence often known as the Tobin tax).[39] The transborder movement ATTAC, founded in France in 1998, has figured especially prominently in this campaign.[40] Certain NGOs have also promoted modest drives for so-called "ethical investment" in global markets. Since the late 1990s several NGOs, including BothENDS (Netherlands), the Fifty Years Is Enough Network (USA), and the Halifax Initiative (Canada), have organized teach-ins about the operations and consequences of global commercial financial markets. A scattering of grassroots activists in North America have advocated "de-globalization", with a turn to local community currencies.[41] On the whole, however, NGOs, religious bodies, and trade unions have accorded little – indeed, surprisingly little – priority to commercial global finance.

A host of civil society concerns about public and private transborder finance have come together in debates regarding the overall global financial regime. Such deliberations have experienced several peaks, including calls in the 1970s for a New International Economic Order, discussions in 1994 to mark the fiftieth anniversary of the Bretton Woods accords, and recent debates on the global financial architecture. Policy think tanks and university academics have figured most prominently in these activities, through a slew of symposia and publications. Some of the more influential participants have included Washington-based bodies like the Brookings

Institution, the Cato Institute, the Institute for International Economics, and the ODC. Among business groups, the Bretton Woods Committee, a Washington-based association of some 600 corporate members, in 1992–94 sponsored a major study of the IMF and the World Bank.[42] More recently, the IIF has convened working groups on financial crises, data transparency, the liberalization of transborder capital movements, and global standards for the soundness of banks. A few NGOs have also conducted critical examinations, in seminars and publications, of general governance arrangements for global finance. Notable activities have come in this respect from the Bangkok-based Focus on the Global South, the London-based Bretton Woods Project, and the Washington-based Center of Concern. Since the late 1990s a number of online discussion and action networks have also played a growing role in civil society engagement of global finance, particularly in the context of the so-called "anti-globalization" protests.[43]

In sum, then, civil society associations have addressed various issues related to contemporary global finance. The scale of these activities should not be exaggerated, and some aspects of transworld finance have received quite limited attention. Moreover, as the chapters in Part 2 of this volume demonstrate, the forms and intensity of civil society activism on global finance have varied considerably between different parts of the world. Nevertheless, these qualifications noted, civil society organizations have become active players in the politics of global finance.

Civil society and global finance: potential benefits

This book aims not only to describe civil society initiatives in respect of global finance, but also to assess them. To undertake such an evaluation we need explicit standards for judgement. The remainder of this chapter outlines some of the criteria that might be considered. This section identifies eight possible positive impacts, and the next section reviews eight potential negative aspects. Only a framework of evaluation is suggested here; later chapters in this book provide relevant empirical evidence with which to determine how far these potentials have been and could be realized in practice.

A first potential positive impact of civil society involvement in global finance concerns public education. Civil society activities might raise citizens' awareness and understanding of global finance and its governance. To this end, CSOs can prepare handbooks and information kits, produce audio-visual presentations, organize workshops, circulate newsletters, supply information to and attract the attention of the mass media, maintain listservs and websites on the Internet, and develop curricular materials for schools and higher education courses.

Second, civil society might make positive contributions to the governance of global finance by giving voice to stakeholders. Civil society associations can provide opportunities for concerned parties to relay information, testimonial, and analysis: to each other; to market actors; and to governance agencies. In particular, CSOs can open political space for social circles like the poor and women, who tend to get a limited hearing through other channels (including constitutional representative assemblies). In this way, civil society activism can empower stakeholders and indeed shift politics toward greater participatory democracy.

Third, civil society associations might fuel debate about global finance. Effective governance rests *inter alia* on vigorous, uninhibited discussion of diverse views. Inputs from civil society can put a variety of perspectives, methodologies, and proposals in the policy arena. Thanks to such contributions, policy deliberations can become more critical and creative. In addition, if we posit that openings for dissent are as necessary to democracy as securing of consent, then civil society can offer sites for objection and challenge.

Fourth, civil society might contribute positively to the governance of global finance by increasing public transparency. Greater visibility of financial market operations and their regulation allows investors and the public at large to make more informed judgements, thereby enhancing both efficiency and democracy. Pressure from civil society groups can encourage authorities in the governance of global finance to be more open about who takes decisions, what decisions they take, from what options, on what grounds, with what expected results, and with what supporting resources for implementation. Civil society actors can also interrogate the currently popular official rhetoric of "transparency" by asking critical questions about what is made transparent, at what time, in what forms, through what channels, on whose decision, for what purpose, and in whose interest.

Fifth, civil society might promote more effective governance of global finance by increasing the public accountability of the agencies concerned. Civil society groups can monitor the implementation and effects of policies regarding global finance and press for corrective measures when the consequences are adverse. To take one specific example, civil society actors can keep a check on the social expenditure that has been promised in connection with recent debt relief packages. In addition, civil society associations can exert pressure directly on global financial corporations, for instance, by spurring consumer boycotts of their services. Through an accountability function, civil society can push authorities in the area of global finance to take greater responsibility for their actions.

Sixth, civil society might enhance the workings of global finance by improving material welfare. For example, service delivery by civil society associations can help to reduce the social fallout (unemployment, cuts in public services, etc.) that often accompanies the macroeconomic adjustments that are undertaken in response to financial crises. NGOs can also urge that global finance flows into channels (like micro-credit schemes, for instance) that may especially benefit vulnerable social groups.

Seventh, civil society might through its various positive influences enhance social cohesion. Contributions to public education, stakeholder voice, policy debate, transparent and accountable governance, and material welfare can all help to counter arbitrary social hierarchies and exclusions that global finance might otherwise encourage. As a result, global finance would contribute less to social conflict and more to social integration.

Finally, civil society might promote legitimacy in global financial governance. Legitimate rule prevails when people acknowledge that an authority has a right to govern and that they have a duty to obey its directives. Legitimate governance tends to be more easily, productively, and nonviolently executed than illegitimate authority. The IMF and the World Bank have recognized this general principle with their recent attention to issues of policy "ownership". Civil society can offer a means for citizens to affirm that certain rules and institutions of global finance should guide – and where necessary constrain – their behaviour. Likewise, civil society can also provide a space for the expression of discontent and the pursuit of change when existing governance arrangements are regarded as illegitimate.

In sum, civil society has considerable positive potential to improve the governance of global finance. It would be naïve to present civil society interventions as a panacea for the global financial order, particularly given the generally modest proportions of this activism to date. At the same time, the possible gains on offer are such that we would be equally foolish to dismiss the inputs of civil society out of hand. We have arguably witnessed only the early stages of a long development. Indeed, the levels of activity and contributions already far exceed the position just twenty or thirty years ago.

Civil society and global finance: possible problems

None of the above fruits of civil society involvement in global finance follow automatically. The positive potentials cannot be realized in the absence of deliberate efforts and ample resources. In addition, civil society might in certain ways actually detract from effective governance of global finance. Eight general negative possibilities can be identified: some of them underdeveloped opportunities; and some of them positive harms.

First, civil society actors might pursue dubious goals. Voluntary associations may not have the public interest at heart in some – or even any – of their activities. To take one striking example of "uncivil society", transborder criminal networks have used global finance to perpetrate considerable damage. Other destructive elements such as racists, ultra-nationalists, and religious fundamentalists can seek to suppress the democratic rights of others. Business forums, professional bodies, and trade unions can focus on narrow and short-term interests of their members, possibly to the detriment of the general welfare. In their efforts to secure special interests in global finance and its governance, lobby groups may bypass – and thereby subvert – democratic processes through the state. In short, civil society is not intrinsically a virtuous force for the collective good and can in some cases do ill.

Second, civil society interventions in respect of global finance might suffer from flawed policy strategy and tactics. True, notions of "flawed policy" are political, and care must be taken that ruling discourses of technocratic expertise do not arbitrarily suppress alternative perspectives. However, we cannot be so relativist as to argue that all policies are of equal quality. Civil society campaigns can be poorly conceived and/or ineptly executed. For example, activists may lack sufficient economic literacy to substantiate certain claims, or they may have little understanding of the mandate and *modus operandi* of institutions of global financial governance. Academics may fail to link theoretical models of global finance and its governance to empirical evidence and political practicalities. On a more specific point of strategy, it might be questioned whether civil society should focus its advocacy regarding global finance so much on the Bretton Woods institutions, to the relative neglect of commercial markets and the other governance actors mentioned earlier. As for tactics, should CSOs perhaps give more attention than hitherto to build coalitions between North and South, as well as between different sectors of civil society? True, ill-informed and misdirected civil society efforts can inadvertently produce beneficial results. More usually, however, low-quality initiatives are an unhelpful distraction and in some cases can cause actual harm, including to vulnerable social circles that well-intentioned civil society associations may be aiming to help.

Third, involving civil society might detract from the governance of global finance if the costs in efficiency outweigh the gains in equity and democracy. If taken seriously, then civil society participation in policy formulation, execution and evaluation demands a substantial commitment of resources. Democracy is not cheap. The expense is justified when it yields benefits in efficiency, security, and social justice, as well as gains in democracy as a value in its own right. However, at some point the marginal returns from civil society participation are likely to decline and may even turn negative. Of course, people will disagree on how to calculate these costs and benefits – and thus on where the points of declining and negative returns lie. That said, these debates can be deferred for the moment: current levels of civil society participation in global finance are in general so modest that efficiency problems are hypothetical to all but the most dedicated technocrats. Nevertheless, it is prudent to remember, even at this early stage of development, that civil society involvement in policy cannot be run on a blank cheque.

Fourth, civil society engagement of global finance might have negligible or detrimental effects if the governance institutions concerned are ill-equipped to handle CSO inputs. Regulatory agencies may lack relevant staff expertise, adequate funds, suitable procedures, or the necessary receptive attitudes to take advantage of the benefits on offer from civil society. Officials can make innumerable mistakes in their dealings with civil society associations. They can treat the dialogue as a public relations exercise, or focus their contacts on sympathetic groups to the exclusion of critics, or dismiss out of hand civil society accounts that challenge "expert" knowledge, or expect immediate results when relationships require time to mature. Needless to say, the onus for corrective action on these problems lies with official bodies rather than with CSOs.

Fifth, civil society inputs to global finance might have negative consequences when CSOs become co-opted, losing their previously highlighted positive potentials to stimulate debate and provide space for dissent. For example, civil society groups may come uncritically to render services to financial governance agencies or take funds from them. Campaigners may meet officials in a continual stream of convivial exchanges, without ever laying down deadlines for action. Certain civil society campaigners may even "cross over" to work for organizations that they previously challenged. Some CSOs have engaged in what they call "critical coop-eration" with global financial institutions; however, beyond a certain point the critical element becomes diluted and eventually lost altogether. Meanwhile, official institutions may co-opt the language of civil society critique, subtly recasting it to their own purposes. Such captures of discourse may have occurred recently, as the Bretton Woods institutions have embraced a rhetoric of "participation", "good governance", "social capital", and "poverty reduction".

Sixth, civil society activity in respect of global finance might be undermined by undemocratic practices. Civil society groups – including those that campaign for greater democracy in global finance – can fall short of democratic criteria in their own activities. A lack of internal democracy within CSOs is not only objectionable in itself, but also contradicts civil society efforts to bring greater democracy to poli-tics at large. For example, civil society associations might offer their members little opportunity for participation beyond the payment of subscriptions. CSOs may purport to speak on behalf of certain constituencies without adequately consulting them. The leadership or group culture of a civil society organization may impose peremptory constraints on debate. Civil society can become a realm of exclusion-ary cliques no less than many political parties and official circles. A CSO can also be run with top-down authoritarianism. In addition, policy making in civil society bodies can be quite opaque to outsiders – or even to some insiders. Civil society groups can further lack transparency if they do not publish financial statements or declarations of objectives, let alone full-scale reports of their activities. Moreover, the leadership of CSOs can be self-selected, raising troubling questions of account-ability and potential conflicts of interest. In short, the operations of civil society are no more intrinsically democratic than those of the public sector or the market. Several codes of conduct for NGOs have appeared in recent years in response to these concerns.[44]

Seventh, civil society involvement in global finance might suffer from inade-quate representation. If civil society is fully to realize its promises, then all interested parties must have access – and preferably equal opportunities to par-ticipate. Otherwise, civil society can reproduce or even enlarge structural inequalities and arbitrary privileges connected with class, gender, nationality, race, religion, urban versus rural location, and so on. The capacities of civil soci-ety to advance social justice and democracy in global finance can be compromised if the participants are drawn disproportionately from middle classes, men, Northern countries, whites, Christians, and urban dwellers. To take one obvious example, civil society pressure for ethical investment in global financial markets tends to involve only those with resources to invest. Hierarchies of social power and associated struggles to be heard operate in civil society no less than in other political spaces.

Eighth, and related to the problem of representation, the civil society that engages global finance might have an overly narrow cultural base. Civil society may not reflect and respond to all of the contexts for which it purports to speak. In particu-lar, there is a danger that civil society in the South and the former communist-ruled countries becomes monopolized by western-styled, western-funded NGOs led by westernized élites. For all that such campaigners might criticize prevailing conditions of global finance, they have stronger cultural affinities with global managers than with local communities. Thus NGOs and other professionalized CSOs may – perhaps quite unintentionally – marginalize grassroots circles that could give better voice to the diverse life-worlds that global finance affects.

Given these potential problems, we do well to balance enthusiasm for civil society engagement of global finance with due caution. Much can go right, but much can also go wrong. Possible benefits can be neglected, and in some circumstances civil society involvement in global financial governance may actually detract from human security, social justice, and democracy. In short, civil society can be a means to good ends, but it is not the end itself. It is quite proper to demand of civil society associations that they not merely assert – but also demonstrate – their legitimacy.

Conclusion

This chapter has set the contemporary rise of civil society relations with global finance in the context of wider historical trends of globalization and its governance. The new geography of finance has raised opportunities for human betterment but also major challenges for efficiency, stability, equity, and democracy. Existing governance arrangements have often failed to deliver the positive potentials of global finance and indeed sometimes have contributed to inefficiency, instability, injustice, and democratic deficits. Global finance as it stands has given civil society ample grounds for dissatisfaction.

Civil society can make important contributions to better governance of global finance. CSOs can advance public education, provide platforms, fuel debate, increase transparency and accountability, improve material welfare, promote social cohesion, and enhance legitimacy. Of course, civil society does not provide a complete answer. Improvements in global finance require not only quality inputs from CSOs, but also the will and capacity for change in official quarters and market circles. However, positive interventions from adequately resourced and suitably accountable civil society can bring much good to global finance, particularly in current circumstances of largely ad hoc and experimental governance arrangements.

But we must retain caution. As we have seen, the promises of civil society for global finance are not realized automatically. A sober assessment of the record to date and the possibilities for the future – as this book attempts to provide – should help us to achieve the promises and avoid the pitfalls of civil society involvement in transworld finance.

Notes

1 I am grateful for feedback from other participants in the Civil Society and Global Finance Project, in particular detailed comments from Barry Herman and Alison Van Rooy.

2 Both cited in Michael Edwards, "Civil Society and Global Governance", in Ramesh Thakur and Edward Newman (eds), *New Millennium, New Perspectives: The United Nations, Security, and Governance*, Tokyo: United Nations University Press, 2000, p. 205.

3 Michel Camdessus, Address to the World Summit for Social Development, Copenhagen, 7 March 1995. Available at http://www.imf.org.

4 Jackie Smith, Charles Chatfield and Ron Pagnucco (eds), *Transnational Social Movements and Global Politics: Solidarity beyond the State*, Syracuse: Syracuse University Press, 1997; Margaret Keck and Kathryn Sikkink, *Activists without Borders: Transnational Advocacy Networks in International Politics*, Ithaca: Cornell University Press, 1998; John Boli and George M. Thomas (eds), *Constructing World Culture: International Nongovernmental Organizations since 1875*, Stanford: Stanford University Press, 1999; John W. Foster with Anita Anand (eds), *Whose World Is It Anyway? Civil Society, the United Nations and the Multilateral Future*, Ottawa: United Nations Association in Canada, 1999.

5 Thomas G. Weiss and Leon Gordenker (eds), *NGOs, the UN, and Global Governance*, Boulder, CO: Rienner, 1996; Peter Willetts (ed.), *"Conscience of the World": The Influence of Non-Governmental Organisations in the UN System*, Washington, DC: Brookings Institution, 1996; Robert O'Brien *et al.*, *Contesting Global Governance: Multilateral Economic Institutions and Global Social Movements*, Cambridge: Cambridge University Press, 2000; Part 3 of this volume.

6 Craig Warkentin and Karen Mingst, "International Institutions, the State, and Global Civil Society in the Age of the World Wide Web", *Global Governance*, Vol. 6, No. 2 (April–June 2000), p. 251; O'Brien, *et al.*, op. cit. Chapter 1; also Michael G. Schechter (ed.), *Innovation in Multilateralism*, Tokyo: United Nations University Press, 1999.

7 Peter Söderholm, *Global Governance of AIDS: Partnerships with Civil Society*, Lund: Lund University Press, 1997; John Borton *et al.*, *NGOs and Relief Operations: Trends and Policy Implications*, London: Overseas Development Institute, 1994; Deborah Stienstra, *Women's Movements and International Organizations*, Basingstoke: Macmillan, 1994; Jan Aart Scholte with Robert O'Brien and Marc Williams, "The WTO and Civil Society", *Journal of World Trade*, Vol. 33, No. 1 (February 1999), pp. 107–24.

8 Jan Aart Scholte, *Globalization: A Critical Introduction*, Basingstoke: Palgrave, 2000, Chapter 2.

9 Ibid, Chapter 3; *Financial Times*, 15 November 2000, Telecoms Supplement, p. XII.

10 Anne-Marie Slaughter, "Governing the Global Economy through Government Networks", in Michael Byers (ed.), *The Role of Law in International Politics: Essays in International Relations and International Law*, Oxford: Oxford University Press, 2000, pp. 177–205.

11 A. Claire Cutler, Virginia Haufler and Tony Porter (eds), *Private Authority in International Affairs*, Albany: State University of New York Press, 1999; Karsten Ronit and Volker Schneider (eds), *Private Organisations in Global Politics*, London: Routledge, 2000; Richard A. Higgott, Geoffrey R.D. Underhill and Andreas Bieler (eds), *Non-State Actors and Authority in the Global System*, London: Routledge, 2000.

12 Cf. Special Issue on "Globalization and Resistance", *Mobilization*, Vol. 6, No. 1 (2001).

13 Unless indicated otherwise, the data below are taken from Scholte, op. cit., Chapters 2 and 3.

14 *Annual Report 2000*, Basle: Bank for International Settlements, 2000, p. 122.

15 Ibid, p. 112.

16 Bank for International Settlements, "Quarterly Review: International Banking and Financial Market Developments", June 2000, p. 26.

17 Actually 11: Belgium, Canada, France, Germany, Italy, Japan, the Netherlands, Sweden, Switzerland, the UK, and the USA.

18 Eduardo Mayobre (ed.), *G-24: The Developing Countries in the International Financial System*, Boulder, CO: Rienner, 1999.

19 The G7 comprises Canada, France, Germany, Italy, Japan, the UK, and the USA. The European Community/Union has participated since 1977. Russia was added in 1998 to form the G8. See further Peter I. Hajnal, *The G7/G8 System: Evolution, Role and Documentation*, Aldershot: Ashgate, 1999; and <www.g7.utoronto.ca>.

20 Membership of the G20 is currently actually 19, comprised of the G7 plus Argentina, Australia, Brazil, China, India, Indonesia, the Republic of Korea, Mexico, Russia, Saudi Arabia, South Africa, and Turkey, plus the EU, the IMF, and the World Bank. See further <www.g20.org/indexe.html>.

21 R. Dale, "International Banking Regulation", in Benn Steil (ed.), *International Financial Market Regulation*, Chichester: Wiley, 1994, pp. 167–96; Ethan B. Kapstein, *Governing the Global Economy: International Finance and the State*, Cambridge, MA: Harvard University Press, 1994, Chapter 5; Joseph J. Norton, *Devising International Bank Supervisory Standards*, London: Graham and Trotman, 1995.

22 Wolfgang H. Reinicke, *Global Public Goods: Governing without Government?*, Washington, DC: Brookings Institution, 1998; <www.oecd.org/fatf>.

23 See <www.fsforum.org>.

24 Tony Porter, *States, Markets and Regimes in Global Finance*, Basingstoke: Macmillan, 1993; Benn Steil, "International Securities Markets Regulation", in Steil, op. cit., pp. 197–232; <www.iosco.org>.

25 <www.iaisweb.org>.

26 <www.bis.org>.

27 IMF, *Annual Report 1966*, Washington, DC: International Monetary Fund, 1966, p. 133; IMF, *Annual Report 2000*, Washington, DC: International Monetary Fund, 2000, p. 95.

28 IMF, *Annual Report 1997*. Washington, DC: International Monetary Fund, 1997, pp. 36–7.

29 See <http://dsbb.imf.org>.

30 Geoffrey R.D. Underhill, "Negotiating Financial Openness: The Uruguay Round and Trade in Financial Services", in Philip G. Cerny (ed.), *Finance and World Politics: Markets, Regimes and States in the Post-Hegemonic Era*, Aldershot: Elgar, 1993, pp. 114–51.

31 Timothy J. Sinclair, "Passing Judgement: Credit Rating Processes as Regulatory Mechanisms of Governance in the Emerging World Order", *Review of International Political Economy*, Vol. 1, No. 1 (Spring 1994), pp. 133–59; Thomas Friedman, *The Lexus and the Olive Tree*, London: HarperCollins, 1999, pp. 32–3, 91–2.

32 G30, *Derivatives: Practices and Principles*, Washington, DC: Group of Thirty, 1993; DPC, *A Framework for Voluntary Oversight of the OTC Derivatives Activities of Securities Firm Activities to Promote Confidence and Stability in Financial Markets*, Washington, DC: Derivatives Policy Group, 1995.

33 Carole J.L. Collins, Zie Gariyo and Tony Burdon, "Jubilee 2000: Citizen Action across the North–South Divide", in Michael Edwards and John Gaventa (eds), *Global Citizen Action*, Boulder, CO: Rienner, 2001, pp. 135–48.

34 O'Brien *et al.*, op. cit., Chapter 4; Durbin and Welch in this volume.

35 O'Brien *et al.*, op. cit., Chapter 2.

36 Paul J. Nelson, *The World Bank and Non-Governmental Organizations: The Limits of Apolitical Development*, London: Macmillan, 1995; Jonathan A. Fox and L. David Brown (eds), *The Struggle for Accountability: The World Bank, NGOs, and Grassroots Movements*, Cambridge, MA: MIT Press, 1998; Diana Tussie (ed.), *Luces y sombras de una nueva relación: el Banco Interamericano de Desarrollo, el Banco Mundial y la Sociedad Civil*, Buenos Aires: Temas, 2000.

37 <www.worldbank.org/poverty/strategies/index.htm>; <www.igc.org/dgap/saprin>.

38 <www.worldbank.org/poverty/strategies/index.htm>.

39 On the Tobin tax, see *inter alia* Barry Eichengreen and Charles Wyplosz, "Two Cases for Sand in the Wheels of International Finance", *Economic Journal*, Vol. 105, No. 1 (1995), pp. 162–72; David Felix, *Financial Globalization versus Free Trade: The Case for the Tobin Tax*, Geneva: United Nations Conference on Trade and Development, 1995; Mahbub ul-Haq, Inge Kaul and Isabelle Grunberg (eds), *The Tobin Tax: Coping with Financial Volatility*, New York: Oxford University Press, 1996.

40 The Association for the Taxation of Financial Transactions for the Aid of Citizens. See <www.attac.org>.

41 <www.ratical.org/many_worlds/cc/>.

42 Bretton Woods Commission, *Bretton Woods: Looking to the Future*, Washington, DC: Bretton Woods Committee, 1994.

43 Cf. Kevin A. Hill and John E. Hughes, *Cyberpolitics: Citizen Activism in the Age of the Internet*, Lanham, MD: Rowman & Littlefield, 1998; Jeffrey M. Ayres, "From the Streets to the Internet: The Cyber-Diffusion of Contention", *Annals of the American Academy of Political and Social Science*, Vol. 566 (November 1999), pp. 132–43.

44 See James Cutt and Vic Murray, *Accountability and Effectiveness Evaluation in Non-Profit Organizations*, London: Routledge, 2000; Michael Edwards, *NGO Rights and Responsibilities: A New Deal for Global Governance*, London: Foreign Policy Centre, 2000.

Part II
Regional experiences

2 Latin American NGOS and the IFIs

The quest for a South-determined agenda

Manuel Chiriboga

Summary	
• Introduction	35
• Global finance, the IFIs and Latin America	36
• Civil society responses to the IFIs	40
• Challenges for the future	46
• In closing	48

Introduction

In 1997 the Rede Brasil sobre Instituções Financieiras Multilaterais (Rede Brasil, Brazilian Network on Multilateral Financial Institutions), a civil society network that specializes in international financial institutions (IFIs), received through NGO colleagues in the North a copy of the secret Country Assistance Strategy (CAS) for Brazil. The CAS is the World Bank Group business plan that establishes and justifies the goals and priorities for a particular country over a given time period. In 1996 the NGO Working Group on the World Bank, a worldwide platform that seeks to influence Bank policy, had made civil society participation in the CAS process and public disclosure of the document two of its main objectives.

After translating the Brazilian CAS, Rede Brasil circulated it widely among Brazilian NGOs, labor and peasant unions, and friendly parliamentarians. It was stressed to the parliamentarians that the CAS had significant implications for budget and loans policies, both constitutional responsibilities of the Brazilian Congress. A legislator then formally asked the Ministers of Finance, Planning, and Budget for a copy of the CAS, which, after some hesitation, they handed over, opening it up for parliamentary discussion. Rede Brasil then requested Congressional authorization to publish the CAS, and this was granted. The World Bank objected that the CAS was an internal Bank document, but the Congress asked the Bank not to interfere in the internal politics of Brazil.[1]

This scenario reveals important changes in Latin American NGO campaigning and was in many senses a turning point in NGO advocacy strategies in Latin America. National agendas became linked with global advocacy campaigns. Significantly, the strategy for this campaign was mainly defined by Brazilian NGOs: Northern NGOs only supplied information. Similar stories have emerged across Latin America, related not only to macroeconomic policy, but also to IFI involvement in sectoral reform and specific projects.

This chapter discusses the evolution of Latin American NGOs as players in global advocacy efforts regarding the IFIs, especially the multilateral development banks (MDBs). NGOs are only part of civil society, but they have played a key role in this policy area. Not only have NGOs been important as activists in their own right, but they have also interested and educated other civil society organizations (CSOs) in issues of global finance.

It is true that, in terms of volume, loans from the IFIs represent but a small proportion of financial flows to Latin America. In 1997 the World Bank and the Inter-American Development Bank (IDB) approved close to $12 billion in loans to the region, while commercial flows reached almost $119 billion.[2] However, these institutions have played an additional key role through their influence on macroeconomic policies. On this count the IFIs have figured crucially in opening the region to global finance.

Southern NGOs are for the most part relative newcomers to the politics of IFIs. The story basically starts in the early 1990s. Nevertheless, this short period has seen significant changes in the relations that Latin American NGOs have between themselves, with governments, with the IFIs, and with Northern NGOs. Engagement with the IFIs has also posed quite an array of challenges at a time of rapid change for the NGO movement itself.

The rest of this chapter is divided into three parts. In the first part we briefly synthesize the main trends in IFI activity in Latin America during the 1980s and 1990s and the different relations with governments that have emerged. In the second part we discuss three phases of Latino NGO activity regarding the IFIs, identifying also the opportunities for civil society engagement that the institutions themselves have opened. In the third section we discuss some of the main challenges that confront Latino NGOs in their advocacy on IFIs.

Global finance, the IFIs and Latin America

The 1980s and 1990s saw an expansion of the role and importance of the IFIs in Latin America. After years of supporting infrastructure projects and agricultural and rural development through loans, from the mid-1980s these institutions shifted their attention to structural adjustment programs and sectoral reforms. In doing so the IFIs opened the doors to increased investment in the region, both foreign direct investment and financial flows (including short-term credits). Flows of private finance capital dropped from an average of $47 billion per annum in 1980–82 to $10 billion per annum in 1983–90. After the IFI-sponsored reforms, private financial flows increased to an average of $43 billion per annum in 1991–96 and $70 billion per annum in 1997–99.[3] As Jahved Burki and Guillermo Perry explain, this turnaround resulted both from external factors linked to global financial markets and from domestic changes.

Yet from the mid-1990s onwards these flows also brought the region an almost forgotten phenomenon: financial volatility and associated costs in terms of banking crises, fiscal deficits, recession and unemployment.[4] In consequence, the IFIs, who prior to 1995 had pushed for deregulation of financial markets and liberalization of short-term capital controls, now pushed further for financial sector reform and anti-cyclical macroeconomic policies.

The International Monetary Fund (IMF), the World Bank, and the IDB are the main IFIs operating in the region. The Caribbean Development Bank (CDB), the Andean Development Corporation (CAF), and the Central American Economic Integration Bank (BCIE) have also played a role in their respective subregional areas. Latin American and Caribbean states are members and shareholders in each of these institutions, but they are also borrowers, subject to IFI influence.

Table 2.1 Latin American and Caribbean states' voting rights in IFIs

	IMF	*World Bank*	*IDB*	*CDB*
Voting rights as % of total	8.2	8.4	51.5	61

The IFIs have five main channels of influence in Latin America. First, they issue loans. During the 1990s the World Bank and the IDB approved over $120 billion in credits to Latin America.[5] For its part, the IMF approves loans for emergency financial assistance and for macroeconomic adjustment operations. In recent years the Fund has extended credits in Latin America to Argentina, Bolivia, Brazil, Columbia, Ecuador, Mexico, Nicaragua, Panama, Peru and Uruguay.[6]

Second, the IFIs exert influence in Latin America through their work on surveillance and policy advice. In this way the institutions influence much economic policy and, increasingly, also social and institutional reform. This role is accomplished through technical assistance, surveillance and policy support missions. These activities may or may not be linked to financial assistance. Increasingly they are executed through an in-country presence and monitoring by IFI resident offices and representatives. The IDB has representatives in every country of the region. The World Bank has offices in Argentina, Bolivia, Brazil, Colombia, Ecuador, Guatemala, Haiti, Jamaica, Mexico, Nicaragua, Paraguay, Peru and Venezuela. Recently the Bank has moved relevant directors from headquarters in Washington, DC, to field offices in Argentina, Brazil, Mexico and Peru. The IMF also has resident representatives in most countries of Latin America.

Third, the IFIs train public-sector officials through specialized training units. These include the IDB's Instituto para Desarrollo Social (Institute for Social Development, or INDES), the IMF Institute and the World Bank Institute.

Fourth, the IFIs issue emergency assistance in response to major natural disasters or, increasingly, when countries face the impact of international financial instability and crisis.

Fifth, the IFIs act as a lender and guarantor *vis-à-vis* private-sector flows and investments to and within the region. This is done through institutions such as the World Bank's International Finance Corporation (IFC) and Multilateral Investment Guarantee Association (MIGA), as well as the IDB's Inter-American Investment Corporation (IAIC). In addition, the IMF's reviews and statements on the economic soundness of each country may encourage private global capital to move into or out of the region.

IFI activities in Latin America have gone through three phases since the mid-1980s. The first phase was marked by stabilization and structural adjustment policies (SAPs) on the pattern of the so-called "Washington Consensus". The second period saw the IFIs shift their reform efforts towards sectoral policies and programs. Emphasis was given to institutional reform, poverty reduction and social development. In the third and more recent period, the IFIs have sought to deepen structural reform in response to international financial instability.

Up to the mid-1990s the IMF and the World Bank stressed a set of policies broadly known as the Washington Consensus. The label, coined by the economist John Williamson, encompassed a package of ten general policy principles: fiscal discipline; public expenditure priorities on education, health and infrastructure; tax reform; exchange rates established by markets; competitive exchange rates; trade liberalization; promotion of foreign direct investment; privatization; deregulation; and the enforcement of property rights.[7]

Although most governments in Latin America followed the general principles of the Washington Consensus, their application was not universal or homogeneous. Interpretations varied considerably between countries. One common characteristic was the emphasis above all else on price stability and the control of inflation. Washington Consensus programs were often applied to countries coming out of hyperinflationary periods, debt crisis and serious political breakdown, followed by some type of political consensus or strong conservative authoritarian regimes. This scenario unfolded in most of the biggest countries of the region (such as Argentina, Brazil and Mexico), in medium-income countries (such as the Dominican Republic, Peru and Uruguay), and in some of the poorer countries (such as Bolivia and El Salvador). On the other hand, countries such as Colombia, Ecuador, Nicaragua, Paraguay and Venezuela resisted orthodox stabilization and adjustment programs until very recently.

In the mid-1990s, IFI reform programs for Latin America started to shift away from a sole focus on macroeconomic adjustment. A new consensus emerged which argued that, while stabilization and economic reforms had produced an increase in per capita growth, the rates were not rapid; nor was this growth reducing poverty. So-called "second-generation reforms" were therefore needed if countries were to combine growth with reductions in poverty and inequality.[8] The new reform packages included more focus on quality investment in human capital, efficient financial markets, enhanced regulatory and legal capacities in areas such as financial supervision and prudential regulation, a new governance style (transparency and corruption control) and quality public services, including decentralization, civil service and judicial system reforms, plus poverty reduction programs and social safety nets. These expanded Washington Consensus programs have normally included a degree of civil society participation, as they have been implemented in the context of strong NGO campaigning for IFI reform.

The change in focus resulted from a double set of pressures: one coming from within the region and the other emerging from civil society in the North. In Latin America itself, political decision makers came under pressure from social and political actors who felt that the gains from reforms were not evenly distributed and that a significant part of the population was excluded from the benefits.[9] Although poverty had declined in some countries, progress was slow, and inequality had grown significantly.[10] In the North, meanwhile, the IFIs were feeling the sting of NGO protests and advocacy around the 50 Years Is Enough Campaign, which drew the attention of Northern politicians to IFI activities.

The second-generation reforms had little chance to take hold before Latin America was hit by global financial instability. Between 1990 and 1995 movements of short-term capital to the region tripled. At first, this injection had positive effects. Latin American countries enjoyed growth and controlled inflation, as the flows helped to finance imports, debt repayments, and credits to the private sector. A sense of prosperity prevailed. However, the volatility of short-term capital soon cut short the dream. Following the Asian crisis of 1997, the Russian crisis of 1998 and the Brazilian crisis of 1999, over $9 billion left the region.[11] As a result, growth was interrupted, unemployment and poverty increased, and the region required fresh IFI financing. In 1999 the World Bank approved large adjustment loans for Argentina, Brazil, Panama and Peru.

These IFI rescue packages carried a new set of policy prescriptions. The programs included monetary austerity, fiscal cuts and new taxes, and anti-dumping trade policies. Such measures generally provoked recession. The IFIs also emphasized a new set of reforms dealing with the financial sector, social security and labor markets. As a consequence, SAP loans in the region increased dramatically: from around 17 per cent of the World Bank's loans to Latin America in 1996 to 29 per cent in 1999 and to 56 per cent in 2000;[12] and, in the case of the IDB, from 37 per cent in 1996 to 39 per cent in 1999.[13] Meanwhile, social lending decreased. What was new in most of these rescue packages was close coordination between the IMF, the World Bank, the IDB, the subregional banks and the US Treasury.

At present, no end to the financial crisis seems in sight, and countries such as Argentina find it difficult to recover their growth patterns. Yet, when stability does return in the coming years, the IFIs will probably return to their previous priority of second-generation reforms. However, the crises will leave a legacy of closer IFI surveillance of macroeconomic policy as well as demands to quicken the pace of reform. The crises appear also to have increased coordination between the global financial institutions. New collaboration between the IMF and the World Bank around the Poverty Reduction Strategy Papers (PRSPs) points in that direction, as do many policy declarations by the G7 finance ministers. Closer coordination between the Bank and the Fund was already evident in the Ecuadorian support package at the beginning of 2000.

Meanwhile, private financial flows to Latin America have slowly started to grow again. Cross-border lending and securities trading have resumed, and foreign direct investment has recovered its growth pattern. So once again the IFIs have played a major role in opening up Latin America to global financial markets.

Civil society responses to the IFIs

Having reviewed global financial flows and IFI activities in Latin America, we now turn to the role of civil society. This section discusses some of the main trends and changes regarding Latin American CSO activism *vis-à-vis* the IFIs. We first discuss the origins of NGO advocacy in the region and then focus on the phases and trends of NGO activism regarding the IFIs.

The main point to emphasize is that, since the mid-1990s, Latino NGOs have moved toward the formation of national and regional coalitions interested in the IFIs. The NGOs have sought to develop a domestically based agenda that looks at the responsibility of Southern governments in respect of international finance. This effort has become part of a struggle to democratize governments: to make them participatory, accountable and transparent. This opens up possibilities for a broader understanding of global finance and development. The new approach also provides the basis for new types of international alliances of NGOs.

Civil society advocacy is a recent phenomenon in most countries of Latin America. Up to the late 1980s, activists in the region were more interested in bringing about radical change through revolution. They mistrusted democracy as a bourgeois institution that only represented the élite and imperial powers and could not respond to the needs of the people. Most NGO activists thought of themselves as intellectuals linked to peoples' organizations.

Albeit with differences from country to country, NGOs and the activists linked to them basically moved through three phases, each marked by a different set of political perspectives. The first, organized around the principle of *asistencialismo* ("assistentialism"), prevailed during the 1950s and 1960s. It focused on the need to support the poor under the guidance of the Catholic Church. The second phase, lasting from the 1960s to the mid-1980s, highlighted the need for radical social change and socialism. It was based on a strong alliance between intellectuals (many of whom had established or were linked to NGOs) and popular organizations (especially trade unions and peasant movements). The third phase, unfolding since the mid-1980s, has centered on principles of inclusiveness, sustainability and democracy. Each of these phases has been associated with the appearance of new groups of CSOs. In the last phase, civil society has grown horizontally, as groups linked to human rights, the empowerment of women, environmental conservation, indigenous peoples, and so on have become active.

Until recently, NGO networks in Latin America have usually been weak. They specialized in comparative analysis or in sharing field practices. The Latin American Council for Social Sciences (CLACSO), founded in 1967, was perhaps the most important older network. It brought together social science researchers from NGOs and universities from across the region. Meanwhile, Solidarios, operating from

1972, and the Asociación Latinoamericana de Organizaciones de Promoción (ALOP, the Latin American Association of Advocacy Organizations), started in 1979, linked development NGOs to share experiences and to train activists. Finally, the Consejo de Educación de Adultos de América Latina (CEAAL, the Council of Adult Education in Latin America), established in 1982, brought together NGOs engaged in popular education. Peoples' organizations were connected through trade union federations (organized on competing ideological lines) and peasant and cooperative organizations. Networks of other actors – such as women, indigenous peoples, squatters, etc. – were weak in the region.

Latino civil society concerns about globalization – and about international finance more specifically – are a recent phenomenon, going back no further than to the mid-1980s. The main pillars of this advocacy have been: (a) the debt campaigns built around the crisis of the mid-1980s; (b) critiques of structural adjustment's impact on the poor and excluded; and (c) discussions of trade agreements, particularly Mexican mobilization around the North American Free Trade Agreement (NAFTA).

The 1980s' debt campaigns were organized with support from European church-linked groups. They argued that debt did not have to be serviced since it had already been paid: through the outflow of private capital to international financial markets; through high and speculative interest rates; and through unjust terms of trade.[14] The campaigns organized strong popular education programs, established alliances that included peoples' organizations, undertook research, and forged links with NGOs from Europe. Eventually, with the support of the Catholic Church, the campaigns promoted debt swaps for social and environmental programs in countries including Costa Rica, Ecuador, El Salvador and Mexico.[15] When the debt emergency receded and NGOs turned to negotiating swaps, these campaigns faded.

A second pillar of civil society mobilization on globalization in Latin America has involved critiques of the neoliberal policy model that was implemented throughout the region from the 1980s. NGOs strongly opposed privatization, as it implied massive layoffs, mostly among unionized workers, the traditional allies of the NGOs. Orthodox adjustment packages also involved reductions in social spending and rural development programs, increasing poverty throughout the region, especially among the peasants. NGOs, particularly those with research capacities, started a thorough critical analysis of the programs in Latin America. These critiques put the IFIs on the radar screen of NGOs and peoples' organizations. NGOs supported education programs on SAPs, links with both old and new social organizations, and the search for alternative development models.

Further concrete NGO advocacy regarding neoliberalism came in response to trade agreements, especially NAFTA in relation to Mexico. When the Mexican government started to discuss the treaty, civil society groups met to consider its implications. While CSOs did not oppose a trade liberalization treaty with the USA and Canada per se, they had many doubts about the terms of the proposed NAFTA agreement. To voice these criticisms and pursue alternatives to NAFTA, these CSOs established the Red Mexicana de Acción Frente al Libre Comercio (RMALC,

Mexican Network for Action on Free Trade).[16] Unlike earlier civil society initiatives on trade policy, RMALC supported citizen rights to participate and intervene in public debates, demanded accountability from government negotiators, and proposed alternative economic models. The network also sought to build international alliances, establishing strong links with like-minded movements in Canada and the USA. Since then, similar groups have been organized in relation to the proposed Free Trade Agreement of the Americas (FTAA): for example, the Rede Brasileira pelo Integração dos Povos (REBRIP, Brazilian Network for Integration among Peoples) and the Central American Civil Society Initiative on Integration (ICIC).

With such experiences and lessons, civil society groups in Latin America started in the 1990s to look directly at the IFIs. Until then, Latin American NGOs had only sporadic contacts with the MDBs. In most cases, these initiatives related to funding and resource mobilization or to specific Northern-led global campaigns.

In regard to funding issues, NGOs had their most structured relations with the IDB and its Small Grants Facility. This program, started in the 1980s, until recently channeled significant resources to NGOs that had a good development proposal and could obtain the backing of their government as guarantor. Most of the operations have been run through a special IDB facility, the Multilateral Investment Fund, working with Northern trust funds to support special pilot programs, including micro-finance schemes.

For the rest, NGO advocacy regarding the IFIs was very slim and generally limited to issues of environmental protection and the rights of indigenous peoples. Moreover, national NGOs in Latin America generally played a secondary role in these campaigns. The Planoforo project, dam construction loans, and the Polonoroeste road project – all in Brazil – are probably the best known cases of 1980s' campaigns. These first experiences of advocacy on the IFIs were initially dominated by international issue networks composed of international and national NGOs, with little significant grassroots involvement. National NGOs and grassroots organizations basically collected information, while international NGOs undertook the policy advocacy.[17]

This pattern started to change with campaigns on SAPs. Latino NGOs documented the social and economic impacts of SAPs and discussed alternative scenarios, partly influenced by proposals from the United Nations Economic Commission for Latin America and the Caribbean (ECLAC) and the United Nations Development Program (UNDP).[18] NGOs also strongly criticized the loss of national sovereignty that SAPs implied. Two cases of Latin American NGO involvement are illustrative: discussions over the Mexican structural adjustment program; and ALOP's campaign on Social Investment Funds (SIFs).

The Mexican SAP analysis was undertaken by Equipo Pueblo, a Mexican NGO and a member of ALOP, as part of a policy discussion supported by the NGO Working Group on the World Bank. Equipo Pueblo documented the impact of SAPs on economic growth, poverty and inequality, social services provision and the health of medium and small national firms. The Bank refused to discuss the document, which it regarded as ideological. Nevertheless, the report involved countrywide discussions with all sorts of grassroots and popular organization groups, which helped to construct a strong constituency in Mexico for national and international advocacy work on the IFIs.[19]

In the case of SIFs, ALOP teamed up with a German NGO, the Evangelische Zentralstelle für Entwicklungshilfe (EZE), to document these MDB anti-poverty programs. SIFs were created to support poor people while SAPs were implemented. ALOP conducted brief studies covering around a dozen countries of the region and then did in-depth work on Chile, Guatemala and Honduras. The research showed that these social welfare programs had limited coverage, failed to generate sustainable poverty reduction, were liable to political manipulation by national governments, and lacked real participation mechanisms.[20] On the back of these studies, ALOP and EZE started a multi-year campaign that emphasized participation and a shift to a more local focus on development. The campaign targeted national governments, the German bank that co-financed such programs, and the World Bank itself.

Much of this advocacy on SAPs and SIFs was pursued through international forums, so that Latino NGOs were exposed to global campaigning. In most cases problem definition, strategy setting and implementation were carried out jointly by Latino and Northern NGOs. The collaboration particularly involved European partners, with whom Latino NGOs had historical partnerships for development work. Such activities were also learning processes for Southern coalition members who, in general, had no previous experience in international lobbying.

In 1995 a key political event triggered a search for more horizontal relations within global coalitions campaigning for IFI reform. The IDA-10 replenishment discussion brought a collision over strategy between Northern and Southern NGOs. Many Washington-based NGOs lobbied the US Congress against further financing of the International Development Association (IDA), the soft-loan facility of the World Bank. In contrast, Southern NGOs argued for replenishment coupled with reform of the policies supported by IDA. These parties included mainly NGOs from Africa, but also Latino groups like ALOP and the Fundación Augusto Cesar Sandino (FACS) in Nicaragua.[21] Although this disagreement allowed the Bank to divide the NGO campaigners, it ultimately helped to change the nature of North–South NGO relations and to increase the initiative of Southern NGOs in global advocacy.[22]

North–South NGO conflicts over the IFIs arose again in 1997 on the Structural Adjustment Policy Review Initiative Network (SAPRIN). On this occasion, ALOP and Rede Brasil clashed with the Development Group for Alternative Policies (D-GAP), a Washington-based NGO that initiated SAPRIN. The Latino organizations felt that D-GAP was unwilling to give Southern NGOs sufficient say in determining priorities, strategy and implementation in SAPRIN.

Another point of continuing disagreement between Northern and Southern NGOs has concerned social policy. Many Northern NGOs have pushed the MDBs to channel more of their portfolio into social programs and poverty eradication rather than adjustment programs and infrastructure projects. In contrast, many Latin American NGOs consider that linking social policy to MDB support allows governments to evade their central responsibility for redistribution. From the

Latino NGO perspective, poverty results from exclusion and inequality, which arise from the prevailing economic and social development model. What is needed is not social policy as a compensatory mechanism within the existing model, but a change of the model itself.

Through experiences like the disagreements over IDA, SAPRIN and social policy, Latino NGOs have developed more autonomy. Increasingly, they have set their own national and regional agendas. Two processes have encouraged this trend: on the one hand, initiatives from the NGO Working Group on the World Bank; and, on the other hand, trends in national NGO networks working on the World Bank that have put pressure on governments in their dealings with the IFIs.

The NGO Working Group on the World Bank, established in 1982 and still active, is a coalition of development NGO networks. Its members include ALOP, the Association of World Council of Churches related Development Organizations in Europe (APRODEV), Coopération Internationale pour le Développement et la Solidarité (CIDSE), the Society for Participatory Research in Asia (PRIA), and the Inter-Africa Group (IAG). Led by Southern associations, the Working Group has pursued a strategy of critical cooperation with the Bank: on the one hand it has supported IDA replenishment, while on the other it has criticized the policies of both the Bank and governments in the North. This NGO coalition has pushed for IDA reform, greater civil society participation in Bank projects, policies and the CAS process, capacity building for Southern NGOs, and policy dialogue with vice-presidencies of the Bank.[23]

The Working Group has engaged in a host of activities. It has pursued regional dialogues with senior regional World Bank officials, discussions that have involved an expanded civil society constituency. It has monitored various projects and policies regarding participation by primary stakeholders. It has monitored SIFs and has held a number of policy dialogues through forums.

These efforts have yielded some policy changes. For example, the Bank has incorporated participation by civil society into the formulation of several CASs, including those for Colombia, El Salvador, Peru and, more recently, Argentina (see Senderowitsch and Cesilini in this volume). Unfortunately, these exercises have not involved significant participation by governments, and NGOs have tended to be excluded from follow-up discussions. The Bank has furthermore increased NGO participation in its projects and has hired several NGO specialists on to its staff.

The shift towards dialogues located in the South, both regionally and nationally, has expanded opportunities for direct exchange between Southern NGOs. It has also facilitated direct contacts and dialogue with World Bank officials and has reduced the role of international and Northern NGOs as intermediaries for such contacts. In turn, Southern NGOs have become empowered to dialogue directly with Bank management, both in Washington and in country offices. Latin American dialogues with senior officials have involved more than 300 groups, including ALOP, Rede Brasil, FACS, Transparencia and Equipo Pueblo from Mexico, the Caribbean Policy Development Center (CPDC), the Fundación Nacional para el Desarrollo (FUNDE, National Foundation for Development) from El Salvador, and the Centro de Estudios y Promoción del Desarrollo

(DESCO, Centre for Studies and Promotion of Development) from Peru. These meetings have helped to reinforce national processes. Thus, the NGO Working Group has been instrumental in expanding the constituency for Bank advocacy and in empowering NGOs for direct campaigning.

Regional dialogues have also opened up new challenges and risks for Southern NGO activism. One problem is the tendency of Bank staff at the regional and country offices to see NGOs basically as service providers. Moreover, in many cases these officials tend to seek out friendly NGOs and government-oriented NGOs (or GONGOs). Meanwhile, many Southern NGOs look to the Bank as a potential source of funding. This situation carries the risk of clientelism, where favorable comments from NGOs are exchanged for funding possibilities from the Bank. In consequence, the World Bank may not hear some of the more critical voices or those representing stakeholders affected by Bank policies and projects. NGOs should continue to press the IFIs for independent NGO processes, such as those found in Brazil, Mexico and Nicaragua.

A second risk is that Southern NGOs may lose allies among international and Northern NGOs, who are more centered on IFI reform than on specific projects or programs. It is therefore necessary to identify particular agenda items that can bring North and South together. This will require that Southern NGOs look at IFI reform and that Northern NGOs support specific regional and national campaigns.

Partly building on the experience of contacts with the World Bank, Southern NGOs have also started to approach the IDB, the regional development bank for Latin America. An NGO alliance has been established to hold regular sessions with senior staff of the IDB. It includes among others Rede Brasil, ALOP, Red-Bancos (Banks Network) based in Montevideo, the Coalición Rios Vivos (the International Rivers Network, based in California and with nodes in Brazil and Paraguay), El Banco en la Mira de las Mujeres (Women's Eyes on the Bank, with a regional base in Mexico) and the Organización Interamericana de Trabajadores (ORIT, affiliated with the ICFTU and linked to the US labor confederation, the AFL-CIO). This group has raised issues such as the impact of big infrastructure projects in the Amazon and the Pantanal (a huge swamp in Brazil where the big southern cone rivers are born), participation policy and an increased civil society presence at the IDB's annual meeting.

In addition, since the mid-1990s some national and regional NGO coalitions have attempted advocacy at relations between governments and the MDBs. Players worth mentioning in this regard are regional groups such as ALOP, CPDC, Red-Bancos, and El Banco en la Mira de las Mujeres. At a national level the active groups have included Rede Brasil in Brazil, the Federación de ONGs (FONG) and the Grupo Propositivo de Cabildeo (GPC), both in Nicaragua, Evaluación Ciudadana del Ajuste Estructural (CASA, Citizen Assessment of Structural Adjustment) and Transparencia in Mexico, and the Bolivian coalition against debt.

All these initiatives have diversified and expanded the civil society constituency for campaigns on the IFIs. NGO advocacy work has also mobilized democratic institutions such as parliaments and the judicial system. Many of these NGOs have reached out to wider civil society. For example, Rede Brasil and CASA include not only NGOs, but also grassroots organizations, church groups, trade unions, research centers, peasant groups, and organizations of people affected by particular MDB projects. In many cases, these campaigns are organized at both national and sub-national levels.

Probably the most significant changes introduced by these groups are the construction of advocacy agendas based on national priorities and an increasing focus on the role of national governments. The agendas no longer come automatically from Northern partners and are more nationally oriented. In some cases the Latino NGOs use international pressure on the IFIs as a way to open up national debate and to highlight the shortcomings of national policies. This strategy recognizes that pressure from the international level alone will not by itself yield results. It must be linked with political advocacy from below and with domestic political processes. This approach recognizes that Southern governments, especially those of medium-income countries, are co-responsible for what IFIs do in a country.[24]

Civil society coalitions in Latin America have directed more attention to national institutions as legitimate mechanisms for accountability and citizen control. As noted at the start of this chapter, Rede Brasil pushed the Brazilian Congress to demand that the CAS be made public. CSOs have also mobilized congressional representatives in Argentina. In Ecuador, CSOs challenged the IMF Letter of Intent in the constitutional court. On other occasions CSOs have asked the Defensor del Pueblo or the ombudsman to intervene. In using this strategy, coalitions have opted to work within established democratic mechanisms.

Thus recent Latin American NGO activism on the IFIs has linked national politics to global finance and seeks better to integrate national and international campaigns. Issues regarding the IFIs are thereby related to questions of national development alternatives and the struggle for democracy and citizen rights in Southern countries.

This trend of "nationalization" does not imply that international campaigns no longer have a role. Civil society organizations still need to press for reform of the IFIs and the way they do their business. IFI accountability, transparency and even the need to change voting rights in order to assure equal power to every state continue to be high on the agenda of Southern NGO advocacy. However, these reform campaigns have to be constructed out of more horizontal relations: both between Northern and Southern NGOs and between NGOs and other civil society organizations.

Challenges for the future

The new roles that Latin American NGOs are constructing require that they give greater attention to a number of issues. These questions relate to:

- the main ideological and political reference points for advocacy on the IFIs;
- how NGOs construct alliances with other stakeholders, especially peoples' organizations;
- the need to work within – and expand – accountability mechanisms in each country;

- the need to strengthen NGO professional capabilities, especially through links with academic circles;
- the need to develop further the campaign capacities of Southern NGOs, for example, by creating more possibilities to network and exchange experiences; and
- the resolution of problems concerning the financial sustainability of NGOs.

Regarding the first of these points, the main paradigm of Latin American NGOs has generally shifted from revolutionary Marxism to what could be described as citizen rights democracy and a more inclusive development paradigm. This new ideological framework is well described by Jorge Castañeda and Roberto Mangabeira when they affirm:

> We favor a more distributional model *vis-à-vis* a productive one. We link it to democracy and overcoming social and economic dualism. It rests on a strong and active state that supports small and medium-sized enterprises.[25]

Additionally, this new perspective emphasizes citizen rights, including political and economic, social and cultural rights. It further promotes active citizenship *vis-à-vis* government and a strong civil society. Transparency and accountability in government are also given high priority. Regarding globalization, the new generation of NGOs are advocates of regional Latin American trade and integration agreements, which they consider a vital step before these countries can be integrated into the wider international system.

Adopting this perspective, today's Latin American NGOs identify strongly with excluded sectors of society, not only in relation to class, but also in regard to gender, ethnicity, generation and the popular rural and urban sectors of society. NGOs in Latin America traditionally conceived of their constituents in terms of workers and peasants, but more recently they see their base in a larger range of development stakeholders. How to construct solid relations with peoples' organizations, many of which have their own advocacy strategies, implies a second challenge: the need to develop more horizontal relations with them.

Meanwhile NGO relations with political parties in Latin America are increasingly marked by some mistrust. This is the case even in relation to new left parties with which NGOs most closely affiliate. NGOs seek to democratize these left political parties.

Since Latino NGO advocacy on the IFIs prioritizes national agendas, the campaigns logically seek to strengthen the internal accountability mechanisms established by national constitutions. These channels include legislatures, constitutional courts, the ombudsmen and, in some cases, the judicial system. This evolution has been most evident in Mexico and Brazil but has started to appear also in other countries. The NGO view is that these institutions will only move and better represent people if they are placed under pressure from civil society. None the less, NGOs need to better understand the roles and procedures of such institutions.

Another major future challenge for Latino NGO advocacy on global finance is to move beyond the IFIs. These agencies will probably continue to play important roles, but their work of the 1980s and 1990s has opened Latin America to private international finance actors. International commercial loans, short-term capital flows, hedge funds, derivatives and risk-assessment firms have become important aspects of global finance in Latin America. Latino NGOs have so far acquired limited knowledge of private global finance and its implications for inclusive development and democracy. Civil society groups in the region need to look more closely at these issues and to explore new rules for global financial markets.

Another challenge that NGOs in Latin America increasingly face is to have more technical and professional support for their campaigns on the IFIs. The research capabilities of most Latino NGOs have decreased in the 1990s as Northern partners cut back funds. NGOs have sought to compensate for this loss by building relations with ideologically sympathetic academic researchers. Indeed, many NGO activists also belong to university staff. Bridging relations between NGOs and academics will require a better understanding of their different approaches, establishing exchanges and, in some cases, joint fund-raising.

Latino NGOs must also build up other capacities for campaigns on global finance. For example, many NGOs need to strengthen their information management and use of electronic communications. Other efforts are needed to improve campaign and lobbying methods, mobilization of public opinion, and relations with the mass media. Many of these areas are new or unevenly developed among Latin American NGOs. In many cases, advances on these points require specialized support.

Finally, there is the challenge of funding. Latin America has an increasingly active community of advocacy NGOs. However, this work remains strongly dependent on external funding. As international aid and cooperation with Latin America decreases, or is linked to political and commercial objectives, resources available for Southern NGOs also decline in most countries.[26] Local groups are therefore pushed to find different ways to sustain their efforts. The new channels include alternative funders like US-based foundations, consultancy work, contracts with states to deliver services, and other income-generating activities. In addition, some funds for Latino NGOs can be obtained from the advocacy departments of Northern NGOs. Meanwhile, the mobilization of local financial support is still very limited. Some modes of financing are more compatible with advocacy than others. Continued NGO efforts on the IFIs will depend very much on how the funding issue is addressed.

In closing

International financial institutions have played a major role in Latin America. Their reform packages have opened up the region to global financial markets and their failures. Financial market volatility and instability strongly hit the region through Mexico in 1994 and Brazil and Argentina in 1999. IFIs have started to look at the conditions necessary to limit the damages of such market phenomena, in most cases through a deepening of structural adjustment policies.

Civil society in Latin America has mainly addressed global finance with a focus on the IFIs. At first Latino NGOs were strongly under the influence of Northern groups. More recently the Latin American associations have constructed a more domestic agenda that seeks to bring the role of the IFIs and the responsibilities of governments into public debate. To that end, NGOs are emphasizing themes of transparency, accountability and participation. They have also developed broad-based civil society constituencies to promote such debates and the construction of alternative development directions.

None the less, Latino NGO coalitions need to pay more attention to a number of areas. They must look at global finance as involving more than the IFIs. They must strengthen their professional capabilities, both within their own organizations and through alliances with universities and academic centers. They must pay more attention to communication with public opinion at large and give increased effort to educating citizens on issues of global finance. Advocacy will require not only technical expertise, but also public mobilization, directly or through parliaments, congresses and judicial systems. Constructing advocacy coalitions along these lines will also help to reconstruct Latin American coalitions with Northern groups on a more sound and sustainable base.

Notes

1 A. Vianna, "Pensar Localmente, Agir Globalmente: A Construção de uma agenda nacional para atuar frente as Instituções Financeiras Multilaterais" ["Think Locally, Act Globally: The Construction of a National Action Agenda regarding Multilateral Financial Institutions"], *Proposta* (December 1998–February 1999), pp. 12–19.

2 World Bank, *En el Umbral del Siglo XXI. Informe sobre el Desarrollo Mundial, 1999–2000* [*Entering the Twenty-First Century: World Development Report 1999–2000*], Washington, DC: World Bank, 1999, p. 270; World Bank, *Informe Annual 1999* [*Annual Report 1999*], Washington, DC: World Bank, 1999, p. 90; Inter-American Development Bank, *Informe Annual 1999* [*Annual Report 1999*], p. 2.

3 S. J. Burki and G. Perry, *The Long March: A Reform Agenda for Latin America and the Caribbean in the Next Decade*, Washington, DC: World Bank, 1997, p. 13; *70th Annual Report*, Basle: Bank for International Settlements, 2000, p. 37.

4 C. Wyplosz, "International Financial Instability", in Inge Kaul *et al.* (eds), *Global Public Goods: International Cooperation in the 21st Century*, New York: Oxford University Press, 1999, p. 156.

5 World Bank, *Annual Report*, Washington, DC: World Bank, various years; Inter-American Development Bank, *Annual Report*, Washington, DC: IDB, various years.

6 International Monetary Fund, *Annual Report 1998*, Washington, DC: IMF, 1998; *Annual Report 2000*, Washington, DC: IMF, 2000.

7 M. Naim, "Washington Consensus or Washington Confusion?", *Foreign Policy*, No. 118, Spring 2000, p. 89. See also B. Martib, *New Leaf or Fig Leaf: The Challenge of the New Washington Consensus*, London: Bretton Woods Project and Public Services International, 2000.

8 S. J. Burki and G. Perry, op. cit.; E. Lora and F. Barrera, *Una Década de Reformas Estructurales en América Latina: El crecimiento, la productividad y la inversión ya no son como antes* [*A Decade of Structural Reform in Latin America: Growth, Productivity and Investment are not as before*], Washington, DC: Office of the Chief Economist, Inter-American Development Bank, 1997; S. J. Burki and G. Perry, *Beyond the Washington Consensus: Institutions Matter*, Washington, DC: World Bank, 1998.

9 Gabriel Casaburi and Diana Tussie, "La Sociedad Civil y los Bancos Multilaterales de Desarrollo" ["Civil Society and the Multilateral Development Banks"], in Diana Tussie, ed., *Luces y Sombras de una Nueva Relación*, Buenos Aires: FLACSO, Temas Grupo Editorial, 2000, p. 17.

10 CEPAL, *Panorama Social de América Latina* [*Social Panorama of Latin America*], Santiago: CEPAL, 1994.

11 World Bank, *Global Development Finance, 1999*, Washington, DC: World Bank, 1999, table 2.8.

12 World Bank, *Informe Annual 2000* [*Annual Report 2000*], Washington, DC: World Bank, 2000, p. 86.

13 Inter-American Development Bank, *Informe Annual 1996 y 1999* [*Annual Report 1996 and 1999*], Chapter 3, p. 1.

14 See, for example, A. Acosta, *La Deuda Eterna* [*The Eternal Debt*], Quito: LIBRESA, 1994, pp. 363–4.

15 ALOP–FOLADE–FEPP, *Fondos de Deuda Externa y de Contravalor para el Desarrollo* [*External Debt and Countervalue Funds for Development*], Quito: Fondo Ecuatoriano Populorum Progressio, 1997.

16 R. Reygadas, *Abriendo Veredas* [*Opening Paths*], Mexico: Convergencia de Organismos Civiles para la Democracia, 1998.

17 Margaret E. Keck, "Planaforo in Rondonia: The Limits of Leverage", in Jonathan A. Fox and L. David Brown (eds), *The Struggle for Accountability*, Cambridge, MA: MIT Press, 1998, pp. 181–218.

18 CEPAL, *Transformación Productiva con Equidad* [*Productive Transformation with Equity*], Santiago: CEPAL, 1990; UNDP, *Informe sobre el Desarrollo Humano* [*Human Development Report*], Madrid: PNUD-CIDEAL, annual since 1990. See also ALOP, *América Latina: Opciones Estratégicas de Desarrollo* [*Latin America: Strategic Options for Development*], Caracas: Nueva Sociedad, 1992, where the first debates between NGOs and the international development agencies took place.

19 See NGO Working Group on the World Bank, *Structural Adjustment*, London: NGO Working Group on the World Bank, 1995.

20 G. Irías, *Ajuste Estructural e Inversión Social* [*Structural Adjustment and Social Investment*], San José: ICCO-ALOP-DEI, 1996.

21 Fundación Augusto Cesar Sandino, *La Restructuración del Banco Mundial, Nicaragua: el caso AIF* [*The Restructuring of the World Bank: The Case of IDA and Nicaragua*], paper presented at the third meeting of the Latin American and Caribbean NGO Working Group, Lima, 1998.

22 Paul Nelson, "Conflict, Legitimacy and Effectiveness: Who Speaks for Whom in Transnational NGO Networks Lobbying the World Bank?", *Non-Profit and Voluntary Sector Quarterly*, Vol. 26, No. 4, December 1997, pp. 426–41.

23 Jane Covey, "Is Critical Cooperation Possible? Influencing the World Bank through Operational Collaboration and Policy Dialogue", in Fox and Brown, op. cit. pp. 81–119. See also Manuel Chiriboga, "NGOs and the World Bank: Lessons and Challenges", in FIM, *Civil Society Engaging Multilateral Institutions, At the Crossroads*, Vol. 1, No. 1, Fall 1999, Proceedings of the First International Forum of Montreal, held on 8 September 1999, pp. 24–32.

24 Cf. Vianna, op. cit., p.19; and F.V. Mello, "Entre a Política de Poder e a Utopía de Governo global: alguns desafios políticos e teóricos para a ação cidadá frente a global-ição" ["Between the Politics of Power and the Utopia of a Global Government: Political and Theoretical Challenges for Citizen Actions regarding Globalization"], *Proposta*, December 1998/February 1999, p. 17.

25 J. Castañeda and R. Mangabeira, *Una nueva visión para el futuro de América latina en el Umbral del Milenio* [*A New Vision for the Future of Latin America at the Dawn of a New Millennium*], Lima: Caretas, 1998.

26 ALOP, *La Realidad de la Ayuda al 2000, Enfoque América Latina* [*The Reality of Aid in the Year 2000: A Latin American Perspective*], Lima: ALOP, 1999.

3 Civil society and global finance in Africa

The PRSP process in Uganda

Zie Gariyo

Summary

Introduction

Africa has generally lain at the margins of contemporary global finance. Africans have owned but a tiny proportion of global savings and have obtained only a small share of global credits. Most of the limited sums of global finance capital in Africa have come from official sources rather than from commercial markets. Loans from the International Monetary Fund (IMF) and the World Bank have figured especially prominently.

Although Africa has had little involvement in global finance when its absolute levels of transborder flows are compared with those of other continents, the sums have been quite substantial in relation to national incomes and export earnings in the region. Indeed, the inability of many African countries to repay their transborder loans has created crippling debt problems since the 1980s. A large proportion of these debts are owed to the IMF and the World Bank.

Civil society in Africa has for the most part remained marginal to serious policy discussions on global financial issues, both at national and at international levels. There has been relatively little engagement between civil society organizations (CSOs) in Africa and key decision makers in the global financial arena, such as multilateral agencies and governments. The main exception to this general rule relates, not surprisingly, to debt issues. Civil society networks on debt relief have been active in a number of African countries, including Angola, Cameroon, Kenya, Mozambique, Nigeria, Senegal, Tanzania, Uganda, Zambia and

Zimbabwe. Often these and other civil society groups have also addressed policies of structural adjustment that the two Bretton Woods institutions (BWIs) have pre-scribed in response to debt and development problems in Africa.

This chapter analyzes one case of African civil society engagement with the debt crisis and structural adjustment. It examines the involvement of CSOs in Uganda in the formulation of the 2000 Poverty Reduction Strategy Paper (PRSP), as required by the IMF and the World Bank before a country can access debt relief under the Heavily Indebted Poor Countries (HIPC) Initiative. The case of the PRSP process in Uganda shows how CSOs can influence policy planning at the macro level.

In examining civil society participation in the preparation of the PRSP in Uganda, the chapter analyzes broader issues, including the achievements, oppor-tunities and challenges faced by CSOs. The chapter then looks at the future prospects for broader participation by Ugandan CSOs and offers insights into critical issues of policy analysis, advocacy for increased social spending, and more. The chapter concludes that the Ugandan experience of CSO involvement with the PRSP presents important lessons that can be utilized in other HIPC countries of Africa, Latin America and Asia.

Debt relief and PRSPs in Africa

Sub-Saharan Africa has been subjected to structural adjustment programmes of the IMF and the World Bank since the early 1980s. These programmes were meant to reorient African economies to the market. However, even a casual obser-vation shows that, twenty years later, these economies are far from being wholly market-oriented.

The BWIs have acknowledged that Africa is an economic backwater and a basket case that is currently incapable of participating beneficially in global finance. In a recent report the World Bank concedes:

> Africa's place in the global economy has been eroded, with declining export shares . . . and massive capital flight and loss of skills to other regions. Now the region stands in danger of being excluded from the information revolution.[1]

Instead, most countries of Sub-Saharan Africa have acquired an unsustainable debt burden. In 1985, the external debts of the region stood at $95 billion. By 1998 this sum had reached a phenomenal $208 billion.[2] In response to the resultant crisis, the World Bank and the IMF in 1996 succumbed to international pressure to grant debt relief to poor Third World countries – many of them in Africa – with the HIPC Initiative. Three years later, as a result of further intense lobbying from civil society to make debt relief more meaningful, a so-called "enhanced HIPC" was announced to make debt relief faster, broader and deeper.

International non-governmental organizations, some Third World governments and other international development agencies have continued to charge that the HIPC scheme is too narrow and inadequate to solve the debt problem of poor countries. Confirming these views, a report to the US Congress states:

> The enhanced Heavily Indebted Poor Countries initiative will provide significant debt relief to recipient countries . . . However, given the continued fragility of these countries, the initiative is not likely to provide recipients with a lasting exit from the debt problems unless they achieve strong, sustained economic growth.[3]

To reverse the economic downturn of most poor Third World countries, the IMF in 1999 renamed the much-discredited Enhanced Structural Adjustment Facility (ESAF) as the Poverty Reduction and Growth Facility (PRGF). In the words of the IMF, this new approach is "results oriented, focusing on the outcomes that would benefit the poor".[4]

At the same time as enhancing HIPC in September 1999, the Board of Governors of the IMF and the World Bank also approved the introduction of the PRSP as the basis on which poor countries would receive the increased debt relief. An aid recipient country is required to prepare a PRSP before it can access financial support from the BWIs. The PRSP provides a framework for IMF lending and the World Bank's Country Assistance Strategy (CAS). The CAS covers the Bank's medium-term business plan and its proposed lending operations.

The PRSP outlines how a country plans to utilize debt savings in order to eradicate poverty. In terms of general principles, the document articulates the government's commitment to poverty reduction. It focuses the priority of public action on reducing poverty. The PRSP also sets out the main elements of the government's poverty reduction strategy. Mainly, the macroeconomic framework and policy matrix focuses on reducing poverty through faster economic growth. The PRSP also asserts the government's commitment to developing poverty reduction policies through a consultative process.

More specifically, a comprehensive PRSP includes poverty diagnostics based on good indicators of poverty and its reduction. It also presents a shared communal vision of desired poverty reduction goals, reached through a participatory process, and it lays out participatory processes to monitor policy implementation and progress in poverty reduction.[5]

As the preceding remarks suggest, governments are enjoined to formulate PRSPs in a participatory manner, involving consultations with other stakeholders including CSOs as partners in development. The BWIs have conceded that economic recovery for poor Third World countries cannot take place unless civil societies in the respective countries are involved in the policy-making process, including, in particular, how macroeconomic policies are formulated and implemented. Thus one of the central features of the PRSP is the requirement that civil society should participate. According to the IMF, the PRSP is "country-driven and owned, based on broad based participatory processes for formulation, implementation and outcome based progress monitoring"; it is "partnership oriented".[6]

The prescription of partnership between government and civil society in the PRSP process is novel. The majority of Third World states have never regarded civil society as a stakeholder. Yet the insistence by the IMF and the World Bank on civil society participation could, in fact, worsen the situation. Countries could be denied access to much-needed aid resources if they fail to build a government-civil society partnership. Alternatively, governments could be encouraged to coerce their civil societies into endorsing the country's PRSP in situations where there has been no dialogue. As the previously cited official report to the US Congress states:

> The desire to receive debt relief quickly may cause some countries to quickly prepare the strategies, which could diminish the strategies' quality or the level of civil society participation.[7]

All countries that are engaged in formulating a PRSP should heed this observation. Uganda's advantage was that the formulation of the country's PRSP coincided with the revision of its Poverty Eradication Action Plan (PEAP). Uganda was not starting from scratch. Even here, it took over two months, from December 1999 to the end of January 2000, to get government, donors and civil society to agree on the conceptual framework. In most countries, where there is no prior dialogue between civil society and government, the possibility of discussing even the outline of such a conceptual framework remains remote.

The demand that civil society should engage government and multilateral financial institutions is neither an innovation nor a change of heart on the part of the BWIs. Their rhetoric on civil society participation cannot be taken for granted, as some studies have shown.[8] In fact, the Bank and the Fund have with the PRSP turned a genuine demand by civil society on its head. Instead of allowing civil society in Sub-Saharan Africa to set the conditions of engagement with their governments, the BWIs' intervention may have disastrous consequences. Civil society is demanding participation in a broad process of dialogue with donors and governments, but the IMF and the World Bank are interested only in preparing a PRSP as an end in itself. They are using these mechanisms as a carrot and stick to restructure the financial regime in Africa. Whether or not they will succeed remains to be seen.

Thus, in most African countries there is resistance from both governments and civil societies to the formulation of PRSPs. For example, a Government of Kenya delegation that paid a visit to the offices of Uganda Debt Network to discuss civil society involvement and learn from the Uganda experience remarked – after a lengthy explanation about the extent of civil society engagement – that civil society could be anti-government. In Kenya it was unheard of for the state to give free reign to civil society organizations to mobilize and engage the government in policy design and planning. The delegation implied that the inclusion of grassroots community people in the Ugandan PRSP consultations was tantamount to undermining the state. Other critics have described IMF involvement in the PRSP process as a usurpation of the power of the governments of the countries concerned. On this diagnosis "in many ways, participation in PRSPs is engineering consent for structural adjustment policies".[9]

The PEAP/PRSP in Uganda

Preparation of the PRSP for Uganda took place in January–April 2000. The consultation process had several dimensions: (a) consultations between government and donors; (b) consultations between government and civil society; and (c) consultations within civil society. The Executive Boards of the World Bank and the IMF approved the Ugandan PRSP in May 2000.

The formulation of the PRSP coincided with the Government of Uganda's revision of its Poverty Eradication Action Plan. Eventually the donors accepted the revised PEAP as the PRSP for Uganda. The PEAP is a broad policy framework paper formulated in 1997 for the elimination of poverty in Uganda.[10] Since that time, Poverty Priority Areas (PPAs) have been selected, and budget resources have been mobilized for these places.

The government made sure that research findings from various institutions were incorporated into the PEAP review process. Particularly important in this regard were materials from the Uganda Participatory Poverty Assessment Project (UPPAP) of the Ministry of Finance, Planning and Economic Development (MFPED). This participatory project was established to collect data and information from poor people regarding their own perceptions and definitions of poverty. Such inputs widened the scope and definition of poverty and broadened ownership of the PEAP. Other research bodies, such as the Makerere Institute of Social Research (MISR) and the Economic Policy Research Centre (EPRC), also based at Makerere University, were actively involved in the analysis and compilation of the PEAP.

The government set up a technical team that worked around the clock to produce drafts at very high speed. The first draft of the revised PEAP in February was a mere seventy pages. By mid-March the number of pages had more than doubled. The final draft in April was more than 200 pages long. Government officials faced intermittent pressure from IMF and World Bank staff to produce a draft PRSP in a period of only three months, so as to present it to their Executive Boards in April–May 2000.

The revised PEAP is a very comprehensive document compared to the earlier version. It identifies the critical poverty areas and prescribes the means for poverty eradication. In broad terms, the plan focuses on: (a) creating an enabling environment for sustainable economic growth and transformation; (b) promoting good governance and security; (c) raising the incomes of the poor; and (d) improving the quality of life of the poor.

The Ugandan PEAP was then turned around and redrafted to become the country's PRSP.[11] One is struck by the difference in language between the two documents. Instead of the plain language in which it was originally composed, the PEAP was rewritten to make it look more acceptable to IMF and World Bank officials. The revised version was presented to the Donor Consultative Group (CG) meetings that were held in Kampala in March 2000 and became the Ugandan PRSP. However, the document that is recognized officially in Uganda is the PEAP, and this plan forms the basis on which donors provide aid to the Government of Uganda.

Sceptics have suggested that the PRSP process might not yield anything new, merely reproducing previous perspectives along the economic growth model espoused by the IMF and the World Bank. Indeed, reading through the Ugandan PRSP one notices that nothing much has changed. The economic growth model still heavily underpins the PEAP and the PRSP.

With the approval of its PRSP, Uganda was able to access debt relief under HIPC II, becoming the first beneficiary of the Enhanced HIPC Debt Relief Initiative. To this effect, the country obtained approximately $46 million in the financial year 2000/1. Relief is projected to increase to $55 million in each of the financial years 2001/2 and 2002/3. Taken together, the HIPC I and HIPC II debt relief initiatives are producing savings of approximately $90 million annually on Uganda's repayments of foreign debts. All the savings from debt relief are being committed to poverty eradication through the Poverty Action Fund (PAF), a Government of Uganda mechanism set up in 1998 for mobilizing savings from debt relief and donors to finance poverty priorities identified in the PEAP. Through the PAF donors have almost doubled their contribution to poverty programmes in the financial year 2000/1.

Civil society participation in the PEAP/PRSP process

In December 1999 the Government of Uganda decided to revise the PEAP and to formulate its PRSP as a precondition to qualify for debt relief. The government also decided to open the process widely and allow CSOs to participate in the exercise. Civil society involvement began in December 1999, when the MFPED invited representatives of CSOs to a consultative meeting to discuss the process of revising the PEAP. In January 2000, CSOs organized a consultative meeting with government and World Bank officials. Over forty-five CSOs attended, and a Civil Society Task Force was formed, with a mandate to organize an all-inclusive consultation process, involving as many sections of Ugandan civil society as possible.

The Task Force was composed of representatives of international and national NGOs operating in Uganda. The international NGOs included Oxfam (UK), Action Aid (UK), VECO Uganda (Belgium), SNV (Netherlands), and MS Uganda (Denmark). The Ugandan NGOs included Action for Development (ACFODE), the Uganda Women's Network (UWONET) and research institutions such as the Centre for Basic Research and MISR. The Uganda chapter of the Forum for Women Educationalists (FAWE), a regional NGO based in Kampala, also joined the Task Force. Later, World Vision International and the Catholic Medical Bureau were co-opted as Task Force members.

The Uganda Debt Network (UDN) became the lead agency for civil society participation in the PEAP/PRSP process. The UDN is an advocacy and lobbying coalition of NGOs (both local and international), academic, research and religious institutions, and individuals. It was formed in 1996, primarily to campaign for debt relief under the HIPC Initiative. The UDN was also the lead organization in Uganda for the Jubilee 2000 campaign for total cancellation of unpayable debts of poor countries. Through these campaigns the UDN engaged government and donors and lobbied to ensure that savings from debt relief are spent on poverty eradication programmes, especially in the areas of education and health. Today the network has more than sixty-six members.[12]

Ugandan CSOs recognized that, in spite of their lack of capacity and the short time available for preparing the PRSP, there were benefits from participation and such an opportunity should not be dismissed. CSOs followed the government example and set up their own technical team to speed up consultations with ministry officials. This step proved very decisive in raising the profile of the CSOs and accelerating the pace of their participation.

CSOs mobilized representatives of their constituents through various forums and engaged them in discussions to solicit their inputs into the PEAP/PRSP. The Civil Society Task Force for the revision of the PEAP and the formulation of the PRSP carried out numerous consultations with grassroots people to collect their views on poverty reduction. It organized numerous workshops, seminars and radio and television discussions. However, the highlight of these consultations were the two-and-a-half-day workshops, at which community representatives were invited to discuss the draft PEAP documents. The Task Force organized eight zonal meetings (where each zone encompassed four to seven districts), which together involved over 644 participants (405 male and 239 female). The UDN used its grassroots campaign experience in the Jubilee 2000 campaign to identify focal points that would mobilize the participants.

It was decided that the meetings should be as inclusive as possible, involving men, people with disabilities, women, youth, elderly people, religious leaders and community leaders. However, to make it a truly civil society input, the invitation excluded local government officials and local political leaders. The MFPED organized consultations with these circles.

The Civil Society Task Force also organized a media campaign, including radio and television phone-in programmes at which government officials were invited to respond to queries from the public and to explain the PRSP process. The Task Force also published information in the media to guide the consultations and invited the general public to make their contribution. Over 40,000 copies of a newspaper pull-out and 10,000 copies of a policy brief were published and circulated to the public.

Other civil society consultations were held in addition to those organized by the Task Force. This was partly because the Task Force had little time to mobilize extensively for the participation of all civil society organizations. Moreover, participation was voluntary, requiring commitment and sacrifice from those involved. Initiative from outside the Task Force was considered a source of dynamism and contributed to the success of the consultations. So the Task Force encouraged its members and other development actors to hold consultations and present findings to the Technical Team for incorporation into the civil society memorandum to government.

In this vein, Oxfam organized a consultation for over forty NGOs and community-based organizations involved in rural water and the improvement of sanitation. DENIVA, the umbrella body of indigenous associations in Uganda, organized a consultation with over fifteen of its members in two districts in North East Uganda. MS Uganda, the Danish NGO, organized and obtained reports from consultations with over 135 community representatives in the West Nile region in North West Uganda.

Furthermore, the Task Force organized consultations with special interest groups, such as those engaged in conflict resolution, environmental issues, and others. Other CSOs such as trade unions – through the National Union of Trade Unions (NOTU) – and the Uganda National Students Association (UNSA) were invited to attend the initial meetings, but they did not actively participate in the consultations. The Uganda National Farmers Association (UNFA) did not organize consultations with its large constituency, although the Task Force encouraged it to do so.

Findings from these civil society consultations were presented to the Technical Committee of the Ministry of Finance, Planning and Economic Development, which was responsible for the drafting of the PEAP document. This committee, in turn, incorporated as much of the inputs as possible into the PEAP draft. Sometimes, civil society inputs were wholly incorporated into the draft. For instance, government incorporated the whole section on participation and monitoring written by civil society. In the first draft, the issue of employment was not seriously discussed. After a seminar organized by the Task Force, at which the government was criticized for ignoring the issue, employment was given much more attention. The government appreciated civil society inputs to get specific areas of interest clarified and others prominently articulated, thus improving the quality of the entire PEAP.

The Ugandan experience of civil society participation in the preparation of a PRSP shows that government commitment to these consultations is essential. In spite of the strict guidelines that civil society participation in the formulation of a country's PRSP is essential, most governments in Africa are not yet ready to accept CSOs as serious stakeholders in policy planning. The Government of Uganda ensured that CSOs were given enough space in the PEAP/PRSP process by organizing independent consultations and incorporating as much of the their inputs into the documents as possible. This was a very important milestone in changing government–civil society relationships in Africa.

The Government of Uganda provided as much information as was required by the CSOs. It also made available the draft PEAP/PRSP for circulation. This document was synthesized, and a four-page summary was produced to guide the facilitators of the consultation workshops. The government furthermore allowed CSOs to attend as full members the meetings of the National Task Force (NTF), comprised of senior government officials. The civil society technical team was also in close and continuous contact with the government technical team, composed of senior technocrats and consultants responsible for compiling the PEAP report. These officials were charged with receiving and reviewing all the inputs from the various stakeholders and incorporating them into the PEAP/PRSP.

Moreover, the government did not dictate the agenda of the CSOs in the PEAP/PRSP consultations, nor the methodology to be used in CSO consultations with community people. The Government of Uganda has recognized civil society as a partner in the development process of the country. The authorities have increasingly widened the space for civil society participation. The Planning Ministry, the lead government agency in these matters, took it upon itself to ensure that CSOs were regularly represented at the table in the PEAP/PRSP process.

Nevertheless, Ugandan CSOs felt left out of the later stages of the process, when they were excluded from the discussions that turned the Ugandan PEAP into the PRSP that was presented to the IMF/World Bank Executive Boards. Although there were numerous contacts with government officials at all stages in the preparation of the PEAP, there were fewer contacts with donors and, more specifically, with the IMF and the World Bank missions in the preparation of the IMF version of the PRSP document. The few meetings that did take place between the missions and CSOs were almost like verification meetings to find out the level of civil society participation and the quality of inputs. Members of the Civil Society Task Force met with various World Bank missions and a mission from the US State Department, but these discussions were more general.

Civil society and the PEAP/PRSP: contributions and problems

Limited capacities notwithstanding, Ugandan CSOs faced the challenge of timely delivery of inputs, critical analysis of draft documents, comprehensive consultations with all stakeholders and the production of materials that would be acceptable to the government technical team. These efforts had a number of positive results. Most of the inputs and recommendations by civil society were incorporated into the final PEAP report that was developed in March 2000.

For one thing, CSO inputs helped to build a consensus on poverty eradication as a priority issue. This consensus between government, civil society and donors did not exist before. Under the Ugandan PEAP/PRSP, the bulk of the government budget will be focused on poverty eradication, while maintaining high levels of economic growth. Growth will be assessed in terms of its effects in reducing the incidence of poverty. Expenditures for the Priority Poverty Areas (PPAs) will be ring fenced and will not suffer routine budgetary cuts or a diversion of funds when emergencies or unexpected expenditures occur. Nevertheless, whether or not this commitment is upheld will depend on the vigilance of civil society in monitoring budgetary expenditure.

In addition, civil society involvement in the PEAP/PRSP process made employment creation and the formulation of an employment policy a priority concern. In the initial drafts, government officials and donors were reluctant to emphasize employment issues. However, after a serious debate led by CSOs, this question now ranks high on the list of critical issues, next to macroeconomic stability.

During the consultative workshops organized by government to discuss the cost of implementing the goals of the PEAP/PRSP, the issue of basket funding rather than project funding for budgetary support became contentious. In the past, most donors have tied their aid to project support. CSOs supported the proposal by government that budget support should be flexible in order to give government a bigger say in the allocation of expenditure for poverty eradication. This is necessary to enable government to redirect over-funded areas to less-funded but equally critical and deserving areas. For instance, in Uganda donors have committed more money to the education sector (and primary education in particular) than to any other sector.[13] So education has become over-funded with donor aid, while other equally critical areas, such as agriculture and rural small-scale industry, have not been similarly privileged. Although one appreciates the importance of education in poverty eradication, that goal involves a whole series of issues that must be tackled simultaneously and not one at a time.

Donors have now accepted a recommendation from the civil society consultations that aid should be provided in one basket, as part of the budgetary resources to be spent in the agreed priority areas of the PEAP. However, it remains to be seen whether they will fulfil their commitment. Donors are worried about the lack of effective accountability and continued reports about misuse of public resources by government officials. Hence, donors are wont to tread cautiously, thereby delaying the implementation of key programmes. Nevertheless, civil society organizations expect that aid and budgetary resources such as taxes will be merged within the Medium Term Expenditure Framework.

Civil society involvement in formulating the PEAP/PRSP has also had positive results in terms of future evaluation of policies. CSOs and other stakeholders in Uganda will be heavily involved in the monitoring of poverty indicators. The government has committed itself to make all relevant information about public policies known to as many stakeholders as possible. The government will also seek to publicize budgetary policies and public expenditure reviews. In addition to this enhanced transparency, the government has committed itself to building institutional capacities for accountability. It will assist local governments to recruit competent staff to help them with accountability and planning.

As a starting point, the Uganda Debt Network is already involved in monitoring the Poverty Action Fund (PAF), which is used for primary education, health, rural roads, agricultural extension services, micro-finance and HIV/AIDS programmes.[14] PAF Monitoring Committees, composed of representatives selected by community people at the grassroots, have been set up to carry out continuous monitoring of the implementation of the programmes under the PAF.

However, along with the benefits, CSO involvement in the formulation of the Ugandan PRSP also produced a number of problems. For example, during the process it was clear that most CSOs lacked staff capacity to engage donors and policy planners in meaningful dialogue about macroeconomic policy issues. This remains a problem at both national and local levels. In Uganda only a few CSOs have the capacity to influence policy planning. The others are not even aware that space is open for them to participate. As a result, there is a danger that CSOs might endorse positions about which they have little knowledge.

Moreover, if the Government of Uganda had not deliberately encouraged the participation of CSOs, no input would have been delivered. In some cases, government officials took the initiative to send drafts of the PEAP/PRSP documents to Task Force members for comments and inputs. In one case, a workshop organized by the Planning Ministry to discuss the draft PEAP was at their request co-facilitated by CSO representatives. In specific goal areas CSO representatives were asked to lead the discussions. These included: (a) improving the quality of life of the people; and (b) raising the incomes of the poor.

In addition, CSO representatives participated in all the discussions that took place either in plenary or in group discussions. Thus, it can be seen that, given the short time available to formulate a PRSP, CSOs are prepared to respond quickly. Moreover, in the case of Uganda, CSOs had participated in formulating the first PEAP in 1997, so they were familiar with the content of the documents. CSOs had also participated in a two-year project, the Uganda Participatory Poverty Assessment Project (UPPAP), which had extensively collected the views of poor people at the grassroots.

The Ugandan experience shows that deliberate efforts are needed first to build the capacity of CSOs, especially the national organizations, if they are to have a greater impact on policy planning, implementation, monitoring and evaluation. Capacity building includes the recruitment of high-calibre, skilled and well-trained staff to implement some of the strategic programmes. Counterparts in government are well trained and knowledgeable in their fields of competence and have little patience for a slow pace on the part of CSOs. At local level, CSOs need to build the capacity of grassroots people to monitor policy implementation. For its part, local government must develop transparent and accountable systems that enable grassroots communities to have access to the information they need to conduct effective monitoring.

Another challenge is to use CSO influence and achievements. CSO inputs should be mainstreamed into policy planning. Some government officials still regard CSO participation merely as an exercise to legitimize the government agenda. They still view criticism from CSOs with suspicion.

Furthermore, CSOs need to fully understand and analyze the donor agenda. Donors retain a strong influence over budgetary and other policy plans in Africa (and elsewhere in the Third World) because they contribute a large portion of the government budget. For instance, in the financial year 2000/1 Uganda's budget was dependent for 53 per cent on donors, including loans and grants, while the government contribution was only 47 per cent.

Civil society organizations in Uganda that participated in the formulation of the Ugandan PRSP believe that there were good lessons to be learned and achievements to be used as a starting point for future engagements with government and donors. Relationships between civil society and government were put on a new footing. Several CSOs became part of the whole budget planning process and are now represented on Sector Working Groups, such as the Macro Working Group and the Poverty Working Group. However, it was also noted that CSOs often lack the necessary skills and knowledge to engage government and donors and that CSOs neglected the engagement with donors.

The future of African civil society participation in the PRSPs

Whether or not civil society continues to play a significant role in future donor–government policy planning process remains to be seen. What is clear is that, for CSOs effectively to influence policies in Uganda and elsewhere in Africa, there must be a conducive policy environment. Thus, to require that governments in Third World countries should prepare a participatory PRSP in a short time – also when such governments do not have respect for their own people's views – is not realistic. The Government of Uganda was central to the participation of the CSOs and was anxious to have their inputs included in the PRSP.

Civil society participation in the formulation of the PRSP increases democratic ownership of the process. Increased ownership enhances policy implementation, so that intended outcomes can be better realized. However, some civil society activists have opposed the timing of PRSPs. They argue that civil society participation is given only cursory attention. For instance, in reference to the Tanzania experience, Charles Abugre has criticized the PRSP process thus:

> Sometimes the IMF and the World Bank make all the important lending decisions for a government just before a PRSP is finalized . . . Tanzania's full PRSP comes to the Board in November 2000, yet before that (from April through June 2000), the IMF and World Bank approved their lending frameworks and programmes for the country. We wonder what purpose the full PRSP will serve in Tanzania.[15]

Such actions undermine the essence of participation in the PRSP process and the paper itself, since the donors have already gone ahead to take care of their own interests in their lending mechanisms. The PRSP then becomes a *dormant paper*. Realistic participation is needed to ensure that the voices of the poor are heard and considered.

If taken seriously, the PRSP marks a fundamental departure from being a donor tool to a tool for evolving the principles of participation in eradicating poverty. It provides a framework for consultations with various stakeholders, including the poor themselves. CSO participation in the development of PRSPs increases the chances that the needs of the poor are considered.

Although civil society participates in the PRSP process, it faces the challenge of sustaining this policy involvement. Many CSOs lack the adequate capacity to engage in quality dialogues with stakeholders such as the donors and even the government itself. A lot has to be done to enhance the capacity of CSOs in the decision-making process. The future of civil society participation in not only the PRSPs but also other development papers depends on initiatives to increase CSOs' capacity in the decision-making process.

The future of participatory PRSPs depends also on how seriously the IMF and the World Bank take them. Stakeholder participation and the outcomes of consultations must be treated seriously not just in words but also in deeds, by making them truly reflect the concerns, demands and interests of the poor. PRSPs must have clearly set goals decided by the governments and people in poor countries. The Bretton Woods institutions should avoid imposing a PRSP, even an interim one, on any country, as it undermines the credibility of such a document and will only perpetuate rather than lessen aid conditionalities.

Notes

1 World Bank, *Can Africa Claim the 21st Century?*, Washington, DC: World Bank, 2000, p. 1.
2 UNDP, *Human Development Report 2000*, New York: Oxford University Press, 2000.
3 *Debt Relief Initiative for Poor Countries Faces Challenges*, United States General Accounting Office (GAO) Report to Congressional Committees, June 2000.
4 *News and Notices for IMF and World Bank Watchers*, Washington, DC: Bread for the World, 2000.
5 For more on PRSPs, see http://www.worldbank.org/poverty/strategies/index.htm.
6 *News and Notices*, op. cit.
7 *Report of the General Accounting Office*,Washington, DC: Department of State, 2000.
8 E.g. Paul J. Nelson, *The World Bank and Non-Governmental Organizations: The Limits of Apolitical Development*. London: Macmillan, 1995; Jan Aart Scholte, "'In the Foothills': Relations between the IMF and Civil Society," in Richard A. Higgott, Geoffrey R. H. Underhill and Andreas Bieler (eds), *Non-State Actors and Authority in the Global System*, London: Routledge, 2000, pp. 256–73.
9 Charles Abugre and Nancy Alexander, "Whitewashing Blackmail: How the IMF and the World Bank Cover up Their Coercive Lending Programmes with Governments of Low Income Countries," unpublished paper, July 2000.
10 http://www.udn.or.ug/peap2/pdf.
11 Government of Uganda, *Poverty Eradication Action Plan and Poverty Reduction Strategy Paper*, Kampala, draft report, 2000.
12 http://www.udn.or.ug/
13 In 1997 the government of Uganda implemented a policy of Universal Primary Education for four children per family. Since then, the number of pupils enrolled in primary schools has jumped from 2.9 million in 1997 to over 6.5 million in 2000. Donors have contributed substantially to funding for primary education. The government now argues that, in order to cope with increased entrance for secondary school education, there is now a need to expand the carrying capacity of the present schools and build new ones. However, donors are not enthusiastic to fund such a programme.
14 For full details see http://www.udn.or.ug/.
15 Charles Abugre, "Who Governs Low Income Countries?", *News and Notices for IMF and World Bank Watchers*, Washington, DC: Bread for the World, 2000.

4 Civil society and the Asian financial crisis

Kamal Malhotra[1]

Summary

• Introduction	64
• Globalization and the East Asian crisis	65
• Civil society responses	69
• The civil society role in the Asian crisis	72
• Future prospects	76

Introduction

This chapter situates its overall analysis in the context of current patterns and processes of economic globalization and its now fractured interface with the East Asian "miracle". Globalization is defined here not just as the liberalization of international trade and finance, but also as a broader process of integrating economy, technology and governance. Globalization encompasses new markets, new rules (e.g. new multilateral agreements), new tools (e.g. information technology) and new actors (e.g. the World Trade Organization [WTO] and so-called "global civil society").[2]

Globalization is a term that is now everywhere but appears to have come from nowhere. In popular consciousness it is associated with the omnipresence and omnipotence of Coca-Cola and McDonald's and a helpless sense of inevitability. However, this chapter takes the view expressed by Rubens Ricupero, the Secretary-General of the United Nations Conference on Trade and Development (UNCTAD), that "globalization is *not* an unstoppable change sweeping inevitably across the face of the world. It is, at least in part, a work of deliberate construction".[3] We therefore need to distinguish the inevitable aspects from those that derive from policy choices.

The first substantive section of the chapter provides an analysis of how current patterns of globalization contributed to the East Asian crisis. This section also summarizes some of the history, chronology, causes and broader systemic implications of the Asian financial crisis. The analysis differentiates between South East and

North East Asia, using Thailand and the Republic of Korea, respectively, as illustrations of these two sub-regions.

The second section describes civil society responses to the Asian financial crisis. This discussion covers the types of civil society actors that became involved, as well as their transnational linkages and alliances. The third section then assesses the role of civil society in the Asian crisis, while the last section offers some reflections on future prospects for civil society influence in the ongoing debate concerning reform of the global financial architecture.

The chapter argues that civil society organizations (CSOs) were active during the Asian financial crisis from the local to the global level, both individually and in strategic alliances with other Southern and Northern organizations. Six key outcomes of the civil society role in the Asian crisis are highlighted. These range from a catalytic role in making links between economic and political democratization issues to the promotion of alternative development strategies. The chapter also summarizes both general principles and specific proposals advocated by some CSOs as a response to the crisis and then concludes with brief reflections on future prospects of civil society engagement on issues of global finance. Civil society mobilization around the Asian financial crisis has already given significant impetus to subsequent civil society activism on broader globalization issues in Seattle, Washington, Prague and – most recently and most importantly – Porto Alegre in Brazil.

Globalization and the East Asian crisis

The current patterns and processes of globalization, while complex and multifaceted, are nevertheless clearly led by economics and finance. The main emphasis has been on the regional and global integration of national economies through the liberalization and deregulation of both product and capital markets. As a result, private capital flows to developing countries increased approximately fivefold before the Asian crisis, from $48 billion in 1990 to $244 billion in 1996.[4]

At the same time, official development assistance (ODA) actually declined, from approximately $60 billion to less than $45 billion, only a little more than the volume of private capital flows in 1996 to just one country, the People's Republic of China, at $42.3 billion.[5] In 1990, ODA accounted for 56 per cent of total financial flows to developing countries and private flows for the remaining 44 per cent. In contrast, by 1998 official and private flows respectively accounted for 16 and 84 per cent of the total.[6] The dynamic between ODA and private capital has therefore totally changed, with significant consequences for the poorest developing countries and for poor and vulnerable population groups within all developing countries, including the so-called "emerging markets" of East Asia. While ODA remains important for the least developed countries, this is not the case – at least in aggregate terms – for the "emerging markets" of East Asia that were in the eye of the financial storm of 1997–8.

Private capital flows have clearly had a major impact on the middle-income countries that were most directly hit by the Asian crisis. The large inflows benefited certain population groups (especially some professionals and the already capital-rich) during the boom period of the early 1990s. However, the positive impacts largely bypassed vulnerable sectors of society. Moreover, on the negative side, the immediate aftermath of the crisis saw net capital outflows of $12 billion from Indonesia, the Republic of Korea, Malaysia, the Philippines, and Thailand in 1997, as against net inflows of $93 billion in 1996.[7] These withdrawals had, and continue to have, a devastating social impact.

The Asian crisis started in July 1997 with the devaluation of the Thai baht. However, the seeds of the debacle were sown many years earlier, and evidence of an impending collapse existed from at least 1995. These warning signs were ignored or glossed over by key decision makers both in Thailand and in the international financial institutions.

During the second half of 1997 the crisis spread from Thailand through a so-called "contagion effect" to the Republic of Korea, Malaysia, Indonesia and the Philippines. Even Hong Kong experienced tense moments when government intervention was necessary in this bastion of "free market" economics to maintain the value of the local currency. In 1998–9, the contagion spread to the Russian Federation, Brazil and other parts of Latin America.

While the worst days of the Asian crisis are clearly over, the recovery remains precarious, partly because these countries lacked any meaningful social security system. As a result, marginalized and socially excluded population groups were made even more vulnerable in the aftermath of the crisis. A few relatively narrow economic and financial indicators have improved, but the enormous social reversals have yet to be recouped.

Indeed, a broad-based recovery in social and human development indicators is likely to take many years. In the Republic of Korea, high unemployment remains a major problem in spite of a return to very high economic growth rates. Thailand has remained flat on most indicators, with very modest economic growth. The situation in Indonesia remains serious on all fronts.

South East Asia: the case of Thailand

The connection between current patterns of globalization and the crisis are clearest in South East Asia. The case of Thailand is particularly instructive. The reasons for the crisis in Indonesia, Malaysia and the Philippines were broadly similar to the Thai experience, albeit with country-specific variations.[8]

The roots of the crisis can be traced to Thailand's addiction to foreign capital. The 1985 Plaza Accord of the Group of Seven facilitated this dependence. This agreement attempted to reduce US trade deficits with Japan by forcing an appreciation of the yen against the dollar. In consequence, the role of Japanese foreign direct investment (FDI) in South East Asia dramatically increased.

A second major cause of the financial crisis in Thailand was the country's three-point "miracle formula": financial liberalization, high interest rates, and a pegged exchange rate. Financial liberalization began in 1989 and found its institutional expression in the Bangkok International Banking Facility (BIBF), created in 1993.

The BIBF embodied Thailand's desire to attract short-term foreign capital flows. It was also meant to provide an offshore finance facility for Thai-based investments in the Mekong basin countries, although that role never really materialized. Meanwhile, high interest rates and the pegged exchange rate (linked to the US dollar for some fifteen years prior to July 1997) attracted approximately $50 billion in speculative portfolio capital to Thailand between 1993 and 1996.[9]

Thailand's problems also emanated from its low-end value added, labor-intensive export growth strategy, its failures of education policy, and its pitiful investment in research and development.[10] This combination of factors contributed significantly to the subsequent loss of Thailand's export competitiveness in a context of global trade liberalization. Thai exports suffered especially from competition with the People's Republic of China, given Thailand's comparatively higher labor costs.[11]

This two-pronged strategy of financial liberalization and low-end value labor-intensive exports brought short-term success, but lacked long-term sustainability. The financial liberalization process was premature and unregulated, while export competitiveness could not be easily or quickly scaled up, given the failures of both education policy and research and development investment.

Hence the experience of Thailand exemplifies the perils of excessive dependency on foreign capital and exports as a soft alternative to progressive domestic taxation and increasing the purchasing power of the poor. The country used foreign capital rather than raising revenue and resources at home. This dependence has been compounded in the Thai case by its striking reliance on both imported skilled labor and the sex trade for export revenues.

North East Asia: the case of the Republic of Korea

North East Asia differed from South East Asia in important respects. South Korea and Taiwan were not addicted to foreign capital, and their "miracles" were substantially financed through high domestic savings and investment. The state played a key role: by supplying subsidized credit to priority sectors and industries; by providing export incentives; by placing controls on foreign borrowing; and by ensuring a stable exchange rate. The state determined capacity and economies of scale in strategic and priority industries.[12]

This approach changed in the early 1990s. The Republic of Korea adopted a more liberal stance towards foreign capital, owing to the pressures of globalization and the requirements of its new membership in the rich countries' club, the Paris-based Organization for Economic Cooperation and Development (OECD). The government relaxed controls, which *inter alia* allowed massive short-term borrowing abroad and excessive investment in a few industries. Further pressure came with the forced appreciation of the national currency, the won, several years prior to the crisis, largely under pressure from aggressive unilateral US trade policy. This combination of factors was aggravated by a failure to maintain adequate levels of investment in research and development and an increasing lack of transparency in the *chaebols*, Korea's large industrial and trading conglomerates. The latter problem became especially acute after many *chaebols* became transnational corporations (TNCs) and thus less subject to effective control by the Korean authorities. Lacking adequate monitoring, many *chaebols* engaged in excessive borrowing and investment. Much of this investment went into hotels, golf courses and real estate rather than research and development or manufacturing. In sum, South Korea's crisis resulted in large part from the forces of neoliberal economic globalization which led the government to abandon the previously successful strategy of state intervention and state-assisted capitalism.[13]

Broader systemic implications

In terms of both scope and impact, the Asian crisis has undoubtedly been the most serious financial breakdown since the collapse of the Bretton Woods regime in the early 1970s. The debt crisis of the 1980s had a profound impact on Northern commercial banks, but the Asian crisis has had far-reaching consequences for Northern economies as a whole. Global financial integration has greatly deepened in recent decades, so that a crisis can readily spread through the so-called "contagion effect". Moreover, the countries of East Asia have over the same period obtained a substantial share of world trade and production, thereby increasing the repercussions that a crisis in this region has for the world economy at large. The financial crisis that erupted in 1997 was therefore a global crisis with a regional trigger in East Asia. It caused a significant drop in global economic growth and made economic recovery in Japan much more difficult.

The Asian crisis challenged key aspects of the "free market" doctrine and the role of the private sector. The collapse of 1997 reflected a clear failure of *laissez-faire* policies to produce an optimal global allocation of capital. The visible symptoms of this failure were excessive lending by international financial markets and excessive borrowing abroad by domestic private sectors.

In spite of these problems of the private sector, the International Monetary Fund (IMF) responded to the Asian crisis – especially in its initial phase – with measures that closely resembled the medicine that the Fund prescribed for the public sector in Latin America in the 1980s. These tight monetary and fiscal policies led to high interest rates, deflation (in the case of Thailand), and big squeezes in social and other budgetary expenditures as national governments tried to balance their budgets or (as in Thailand, at least initially) to generate a budget surplus. This approach compounded the problems of the Asian crisis, both deepening difficulties of the private sector in the afflicted countries and extending the crisis to the public sector as well.[14]

The Asian crisis also aggravated Japan's difficulties. Japanese firms were not able to respond to their loss of competitiveness by outsourcing through FDI to South East Asia as they had done following the Plaza Accord. The companies were already heavily financially exposed in South East Asia, which moreover had excess capacity in manufacturing.

Most importantly, the Asian crisis highlighted the systemic weaknesses of current global monetary and financial regimes. Contemporary globalization has made world financial markets much more integrated than world product markets, so that capital has gained greater mobility relative to other factors of production. Yet international financial transactions lack the degree of global governance found – however imperfectly – in the trade area.

The Asian crisis also made clear, beyond a shadow of a doubt, that current international arrangements are asymmetrical. They punish borrowers rather than regulate lenders. In the name of maintaining the stability of the international financial system, IMF prescriptions have prioritized the interests of international banks, often at the expense of living standards – especially of the poor – and of development in debtor countries. IMF rescue packages have tended to rescue profligate and irresponsible international foreign creditors at the expense of domestic financial institutions. Nor has the IMF developed effective policies to prevent "beggar-thy-neighbor" strategies affecting key monetary and financial variables. In addition – and again in contrast to the trade arena – the current global financial regime lacks a dispute settlement mechanism that could deal, for example, with competitive devaluations and unsustainable debt burdens.

The IMF is also increasingly unable to play an effective surveillance role. Indeed, it cannot even monitor, let alone regulate, international financial flows. Yet the Fund has continued to advocate capital account liberalization, even though premature and unregulated financial liberalization is widely acknowledged to be a problem rather than a solution.[15] Political circumstances have forced the IMF to temper such advocacy for the moment, but the pursuit of financial liberalization will continue as an implicit part of IMF conditionality, albeit more discreetly than before.

Finally, the Asian crisis has shown that major contributors to IMF rescue packages can take advantage of this opportunity to push their own geopolitical and geoeconomic interests. For example, the US government used this crisis and IMF conditionalities as a golden opportunity to achieve benefits for its financial sector and its TNCs – objectives that it had pursued unsuccessfully for over a decade previously in the Republic of Korea.[16] The Japanese government also exploited the trade and other economic opportunities that the crisis presented in the Republic of Korea.

Civil society responses

Civil society means different things to different people and in different political, cultural and social contexts. Used descriptively, the term is a hat-stand of limited value, since it then covers all types of non-state actors regardless of their value orientations, motives and agendas. This catchall is neither analytically nor practically useful.

For the purposes of this chapter, civil society is therefore defined as a political project of democratization and development. From this perspective CSOs encompass the range of non-state actors that are committed to the democratization of political, economic, social, cultural and environmental policies, at all levels from the local to the global. This democratization will pave the way for reductions of poverty and inequality in a manner consistent with long-term sustainable human development.

In the context of the Asian crisis, such CSOs included trade unions, women's and gender networks, human rights and environmental networks, academics, policy research institutes, other nongovernmental organizations (NGOs), and community-based organizations (CBOs). These civil society organizations operated at all levels: local, national, regional and global. They worked both alone and in alliances.

Examples of groups active at the local level during the Asian crisis included the Local Development Institute (LDI) and the Alternative Local Currency Project in Thailand. The latter project, which was conceived in direct response to the crisis, explores how local communities can de-link from use of the baht in order to protect themselves from the volatility of national currency movements and to enhance their control over decisions that affect their lives. Local chapters of the Consumer Association of Penang (CAP) were active in Malaysia in a variety of ways. Farmers, religious, cultural and environmental groups in Indonesia can also be counted among the local CSOs that mobilized in response to the Asian crisis. A wide range of peasant, labor and other movements in the Philippines and the Republic of Korea were also involved at the local level.

Prominent CSOs at the national level during the Asian crisis included the Assembly of the Poor in Thailand, a fascinating coalition of over a hundred groups affected by real-estate encroachment, environmental degradation and other negative aspects of Thailand's "economic miracle". The Assembly of the Poor highlighted the social costs of both the crisis and the policy responses to it by the IMF and the Thai government. It led rallies and organized sit-ins outside Government House in Bangkok.

In the Republic of Korea, organized labor took a leading role in national civil society mobilization through the Korean Confederation of Free Trade Unions (KCFTU). This labor movement was at the forefront of street demonstrations against IMF prescriptions, which (in a play on the institutional acronym) they dubbed "I Am Fired". The KCFTU was particularly concerned about the IMF demand for labor market flexibility, which in effect meant an end to the long-standing compact between government, business and labor in the country. In addition, the KCFTU addressed broader issues related to the crisis, such as the undemocratic character of the *chaebols* and the IMF demand for further liberalization of the financial sector.

Important national CSOs in Indonesia included Wahana Lingkungan Hidup Indonesia (WALHI, Indonesian Forum for the Environment) and the International NGO Forum on Indonesian Development (INFID).[17] In addition to spearheading the struggle to remove President Suharto and increase political democracy in Indonesia, CSOs like WALHI brought public attention to problems of food security and environmental degradation that had direct links to the financial crisis in the country.

National policy advocacy and campaign groups active in the Philippines included the Freedom from Debt Coalition and Action for Economic Reforms. These groups used the crisis to escalate their demands – already made during more than a decade prior to 1997 – for fundamental change in Philippine economic and financial policies. Interestingly, some key members of these groups joined the government shortly before the crisis in important cabinet and other senior posts, like the National Treasurer. From these positions of influence the activists-turned-officials were able to direct policy in crucial areas. For example, they kept interest rates on Philippine Treasury bills low, even against the wishes of the IMF.

Several important CSOs in Asia responded to the crisis through regional and global channels. Examples include Focus on the Global South (based in Thailand), Third World Network (TWN, based in Malaysia), Development Alternatives with Women for a New Era (DAWN) – South East Asia (based in the Philippines), and Forum Asia (a regional human rights network headquartered in Bangkok). Focus on the Global South and TWN issued particularly vocal critiques of the financial policies that led to the crisis and the IMF response that aggravated it. They also advocated alternative responses such as the selective use of capital controls and specific reforms of the global and regional financial architecture. Critiques by Focus and TWN gained wide media coverage and reached policy makers at the highest levels. Many of their analyses and proposals continue to be published in books and international journals, carrying an influence well beyond Asia and the Asian crisis.

Many national and regional civil society groups that were active in the Asian crisis formed alliances: both between themselves and with partners from outside the region. The external links included bodies based in the North, such as Oxfam International, British church groups, and the International Confederation of Free Trade Unions (ICFTU). The outside partners also included CSOs from other regions of the South: for example, Instituto Brasileiro de Análises Sociais e Economicas (IBASE) in Brazil; Red-Bancos in Uruguay; the Centro de Estudios y Promoción del Desarrollo (DESCO) in Peru; and Equipo Pueblo and Red Mexicana de Acción Frente al Libre Comercio (RMALC) in Mexico. Information technology greatly facilitated such alliances.

Many academics from the region and outside it (for example, in India and the Russian Federation) also provided analysis and got involved in activism on the issues raised by the crisis.[18] Progressive media organizations also played a prominent role in the region, especially daily newspapers in the Philippines (e.g., the *Philippine Daily Enquirer*) and Thailand (e.g., *The Nation*). Also important were regional and global Third World media networks such as the Inter-Press Service (IPS). *The Hindu* in India was another South-based media group with international circulation that regularly carried news and commentary on the Asian crisis.

Indeed, one beneficial and unintended consequence of the Asian crisis is that it facilitated linkages and alliances between very different types of CSOs: trade unions, academics, human rights networks, development NGOs, people's movements and policy research institutes. Such coalitions were not always easy or successful, owing to their different histories and constituencies. However, more progress was achieved in response to the Asian crisis than had previously been possible.

The crisis also catalyzed inter-regional alliances, especially between North East Asia and South East Asia. Such ties resulted partly because the South Koreans were forced to look southwards within Asia to learn from CSOs, rather than towards the OECD countries. Inter-regional collaboration has continued to strengthen within the growing global mobilization against current patterns of globalization. This movement was highly visible and successful at the WTO Ministerial Conference in Seattle in November 1999. It continued to gain momentum in 2000 through actions against the Bretton Woods institutions in Washington, DC, and Prague.

One event that substantially furthered these regional and global alliances was the landmark conference on "Economic Sovereignty in a Globalizing World: Creating a People-Centered Economics for the 21st Century". This meeting was organized by Focus on the Global South, with co-sponsorship from DAWN and the Structural Adjustment Participatory Review Initiative Network (SAPRIN). Held in Bangkok in March 1999, the conference brought together over 300 activists, academics and even governmental representatives from around the world.[19]

It is noteworthy that many of the Asian participants in this meeting also traveled to Seattle, where they were active both inside the convention center and on the streets. Indeed, contrary to the popular perception that the Seattle demonstrations involved only Northern protestors, many Southern CSOs participated. Among these, the largest regional contingent came from Asia.

The civil society role in the Asian crisis

Not surprisingly, it is difficult conclusively to ascertain the precise influence of civil society advocacy on the course of the Asian financial crisis and the soul-searching by the international community that has gone on after it. So many variables simultaneously impacted the situation, making it hard to establish the direct cause and effect of any one factor, like civil society advocacy, with any degree of certainty. Nevertheless, there is widespread agreement that CSOs have had and will continue to have a number of significant impacts. In addition, the Asian crisis had several important impacts on civil society development in the region. Six key outcomes of civil society activities in the Asian crisis are highlighted here.

First, as suggested in the previous section, the crisis of the late 1990s played a catalytic role in shifting the approach of civil society to societal problems from a politics-centered to a political economy perspective. Previously, given the nature of the regimes in Indonesia and the Republic of Korea over much of the late twentieth century, the bulk of civil society energy in these countries had focused primarily on issues of political democratization. In Thailand, too, the fragility of democracy and the unforgotten bloody legacy of the mid-1970s prompted civil society to devote most of its efforts to issues of political democratization and the need for a much more progressive constitution. The rhetoric and reality of the East Asian "miracle" reinforced this preoccupation with politics to the neglect of economics. The economic boom in many of these countries made it extremely difficult to find and sustain a constituency for mobilization on economic democratization issues. Moreover, most CSOs in these countries had very limited economic literacy.

The Asian financial and broader economic crisis encouraged both local and national civil society groups to make the essential interconnections between political and economic democratization issues. By understanding these linkages, CSOs have gained a more holistic and coherent critique of globalization in general and the East Asia "miracle" more particularly, as well as the fractured interface between the two. This change has been especially evident in Thailand and the Republic of Korea, where CSOs that previously focused on specific concerns (such as the environment or labor) began to articulate connections between these narrow issues and the broader political and economic models that their governments espoused, often with explicit support from international donors.

A second outcome of the crisis was that the financial and associated economic collapse enabled civil society groups to advance their democratization struggles with important tangible successes and victories in both Thailand and Indonesia. Many of these associations had been opposing dictatorship in their countries for decades. For example, the crisis clearly hastened and facilitated the early adoption of Thailand's progressive new constitution in November 1997. Even more explicitly, the crisis facilitated the overthrow of the Suharto regime in Indonesia in May 1998. Arguably, the crisis has also increased the space for democratic debate in Malaysia and has helped consolidate hard-won democratic space in the Republic of Korea.

Third, the Asian crisis spurred civil society education campaigns on financial and broader economic issues.[20] These activities enabled and catalyzed many ordinarily passive citizens to think critically about "development", "globalization" and the "East Asian miracle". These people became part of expanded ranks of activists and educators. In this way, CSOs provided an important public good in the aftermath of the crisis. Such economic and financial literacy work has accelerated not only in the directly affected crisis countries, but also in indirectly affected countries such as the Lao People's Democratic Republic, Vietnam and Cambodia.

Fourth, the Asian crisis provided a crucial stimulus for increased links between academics and activists in the affected countries. Both of these groups are normally a very small category of people in a country. Contacts between them increased the numbers of academic activists on the one hand and activist thinkers and writers on the other. This development has had important positive implications for economic literacy work in the region. Increased linkages between activists and academics have been quite significant in Thailand, a country that historically has been very weak in achieving such positive relationships.

This economic literacy work continues today and offers huge positive future potential for long-term civil society capacity on complex economic issues. This greater strength should increase the effectiveness of future civil society campaigns, lobbying and advocacy activities on macroeconomic policies and economic globalization issues. Higher economic literacy should also lead to greater and more effective participation of CSOs in national, regional and global economic and financial policy making than has hitherto been the case – or considered possible by mainstream policy makers and commentators.

Fifth, the crisis led to significant involvement of CSOs in the monitoring of the social impact of the crisis, especially through the provision of qualitative grassroots data. This activity led, for example, to civil society critiques of both conceptual and operational aspects of the World Bank's Social Investment Funds (SIFs) and social safety net measures, such as those in Indonesia and Thailand. These civil society inputs brought some modifications to these programs. For example, the final design of the SIF in Thailand incorporated development measures such as micro-credit and income-generation programs, rather than merely relief handouts.

Sixth, and perhaps most importantly, the Asian crisis gave an impetus to the civil society initiatives to promote alternative national development strategies, different from those that held sway in official circles. For example, the March 1999 conference organized by Focus on the Global South produced not only critiques of mainstream financial globalization strategies, but also the articulation of a range of alternative proposals.[21] Some civil society groups, notably key regionally based policy research institutes – such as Third World Network, Malaysia and Focus on the Global South, Thailand – have furthermore put forward proposals for strengthening regional and global governance, based on a range of principles.

Reimagining the Future: Towards Democratic Governance (a book jointly produced by Focus on the Global South, La Trobe University in Australia, and the Toda Institute for Global Peace in Hawaii, USA) highlights the following guiding principles:[22]

- Subsidiarity: that is, what can be done at the local level should not be done at the regional or global level.
- Sustainable human development: that is, economic and financial policies should be the means to sustainable human development and not ends in themselves.
- Priority to the real economy: that is, financial flows should support transactions in the real economy of goods and services and not take on a life of their own.
- Autonomy: that is, states and governments should be able to exercise greater national autonomy in determining policy.
- Pluralism: that is, governments should have a variety of economic policies available to them.
- Democracy: that is, national, regional and global governance mechanisms should – as part of the achievement of sustainable human development – be more participatory and accountable to citizens.
- Priority to the United Nations: that is, the UN (as a relatively more democratic and representative body) should have a greater role in economic and social policy than the Bretton Woods institutions and the WTO.

CSOs in Asia have advocated a number of specific policy proposals for alternative approaches to global finance, based on or consistent with the preceding principles. One example is a currency transactions tax on international foreign-exchange dealings, to be implemented nationally, within the framework of an international cooperation agreement. An International Taxation Organization, with participating member states as its Board of Governors and with accountability to the UN, would be responsible for the allocation of revenues to be used at the regional or global level.

Other CSO proposals have urged that governments should not phase out national capital controls, especially on inflows.[23] Moreover, they should be abolished only when and if the institutional capacity exists at national, regional and global levels to manage such a development as part of a coherent and comprehensive world financial framework.

On debt burdens, CSOs have called for an independent international debt arbitration mechanism under the auspices of the United Nations. Such a mechanism would redress the invidious current situation where creditors are the unilateral judges of debt problems.[24]

On international monetary arrangements, CSOs in Asia have urged the creation of regional – or, where appropriate, sub-regional – institutions. The objective would be to have agencies that are more responsive than the IMF to regional and country-specific circumstances, thereby encouraging greater policy pluralism.[25] A regional monetary institution appears most immediately necessary and feasible in "emerging" Asia (including parts of South Asia such as India), since this region already has the financial reserves and the political will to undertake such a project. A regional monetary regime should also be feasible in the short-to-medium term in Latin America (for example, among the Mercosur countries). A regional arrangement is less pressing for Africa, given that this continent includes few "emerging market" countries; however, Africa can and should pursue a regional monetary arrangement in the medium-to-long term.

With respect to the IMF, many have argued for a limitation of its mandate to stabilization and the current scope of surveillance. The Fund's Articles of Agreement should not be amended in respect of capital account convertibility. Meanwhile, IMF surveillance should be much strengthened in respect of the monetary policies of and capital flows from the industrialized countries. In this connection, Northern NGOs would do well to direct much more attention to IMF surveillance and other activities in their own countries. For example, they could demand participation in the IMF's Article IV surveillance missions, and they could issue assessments of the IMF reports after they are published.

Most importantly, CSOs have advocated the creation of a broadly based Economic and Social Security Council as a principal entity of the UN, in place of the current Economic and Social Council (ECOSOC). The new body would in the longer term acquire a key decision-making role in global economic governance. It would operate without a veto power and be accountable to the General Assembly.[26]

CSO proposals like the above have gained wider attention following the Asian crisis. Policy research institutions in the region such as Focus on the Global South and Third World Network have received many invitations to address key policy forums. These events have been organized by governments, regional multilateral organizations, civil society organizations at all levels, the Bretton Woods institutions, the UN and bilateral donor country institutions, and even the Group of 77 and Group of Eight at senior levels. CSO analysis and proposals for change have also received considerable media coverage, for example, in *The Nation*, the *Far Eastern Economic Review* and the *Asian Wall Street Journal*.[27]

Future prospects

Civil society engagement on issues of global finance did not begin with the Asian crisis. Nor will it end after the crisis has receded. However, the crisis gave the previously nascent civil society movement on global economic and financial governance a major boost, generating a momentum that would otherwise have taken years to generate.

CSOs campaigning on the Asian crisis have contributed significantly to the highly visible subsequent mobilizations on the WTO in Seattle in December 1999, the Spring Meetings of the World Bank and the IMF in Washington, DC in April 2000, and the Annual Meetings of the Bretton Woods institutions in Prague in September 2000. The proposed inter-governmental UN Financing for Development (FfD) conference and its Preparatory Committee meetings in 2001 provide a further focus for CSOs concerned with influencing policy on global financial architecture issues (see chapter by Herman in this volume).

True, such activities are not entirely new. Notable civil society mobilizations also occurred around the IMF/World Bank Annual Meetings in 1988 (Berlin) and 1994 (Madrid). However, the recent mobilizations have gained a much higher profile in public and official consciousness. The present campaign has mobilized large Northern constituencies and involves an almost continuous string of demonstrations.

Other recent meetings have focused on building civil society alliances. One such meeting was held in Geneva around the "Copenhagen+5" event in June 2000. A plan was announced at this conference to hold a World Social Forum in Porto Alegre, Brazil every January on the same dates as the World Economic Forum in Davos, Switzerland. Supported and facilitated by the municipality of Porto Alegre, the first World Social Forum in January 2001 was a big gathering of different civil society groups who are critical of current patterns and processes of economic and financial globalization.

Increasingly frequent teach-ins are also being organized by civil society groups such as the International Forum on Globalization (IFG). These meetings focus critically on globalization issues in general as well as more particularly on the World Bank, the IMF, the WTO and even parts of the UN. That said, many CSOs see the UN as a potential ally on economic and financial architecture issues and want to see its role strengthened in this area *vis-à-vis* the Bretton Woods institutions and the WTO.

Civil society meetings and teach-ins have helped to build both the organizational and the substantive capacities of activists on the issues. These events have also helped to strengthen the alliances between a broader range of CSOs around the world. Such alliances have increasing participation and representation from the South, including from regions such as the Arab world and Eastern Europe that only a few years ago were conspicuous by their absence at such global gatherings.

Civil society mobilizations on global finance will no doubt continue to generate their own momentum. The movement will be hard to stop, let alone roll back, unless significant changes are made in current global economic and financial governance. The present mobilization is injecting young blood into global civil society at a time when the luminaries who have long led the movement on these issues are aging.

Moreover, the demonstrations in Seattle and Washington showed that a larger number of US citizens are joining this campaign. There have been upsurges of involvement by US citizens before: for example, in several NGO campaigns since the late 1970s to oppose IMF quota increases; in the mid-1980s US Debt Crisis Network; and in the mid-1990s with the birth and rapid growth of the Fifty Years Is Enough network. However, the number and varied range of US citizens who are joining current mobilizations are unprecedented. This trend is vitally important, because the post-Cold War period knows only one superpower, the United States, many of whose policies pose problems for the poor and powerless of the world. It is therefore crucial that US citizens continue to press their government to change policies that work against the interests of developing countries and their peoples.

While it may be too early to conclude that Seattle was a watershed for civil society influence on globalization issues, it has clearly reinvigorated social movements. This augurs well for future civil society mobilizations on global finance. Nevertheless, the ability of civil society tangibly to influence the future financial architecture will depend not only on bringing people on to the streets, but also – if not more importantly – on economic literacy and the ability of CSOs to offer substantive proposals for alternatives to the current economic orthodoxy. Street-level pressure must move in tandem with lobbying in the corridors of power.

In order to achieve change in global finance, civil society groups will need – selectively and strategically – to make alliances with some Southern governments. An increasing number of Southern CSOs are recognizing this need and building such links on a more regular basis. For example, important Southern CSOs like Third World Network and the Southern and Eastern African Trade Information and Negotiations Initiative (SEATINI) have developed strategic collaboration with key Southern governments on trade issues.

In conclusion, while we should not overly credit the Asian crisis for generating the current civil society mobilization on global economic and financial governance issues, it did provide a very important impetus for civil society mobilizations. As such, the crisis was a painful but essential building block for future civil society advocacy and action to change the global financial architecture.

Notes

1 This chapter is based on the author's experience between August 1995 and July 1999 as Co-Director of Focus on the Global South, Chulalongkorn University Social Research Institute, Bangkok, Thailand. The views expressed here do not necessarily reflect the views of UNDP; nor do they necessarily represent the institutional views of Focus on the Global South or Chulalongkorn University.

2 UNDP, *Human Development Report 1999*, New York: Oxford University Press, 1999.

3 Closing statement at UNCTAD X, Bangkok, 19 February 2000. See <http://www.unctad.org/sg/statements.en.htm>.

4 UNCTAD, *Trade and Investment Report 1997*, Geneva: United Nations Conference on Trade and Development, 1997.

5 Kamal Malhotra, *East and Southeast Asia Revisited: Miracles, Myths and Mirages*, Bangkok: Focus Papers, Focus on the Global South, November 1997.

6 UNCTAD, *Trade and Investment Report 2000*, Geneva: United Nations Conference on Trade and Development, 2000.

7 *The Economist*, Vol. 346, No. 8054, 7 February 1998, p. 142 [citing the Institute of International Finance].

8 Cf. K.S. Jomo (ed.), *Tigers in Trouble: Financial Governance, Liberalisation and Crises in East Asia*, London: Zed Books, 1998.

9 Malhotra, op. cit. p. 24.

10 Ibid, pp. 21–2.

11 Ibid.

12 Walden Bello and Stephanie Rosenfeld, *Dragons in Distress: Asia's Miracle Economies in Crisis*, San Francisco: Institute for Food and Development Policy, 1990.

13 Chang Ha-Joon, "South Korea: The Misunderstood Crisis", in Jomo, op. cit., pp. 222–31.

14 Cf. Jeffrey D. Sachs, "The Wrong Medicine for Asia," *New York Times*, 3 November 1997; Yilmaz Akyüz, "The East Asian Financial Crisis: Back to the Future", in Jomo, op. cit., pp. 33–43; Nicola Bullard with Walden Bello and Kamal Malhotra, *Taming the Tigers: The IMF and the Asian Crisis*, Bangkok: Focus Papers, Focus on the Global South, March 1998; C.P. Chandrasekhar and Jayati Ghosh, *Hubris, Hysteria and Hope: The Political Economy of Crisis and Response in East Asia*, Delhi: Jawaharlal Nehru University, 1998.

15 Alex Cobham, "Capital Account Liberalisation and Poverty", draft paper, December 2000.

16 Michel Chussodovsky, "The IMF Korean Bailout", e-mail of 1 January 1998; "Koreans Ask: Who's to Blame?" *The Nation*, 6 December 1997.

17 <http://www.walhi.or.id/>; <http://infid.ngonet.be/>.

18 Chandrasekhar and Ghosh, op. cit; Jayati Ghosh and C.P. Chandrasekhar, *Crisis as Conquest: Learning from East Asia*, London: Sangam Books, 2000.

19 For a selection of papers and proposals from this conference, see Walden Bello, Nicola Bullard and Kamal Malhotra (eds), *Global Finance: New Thinking on Regulating Speculative Capital Markets*, London: Zed, 2000.

20 Cf. Najma Sidiqque, *How "They" Run the World*, Pakistan: Shirkat Gah, Women's Resource Centre, 1998 [translated into Thai by Chanida Chanyapate Bamford at Focus on the Global South, Bangkok].

21 Bello *et al.*, *Global Finance*.

22 Joseph A. Camilleri, Kamal Malhotra and Majid Tehranian, *Reimagining the Future: Towards Democratic Governance*, Bundoora, Australia: La Trobe University Department of Politics, 2000.

23 Sumangala Damodaran, "Capital Account Convertibility: Theoretical Issues and Policy Options," in Bello *et al.*, *Global Finance*, pp. 159–76; Martin Khor Kok Peng, "Why Capital Controls and Debt Restructuring Mechanisms Are Necessary to Prevent and Manage Crises" in ibid, pp. 140–58.

24 Camilleri *et al.*, op. cit. p. 56.

25 Ibid. See also E. Altbach, "The Asian Monetary Fund: A Case Study of Japanese Regional Leadership," *Japan Economic Institute Report*, No. 47A, 19 December 1997.

26 Camilleri *et al.*, op. cit. p. 56.

27 Cf. numerous articles by and citations of Walden Bello and Kamal Malhotra, Co-Directors of Focus on the Global South, and Martin Khor Kok Peng, Director of Third World Network, Malaysia.

5 Global finance and civil society deficits in Russia

Nodari Simonia

Summary	
• Introduction	79
• Global finance in post-Soviet Russia	80
• Global finance and crisis in Russia	83
• Civil society development in Russia	85
• Civil society and global finance: non-engagement in Russia	91
• Conclusion	92

Introduction

Why, in contrast to many other transition countries, did Russia fail to achieve any considerable success in economic development during the 1990s? Why does Russia remain in a deep structural crisis that embraces all spheres of its socio-economic and political life? Why has civil society responded so inadequately to these problems?

In a September 1999 article in *Vedomosti*, the First Deputy Managing Director of the International Monetary Fund (IMF), Stanley Fischer, argued in effect that all progress made by Russia in 1992–97 was thanks to his organization, while all failures and miscalculations were the fault of Russia itself.[1] However, things are far more complicated than that. Developments up to the collapse of August 1998 happened as a result of the joint and absolutely uncontrolled activities of the Russian and international financial bureaucracies.

Of course, no one can or should carry out reforms in Russia except the government and people of Russia. Nevertheless, international financial institutions (IFIs) and the West in general have had considerable impact on the nature, the course and the results of reforms in Russia. After all, officials of the IMF and a whole crowd of Western (especially American) scholars and specialists constantly tutored the "independent" Russian government from its inception in 1991 – and at quite a cost. What have these international actors contributed to the sad situation that we witness today?

This chapter presents first a brief analysis of the global financial streams that came into Russia during the 1990s. Then we dwell on the main reasons for the inefficient utilization of credits and loans received by the country. Finally, we explain why civil society in Russia – and public opinion generally – have failed to exert even marginal influence to improve the economic situation in Russia, in particular to promote more productive use of global financial inflows.

Global finance in post-Soviet Russia

In July 1991 the USSR applied for membership of the IMF and four agencies of the World Bank Group. In November 1991 the Soviet government and the World Bank signed an agreement on technical co-operation. Parallel to this, in October 1991, Russian President Boris Yeltsin addressed the West, and especially the IMF, with a request to render Russia assistance and to supervise the construction of a new society. After the disintegration of the USSR in December 1991, the Russian Federation joined the IMF in April 1992. In June 1993 it also became a member of three parts of the World Bank Group. Russia joined the International Bank for Reconstruction and Development (IBRD), the International Finance Corporation (IFC) and the Multilateral Investment Guarantee Agency (MIGA), but not the International Development Association (IDA). Russia also became involved in meetings of the Group of Seven (G7), although the Yeltsin government had no significant direct participation in G7 discussions concerning global finance.

The general (though not quite complete) picture of financial inflows into Russia up to 1998 can be gleaned from Table 5.1. The sums cover only loan principal and exclude accumulated interest.

The "Soviet debt" was accumulated mainly during the last years of Gorbachev's *perestroika*. These loans chiefly went to purchase equipment for industry: that is, to promote production. Later on, with economic collapse and practically uncontrolled privatization in Russia, most of these investments became easy prey for bureaucrat-capitalists, and the state found itself unable to repay the debts on time.

In contrast to Soviet debts, a lion's share of the Russian Federation's foreign borrowings went for consumption: that is, to patch up budget holes and to service past loans. Moreover, Table 5.1 does not include private foreign borrowings that were made against sovereign guarantees. It is difficult to determine exact figures for such loans, but the following data give an approximate idea. After 1992 hundreds of Russian enterprises together received over $15 billion in tied credits; however, it was mainly the state that repaid these sums. For example, in 1998 the Russian government paid $625 million to foreign creditors for these debts, while the relevant enterprises paid it only $65.2 million on these accounts (i.e. little more than 10 per cent of the amount due). In addition, about 30 regional governments of Russia failed to repay international credits received by local authorities.[2]

Table 5.1 External debt of Russia[3] ($ billion)

	1992	1993	1994	1995	1996	1997	July 1998	Dec 1998
State sector	**107.7**	**120.6**	**127.5**	**128.0**	**143.3**	**153.6**	**176.4**	**164.3**
Federal debts								
Former USSR debt[a]	104.9	103.7	108.6	103.0	100.8	91.4	91.8	93.6
Russian Federation debt	2.8	9.0	11.3	17.4	24.2	32.1	51.2	51.4
from IFIs[b]	*1.0*	*3.5*	*5.4*	*11.4*	*15.3*	*18.7*	*26.2*	*26.0*
from eurobonds	*0*	*0*	*0*	*0*	*1.0*	*4.5*	*15.8*	*16.0*
from other sources[c]	*1.8*	*5.5*	*5.9*	*6.0*	*7.9*	*8.9*	*9.2*	*9.4*
Other state debts								
Debts of local government	0	0	0	0	0	1.3	2.2	2.4
Foreign holdings of domestic state bonds	0	0	0	0	7.2	17.7	20.1	5.8
Ministry of Finance hard-currency bonds	0	7.9	7.6	7.6	11.1	11.1	11.1	11.1
Private sector	**4.5**	**4.3**	**4.9**	**6.3**	**11.3**	**50.9**	**57.3**	**43.4**
Banks	n.a.	n.a.	n.a.	n.a.	n.a.	37.2	34.5	20.2[d]
Other enterprises	n.a.	n.a.	n.a.	n.a.	n.a.	13.7	22.8	23.1
Total	**112.2**	**124.9**	**132.4**	**131.3**	**154.6**	**164.9**	**233.7**	**207.7**

Notes
a Including interest arrears
b IMF, IBRD and EBRD
c Bilateral agreements and commercial credits
d As of 1 July 1998

Table 5.1 shows that the main "culprits" of the headlong growth of state debt up to July 1998 were the IFIs, with the leading role played by the IMF.[4] Russia's debt to the Fund amounted to $19.9 billion as of 1 August 1998. This debt increased particularly quickly during the 1995–96 election campaigns to the State Duma and the Russian presidency, as the West sought to shore up the Yeltsin government.

At $6.15 billion, Russia's debt to the IBRD as of mid-1998 was comparatively modest. Moreover, the government consistently delayed the execution of loans agreed with the IBRD. In some cases it asked to redesign projects. On other occasions it even annulled loans either partially or completely. Generally speaking, Russian governments of the 1990s did not have an industrial policy and more or less ignored restructuring and development of production. Hence they were barely interested in IBRD credits which, besides, stipulated requirements of co-financing and the implementation of economic reforms.

The IMF both directly and indirectly promoted the growth of Russia's foreign debt. Within the framework of its concept of financial stabilization the Fund tenaciously recommended that the Russian government pursue outside sources of finance to cover its budget deficits and to support the rouble within a set band of foreign-exchange rates. To this end, starting in 1996, the government undertook increased eurobond borrowings on the private money markets.

In the same year, and again following IMF advice, the government eased restrictions on the access of nonresidents to the market of internal state borrowings: that is, short-term State Treasury Bills (GKOs) and long-term Federal Loan Bonds (OFZs). Before 1996, non-residents had faced considerable restrictions, including a requirement to hold these bonds until their redemption date. As a result, foreign investors in GKOs and OFZs sometimes acted via intermediary Russian banks. However, when the restrictions were lifted, foreign capital gushed into the market for Russian state securities. In the course of 1996 alone, investments in GKOs by nonresidents reached $6.7 billion through official so-called "S" accounts. Including investments made through "gray" accounts, the estimated total came to some $13 billion.[5]

So, encouraged by the IMF, the government of Russia constructed a financial pyramid, justified by the presumed necessity to stabilize the rouble. Later, when "stabilization" had brought Russia to default, further borrowings were justified by the necessity to "save" the ill-starred rouble. The first half of 1998 saw Russia's largest external borrowings: from the IFIs; on the eurobond markets; and from nonresidents on domestic bond markets. At the end of July 1998, outstanding borrowings from these three sources amounted to $73.2 billion, out of a total post-Soviet state debt of $84.6 billion.

From 1997 a number of additional Russian official players joined the central government on global financial markets. A presidential decree allowed the city authorities of Moscow, St. Petersburg and Nizhny Novgorod to issue and place eurobonds abroad. Certain restrictions were introduced on the size of borrowings and annual payments of debt service, depending on the income levels of the respective territories. Yet, with the general weakness of the central government, local authorities cast prudence to the wind and borrowed extravagantly from foreign banks and investment corporations.

After 1996 around fifteen large Russian commercial banks began actively to use foreign sources of finance, but by no means for investments in the real economy. In most cases (up to 80 per cent) the banks took short-term credits, converted them into roubles, and invested the money in state bonds. These banks also acted as the primary providers of financial intermediation for nonresidents. Especially after August 1996, the Bank of Russia itself began to stimulate the development of a private market in short-term credits. Out of the total foreign debt of Russian banks as of 1 January 1998 ($37.2 billion), nearly half (up to $18 billion) went to foreign currency forward contracts. When, from 1 January 1998, all participants in the GKO market gained equal rights, foreigners had the possibility to convert profits on GKO dealings into foreign currency on both the spot and forward markets. This situation left Russia defenseless and vulnerable to an abrupt reversal of capital flows. By the end of July 1998, debt on forward contracts had decreased to $14 billion, out of a total bank debt of $34.5 billion.[6]

In addition to Russian commercial banks, several of the largest Russian corporations also started borrowing on private global financial markets. These firms mainly came from the energy sector: Gazprom, LUKoil, Tatneft, Sibneft, Mosenergo, etc. Some of these borrowings undoubtedly went to promote real production, but not all of them. For example, in early 1997 Gazprom used a syndicated loan of $2.5 billion to pay overdue taxes.[7]

Taking all borrowings together, Russia's foreign debt amounted to 54.7 per cent of GDP in 1998. Yet, in spite of this major injection of funds, Russia's GDP in 1998 was 42.2 per cent lower, in real terms, than it had been in 1990. Industrial production was down by 53.9 per cent. Investments in fixed capital had fallen by 77.7 per cent. While foreign borrowings were steadily increasing, home investments were sharply declining, on average by 15.2 per cent a year between 1994 and 1998.[8]

Global finance and crisis in Russia

Why did Russia find itself in such sorry circumstances? What put the country into a permanent crisis situation throughout the 1990s?

Some of the factors were internal. Chief among these was the type of capitalism that prevailed in Russia, namely, bureaucratic capitalism, a synthesis of bureaucracy and *nouveau riche* business in its worst form.[9] At a time when Russia lacked social consensus and political stability, the so-called "oligarchs" held sway. Unsure of the situation in Russia, they built "reserve airfields" abroad (in real estate, offshore accounts, etc.). Enormous outflows of illegal and "gray" capital left Russia, frequently considerably exceeding the sums of official foreign borrowings. The Moscow-based Bureau of Economic Analysis has estimated capital flight from Russia at $28.9 billion in 1996, $27.2 billion in 1997, $24.9 billion in 1998, and $18–20 billion in 1999.[10]

Among negative external factors it is necessary first of all to cite the politicized nature of the IMF's approach to Russia. In complete correspondence with the geopolitical and geoeconomic interests of the G7, and especially those of the US Administration, the IMF invariably supported the corrupt regime of President Yeltsin up to the August 1998 crisis. From 1992 a crowd of American advisers, IMF technical missions and IBRD experts taught, counseled, financed and directed the activity of the Russian government and the so-called "reformers". (I deliberately put the word in quotation marks, as true reformers usually reform, modernize and improve something.) Foreign financial support was rendered through many channels, including illegal ones, but the IMF provided the main funds.

It is noteworthy that flows from the IMF became particularly strong on two occasions, each time during an aggravated political situation. The first occurred during the election campaigns of 1995–96. The second happened when financial crisis was brewing in the first half of 1998.

Yet the IMF took a contrary approach when Yevgeny Primakov became Prime Minister of Russia. His government (in office from September 1998 until April 1999) took the first steps to outlaw corruption, reoriented economic policy to support the real sector, and injected greater independence into Russian foreign policy. In this situation the IMF postponed the release of a regular tranche of credits, even though the money was earmarked not for the government budget, but for servicing Russia's debt to the Fund itself.

Finally, following the default of 1998, the West suddenly "noticed" corruption in

Russia. It "opened its eyes" only when the supposed "liberal reformers" that it had backed "swindled" (in the words of Anatoly Chubais[11]) both the IMF and foreign investors as soon as the financial disaster hit.

The IMF has also contributed to Russia's distress by imposing its universal formula of "stabilization" and "structural adjustment". Russia was treated in the same way as Africa, Latin America, Asia and Eastern Europe. Yet in many cases the IMF model has proved to be unadaptable and unacceptable.

The IMF boasts that it assisted Russia to curb inflation. In fact, inflation in Russia spurred widespread non-payment of bills, barter exchange and money substitutes. Inflation is rooted in the sphere of production, so purely monetary methods are not sufficient to eradicate it. Obviously, the problems of Russian production do not lie within the IMF's sphere of competence, but its advice has to take them into account. However, in 1994–95 the IMF insisted that the Bank of Russia cease direct financing of the government budget. In the absence of the institutional fundamentals for a market economy, this policy provoked large-scale corruption and an enormous rise of financial bureaucratic capital. Russia became "addicted" to foreign financial borrowings. The money supply (M_2) became concentrated on the GKO market, while the major part of the real sector was forced to resort to barter and to use money substitutes.[12]

In addition, the IMF debauched the Russian ruling élite by continuing to extend loans, even though none of a succession of approved programs was fully implemented.[13] Numerous Russian publications report that the prospect of default was elaborated during close contacts with IMF leaders and the US Treasury Department.[14] Although the IMF was aware that the rouble could not be saved, it nevertheless gave Russia $4.8 billion in July 1998. This loan did not go to the Ministry of Finance, headed at that time by Mikhail Zadornov, who was not associated with any oligarchs. Instead, the IMF *for the first time* sent its monies to the Central Bank, headed by Sergei Dubinin, who came from oligarchy circles and who returned there after the crisis. It is widely believed that this money later, through "legal channels" (probably the currency market), came into the hands of the oligarchs and was exported to their offshore accounts.

Another international financial institution, the European Bank for Reconstruction and Development (EBRD), acted in close contact with financial–bureaucratic capital in Russia. One of the EBRD's most important tasks in Russia was to encourage small and medium enterprises (SMEs). Between 1994 and 2000 it extended over 32,000 loans to SMEs, to a total of $400 million.[15] However, the credits flowed through large Russian banks such as Rossijsky Kredit, Toribank and Inkombank. The trouble is not that all these "partners" went bankrupt and that the EBRD lost part of the granted sums. Rather, these Russian banks often funneled EBRD money to businesses with which they were connected, instead of to independent small and medium producers.

Clearly, much has gone wrong – in terms of both internal and external factors – when it comes to post-Soviet Russia's involvement with global finance. The question then arises: why have the people of Russia not reacted effectively to this negative situation? In particular, why has civil society played such a small role?

Civil society development in Russia

"Civil society and global finance" is not a well-studied subject in Russia. For example, at the Second All-Russian Congress of Politologists, held in Moscow in April 2000, only one out of approximately 550 papers (including those delivered on panels devoted to international economics) touched upon this topic. The paper in question addressed "Gender Policy in Russia and the International Financial Institutions".

The cardinal difference today between Russia and Western countries is that the formation of a civil society is still at an initial stage in Russia. The country has developed, and continues to develop, according to a "catching-up model". Russia has borrowed many attributes of Western political life, and this produces an illusion that Russia is aligned with the West. However, these borrowings have so far been rather superficial and to a great extent are filled with traditional Russian and Soviet content.

Numerous public organizations existed in Russia even during the Soviet period, of course. However, they had nothing in common with what are known in the West as "nongovernmental organizations" (NGOs). The associations were all included in the framework of a single bureaucratic public organism led by the Communist Party. Thus, regardless of the sphere of activity – whether it be collective farmers, blue-collar workers or persons engaged in cultural activities and sports – all the staff of these organizations were in fact civil servants.

The beginning of Gorbachev's *perestroika* ("restructuring") marked the advent of the second "epoch of Russian awakening". *Perestroika* provided many important prerequisites for an acceleration of the process of civil society formation. Many factors fostered an atmosphere of nation-wide emancipation and the broadening of the people's range of vision at this time: *glasnost* (openness); pluralism; the weakening of the Party and its separation from the state; openness to the outside world; and the emergence of nonstate subjects of economic activity such as cooperatives, commercial banks, and small and medium enterprises.

One of the brightest manifestations of "Russia's awakening" was the emergence of veritable NGOs: that is, autonomous associations that were neither created nor dominated by the state. During the *perestroika* years (1986–91), Russia witnessed the birth of an embryonic civil society. That process unfolded not only in the center of the country, but also in its outlying districts.

Examples of these early NGO initiatives include Meeting 87, a group launched in 1987 in Sverdlovsk (now called Yekaterinburg). This association later served as the basis for a civil society organization, the Regional Center to Support Civil Initiatives, that has provided organizational, technical, informational and legal assistance to NGOs. In Moscow, Memorial – Historical, Educational and Charitable Society – was set up in 1988 to commemorate the victims of Stalin and to defend those who had suffered political persecution in more recent times. In 1989 the Society for the Defense of Convicted Businessmen and Economic Freedom was founded, as was the Committee of Soldiers' Mothers, which has worked to expose human rights violations within the Russian military, including the high number of deaths from hazing and severe punishment. Regional branches of this Committee are active throughout Russia. In 1990 the Russian Association of Business Education was established. It now encompasses over fifty business schools and commercial centers and maintains business contacts with other Russian organizations and associations like the Chamber of Commerce and Industry and the Association of Joint Ventures. The Russian Association of Business Education also cooperates closely with training centers and business schools in Europe, the USA, Canada, India and Eastern Europe. The year 1990 also saw the establishment of Civic Assistance – the Committee for Helping Refugees and Forced Migrants.

Concurrent with the emergence of new NGOs during the *perestroika* years, the traditional Soviet public organizations underwent a peculiar process of renovation, disentangling themselves from strict party/state control. For example, the election of Elem Klimov as First Secretary of the Film Makers Union in 1986 gave that organization an independent voice. These organizations proceeded to use such influence as they possessed to advance the cause of cultural liberalization.

Of even greater importance was the establishment of a free press on the basis of pre-existent publications. Examples included the magazine *Ogonek* and newspapers such as *Moskovsky Komsomolets* and *Argumenty i Facty*. Thanks to Gorbachev's *glasnost* policy a paradoxical situation developed. Mass editions that relied on state support in order to reach many millions of people conducted an active and progressively more intense campaign against the regime.

Considerable changes also took place in the trade union movement under *glasnost*. Here, too, there was slow renovation of the existing organizations as well as the emergence of new bodies. In 1989, for example, the Union of Trade Unions of USSR Cooperative Enterprise Workers (with 200–250,000 members), the International Confederation of Trade Unions of Joint Ventures (with 120,000 members), and the Union of Trade Unions of Medium- and Small-Scale Business (with 1.3 million members) came into being. In 1990 the Trade Union of Workers of Venture Firms and Small Enterprises was founded. Two years later, after the disintegration of the Soviet Union, this body was transformed into the International Union for those sectors, with 200,000 members in Russia and 350,000 members spread across Armenia, Belorussia, Kazakhstan and Ukraine. Also in 1992, the Russian part of that union – together with the trade union of medium- and small-scale business and construction organizations – created the Congress of Russian Trade Unions, encompassing 3.5 million members.

After 1990 the old trade union organization, the All-Union Council of Trade Unions, also began a gradual transformation. This Soviet inheritance served as the basis for the Federation of Independent Trade Unions (FITU), with 55 million members. The FITU soon joined the larger General Confederation of USSR Trade Unions, with 90 million members across seven republics. So trade unions created on a traditional basis had the largest membership. By the end of 1992 the ranks of the FITU had grown to 67 million. Many new trade unions (like that of the venture firms and small enterprises) also joined the General Confederation, in large part since it held the main social security resources.

Meanwhile, 1990 also saw the emergence of a quite radical Independent Trade Union of USSR Miners, with 70,000 members. This trade union was initially used as a powerful weapon of Yeltsin and his supporters in their struggle against Gorbachev. During the *perestroika* period Yeltsin won miners over to his side through purely populist means. By arbitrary decrees in 1990–91 he turned the mines from Soviet (that is, all-Union) into Russian Republic property and also gave miners the control of coal marketing. Hence it is no wonder that he easily managed to raise the miners in a strike movement, with political demands for Gorbachev's resignation and the like. However, when the situation of the miners hardly improved under Yeltsin's rule, they increasingly opposed him and his governments.

In its turn, the largest trade union, the FITU, which had declared itself to be nonpartisan, in fact aligned with left-centrist and left political forces like the Civil Union, the Communist Party of the Russian Federation (CPRF) and the Agrarian Party. Only with the general strike held on 7 October 1998 did the FITU leadership for the first time separate from the CPRF. Thereafter the integration of this largest trade union's leadership into the official political establishment accelerated considerably.

The *perestroika* period also brought increased activities of Western NGOs in Russia. During the epoch of bipolar ideological confrontation, Western NGOs concentrated their efforts on the protection of human rights in socialist countries and on rendering assistance to dissidents. Those human rights NGOs were based in the West and enjoyed foreign state support, including financial assistance. Their activity could in fact be seen as an extension of state policy within the framework of struggle between the two ideologies. Support of these NGOs by bodies like the Ford and MacArthur Foundations and the International Research and Exchange Board (IREX) also fits this pattern.

With *perestroika* such NGOs had a chance to act in Russia on a wider and more legal scale, intensifying their advocacy of Western liberal and democratic values. For example, the Independent Women's Forum, established in 1991 with support from the Ford Foundation, now serves as an umbrella organization for more than 200 women's organizations throughout Russia.

Perestroika also brought to life some new, completely independent, NGOs, created especially for Russia and other newly independent states. The activities of George Soros provide a shining example in this regard. Inspired by what he called Gorbachev's "romantic period", Soros in 1987 established a foundation in Russia called the Cultural Initiative. Within this framework he spent up to $100 million on fundamental sciences: for support of libraries; the introduction of the Internet in research institutes; financial support of students and professors, etc. However, one peculiarity developed. The foundation quickly "assimilated", turning into a Soviet-like institution. To combat this trend Soros twice changed the leadership of the Foundation, but to no avail. Finally, he transformed the foundation into the Open Society Institute, with headquarters abroad. In total, Soros has spent over $750 million in Russia over a thirteen-year period.[16]

However, the West and Russian liberal democrats (a very small group) made a fundamental mistake. They presumed that an awakening of social consciousness at the top indicated a readiness of the whole, or at least the bulk, of Russian society to accept drastic changes in the social order and the economy. The liberal reformers disregarded the continuing predominance of a mass paternalistic consciousness, involving almost total delegation of authority to the state. The apparently mass character of the democratic trend was deceptive. This "mass" was quickly formed due to trimmers, who had previously been very loyal servants of totalitarianism.

Besides, even the few elements of a future civil society that did emerge during this period – that is, independent trade unions, associations of entrepreneurs, war veterans groups, etc. – soon found themselves caught up in political confrontation. The radical liberals involved these groups in struggles for power between Gorbachev (as President of the Soviet Union) and Yeltsin (as President of the Russian Republic). As a result, the incipient civil society organizations lost their independence.

Numerous other conditions also militated against the speedy development of a genuine civil society under the *perestroika* years. They included problems of establishing legal guarantees, developing a social contract, and creating the institutional and legislative infrastructure for a market economy. As a result, civil society became a subject for largely theoretical – but alas fruitless – discussions in the mass media.

After Yeltsin's "enthronement", the process of civil society formation in Russia began to recede. Paternalistic sentiments were cultivated in every possible way, both from the top (in presidential circles) and from the bottom (through the loyal press). Hopes for further democratization of society faded away as bureaucratic capitalism strengthened and corruption and crime burgeoned. An independent middle class, the basis of democracy, failed to develop. It was trampled by bureaucratic capital and criminal structures.

Following a familiar pattern in the history of Russia, paternalistic politics took over. "A kind-hearted and just tsar" reigned over "a loyal and patient people". Meanwhile, the bureaucratic state became further alienated from the real society. The bureaucracy became totally engrossed in problems such as the maintenance of its power, internal factional confrontation, unrestrained accumulation of wealth through corruption, and saving the face of their patron president abroad. In the process, the bureaucracy ceased to perform a number of important state functions, such as guaranteeing law and order, collecting taxes, and regulating the economy.

The formation of a genuine civil society in Russia has also been hindered by many other, no less important, obstacles. One such factor is the absence of social and political consensus in Russian society. Another is the predominance of primordial ties to family, ethnic and religious groups over general civil bonds. Ethnic and confessional heterogeneity in Russia have further militated against civil society development, as has social and economic unevenness across the eighty-nine regional units of the Russian Federation.

Regarding the latter point, many in the West have mistakenly welcomed decentralization in Russia as a sign of democratization and a source of opportunity for NGOs. Yet the opposite has rather been the case. Rapid decentralization has tended to leave public institutions under the even more severe and despotic rule of regional governors. Some Russian analysts have even talked in this regard of "feudalization".

Given the circumstances just described, the establishment and development of real NGOs in Russia proved to be quite a complicated business. Formally, on the surface of public life, a proliferation of NGOs occurred in the country after 1992. However, the form frequently deviated from the content. Most "civil society" organizations became not only politically engaged, but also financially dependent on parties and official agencies. Under drastically worsening economic conditions in Russia, NGOs failed to overcome a "held-out-hand" syndrome. Many civic organizations have survived only due to support from one of three sources: (a) government subsidies and tax exemptions; (b) funds from bureaucratic capital; and (c) foreign contributions, both public and private.

Regarding the first source of funds, financial support from the Russian state to NGOs has decreased to a minimum. Yet NGO dependence on paltry state doles has increased, with unhappy consequences. For example, in the *perestroika* years the previously mentioned Film Makers Union and other organizations in the cultural sphere consistently urged the abolition of bureaucratic interference in their business. However, in May–June 2000 the very same people took to the streets to protest against the abolition of the *State* Committee on Cinematography. Likewise, the Russian greens now want to restore the *State* Committee on Ecology – and even tried to appeal to President Clinton for support in this cause.[17] Such developments are evidence of the increasingly anti-civil nature of Russian society today.

Of course, certain "civil society" organizations have enjoyed the government's favor. Examples include sports associations, the Afghanistan war veterans organization and the Russian Orthodox Church. By Yeltsin's decrees they were exempted from taxes on alcohol, cigarettes, etc. These privileges have allowed them to carry out extremely profitable business. In some cases these activities have turned criminal.

The situation of the "independent" mass media has hardly been better. Most major media organs in Russia have been divided between various groups of bureaucratic capital: that is, the oligarchs. Moreover, the high cost of newspapers has greatly depleted the readership of most of the press. In addition, in 2000 the state commenced methodical attacks against the mass media with the help of political, administrative and financial pressure. The more stubborn journalists have even faced criminal prosecution and open intimidation.

So, whereas *perestroika* gave birth to *glasnost*, the post-Soviet period has brought the problem of preserving *glasnost*. Nowadays there is even a special Glasnost Protection Foundation. Recently some human rights activists even discussed whether or not it was time to go underground.

Another group of NGOs – those that lobby for the corporate interests of certain bureaucratic capitalist groups and certain branches of commerce and industry – has fared somewhat better. These bodies target the State Duma, the Council of the Russian Federation, the government, and the presidential administration. Examples of these actors include the Association of Russian Banks, the Russian Association of Small and Medium-Size Businesses, and the All-Russian Association of Privatized and Private Enterprises.

Yet business clans in Russia exert most of their influence on government by means of direct lobbying rather than through corporate associations. Those elements of bureaucratic capital that are well received in the presidential administration and the government have a great advantage over the rest. Others act through the Duma and the Federation Council in order to make desired amendments to laws and/or to delay their enactment. The most vivid efforts in this respect have consisted of attempts to delay the adoption of laws concerning foreign investment.

Finally, a further circle of NGOs in Russia encompasses numerous organizations that have appeared with financial support from the West. They include human rights organizations, foundations promoting business development, and training centers that aim at the dissemination of democratic and free-market ideals. Neoclassical economics are actively advocated in Russia by such institutions as the American Chamber of Commerce, the US–Russia Business Council, and the Foreign Investors Advisory Council. Many of these Western-supported NGOs act under the aegis of the Center for Civil Society International. Several are branches or departments of noted American establishments such as the Carnegie Endowment, the Ford Foundation and the MacArthur Foundation. In 1993 the US government established the Eurasia Foundation, funded by the Agency for International Development (USAID) and other public and private donors. This foundation has also supported the development of NGOs in Russia.

Foreign-supported NGOs are large in number, but they are largely underproductive from the point of view of developing civil society in Russia. The problems begin with their foreign origin. They were not grown on Russian soil and often do not reflect Russian needs. As a result, Russian NGOs that act under the aegis of and with financial aid from the West easily become objects for accusations of "anti-patriotic sentiments" and even "treachery". They are often prosecuted by local authorities. Even certain Russian NGOs (like the Union of Soldiers' Mothers) face such difficulties.

A second problem with the Western NGOs is that they try to inculcate liberal values through Russian associations in a situation where dozens of millions of people are daily preoccupied with basic needs of food, dwelling, work and personal security. For such people, talk about democracy is just empty words, all the more so after the disappointing experience with Russian democrats during the period of *perestroika*.

A third problem is that the Western NGOs try to impose a liberal economic model on Russia. They try to teach Russians according to alien textbooks that do not correspond with Russian realities. Practically all Russian businessmen and financiers questioned by the American–Russian paper *Vedomosti* in June 2000 about the role of foreign consultants and economists were skeptical regarding mechanical borrowing of alien experience.[18] Instead, these NGOs would do better to start by learning and examining Russian realities. Then they could find appropriate (not textbook) solutions to peculiarly Russian problems. Historical experience shows that borrowing from abroad is profitable when it synthesizes with positive elements of local experience.

Civil society and global finance: non-engagement in Russia

Bearing in mind all of the above, it is no wonder that most of the population of Russia is absolutely indifferent to the problems of global finance, including negotiations with the IMF and other IFIs. Such issues seem very distant from people's constant concern with a chronic lack of money. They have learned a lesson: whether or not Russia gets the next foreign loan, their financial position will not improve. Most people are convinced that the allocated funds will eventually fill the pockets of officials and the oligarchs. Besides, all negotiations are conducted in strict secrecy, and the contents of the agreements seem too complicated and incomprehensible for non-specialists.

As for the press, it is mostly politically engaged. The media presents materials on financial talks according to the interests of its patron clan. Independent editions are few in number, have limited circulation, and are published for a very narrow circle of intellectuals.

Against this backdrop, the bulk of the Russian population has – contrary to the early 1990s – formed a negative attitude toward international finance. The following opinions of "people in the street" were published by *The Russia Journal* in November 1999. Office worker Galina Panko declared, "I am against dollars anyway. It will only push us to debt slavery." Doctor Alexander Sokolov asserted, "We don't need these credits because, with this money, Russia is being pushed into a financial circle where this whole tranche goes to pay off the debts we already have." Teacher Vladimir Schvaitzer argued, "In principle Russia doesn't need the credits." Meanwhile, graduate students Alexei and Inna Chebotaryova concluded, "Russia doesn't need IMF money. It's a major insult for the great power . . . The credits benefit only the government, not the people, IMF money undermines the country, its economy and its international status."[19]

So it is mostly academic circles in Russia that are concerned with problems of global finance. Contrary to Soviet times, when economists worked under the order of the Central Committee of the Communist Party, today they are divided into competing factions. Some economists are members of centers and councils attached to the presidential structures. Some work for the government. Some work for the left majority in the Duma and the Federation Council. Some serve in think tanks for various clans of bureaucratic capital. A few remain independent of any of these "customers", retaining substantial autonomy from commercial and official circles. On the whole, however, genuine scholars do not play an important part in the formation of the economic strategy of the Russian government.

Russian economists have engaged in active discussion of global financial issues in the mass media, in response to the IMF's unwillingness to release a tranche of credits since the autumn of 1999. The Director of the Institute of Economic Analysis, Andrei Illarionov, and the President of Alfa Bank, Piotr Aven, have severely criticized the IMF as a source of foreign debts and have blamed it for crisis situations.[20] Mass-media organs controlled by the notorious Boris Berezovsky have also regularly criticized the IMF.[21] Attempts by the IMF to foist terms that run counter to the economic interests of Russia have also attracted criticism from the Director of the Institute of World Politics and Economy, Alexander Nekipelov, who has cooperated closely with the President of the National Reserve Bank, Alexander Lebedev.[22]

A quite curious episode occurred in Russia regarding Joseph Stiglitz, the former Chief Economist and Vice-President of the World Bank, who severely criticized the IMF and US administration policies concerning developing countries and Russia. Immediately after Stiglitz's resignation in November 1999, an already traditional link between Washington and Russian liberal economists occurred. Just as in good old Soviet times, the Higher School of Economics in Moscow gathered a "party meeting" (i.e. "an academic symposium") and unanimously reprimanded Stiglitz for his "anti-party" line. Among the few who expressed support for Stiglitz (or, to be more precise, for his position on the IMF) was Alexander Astapovich, head of department in the Bureau of Economic Analysis.[23]

Conclusion

This chapter has not told a happy story. Russia's encounter with global finance in the 1990s brought the country major debts and deep crisis, no economic gain and high social costs. Civil society has had little response to this situation, in large part since civil society itself has been so weak in Russia.

How can Russia move forward from these sorry circumstances? Before closing I would like to suggest several proposals and to reflect on the future development of civil society in Russia.

My first proposal is to urge a major redefinition of priorities in Russia's reforms. Social and human aspects of development need to be seen not merely as important, but as the foremost concern. Without this priority, no amount of financial stabilization and structural adjustment will solve anything in Russia.

Second, the organization of the reform process in Russia needs to be changed. It is not sufficient merely to coordinate the efforts of the multiple organizations involved. These activities must be united under one center.

Third, it is necessary to abandon the universalist approach to socio-economic development. The particularities of each country must be understood and respected – and policy adjusted accordingly. It would be helpful in this regard to establish a global research center to study these issues and to make relevant policy recommendations. This center would be a forum of prominent scholars who are experts on different groups of countries. The work of the center would be absolutely autonomous. Its recommendations would be nonbinding. They would also be completely open and accessible for the world public, who would use the knowledge as an instrument of popular pressure and control on policy.

Finally, what of the future of civil society in the Russian Federation? Recent tendencies suggest that Russia is probably doomed to pass through a new stage of authoritarianism. Two possible scenarios suggest themselves. In the first, bureaucratic capital will strengthen its grip of the economy and establish its full dominance over political power, too. In the second scenario, the new President,

Vladimir Putin, will manage to reduce the influence of the oligarchs and regulate their business activity in the interests of the Russian economy.

Neither of these scenarios includes much room for a free evolution of civil society. Most likely, NGOs will for some time fall under strict state control. Problems concerning global finance in Russia will be discussed only in very narrow circles of intellectuals, and all decisions on these matters will be taken at élite level, with minimal input, and no consent, from civil society.

Notes

1 *Vedomosti*, 29 December 1999.
2 *Vedomosti*, 24 December 1999; *Trud*, 22 February 2000.
3 *Survey of Economic Policy in Russia 1998*, Moscow: Bureau of Economic Analysis, 1999, p. 34 [in Russian].
4 Figures are obtained from *Survey of Economic Policy in Russia 1998*, p. 499.
5 *Economic Survey of Europe in 1996–1997*, New York: United Nations, 1997, p. 172.
6 *Survey of Economic Policy in Russia in 1998*, pp. 323, 500–1.
7 *Economic Survey of Europe in 1996–1997*, p. 165.
8 *World Economic Outlook*, Washington, DC: International Monetary Fund, 1999, p. 62; *Bureau of Economic Analysis Information–Analytical Bulletin*, No. 15, June 1999, p. 2.
9 For more about bureaucratic capitalism in Russia, see N. Simonia, "Domestic Developments in Russia", in G. Chufrin (ed.), *Russia and Asia: The Emerging Security Agenda*, Oxford: Oxford University Press, 1999, pp. 52–80.
10 *Segodnya*, 9 February 2000.
11 *Profil*, No. 44, 22 November 1999, p. 33.
12 Cf. M.V. Ershov, *Currency–Financial Mechanisms in the Contemporary World: Crisis Experience in the 1990s*, Moscow: Economica, 2000, ch. 8 [in Russian].
13 Cf. *Expert*, No. 48, 20 December 1999, p. 10.
14 *Survey of Economic Policy in Russia in 1998*, pp. 75–6; *Expert*, No. 1–2, 18 January 1999, pp. 8, 10; *Expert*, No. 32, 31 August 1998, p. 11; *Russkiy Telegraf*, 27 August 1998; *Moskovsky Komsomolets*, 26 August 1998.
15 *Vedomosti*, 14 February 2000.
16 <http://www.osi.ru>.
17 *The Economist*, 3 June 2000, p. 52.
18 *Vedomosti*, 21 June 2000.
19 *The Russia Journal*, Vol. 2, No. 39, 22–28 November 1999.
20 *Expert*, No. 38, 11 October 1999, p. 8; *Expert*, No. 48, 20 December 1999, p. 10; *Profil*, No. 44, 22 November 1999, p. 77.
21 Cf. *Kommersant-Vlast*, No. 31, 10 August 1999, p. 27; *NG-Politekonomia*, No. 3, 15 February 2000.
22 *VEK*, 3–9 December 1999.
23 *Vedomosti*, 26 November 1999.

6 Global finance and incipient civil society in China

Yu Yongding

Summary

•	Introduction	94
•	Global finance in China	95
•	China's policies towards global financial governance	100
•	Civil society responses to global finance in China	104
•	Conclusion	107

Introduction

Since 1978, China has adopted a new approach to economic development. The essential elements of the new approach are market-oriented reforms and opening up to the outside world. Sustained economic growth and significant improvement of the Chinese people's living standards over the past two decades have fully vindicated this approach. Owing to the Asian financial crisis in 1997–98, China slowed its pace of capital liberalization for a short period. However, following the recovery of the Asian economies, and with negotiations for its accession to the World Trade Organization (WTO), China has reinvigorated its efforts to integrate itself into the global economy.

Against this general backdrop, this chapter first gives an account of China's opening up to global finance. The second section discusses Chinese policies towards global finance, in terms of capital account liberalization, the exchange rate regime, and regional monetary cooperation. The third section discusses civil society and its response towards global finance in China. Owing to the fact that civil society is a newly emergent phenomenon in China, the bulk of this section addresses the existence of civil society in China and its role in the social life of the country. On the whole, global finance has not as yet been an object of civil society activities in China.

Global finance in China

Before 1978, China was a closed economy. It had no foreign debt and no foreign direct investment (FDI). In other words, China had virtually no relationship with global finance. However, since the reforms and opening up, China has become a full member of all the key international financial organizations. Various forms of foreign capital have flowed into the country. China has become increasingly active in international financial markets. It has participated vigorously in discussions on regional monetary cooperation and reform of the international financial system. Financial markets in China have partially opened up – and will open up further – to foreign capital. More and more Chinese investors have begun to invest abroad. In short, China has increasingly integrated itself into global finance.

Cross-border financial flows

Since 1978, China has obtained various forms of global finance capital: loans, bonds and securities. These flows are discussed in turn below. In addition, China has attracted major inflows of FDI, which are also mentioned briefly, although these investments otherwise fall outside the scope of the present book.

External official loans, consisting of loans from foreign governments and international financial organizations with concessional terms, have been important components of capital inflows into China. In the early 1980s, official loans played a very important role in Chinese efforts to acquire foreign capital. After two decades, external official loans continue to be significant in the Chinese economy (Table 6.1). However, the share of official loans in China's total capital inflows has dropped considerably, due to the fact that other forms of inflow have been increasing much more dramatically.

Table 6.1 Official loans to China ($ billion)[1]

	1984	1985	1986	1987	1988	1989	1990	1991	1992	1993	1994	1995	1996	1997	1998	1999
G	0.7	0.5	0.8	0.8	1.2	2.1	2.5	1.8	2.5	3.0	2.4	2.7	3.4	3.6	2.9	3.3
I	0.2	0.6	1.3	0.7	1.1	1.0	1.0	1.3	1.3	2.2	1.4	2.7	3.0	1.6	3.0	2.0

Notes
G Net loans extended by foreign governments.
I Net loans extended by international financial organizations.

The Ministry of Foreign Economics and Trade is the only window for foreign government loans to China. The Ministry of Finance is the only window for loans from the World Bank. The People's Bank of China (PBC) is the only window for loans from the International Monetary Fund (IMF) and the Asian Development Bank (ADB). The State Development Planning Commission (SDPC) is in charge of compiling annual plans of foreign borrowing. After reconciling the borrowing applications from different government departments and provincial governments, the SDPC determines the total amount of borrowing and the allocation of loans among different final users.

Commercial loans – consisting mainly of borrowings from foreign banks, trade credits and loans by foreign enterprises and foreign exporters, and other private loans – are more important components of China's capital inflow than official loans. After 1978, commercial loans increased steadily, to a peak of $7 billion in 1994 and 1995.[2] Thereafter these inflows began to lose momentum, but in 1999 China still managed to obtain $3.5 billion of commercial loans.[3]

The Chinese government exerts very strict control over foreign commercial borrowing. Only after having obtained authorization from the State Administration of Foreign Exchange (SAFE) can financial institutions and enterprises take loans from foreign banks and other financial institutions. Chinese residents are not allowed to borrow from foreign banks and other foreign financial institutions without prior government approval. The State Council must approve any borrowings above $100 million. Authorized departments and local governments must approve borrowings under $100 million. The approval procedure involves inter-departmental work between the SDPC, the PBC and the SAFE. All borrowing and lending agreements that lack prior approval by the authorized government organizations are not legally binding. The SAFE will refuse to recognize these agreements and will register the loans as foreign debt. Foreign companies with investments in China can borrow directly from abroad; however, they must register the borrowings with designated branches of the SAFE.

China's first issuance of bonds on international markets came in 1982, when the China International Trust and Investment Company (CITIC) issued 10 billion yen bonds in Japan. Owing to a lack of experience in international bond markets, China has been very cautious in raising money there. In the mid-1980s, China's sale of bonds on international markets once surpassed $1 billion per year, but until 1991 the value of China's issuance of foreign-currency-denominated bonds averaged less than $1 billion per year. Since then, money raised for China from international bond markets has increased significantly. In 1994, China's issuance of foreign bonds reached a record high of $2.8 billion. The contagion effect of the Asian financial crisis and the vulnerability of China's international trust and investment companies (ITICs) had a negative influence on the credibility of Chinese institutional borrowers. However, on bond markets China still succeeded in raising $2.6 billion in 1997, $1 billion in 1998, and $2 billion in 1999.[4]

In China, the issuance of foreign-currency-denominated bonds is limited to ten authorized window financial institutions, the Ministry of Finance and the state policy banks. Other borrowers can ask the ten window institutions to issue bonds for them. If they wish to issue bonds themselves, they must obtain special approval from the SAFE.

Turning to portfolio investment, there are two stock exchanges in China: the Shanghai Stock Exchange and the Shenzhen Stock Exchange, established in 1985 and 1987, respectively. In 1991, these two stock exchanges began to offer so-called "B shares" for foreigners to invest in China's capital markets. B shares are denominated in US dollars. Any flotation of B shares above $30 million is subject to approval by the Securities Supervision Committee of the State Council. The total amount of B shares floated each year must remain within the quotas set by the government. By the end of 1998, 106 companies had between them issued 9.6 billion B shares and raised $4.8 billion.

A small number of Chinese companies are allowed to list on the Hong Kong Stock Exchange and New York Stock Exchange. The shares sold in Hong Kong are called "H shares", and those in New York are called "N shares". By the end of 1998, thirty-one Chinese companies had listed in Hong Kong, eight had dual-listed in Hong Kong and New York, one had listed in New York, two had dual-listed in Hong Kong and London, and one had listed in Singapore. By the end of 1998, these companies had together raised $10 billion.[5] In 1999, Chinese companies raised a further $0.6 billion from foreign stock exchanges.

Finally, although the present book is concerned with finance capital, brief mention should be made of FDI, since it is by far the most important form of capital inflow into China. Passage of the Law of the People's Republic of China on Joint Ventures Using Chinese and Foreign Investment in 1979 ushered in a period of persistent large-scale FDI inflow into China. In 1986 the Law of the People's Republic of China on Enterprises Operated Exclusively with Foreign Capital permitted, for the first time, wholly owned foreign enterprises (WOFEs) to operate in China. In 1996, China signed Article VI of the IMF, establishing currency convertibility for current account transactions, a measure that significantly increased the country's attraction to FDI. Even during the Asian financial crisis, the momentum of the FDI inflow into China was maintained. (See Figure 6.1.)[6]

With regard to capital outflows from China, only authorized financial institutions engaged in foreign borrowing and large enterprise groups are allowed to buy foreign securities of any kind, including derivatives. Chinese residents are not allowed to open personal foreign-exchange accounts abroad. Chinese financial institutions must obtain approval from the SAFE before they can open foreign-exchange

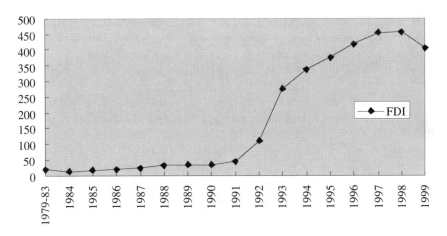

Figure 6.1 Foreign direct investment in China ($100 billion).

accounts abroad. China's outward FDI is under strict regulation and supervision. All investment income must be repatriated back to China within six months of the end of the fiscal year of the host country. Foreign exchange needed for business operations abroad can be kept in the host country only after obtaining the approval of foreign-exchange authorities.

However, despite strict capital controls, capital outflows from China have steadily increased. The situation greatly worsened during and immediately after the Asian financial crisis. Due to capital flight and normal capital outflows in the form of short-term lending to foreign borrowers in 1998, China's capital account turned negative for the first time in decades. Only frantic efforts by the SAFE and other departments of the government allowed the government to return the capital account into the black again (just) in 1999.[7]

Taking into consideration the changes in global finance and the changes in China's domestic situation, it seems that the time for plain sailing in the introduction of foreign capital into China has ended. However, whatever may happen in the future, China's achievement in attracting foreign capital since 1978 has been truly amazing (see Figure 6.2).[8]

Opening up financial services to foreign financial institutions

China has adopted a gradualist approach to opening up its financial services to foreign participation. Broadly speaking, the process can be divided into four stages. In the first stage (1979–82), thirty-one foreign financial institutions were allowed to set up representative offices in China.

The second stage (1982–90) was an experimental period, when a small number of foreign banks were given licences to operate in Shenzhen, and in Shenzhen only. In 1982, a Hong Kong-based commercial bank set up a branch in Shekou, a small town located in the Shenzhen area bordering on Hong Kong. The branch was the first foreign financial institution allowed to operate in mainland China since the creation of the People's Republic. Owing to strict capital controls, foreign banks were prohibited from conducting business in local renminbi yuan (RMB). As a result, the operations of foreign banks were confined to providing foreign firms and joint ventures with services related to foreign-currency transactions.

Soon the regulation of foreign financial institutions began to have a legal basis. In 1983, the People's Bank of China issued Administrative Rules on the Establishment of Permanent Representative Offices in China by Overseas Chinese and Foreign Financial Institutions. Two years later, the PBC issued Administrative Rules on the Operations of Foreign and Joint Venture Banks in Shenzhen Special Economic Zone.

During the third stage (1990–94), the scope of opening up was significantly extended, in terms of the number of foreign financial institutions allowed to operate in China and the cities where they could conduct business. In 1990, the PBC issued Administrative Rules on the Operations of Foreign and Joint Venture Banks in Shanghai. As a result, Shanghai became the second city, in addition to Shenzhen, where foreign banks could operate. Subsequently, a further seven coastal

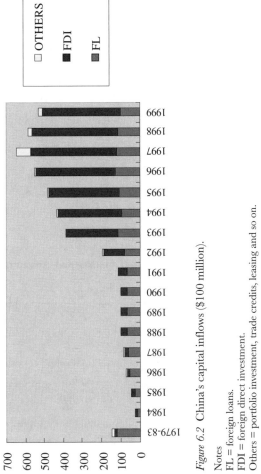

Figure 6.2 China's capital inflows ($100 million).

Notes

FL = foreign loans.

FDI = foreign direct investment.

Others = portfolio investment, trade credits, leasing and so on.

cities were opened up to foreign banks. During the third period, an insurance company from the USA also obtained a licence to operate in China.

The fourth stage (1994 to the present) has been characterized by China's formal opening up to foreign financial institutions on a comprehensive legal basis. In 1994, the State Council promulgated the People's Republic of China's Administrative Rules on Foreign Financial Institutions. In this period, a large number of metropolitan centers in China have been added to the list of cities that are open to foreign financial institutions. The types of business that foreign financial institutions are allowed to conduct has also increased.

By the end of 1999, 284 foreign financial institutions from thirty-nine countries or regions were established in China, spread across twenty-four cities. Japanese financial institutions maintain the largest presence, with seventy companies in total, followed by Hong Kong (thirty-three), the US (twenty-three), the UK (nineteen), France (sixteen), Italy (fourteen), Germany (twelve), Thailand (eleven), the Netherlands (ten) and others. Of the 284 foreign financial institutions, 257 are banks, ten are credit companies, eight are financial companies, and nine are other types of firms.[9]

Another important development during this period has been the opening up of the RMB business to foreign financial institutions in Shanghai Pudong Development Zone, a newly designated experimental area with special policy concessions. Starting from 1999, China's monetary authorities are relaxing the restrictions on the operations of foreign financial institutions. Measures have been taken to pave the way toward enabling foreign financial institutions to conduct RMB lending business.

China's policies towards global financial governance

China is determined to embrace globalization and to participate in global finance. There is no doubt about that. The question is how to do it. China's policy towards global finance has three major pillars. First, China needs to maintain capital controls to buy time to carry out reforms, especially financial reforms, while gradually liberalizing its capital account and its financial services sector. Second, China needs to maintain a stable currency *vis-à-vis* the US dollar, while gradually shifting to a more flexible exchange-rate regime. Third, China supports the role played by key global financial organizations, while also being actively engaged in regional monetary cooperation.

Capital controls

Two experiences had an important influence on the Chinese leadership's thinking in the early 1980s when China was formulating its policy regarding foreign capital. On the one hand, the enviable success of East Asian economies – including their policy of introducing foreign capital – encouraged China to follow suit. On the other hand, the debt crisis of Latin American countries taught China to be cautious about integrating into global finance.

Today, the Chinese economy is very similar to the crisis-affected Asian economies, in terms of its weak financial system, its high level of nonperforming loans (NPLs), and its high debt–equity ratio. During the Asian financial crisis, many foreign observers predicted that China would also collapse. However, China has suffered neither a fall in the RMB nor a financial crisis. With the benefit of hindsight, most economists would agree that capital controls were the key that enabled China to weather the storm of the Asian financial crisis.

The Asian crisis shows that developing countries should not relinquish capital controls too hastily. If a country still needs to maintain a fixed exchange rate, the removal of capital controls will deprive the government of its independence in monetary policy. Moreover, if left unregulated, inherently unstable flows of short-term capital will bring undue disruption to an economy where the market mechanism is imperfect and capital markets are shallow and underdeveloped. Without capital controls, economically and financially weak countries are exposed to attacks from international speculators and suffer huge losses of foreign-exchange reserves. As a result, the level of economic development of these countries can be set back for decades.

Since China's financial reform is far from complete, capital controls should be kept. International speculators could exploit the points of vulnerability in China's financial system more easily than they did in other countries of the region during the Asian financial crisis. Therefore, China should not open this door before its house is in order.

However, capital controls are very costly and are becoming increasingly difficult to implement. Without doubt, China needs gradually to liberalize its capital account. In 1998, alarmed by the prevalent evasion of capital controls, the SAFE and the PBC issued a series of circulars on foreign exchange that aimed to strengthen the control of capital flows. All foreign-exchange transactions under the current account as well as the capital account had to undergo stricter checking and clearing procedures.

Although these efforts succeeded in stemming capital flight, they placed an unbearable workload on the staff of the SAFE. They also caused great inconvenience to enterprises and banks. According to a survey published by the US–China Business Council, over 80 per cent of companies were adversely affected by the new restrictions. Nearly half of the companies surveyed had decided to reconsider, delay or even cancel intended investments and/or financing involving foreign currency.[10] Indeed, tougher capital controls may lead to more evasions. Control helps, but it is not a panacea. In 1999, the SAFE had to relax the controls.

The WTO adds further urgency for capital account liberalization in China. After China's accession to the WTO, it will have to further open up its financial service sector. Under these circumstances, the task of maintaining effective capital controls will become more difficult.

So capital account liberalization is inevitable for China. The question is how it should be sequenced. The basic problem in this regard is to strike a balance between finally liberalizing the capital account and maintaining financial stability to maximize the welfare of the country during the transition.

Exchange rate regime

The experience of Asian countries shows that a regime of fixed exchange rates may cause excessive capital inflows and facilitate the creation of a bubble economy. The fixed exchange rate may also undermine a country's competitiveness which, in turn, would lead to a current account crisis. The Asian crisis also shows that governments tend to postpone the transition from a fixed exchange rate regime (or a de facto fixed exchange regime) to a more flexible exchange rate regime until the change is forced upon them, by which time irretrievable damage may have been done. Therefore, the government must have the courage to act when change is needed.

However, China's experience also shows that specific problems should be specifically analyzed. During the Asian financial crisis, the Chinese government reckoned that maintaining the RMB's peg to the US dollar was a much better alternative than floating or devaluing the RMB. Subsequent events have fully vindicated this policy.

Two factors must be taken into consideration when judging whether the RMB will be devalued in the future. First, the RMB is not convertible under the capital account. Residents of China are subject to strict restrictions in converting RMB to US dollars. Until now, capital controls have remained effective, and the Chinese government can make sure that the capital account will not exert large pressure on the RMB. Hence, in China the exchange rate is mainly determined by the trade account.

Second, even if the Chinese government wants to devalue the RMB to stimulate exports, the cost of doing so is too high. China's foreign exchange market is an inter-bank market. The function of the market is to balance each bank's required foreign exchange position. Banks that are short of foreign exchange can borrow from those with excess foreign exchange. If the net balance of foreign exchange positions of all banks is positive at a given exchange rate, the central bank will buy up that net balance. For example, in 1999 China's inter-bank foreign exchange market had an excess supply of US dollars, due to the balance of payments surplus. To prevent the RMB from appreciating, the central bank bought up to $9.7 billion. A similar scenario unfolded in 2000.

A devaluation of the RMB is therefore unlikely. However, the Chinese government will pay greater attention to choosing a proper exchange rate regime. In 1994, the Chinese government merged the official exchange rate with the swap market exchange rate and devalued the official exchange rate from 5.5 yuan to the dollar to 8.7 yuan to the dollar. At the same time, the government created the inter-bank foreign-exchange market, and China's exchange rate regime became one of "managed floating". However, the need for macroeconomic stability has made the regime a de facto fixed exchange rate regime.

During 1999–2000, when the current account surplus bred widespread fears of an RMB devaluation, the actual pressure on the inter-bank market was to appreciate rather than devalue the currency. To prevent the RMB from appreciating, the central bank has to soak up the excess foreign exchange, which other banks are not allowed to hold. Due to active PBC intervention, the fluctuation of the RMB *vis-à-vis* the US dollar has been extremely small.

Although the government definitely wishes to emphasize that China has a regime of managed floating, under current circumstances it is difficult to let the RMB fluctuate in a meaningful way. A first step in this direction would be to widen the target band. It is reported that the operational principle adopted by the PBC is that the spread between the current day and last day's exchange rates in the inter-bank market should not exceed 0.3 per cent. This rule may change in the future. A second step that the Chinese government may take would be to let the RMB peg to a trade-weighted basket of currencies, with much greater weight than before placed on the euro and the Japanese yen.

After China's entry into the WTO, and the consequent opening up of China's financial services sector, the authorities are bound to have less ability to control capital flows. China's trade balance may also be negatively influenced. In these circumstances, China's foreign exchange market will become much more active, and China's exchange rate regime will truly become one of managed floating.

Regional monetary cooperation

The IMF and the US government made rather disappointing responses to the Asian financial crisis. For some Asian economies, the IMF's rescue package came too late and was too little, and the conditionality was too harsh. Compared with their responses to the Russian and Brazilian crises, it is fair to criticize the IMF and US approach to the Asian countries' plight as indifferent.

In the aftermath of the Asian crisis, China has supported reform of the present international financial architecture, in terms of transparency, data dissemination, international supervision and regulation. In addition, China has shown great enthusiasm for participating in Asian regional cooperation on monetary and financial matters.

The Asian crisis showed that Asian economies, especially East Asian economies, are already closely integrated with each other via their trade and financial ties. No country in Asia could completely avoid the so-called "contagion" effect. As a member of the Asian community, China cannot completely insulate itself from any major Asian economic crisis.

China is very positive about regional monetary cooperation in Asia. However, the Chinese government holds the view that trade and technological cooperation is the basis and precondition for close monetary cooperation. While supporting regional monetary cooperation, the Chinese government is very cautious about any form of institutionalized monetary cooperation. The Chinese government emphasizes the importance of dialogue and patience and prefers to build up Asian monetary cooperation within the IMF framework.

One important milestone for global finance in Asia was the "ASEAN+3" meeting of finance ministers held at Chiang Mai, Thailand in May 2000. This meeting agreed to strengthen policy dialogues and regional cooperation in respect of capital flows monitoring, self-help and support mechanisms, and international financial reforms. The ministers recognized a need to establish a regional financing arrangement to supplement existing international facilities. They agreed to establish a network of research and training institutions to work on issues of common interest. In addition, the Chiang Mai Initiative created an expanded ASEAN Swap Arrangement and a network of bilateral swap and repurchase agreement facilities among the ASEAN countries, China, Japan and the Republic of Korea. The swap arrangement marked an important turning point on the road of Asian monetary cooperation. China firmly believes that regional monetary cooperation can play a very important role in shaping global finance in the twenty-first century.

To implement regional monetary cooperation, Asian governments can first try to put the relevant communication and consultation on a regular basis, such as holding quarterly or annual meetings. Next they can establish a research institute with representatives from major Asian economies who are highly qualified scholars with official positions and officials from financial authorities. This institute should have its own publications, such as newsletters, reports, and so on. The institute should keep a close eye on the economic situation of major Asian countries and issue evaluations of circumstances. The institute should formulate emergency plans in case a crisis erupts. The institute could also help to coordinate different rescue packages that are based on bilateral agreements.

In sum, China fully embraces financial globalization. At the same time, China will work hard to achieve an equitable international financial system that benefits all countries in the world and all strata of people in every country.

Civil society responses to global finance in China

Civil society is a foreign notion for China. The concept came to us from Hegel via Marx. To most Chinese scholars, "civil society" refers to the bourgeoisie in eighteenth-century Western Europe: a class that was becoming a strong economic force but remained excluded from the political establishment. Until now, Chinese intellectuals have only occasionally discussed civil society.[11]

On the other hand, political reform has been intensively discussed since the 1980s. Basically, there are two schools of thought in China about the role of the state, the relationship between economic reform and political reform, and the way to improve governance. The majority view is that the state should be the prime mover in China's modernization drive, that political stability is the precondition for economic progress, and that existing channels and mechanisms are sufficient to improve governance in China. The minority view holds that fundamental political reform should be carried out first and that it should be based on universal principles.

In the early 1990s, a small number of writers took a middle stand and raised the issue of the development of civil society in China. They argued that both the new authoritarianism and the democratization-first approaches ignore the fact that there can be a sphere between the state and the economy, where a large number of independent associations can be established. These associations would constitute China's "civil society".[12]

Civil society can play several important roles in China. First, it can help to cultivate the market economy in China by filling the gaps that result from the state's withdrawal from the economic sphere. Second, civil society can restrain excessive interference by the government into civil life and help to protect the legitimate rights of the common people. Third, as pressure groups and whistle blowers, civil society organizations can push government to improve its governance. Fourth, civil society can reduce social tension and help to form social consensus, thereby playing the role of stabilizer in society. Fifth, the development of the market economy and the existence of an apolitical, autonomous and rule-based civil society can be conducive to further political reform in the future.[13]

In China, nongovernmental organizations (NGOs) are also called nonprofit organizations (NPOs) or the "third sector". Most Chinese NGOs are in fact more or less affiliated to, and funded by, certain government departments. These sorts of associations include national and local academic societies, sectoral business organizations, trade unions (semi-official), nationwide women's associations, athletic and cultural clubs, associations for the disabled, religious groups, and so on. Most of these associations are established from the top down.

Since the early 1990s, a few grassroots NGOs have appeared. These NGOs are mostly apolitical. They have a specific agenda and are not funded by the government. The most notable NGOs of this kind are some foundations, environmentalist groups, independent research institutes, consumer protection associations, and various charities.[14]

Perhaps the most famous endeavour carried out by a Chinese NGO is "Project Hope". This initiative aims to provide financial support for children who leave school due to poverty. The NGO that launched the project is the China Youth Development Foundation (CYDF). Founded in 1989, the CYDF is run by a group of young people who share a common commitment to the betterment of society. Over the past decade, the CYDF has raised funds to enable hundreds of thousands of children to return to school, thereby assisting the government to implement its policy of nine years of compulsory education. Since 1995, the CYDF has established wide connections with foreign NGOs. These links have enabled the CYDF to obtain foreign experience in organizing activities and setting rules to guide the activities. Project Hope is widely regarded as a huge success.[15]

Another famous NGO activity in China is the Happiness Project, organized by the China Population Welfare Foundation (CPWF). This initiative aims to raise funds to provide impoverished women with micro-credits. Project Happiness has helped to lift 40,000 women out of poverty and has reduced poverty for another 180,000.[16]

There are also many less famous NGOs that are very active in China. For example, in 1992 the Maple Women's Psychological Counseling Center established the Women's Hotline in Beijing, maintained by volunteers, without any government funding. The Law School of Beijing University has established a Center for Women's Law Studies and Legal Services to provide services and research on women's issues. In addition, some foreign NGOs have in recent years launched activities in China. For example, the Save the Children Fund (SCF) has carried out several projects in China.

The Chinese government is adopting an increasingly positive attitude towards NGOs. On 17 October 2000, the Third International Seminar on NGO Cooperation was held in Beijing. At the meeting, Mr Wang Wendong, a former Vice-Minister of Foreign Trade and Economic Cooperation, pointed out:

> The non-profit and non-governmental sector in China has shown significant growth in recent years since it has attracted more financial help and technical services for poverty-stricken, remote and ethnic-inhabited areas.[17]

In recent years, the government has encouraged NGOs to play a big role in fighting poverty in China. According to Chinese officials, "A seven-year poverty-reduction project between 1993 and 2000 has culminated in Chinese NGOs pouring at least 30 billion yuan [US$3.6 billion] into helping the country's poor".[18] Successful NGO projects have also raised public awareness of Chinese NGOs and the necessity for the development of NGOs in China. However, despite this increased public attention, the role played by NGOs in China remains very limited.

Meanwhile, NGO engagement of global finance in China is nonexistent. Since the Asian financial crisis, people in China have become significantly more aware of the existence of global finance and its impact on their lives. However, the concern is still limited, and NGOs in China have never been actively involved in discussions of global financial issues.

The explanation for this lack of engagement is simple. First, the Asian financial crisis had only a very indirect and limited impact on the Chinese people, partly due to China's success in dealing with the crisis. Second, global finance is a highly technical issue that is very difficult for nonprofessionals to grasp. In China, almost no NGO has the necessary competence to contribute to the debate.

However, as China gradually opens up its financial services sector and liberalizes its capital account, global finance will have an increasingly important influence on the daily lives of the Chinese people. Consequently, people in the street will respond more vehemently to developments in global finance. Only then will NGOs in China take up the issue and participate in the debate.

That said, a large number of research institutes in China have long participated in debates on global finance. They include thirty-one institutes under the umbrella of the Chinese Academy of Social Sciences. According to the strict definition, these research institutes are not part of civil society, since they are affiliated to the government. However, in terms of the independence of their research, they might still be loosely regarded as civil society organizations.

These institutes have been very active in discussions of global finance in recent years. The mainstream view in these bodies regards financial globalization very positively, although it advocates a gradualist approach to capital liberalization. Meanwhile, a minority of these scholars are very doubtful about the benefits that globalization can bring to China. The mainstream researchers in these institutes have influenced the Chinese government's policy towards global finance, as discussed in earlier sections of this chapter.

Conclusion

Over the past two decades, China has gone a long way towards integrating itself into the global economy. The country has basically completed a transition from a closed economy to an open economy. The value of foreign trade in China now amounts to more than 30 per cent of GDP. By the end of 1997, China had absorbed a total of $217 billion in FDI.[19] Most Fortune 500 companies have now invested in China. By the end of 1997, China's accumulated outward FDI had reached $20.4 billion. China has joined almost all of the key international economic organizations. Once it has joined the WTO and liberalized its capital account, China will finally complete its integration into the global economy.

Although civil society has not become a focal point in China, its emergence is definitely a positive development. Civil society has been playing a constructive role in China's economic and political reforms. I believe that the Chinese government will encourage the growth of civil society and establish an appropriate legal framework to accommodate its development. With time, civil society in China will be increasingly involved in important issues such as global finance.

Notes

1 *China Statistical Abstract* [*Zhongguo Tongji Zhaiyao*] (Beijing: National Bureau of Statistics [Guojia Tongjiju], 1997), p. 245; ibid. (1999), p. 137; *China Statistical Yearbook* [*Zhongguo Tongji Nianjian*] (Beijing: National Bureau of Statistics, 2000), p. 605.
2 *China Statistical Abstract* (1997), p. 245.
3 *China Statistical Yearbook* (2000), p. 605.
4 *China Statistical Yearbook* (1999); Wang Luolin and Pei Changhong (eds), *Foreign Direct Investment in China* [*Zhongguo Waiguo Zhijie Touzi Baogao*] (Beijing: Publishing House of Finance and Economics, 2000).
5 Gao Haihong, *Liberalising China's Capital Account: Lessons Drawn from Thailand's Experience* (Singapore: Institute of Southeast Asian Studies Working Papers, 2000), p. 20.
6 *China Statistical Yearbook* (1999), p. 594; *China Statistical Yearbook* (2000), p. 604.
7 State Administration of Foreign Exchange, *Balance of Payments Annual Report 2001*, p. 29. See also Yu Yongding, "China 1999–2000: Macroeconomic Situation and Financial Reform", *World Economy and China* (March–April 2000), pp. 6–14.
8 *China Statistical Yearbook* (1999), p. 594; *Balance of Payments Annual Report 2001*, p. 13.
9 *China's Financial Outlook* [*Zhonguo Jinrog Zhanwang*] (Beijing: People's Bank of China, 1999), p. 94.
10 *Impact of Recent Foreign Exchange Circulars on US Companies* (US–China Business Council, December 1998) – at http://www.uschina.org/public/fxsurveyresults.html.
11 Important writings on this topic include: Du Zangqi, *Cultural, Power and State* (Jiangsu: Jiangsu People's Publishing House [Jiangsu Renmin Chubanshe], 1995); Deng Zhenglai, *State and Civil Society* (Sichuan: Sichuan People's Publishing House [Sichuan Renmin Chubanshe], 1997); Zhang Shuguang, "Government, Farmers and Markets", *Chinese Social Sciences Quarterly* [*Zhongguo Shehui Kexue Jikan*] (August 1997); Fang Chaohui, "Reflections on Studies of Civil Society in the 1990s", *Tianjing Social Sciences* [*Tianjing Shehuikexue*], No. 5 (1999). See also Timothy Brook and B. Michael Frolic (eds), *Civil Society in China* (Armonk, NY: Sharpe, 1997).
12 Deng Zhenglai, op. cit.
13 Ibid.

14 See Nick Young (ed.), *250 Chinese NGOs: Civil Society in the Making* (Beijing: China Development Brief, 2001).
15 China Youth Development Foundation and UNDP, International Conference on the Development of Non-Profit Organizations and the China Project Hope, 1999. See also http://www.project-hope.org/.
16 Ibid.
17 *China Daily*, 18 October 2000.
18 *China Daily*, 11 June 2001.
19 *World Investment Report 1999* (New York: United Nations, 1999).

Part III

Perspectives from multilateral institutions

7 The World Bank and civil society

An evolving experience

John D. Clark[1]

Summary	
• Introduction	111
• How the Bank–civil society relationship evolved	112
• Why civil society campaigns have targeted economic justice and the Bank	114
• Civil society campaigns on the Bank and their impact on global finance	118
• Where civil society has been successful in changing global finance	119
• Civil society, the Asian crisis and the globalization debate	121
• The civil society case against neoliberal globalization	123
• Conclusion – how much is the Bank changing?	124

Introduction

No inter-governmental organization has experienced a more diverse relationship with civil society than the World Bank, ranging from close collaboration to hostility. This chapter examines the evolving threads of that relationship and how it has impacted on the Bank's programs, policies, operational norms and institutional culture. Civil society organizations (CSOs) of different forms have had a profound impact on many aspects of the Bank's business and have exposed and widened the heterogeneity inherent in an institution whose professional staff come from a wide variety of disciplines and whose management ethos encourages innovation.

In its operations, including country-level analytical and research work, the Bank now frequently works with CSOs, in particular community-based organizations (CBOs), local and international NGOs, foundations and independent think tanks. Although clashes of style, different institutional scales, and the Bank's cumbersome business processes often create frictions, the Bank has strengthened collaboration throughout the 1990s.[2]

In its dialogue with civil society on practices, policies and paradigms, the Bank has found the ride much rougher. Advocacy groups, NGOs with research and lobbying capacity, trade unions, politically linked think tanks and religious bodies have raised a wide array of issues and influenced considerable change, but the disputes have often been bitter.

Inherent in the increasingly sophisticated and increasingly global campaigns to reform the Bank lies a tension that this chapter seeks to dissect. On the one hand, the Bank clearly does have a view in the high-profile debate about globalization. It is influential with many ministers in many governments. It has admitted to many mistakes that entailed serious social or environmental harm. It also has a tendency to arrogance. So it is understandable that the Bank has galvanized civil society campaigns. But on the other hand the Bank has nowhere near the sweeping influence that critics often assume (or infer) it has. Its direct financial muscle – once substantial – is now quite modest. Moreover, on many issues it now argues a similar case to its critics.

This chapter describes how campaigns on international development have shifted towards generic questions of economic justice and why, therefore, international financial institutions (IFIs) have become a prime target. But it questions how appropriate it remains for the Bank to be quite the *bête noire* it is portrayed to be. Paradoxically, because the Bank has become a much more open institution, because many staff prioritize social development, participation and civil society, and because the Bank invites CSOs into so many meetings and shares so many documents, it is much more familiar territory to civil society and therefore an easier target for criticism.

In shifting to a more poverty-focused agenda and in seeking to make peace with CSOs, the Bank has focused more and more on the "soft" development issues, such as vulnerable groups, basic social services, gender equity, environmental protection, inclusion, participation, and community-driven development. Some in civil society are suspicious – even angry – that the talk outstrips the action and that a yawning rhetoric–reality gap has opened. They accuse the Bank of hijacking civil society language, but greatly diluting the conclusions.[3]

The role of civil society during the recent East Asian Economic Crisis, and how the Bank engaged with this scenario, illustrates many of these facets and also underlines why strong relations between IFIs and civil society are vital. Finally, the concluding section of this chapter sets out some challenges for a critical though constructive engagement in the future.

How the Bank–civil society relationship evolved

Before the early 1980s, CSOs gave little attention to the Bank. Thereafter, with its new poverty-reduction mandate, the Bank sought to increase operational links. NGOs were typically viewed as potential low-cost subcontractors that could be engaged at project implementation stage to deliver services to hard-to-reach groups. At the same time, a parallel phenomenon emerged: hard-hitting CSO criticisms of perceived negative environmental and social impacts of many operations, particularly adjustment programs designed to help countries in economic crisis restore balance.[4]

These campaigns of the 1980s threatened parliamentary support for the Bank's budget replenishments in some Northern countries (especially the USA), and the Bank realized it was time to seek peace and mount a more credible public defense. At the same time, a group of Bank staff who shared a vision of participatory development were carving out stronger, more partnership-based links with NGOs and community groups, which started at the project concept stage and emphasized community empowerment and people's choice.

Paradoxically, although 1994 was a low-point in terms of the Bank's public image – due to a widespread opposition campaign that greeted its fiftieth anniversary – this moment also brought a more constructive strategy for Bank–civil society relations. The new approach has helped to tone down the hostility and enable a more reasoned dialogue with its critics. Progress was due to a number of factors, chief of which was the leadership of James Wolfensohn, appointed Bank President in 1995, who engaged earnestly with leading Bank critics and met civil society leaders wherever he traveled. He insisted that the Bank take critics at face value, agreeing sometimes to work together – as in mounting the Structural Adjustment Participatory Review Initiative, in which the Bank and a global civil society alliance are jointly analyzing the impact of adjustment in a range of countries.

The Bank's civil society strategy has had five strands.[5] First, it has improved and expanded operational collaboration, emphasizing early civil society involvement in project design, up-front treatment of concerns about negative impacts, and enhanced use of participatory development approaches (guided by a high-profile internal "learning group").

Second, the Bank has engaged civil society in country-level strategy and policy formulation, in particular through participatory or consultative approaches to sector studies, poverty assessments and country lending strategies.

Third, a new disclosure policy has made public a much wider array of information, particularly in developing countries (increasingly in local languages), about the Bank's programs and analysis.

Fourth, the Bank has been pro-active in establishing international, structured dialogue on major topics and policy initiatives, including on-going consultative forums concerning gender, the environment, forest protection, debt relief and population activities. Shifting from ad hoc, reactive dialogue with civil society helped ensure that the Bank was less exclusively focused on Washington groups, that Southern voices became well represented, and that the Bank became more influential and therefore more respected by civil society.

Fifth, the Bank has sought opportunities in its policy dialogue with governments to urge greater respect and tolerance of civil society, and admission of CSOs into significant policy forums (such as consultative group meetings with donors). By inviting government participation in its discussions with civil society, the Bank has often brokered policy "trialogue" in which – perhaps for the first time – government discusses serious policy issues with its own civil society. The Bank has often urged governments to foster a more enabling policy environment for CSOs by reforming laws and policies.

Critical to this five-pronged strategy have been efforts to reach out to Southern

CSOs, especially those who work with the poor, for which the Bank needed fuller knowledge of the sector. Hence, from 1994 onwards, the Bank started appointing NGO/civil society specialists in its Resident Missions. Now most field offices have such a specialist, who usually comes from a civil society or related background. As a result, the Bank has become much more familiar with civil society, its views and its personalities. While major differences persist, in most countries there is now more constructive dialogue and, as a result, the Bank frequently modifies its work to accommodate CSO ideas.

In Washington, too, Bank staff engage more substantially with CSOs. The units responsible for regional management and sector policies often employ civil society specialists, and so throughout the institution about ninety staff now have civil society issues as their primary focus. Copious management signals make it clear that staff *are expected* to be responsive to CSOs who express interest or concerns. As one old hand recently put it, "when I joined the World Bank you could be sacked for talking with an NGO; now you can be sacked if you don't." It is very rare that the Bank holds a conference or establishes a working group without civil society representation. New policy papers get copied in draft stage to selected CSO specialists for their comments. CSO speakers are frequently invited to give seminars or make presentations at Bank events. NGOs may get detailed briefings on confidential documents and may in some cases have much greater access to top Bank managers than do the Bank's own senior staff.

Something of a backlash occurred in 1997. A number of Executive Directors (the permanent representatives of governments on the Bank's Board) argued that the Bank had gone too far, that it now listened more to NGOs than to them. Representatives of the developing countries, in particular, felt that their own role was undermined by the frequent practice of civil society consultation prior to Board deliberation. The following months saw considerable discussion and the painful evolution of a revised Bank strategy toward civil society.[6] Henceforth the Bank would continue to seek stronger operational links with experienced NGOs and to build dialogue on controversial policy matters. However, it would give much more attention to bringing governments into these arrangements and to analyzing and describing the important contributions that civil society can make to development through practical partnership, shaping public policy, advocacy and strengthening instruments of "good governance". This internal controversy was a salutary reminder of the pitfalls of trying to move faster than the member governments wanted.

Why civil society campaigns have targeted economic justice and the Bank

Prior to the 1990s, public pressure for global justice focused on multinational corporations (MNCs). Campaigns targeted Nestlé for baby-milk promotion, Brooke Bond for conditions of tea-workers, Barclays Bank and Outspan in respect of apartheid, and ITT for destabilizing Allende's government in Chile. Opposition also attacked associated G7 governments such as the USA for neo-colonialism and the UK for old-fashioned colonialism.

However, during the 1990s G7 governments and some multinationals targeted by campaigns engaged CSOs in serious dialogue. This led some critics to shift from high-profile activism to high-level advocacy. The public in G7 countries also became more inward looking, less interested in global issues, and more concerned with finding a job, as the radical spirit of '68 evaporated. International campaigns that linked with their domestic concerns became more effective. Hence campaigns *against* aid that damaged the environment became more popular than campaigns *for* aid. Critics from both left and right criticized the failure of aid and loans in many instances, particularly in regard to Russia and the Asian Crisis, and an uneasy left–far right alliance emerged in the USA against the funding of multilateral organizations.[7]

The changing dynamics of international civil society have also been important, leading to increased prominence of Southern voices.[8] Improved global communications and information technology exposed Northern activists to the agenda of their Southern counterparts.[9] The latter pointed out that domestic companies usually exploit workers and customers more than multinational corporations do, and that the problem is not isolated, specific injustices but the market mechanisms themselves (determined by Northern actors), which are biased against poor people and poor countries. The Latin American debt crisis starting in 1982, followed by a parallel African crisis, underlined this case and pointed CSOs towards systemic economic justice issues.

Effective campaigning on this subject required clear institutional targets, specific events to showcase inherently complex issues, and winnable battles to keep troops motivated. Long-term campaigns – for an elusive goal like an improved international economic order – need to be broken into "bite-size pieces". The World Bank, the IMF and (more recently) the WTO have proved to be attractive targets. Campaigners see these institutions as principal architects and proponents of a kind of globalization that favors the rich at the expense of the poor. The global economic agencies allegedly corrode state-level democratic processes and serve as powerful levers of financial/corporate interests and US foreign and economic policy. They produce social and environmental damage, widen inequities and contradict public interests. They are shadowy, unaccountable bureaucracies compared with institutions of democratically elected governments, and they enjoy weaker constituencies of support than do G7 national institutions such as bilateral aid or export credit agencies.[10]

Of all the inter-governmental agencies, the World Bank has commanded by far the most civil society attention. In 1985 only a handful of CSO staff worldwide focused on the Bank (almost all in OECD countries). By 2000 this had risen to many hundreds, including Bank-specific pressure groups in dozens of developing and transition countries.

The Bank's appeal to civil society owed much to four internal contradictions. The Bank was widely seen as aloof and arrogant; yet it was relatively accessible. It appeared to have a monolithic worldview; yet its staff were diverse and included many friends of NGOs. It was a force in global policy; yet it worked on specific projects that could be scrutinized locally. And its financing decisions were shrouded in secrecy; yet its funds (especially for the International Development Association, IDA) required authorization by democratic governments and parliaments. Moreover, the Bank cared about its image.

Many supporters and staff of the Bank are puzzled why the Bank so firmly occupies the "hot seat" *vis-à-vis* civil society. First, the Bank is not the volume player in global finance that it is often assumed to be. At its outset in 1944, besides its role in financing reconstruction and development, the Bank was designed to help stabilize the world economy through acting as a conduit for a significant proportion of international financial flows.[11] However, that notion has faded as global financial flows have expanded beyond the dream of the institution's founders. Today the average volume of foreign-exchange dealing exceeds $1,200 billion per day – equivalent to the entire 55 years of World Bank lending every eight hours.

Second, the Bank's policy influence is overshadowed by others at both country and global level – in particular the US government and Congress, the EU, Japan, bankers' consortia and MNC leaders. The G7 governments are more intent on globalization than the Bank is, and they are more dismissive of civil society objections. True, the Bank has a role, but as a development pace and standards setter. It encourages Southern governments to accept the rules of global finance, but it does not make those rules. Small countries with limited capacity to borrow on domestic or international markets and medium-sized low-income or severely debt-distressed countries are disposed to heed the Bretton Woods institutions. They need their credit, whereas larger, healthier borrowers have other options and will not be pushed by the Bank to adopt policies that they do not like.

Third, the Bank's supporters think the institution deserves greater recognition for reforms it has made, many of them prompted by civil society. Privately, campaigners often applaud such changes and compare the Bank favorably with other donors or governments (for example, regarding transparency, accountability mechanisms, civil society dialogue, debt relief, participatory processes, poverty focus and environmental and social assessments). CSO leaders in developing countries often welcome the Bank's efforts to improve the policy environment for civil society and urge governments to take them seriously. Recognition for these trends has been voiced by NGOs in both the North and the South, including Inter-Africa Group and other African NGOs, during discussions about the replenishment of the Bank's lending arm for low-income countries, and the US National Wildlife Federation in its Congressional advocacy. Yet, publicly, most campaigners just voice criticism. There is much for which the Bank deserves criticism, but it is often condemned for crimes it no longer commits, or which it speaks out against itself. Indeed, over recent years the President (James Wolfensohn) has appointed many challengers of the "Washington consensus" and social reformers to key management positions, including Joe Stiglitz and Nick Stern as successive Chief Economists and Ramphele Mamphela as Managing Director. The Bank is now arguably the most dissenting voice at the G7 Finance Ministers' Summits and similar occasions. Pressure on the Bank from its most powerful shareholders runs counter to that from civil society on matters of global architecture and neo-liberal economic orthodoxy.

"Bank-bashing" attenuated considerably in the late 1990s, with more criticism being directed at the IMF, but it now appears to be growing again. This turn reflects general citizen anxiety about the juggernaut of globalization more than specific Bank criticisms. Today's protestors tend to fall into three schools. The first is the "head" school, the studied challenge based on critiques of adjustment programs or projects with heavy social or environmental costs, and "alternative economic paradigms". This group includes most of the environment and development NGOs who focus on the Bank. The second is the "fist" school – anti-establishment activists comprising largely Western youths with little development experience, variously motivated by hostility to capitalism, outrage against injustice, and a penchant for anarchy and trouble-making. Though somewhat embarrassed by the "fists", the "head" school provides them – perhaps unwittingly – with something of an intellectual justification. Between these extremes is a large, middle school – the "heart" school. It comprises churches, trade unions, community organizations in poor neighborhoods, and many others who sense a deep injustice in the way that economic orthodoxy drives exclusion, and who strongly believe that the Bank is part of this, while mouthing development and poverty reduction. Many in the Bank would like to believe that the street protestors are overwhelmingly of the "fist" school, but in reality the "heart" school is probably largest.

The fiftieth anniversary of the Bank in 1994 was notable for large-scale street protests at the Bank/Fund Annual Meetings in Madrid. This was the high-point of the US-based "50 Years Is Enough" campaign. In addition to the hundred or so lobbyists from development groups, thousands of student activists from around Europe orchestrated numerous mass demonstrations. After 1994 these mass protests subsided and lobbying became higher level and more focused, particularly on the debt issue.

The next major occasion when institutions of global finance featured in street protests was the WTO meetings of 1999. The extent of protest took everyone by surprise. There was no single organizing group, but word got around labor activists and dissatisfied youth (overwhelmingly from North America) that the occasion was not to be missed. The Battle of Seattle was drawn. Its general themes were: hostility to faceless international institutions "running our lives"; the fear that free trade would lead to job losses in America; and the conviction that the WTO would sacrifice environmental and social standards on the altar of globalization. The more analytical groups present also challenged the threat to national sovereignty posed by international bodies.

Many Southern civil society groups were irritated by the whole show in Seattle. They, too, hated this powerful new institution whose mission was to harmonize trade regimes. But they also deeply resented the blatant national self-interest inherent in the activism. US protestors were fighting to protect their jobs, their markets, their environment, and their consciences (to remain untainted by child labor, for example), but they appeared disinterested in the agenda of Southern civil societies. As became clear six months later at the UNCTAD meeting in Bangkok, the focus of Southern activists was on topics like agriculture and intellectual property rights. They argued in particular that, since Northern governments subsidize farmers so heavily, agricultural trade should be left out of WTO rules until there is a truly level playing field.

The Ruckus Society (which came to prominence by coordinating the program of demonstrations and organizing training in non-violent direct action for Seattle) sought an occasion to mount a repeat performance. The Bangkok meeting was too far for their largely US constituency, so they selected the 2000 IMF/Bank Spring Meetings. These events are usually muted affairs compared with the Annual Meetings, with only dedicated lobbyists attending to inch forward the campaign for debt relief. However, in April 2000 thousands of people gathered. Some took up the chants and brick-throwing of Seattle. Citizens groups held prayer vigils and seminars about economic justice. The seasoned Bank/Fund reformers mingled somewhat uneasily with the crowds.

The veteran civil society campaigners had mixed feelings. The street events put the right issues on to the public agenda, but did they single out the right institution? In recent years the Bank has added its voice to NGO pressure on G7 governments for debt relief. It has called for a "comprehensive development framework" that gives civil society a role in formulating development strategy. It has helped to level the playing field in information technology by bringing computers and the web to poor countries. It has pioneered Participatory Poverty Assessments to listen to poor people's priorities for fighting poverty. In many other ways, too, the Bank talks the language of NGOs. Veteran campaigners still see much in the Bank to criticize, but they want to reform, not abolish, the institution, and they prefer argument to abuse. Hence the main US operational NGOs wrote to the Bank to distance themselves from the protest.[12] Many advocacy NGOs (who were asked by the protestors not to meet with Bank staff during the demonstrations) decided not to cross any picket line but requested meetings off-premises. Other NGOs (such as Jubilee 2000 and Save the Children UK) were prepared to have meetings inside the Bank. Friends of the Earth–US endorsed the protests, but wrote to the Bank afterwards to say that they had done so because of concerns "that there would not [otherwise] be enough emphasis on the issues since many of the groups involved in organizing the [protest] activities do not necessarily have an expertise with the institutions".[13]

This reveals the dilemma facing many Bank reformers: do they attempt to present a unified civil society stance, justifying hostile protesting? Or do they distance themselves and concentrate on advocacy and debate? If they do the latter they might be accused by some of having become too cozy with the Bank, but if they do the former they may lose the credibility they have established with Bank leadership and with governments.[14]

Civil society campaigns on the Bank and their impact on global finance

Many civil society campaigns seek to influence the direct role of the Bank: that is, specific operations or analytical work. In addition, some hope to mould the Bank's broader, policy-shaping role, especially regarding the processes and institutions of global finance.[15] The latter role is largely indirect, undertaken as the Bank encourages borrowers to open markets and reform their financial sectors and as it provides "seals of approval" for economic policy. Civil society can influence both the direct and indirect roles of the Bank, especially by acting through global networks. CSOs can:

- elevate items on the international agenda through influencing public opinion and the media, as witnessed in the campaign for debt relief;
- promote economic alternatives, as illustrated by campaigns for a Tobin tax and "heterodox" forms of structural adjustment;
- inject local knowledge and foster grassroots contacts to influence the Bank's lending operations – e.g. opposing specific projects on social grounds or promoting popular participation;
- strengthen mechanisms of governance by promoting greater public accountability, transparency, due process and voice, both within the Bank and in borrowing countries (e.g. campaigns for greater Bank disclosure, for an independent Inspection Panel and for weeding out corruption from loans to Indonesia);
- offer alternative conduits for development resources, such as in the provision of services, in social funds, and in participatory project processes.[16]

In these activities CSOs have displayed varying quality, often weakly correlated with policy impact. Some CSOs draw on impressive field experience, while others have none. Some relay the experience and insights of their grassroots partners, while others are purely Northern associations, with few contacts in the South. Some CSOs have large memberships, while others are small cliques. Some practice democratic decision making, while others are autocratic. Some have sophisticated research and policy wings, while others launch high-profile media campaigns backed by flimsy evidence. The strength of civil society varies enormously by country and, hence, there is inherent geographic inequity in people's ability to influence global (or national) decisions through citizens' organizations. In some countries, such as the UK or the Philippines, civil society is advanced, strong and diverse. In others, such as Japan or Congo, it is weak. In still others such as Saudi Arabia or Vietnam, civil society is virtually nonexistent. Access to resources, technical skills and influential media is generally far greater in the North than the South; hence power differentials in civil society parallel those in other aspects of world politics.[17]

Where civil society has been successful in changing global finance

In the OECD countries, in spite of the profusion of center-left governments, few in public office (still less in the private sector) today challenge market deregulation and the need for global competition. Indeed, center-left governments are stronger advocates of free trade than their neo-liberal predecessors. What challenge there is to the free market comes from civil society: NGOs, trade unions, advocacy groups, leftist academics, religious leaders, etc. Although these voices have not stemmed the tide, they have won significant concessions with respect to internationally accepted rules of finance on at least three points.

First, civil society has shown that, contrary to conventional wisdom, the poor are indeed creditworthy. Bankers throughout the world are trained to require collateral from borrowers commensurate with the assessed risk of default. This approach has effectively deprived the poor of formal sources of credit. Yet a number of micro-finance programs run by CSOs have demonstrated that, in many cultures, peer pressure, the desire for future banking services, or even the social stigma of defaulting can be sufficient to make the poor a *better* credit risk than the non-poor. Some micro-finance schemes have operated by providing collateral to commercial banks on behalf of poor borrowers and have been able to reduce to near zero the collateral/loan ratio required by the bank, as credit-worthiness is demonstrated. Such a demonstration effect has helped change the theory regarding banking services to the poor.

Second, civil society has established the principle that economic reform needs to be tempered by social priorities and political realities. In the 1980s, NGOs, UNICEF and others sharply criticized structural adjustment lending for its harsh social impact and for failing to balance economic imperatives with political realities. Some in civil society attacked the principles behind the Washington consensus and its uniform promotion of public spending cuts, devaluation, increased interest rates, privatization and market liberalization. These critics called for "heterodox" approaches that would be tailored to the specific needs of the country in question. Other critics recognized that macroeconomic imbalances should be corrected, but argued for adjustment "with a human face" or "at a human pace". In other words, adjustment should be designed to apportion the pain of recession so as to protect vulnerable groups. The World Bank initially rejected these arguments, saying that the introduction of sound economic fundamentals was the paramount necessity and would quickly herald new growth. Associated social costs would be but transient until the rising tide of growth lifted all boats. As the painful transition lingered, and as the voice of trade unions, opposition parties and others grew louder, the Bank recognized the need to adjust adjustment. From the late 1980s, serious efforts were made to monitor the social impacts of adjustment. Strategies for meeting budget imbalances had to demonstrate that basic social services were not interrupted. The political economy of reform was given more prominence, and in some countries public debate on the reform imperatives was encouraged. Structural adjustment was not abandoned, as some critics wanted, but limits were set on adjustment lending, and efforts to give it a human face went well beyond cosmetic surgery. Few question that massive imbalances in an economy need to be corrected and that a failure to do so is likely (through inflation) to hit the poor hardest. Now there is broader agreement that *how* the balances are made is also important.[18]

Third, contrary to conventional wisdom, IFIs are able to provide debt reduction. From the birth of the debt crisis in 1982 to the mid-1990s, the World Bank maintained that multilateral debt should be excluded from rescheduling or reduction because of the way the funds are mobilized. Moreover, its inclusion might lead to a dangerous contagion and the loss of the Bank's all-important high "triple A" credit rating. However, as popular and parliamentary pressure mounted, the Bank's response shifted and some of its most talented economists sought exit strategies for high IFI debt burdens. These officials found encouragement in President Wolfensohn, who realized shortly after his appointment that there was urgent need for decisive leadership and a change of strategy on this issue, since the greater danger of contagion and erosion of confidence came from *inaction*. A scheme was sketched for comprehensive debt relief for the Highly Indebted Poor Countries (HIPCs). Traditional economists, particularly at the IMF, doubted the need for a new approach, and there was some resistance from the G7 because of the share of the burdens that they would have to meet. The G7 insisted that the two Bretton Woods institutions reach a common view, and so compromise was sought. Had it not been for the mounting international debt campaign, particularly in Europe, the scheme may have been stillborn. The Jubilee 2000 campaign, its endorsement by prominent religious leaders, and growing parliamentary support together had a crucial impact.[19]

Civil society, the Asian crisis and the globalization debate

The Bank's response to the Asian crisis illustrates both how it has come to work closely with civil society and also how influential civil society advocacy has become in the economic arena. At the outset of the Asian crisis – with the devaluation of the Thai baht in July 1997 – the IFIs mounted a conventional response to a currency crisis. Massive balance of payments support was provided on the condition that governments took urgent steps to restore macroeconomic stability (increasing interest rates, cutting public spending, rescuing strategically important banks and instigating swift bankruptcy actions to eliminate the rotten apples). Within a few months, however, the Bank realized that East Asia was gripped by not just a financial, but also a *social* crisis. The speed of this realization owed much to the Bank's strong links with civil society and independent academics, its recent decentralization, and the recent appointment of many social development and civil society specialists at headquarters and in the field who amplified the civil society messages.

The Bank therefore became the first international institution to start systematic, country-level analysis of the social impacts of the crisis.[20] It often worked with CSOs and independent social scientists in investigations which revealed that vulnerable groups were hit in various ways:

- Price escalation made it difficult for normal household consumption to be maintained.
- Large numbers lost their jobs, particularly in urban areas and especially in the construction sector.
- The new jobless often went to stay with rural relatives and/or to smaller cities.

- Formal safety nets proved weak, necessitating dependence on household and community coping strategies.
- Employers often used the fear of unemployment to impose more flexible contracts.
- Social services declined as government budgets were cut and imported drugs and equipment soared in price.
- Household credit became scarce and interest rates prohibitive.
- Crime, prostitution, drugs-dealing, violence and other anti-social activity grew.
- Community-level groups often dwindled as people switched from social capital to survival activities.

In most crisis countries the Bank debated these issues publicly and with government, and sought emergency responses. Often programs emerged which forged partnerships or channeled resources through CSOs (e.g. the Community Recovery Project in Indonesia and social funds in Thailand and Cambodia). Sometimes there were teething problems (e.g. the Social Investment Project in Thailand), and sometimes CSOs thought the Bank took the wrong approach (e.g. the Social Safety Net Adjustment Loan in Indonesia). However, in general CSOs welcomed the Bank's direction. Interaction with civil society also exposed the Bank to important political economy factors. The economic decay eroded national morale and precipitated anger with authority, so challenging the technocratic and elite orientation of governments, and bringing issues of corruption to center-stage. Particularly in Indonesia, interaction with civil society helped the Bank appreciate how such issues needed to be factored into its response to the crisis.

The more analytical CSOs were surprised and encouraged by the challenge that a few leading Bank economists presented to the Washington consensus. In particular, they welcomed public criticism by the Chief Economist, Joe Stiglitz, of using high interest rates and fiscal contraction as principal response mechanisms. Stiglitz stressed that the origin of the problem in Asia was not the same as the debt crisis of Latin America and subsequent economic crises. The problem largely lay not in government profligacy and budget deficits, but in an overheated *private* sector, especially in the bursting of real-estate and construction bubbles. Stiglitz and others reoriented attention to these issues and their root causes: weak regulation and opaque decision making in the banking sector; and unrestricted, volatile international capital flows, particularly in banking, derivatives and other "hot" investments.[21] Stiglitz declared that there had been too many banking crises in the twentieth century and that it was time to change the rules of capital trade and banking. Had there been just one or two such crises, it would have been justifiable to blame the individual banks, governments and banking regulators, but with so many crises, he argued, it was time for a radical rethink. As he put it, if a single driver has an accident on a bend in the road, then you blame the driver. But if sixty accidents occur at the same spot, then it is time to redesign the road.

Coming from one of the world's most influential economists, this attack on a hallowed tenet of global finance was music to the critics of economic orthodoxy. The very person charged with being the defender of faith of the Washington consensus had become a dissenter. Though Stiglitz stressed the importance of free trade and market openness, his stance enhanced the acceptability of heterodox approaches, such as capital controls, new requirements for transparency, and greater attention to the social consequences of global economic decisions. The Chief Economist also aligned himself with those in the international labor movement who voiced concern that open capital markets and flexible labor markets would precipitate a "race to the bottom".[22] If comparative advantage is to be reduced to low wages and weak labor standards, then the workers of the developing world would be forced to outdo each other in accepting sweatshop conditions.

The civil society case against neoliberal globalization

Civil society lobbyists have used Stiglitz's analysis in building their case against unbridled globalization. Some also started to reflect on the apparent hypocrisy of free-market advocates. Classic economics describes productivity as being determined by the factors of production – raw and semi-processed inputs, capital, labor, and intellectual property – where each is governed by its own factor market. The keenest advocates of free trade seek unrestrained global markets for *capital*, but remain silent about prevailing selective controls on the trade of commodities and inputs (depending on the vulnerability or power-base of corresponding Northern producers). Neoclassical economists also say nothing about strict patent rights that produce monopolies and limit access to intellectual property, or about highly restricted trans-boundary movement of labor. In spite of much talk about liberalization of markets, there is in practice *less* labor mobility now than in past decades, and there are *more* barriers to trade in developing country exports. The net effect is to distort the relative prices of the factors of production: to maximize the returns to capital and intellectual property and reduce the returns to labor. Hence, across the world, gaps between rich and poor have widened as the richer populations and countries have raced ahead of the poorer.

The Asian crisis has deepened civil society criticism of the inherent weaknesses and inequities in the Washington Consensus worldview. This opposition has drawn at least some in the Bank to be allies – albeit cautious ones – in the cause of a more human-kind economic strategy. At the country level, Bank social assessments have helped CSOs convey their experience to decision makers. Social mitigation programs have often demonstrated CSOs' implementation capacity and provided substantial resources to them. Bank support for community initiatives has led governments to respect more genuinely participatory approaches. The Bank and other donors have enhanced the status of civil society leaders by engaging them in high-level dialogue. There was a backlash, however. The Boards of the IMF and the Bank disliked publicity that implied a gulf between the two institutions. In time, Stiglitz decided he would be freer to pursue his critique of the Washington Consensus outside the Bank.

The Asian crisis also strengthened civil society voice on the national stage in the afflicted countries. For example, civil society associations – including students, labor groups, NGOs and others – were major players in exposing the inequities and corruption of the Suharto regime and precipitating Indonesian democracy.[23] Similarly, trade union and public protests in South Korea prefaced the surprise election of a life-long union leader as President. In Thailand, civil society pressure precipitated a new constitution, adopted in October 1997, that explicitly gives civil society a role in national policy making. Civil society mobilization also accelerated the departure of the Chavalit government in November 1997. Thailand, Indonesia and the Philippines now have civil society representatives in their Upper Chambers, and their governments include senior ministers from civil society backgrounds. Civil society interests also featured strongly in the highly publicized battle in Malaysia between the Prime Minister, Mahathir Mohamed and his former Deputy, Anwar Ibrahim. Civil society has emerged from relative obscurity to become a powerful force in most countries in the region.

Conclusion – how much is the Bank changing?

Two factors might explain why civil society criticism of the World Bank remains at a high pitch. First, the Bank is a convenient icon of the prevailing global economic system that is inherently unjust and has failed the poor. To target "market forces" would be too abstract. To target the Clinton administration would be too partisan. To target world financiers would be too diffuse. In contrast, the IFIs are specific institutions, with real addresses, whose leaders are not publicly elected, who attract criticism from both right and left, and who are not good at fighting back.

The second factor in continuing criticism is a yawning gap that many Bank-watchers describe between what the Bank *says* and what it *does*. Most CSOs accept much of the rhetoric and many recent policies. They recognize NGO-like language in these statements, but therein lies the rub. Many argue that the Bank is *hijacking* civil society language, that it means very different things by the terms, and that it further devalues the currency during implementation. In a word, civil society leaders think the Bank is trying to pull the rug out from under them.

Yet matters are far from clear-cut. The Bank as an institution has certain *policies*, but what it *does* is the net effect of several thousand staff. Contrary to popular expectations, the Bank is far from monolithic. Different staff do different things in different ways. Many officials – particularly those responsible for health, education, rural development, poverty, or environmental programs – have seriously embraced CSO views and have shifted markedly over the 1990s. In other fields, staff have changed much less and are somewhat cynical about the "civil society fashion".

Overall, Bank staff behavior today is very different from that of ten years ago. The change is due partly to staff turnover, partly to changed management signals, and partly to new experiences. A massive staff turnover, prompted by President Wolfensohn's personnel policies and institutional change program, has allowed a rapid change of skills-mix. The Bank now has hundreds of social scientists and staff with civil society backgrounds, compared with a handful ten years ago. Management signals now make clear that partnership with civil society is a critical business element, and staff are now expected to use participatory approaches, stakeholder consultations, and even to spend weeks living in poor communities.

Changes in language are not enough by themselves, but they can be important harbingers of new initiatives and policies. For example, a major anti-corruption program developed after President Wolfensohn broke the taboo on corruption in his speech to the 1997 Annual Meetings. Wolfensohn has instructed staff that a partnership approach to development (with civil society as a key partner) must replace the arrogant "go it alone" style of old.[24] He has endorsed the "participatory development" and "community-driven development" messages of Bank pioneers in these fields, and he has now broached the thorny subject of human rights.

Since the majority of senior Bank managers have been appointed during Wolfensohn's tenure, there are generally strenuous efforts to translate these new policies into country strategies. However, problems often arise in their implementation. This is due partly to a tendency of managers to exaggerate the progressive nature of their programs and claim to be ahead of the curve in embracing new priorities. It is also partly because task managers of specific loans are frequently the most resistant to change.

Task managers have the exceedingly demanding responsibility for large loans. To observe scrupulously all Bank policies would necessitate hundreds of complex actions, for which loan-preparation resources do not allow. These staff are the Bank's technicians, and most have been at it for decades. For them, Bank rhetoric changes as leaders change, policies come and go. The art of survival consists of doing what they know well and have always done, but describing their loan in the context of the new fashions. This is another source of claim inflation.

Hence loan task managers, country or sector directors, and top management all have a tendency to want to believe that change is faster and deeper than it probably has been. Perhaps the most important challenge for civil society commentators on the Bank, therefore, is now to provide objective feedback on how far the new priorities are reflected in actions on the ground, and how far these actions are producing results. The institution needs such a mirror. And management is likely to find local insights concerning progress on the ground to be useful reality checks.

However, playing such a role may present CSOs with a dilemma. Harsher critics might accuse them of being co-opted. Strident attacks on the Bank are also more likely to win media attention, to be popular with other CSOs, and may help in the recruitment of new (especially younger) members. The language of street activists is more accessible than that of the lobbyists who have access to policy makers. But CSOs can make an important and *deeper* contribution to the reforms underway in the Bank, many of which respond, in part, to civil society criticism. CSOs can be more involved in guiding the direction of these changes and can influence more profoundly what the Bank does on the ground, in particular by accepting the invitation to engage in the preparation of Poverty Reduction Strategy Papers, which are to guide the Bank's operations at the country level.

To provide inputs that contribute to these new emphases and genuinely help management monitor and better implement the Bank's poverty mission requires of CSOs the discipline of greater objectivity and of presenting the record as various shades of gray, rather than purely black and white. It is important that civil society continues to criticize Bank staff and institutional failings, but it should not just criticize. It should also praise initiatives of the poverty pioneers in the Bank and others who are devising progressive approaches. It can suggest positive things that the Bank *should* do, new fields where the Bank should be bold. As any CEO of a sizeable organization knows, managing a change process is more about giving signals and incentives to staff about what they are expected to *do* – not what they should refrain from doing. Hence drawing attention to the positives – and pressing management to ensure that the cutting-edge, best practice of today becomes the normal practice of tomorrow – should be an important objective of CSO engagement. Helping to foster future virtues could be more rewarding to CSOs than curing the Bank's past vices, and these could be of more immediate benefit to the world's poor.

Notes

1 This paper reflects the author's views and not necessarily those of the World Bank or its affiliated organizations. He thanks Doug Porter, Veena Siddharth, Nancy Alexander, other chapter authors and World Bank colleagues in the NGO/Civil Society Thematic Team for their comments on an earlier draft, though stressing that all errors and opinions can be attributed only to him.

2 World Bank, *World Bank–Civil Society Relations: Fiscal 1999 Progress Report* (draft), Washington, DC: World Bank, 2000; see also previous year's annual progress reports.

3 J. Covey, *Accountability and Effectiveness of NGO Policy Alliances*, Boston: Institute for Development Research, 1994; J.A. Fox and L.D. Brown (eds), *The Struggle for Accountability: the World Bank, NGOs, and Grassroots Movements*, Cambridge, MA: MIT Press, 1998.

4 B. Rich, *Mortgaging the Earth: the World Bank, Environmental Impoverishment and the Crisis of Development*, Boston: Beacon Press, 1994.

5 World Bank, *NGOs and the Bank*, NGO Unit, Washington, DC: World Bank, 1996.

6 World Bank, *The Bank's Relationship with NGOs*, Washington, DC: World Bank, 1998.

7 New Economics Foundation, *Towards Understanding NGO Work on Policy*, London: NEF, 1997; M. Lockwood and P. Madden, *Closer Together, Further Apart: a Discussion Paper on Globalization*, London: Christian Aid, 1997.

8 R. Tandon, *Networks as Mechanisms of Communications and Influence*, New Delhi: Society for Participatory Research in Asia, 1995.

9 J. Clark, *Democratizing Development: the Role of Voluntary Agencies*, London: Earthscan and West Hartford: Kumarian Press, 1991.

10 P. Nelson, *The World Bank and Non-governmental Organizations: the Limits of Apolitical Development*, Basingstoke: Macmillan, 1995.

11 D. Kapur, J.P. Lewis and R. Webb (eds), *The World Bank's First Half Century*, two volumes, Washington, DC: Brookings Institute, 1997.

12 S. Moseley *et al.*, letter to Mr Wolfensohn signed by 22 major operational NGOs, Washington, DC, 14 April 2000.

13 A. Durbin, "Clarifying Friends of the Earth's Position Regarding A16" [e-mail to the World Bank], Washington, DC, 27 April 2000.

14 Nelson, op cit.

15 F. Santa Ana (ed.), *The State and the Market: Essays on a Socially Oriented Philippine Economy*, Manila: Action for Economic Reforms, 1998.

16 C. Malena, *Working with NGOs: a Practical Guide to Operational Collaboration between the World Bank and NGOs*, Washington, DC: World Bank, 1995.

17 M. Edwards and D. Hulme (eds), *NGO Performance and Accountability: Beyond the Magic Bullet*, London: Earthscan and West Hartford: Kumarian Press, 1995.

18 K. Watkins, *The Oxfam Poverty Report*, Oxford: Oxfam, 1995.

19 Jubilee 2000, website: <www.oneworld.org/jubilee2000/> or [in USA]: <www.j2000usa.org/j2000>.

20 C. Robb, *Participatory Poverty Assessment Report*, Washington, DC: World Bank, 1999.

21 J. Stiglitz, "Towards a New Paradigm for Development: Strategies, Policies and Processes", Presented as the Prebisch Lecture at UNCTAD, Geneva, October 1998.

22 J. Stiglitz, "Democratic Development as the Fruits of Labor", speech to the Industrial Relations Research Association, Boston, January 2000.

23 International Confederation of Free Trade Unions, "Statement to the 1998 APEC Leaders' Meeting" – at website: <www.icftu.org/>.

24 J. Wolfensohn, *A Proposal for a Comprehensive Development Framework* (discussion draft, 21 January 1999), Washington, DC: World Bank.

8 Civil society and the World Bank's Country Assistance Strategy in Argentina

Roberto Senderowitsch and Sandra Cesilini[1]

Summary

• Introduction	128
• Lessons of the past	129
• The Argentinean consultation	130
• Lessons learned	136
• An emerging model: avoiding representative chaos	139
• Conclusion	141

Introduction

Much evidence demonstrates the advantage of civil society participation in World Bank activities. Participation provides key information for the planning of projects and makes programs more sustainable. Usually, projects that include the voices and perspectives of those who will be affected are more effective and efficient. By taking into account different perspectives and opinions, the Bank can better design projects to address real needs and put more efforts where they are needed.

The World Bank has taken steps to involve civil society in the formulation of the Country Assistance Strategy (CAS). The CAS is a document through which the Bank presents its "business plan" to client governments, and in which it details its planned financial assistance for the next three to four years. This "business plan" can benefit from consultation with as wide a range of stakeholders as possible. Consultation in the CAS enables the World Bank to hear a range of opinions about priority development areas, to discuss advantages and disadvantages, and to identify obstacles and implementation problems before deciding with the client government where the Bank is best placed to help.

Previous experience with consultative CAS processes in Latin America has pointed to the challenges of achieving representation by involving a broad swathe of participants.[2] In addition, experience has revealed a tension between working with a wide range of participants and producing a coherent set of recommendations for the Bank. Implementing participatory processes constitutes a complex task that requires professional expertise and strategic thinking, especially when dealing with various groups and actors representing different political views and interests.[3]

This chapter offers a field perspective on interactions between the World Bank and civil society, focusing on the consultation process in the Bank's Country Assistance Strategy for Argentina. In particular, this study explores the challenge of using highly heterogeneous participation to build a good-quality product. It argues that a high level of heterogeneity can enrich the CAS process only when clear rules of the game exist and that these, in turn, increase the level of predictability. Other crucial elements for successful interactions between civil society and the World Bank include a favorable background environment, successful planning and timing, adequate resources, thorough preparation, clear structure, careful selection of participants, well-organized forums, and well-designed follow-up activities. Furthermore, consultations convened by the Bank can create capacity within civil society and build social capital in the community, although the Bank's consultations with civil society should not replace the responsibility of governments to listen to their citizens. The Argentinean experience shows that, despite partial mistrust between civil society organizations (CSOs) and the World Bank, a participatory process can be conducted in a highly collaborative and fruitful manner.

The research was conducted in three stages: literature review; collection of qualitative data; and data analysis. First, an important volume of theory related to organizational psychology, institutional analysis and sociology was reviewed. In addition, World Bank experiences on participatory CASs were analyzed. Second, using a wide range of instruments, qualitative data was gathered in Argentina. These instruments included: (a) personal interviews, which were conducted with World Bank Resident Mission officers, forum coordinators, process facilitators, NGO representatives and journalists;[4] (b) an evaluation survey that was distributed among participants; (c) observation of the participation process itself, during both plenary sessions and team workshops organized around ten thematic areas; and (d) observation of a final evaluation meeting with members of the Argentinean NGO Working Group and Bank personnel involved in the consultation. All of this information was analyzed with the aim of drawing lessons from the Argentinean case and presenting a deductive model useful to organize future consultations.

This chapter develops its analysis in four parts. The first part presents lessons learned in the past regarding civil society participation in Bank products. The second section describes the Argentinean CAS consultation of January–March 2000. The third part draws new lessons from the Argentinean case. The final section suggests a model for use in future World Bank consultations with civil society.

Lessons of the past

Civil society participation in Bank projects and products is increasingly becoming common practice. Past experience of Bank consultation of civil society has yielded important lessons. Analyzing the benefits of enhanced participation, Alan Fowler states that, "increasing evidence indicates that enhanced participation can make country operational strategies better, with stronger development country member ownership and commitment and a sharper focus on the Bank's strategic development objectives".[5] John Clark and Winona Dorschel have also identified several factors in the success of CAS consultations.[6] The benefits of enhanced participation and the lessons learned in the past can be summarized in four main points.

First, engaging with and listening to local stakeholders show respect for their views, promoting local interest and involvement. When people participate and their opinions are taken seriously, they develop a sense of ownership over the product of the consultation. In addition, enhanced participation promotes social learning.

Second, involving a wide array of participants generates a clearer understanding of the complexities of the context. This enables strategies to be more tailored to the specific needs of the population. Wide participation increases the diversity and availability of information, improving the foundations on which strategic decisions will be made, while strengthening their link to their subsequent CAS. Sharing information is crucial to the success of any consultative exercise.

Third, participation makes the interests of other actors more transparent, allowing them to be taken into account early on. By recognizing different interests involved in the consultation, discussions can be more focused on underlying issues, and participants can contribute in a more substantive way.

Finally, preparation and organization are essential elements to the CAS consultation process. In addition to the key role that the World Bank's Civil Society Specialists (CSSs) play in organizing successful consultations, external facilitators can help the discussions to be open and focused.

The Argentinean consultation

This section describes the consultative process initiated by the World Bank in Argentina around the CAS between January and March 2000. This discussion covers the antecedents of the consultation and several aspects of its preparation and implementation.

Context

Argentina has a strong and relatively well-articulated civil society. Argentinean civil society has its roots in colonial times,[7] but the return to democracy in the mid-1980s and a progressive reduction of the state in the early 1990s spurred the growth of a strong sector. Civil society in Argentina is today able both to articulate social demands and to provide social services to various segments of the population, especially in health and education.[8]

In recent years, several factors have fostered a positive relationship between the World Bank and civil society actors in Argentina. First, the Bank has shown clear signs of changing policy in favor of broader civil society participation. Second, the Bank's representative in Argentina, Myrna Alexander, has demonstrated a positive attitude to engaging CSOs in the Bank's operations, *inter alia* as a member of the World Bank Regional Civil Society Steering Committee. Third, a local CSS has successfully mapped CSOs and established an open and ongoing relationship between civic associations and the Bank. Finally, civil society organizations in Argentina have shown increased interest in both monitoring Bank projects and participating in the definition of policies at the macro level.

These factors together promoted the creation in 1998 of a Grupo de Trabajo de ONG sobre el Banco Mundial (NGO Working Group on the World Bank), or GTONG. This body monitors the projects of the Bank in Argentina and actively engages in policy dialogues with the Bank.

In 1998, the Resident Mission in Buenos Aires held a meeting in which Bank officials shared a draft of the CAS with members of the GTONG. Although a dialogue around the CAS took place on this occasion, all parties agreed that the meeting was "nonconsultative", mainly because civil society input was not expected to be included in the final document. Marta Baima de Borri, chairperson of the GTONG, characterizes the 1998 meeting as merely "informational". However, in early 2000 the Bank invited – for the first time – the GTONG to organize a series of consultations with a wide range of CSOs around the formulation of the CAS for Argentina covering fiscal years 2001–4.

The consultation

The Argentinean consultation was unique for several reasons. It was the first to be convened jointly by the World Bank and an NGO Working Group. In comparison with previous CAS consultations in other countries, the exercise in Argentina involved an unprecedented degree of heterogeneity of participants, including a wide range of members of civil society. In sheer numbers, participation in the Argentinean CAS consultation was remarkable: 4,000 people attended. The scope of the consultation was also broad, including seventeen provincial pre-forums, five regional forums and one national forum. And all types of participants were included in the various forums and working groups (see Table 8.1).

Katherine Bain and Estanislao Gacitua have presented a comparison of several CAS consultations in Latin America in 1996–97.[9] Table 8.1 compares their cases with the Argentinean experience. As Table 8.1 indicates, the Argentinean case presents unique characteristics in its mode of organization, the quality of the participants involved, the participation structure, the regional focus, and the number of stakeholders who participated.

Various aspects of the consultation are discussed in the remainder of this section: the planning and timing of the consultation; the selection and invitation of participants; the dissemination of information; resources; the "rules of the game"; the organization and facilitation of the forums; forum procedure; and follow-up activities.

Planning and timing of the consultation

The whole CAS consultation process took less than two months, including the preparation phase, the convening process, the implementation of several pre-forums in remote provinces, five regional forums, and a national meeting in Buenos

Table 8.1 Key features of CAS consultations in Latin America[10]

	El Salvador	Colombia	Peru	Argentina
Mode of organization	World Bank unilaterally convened	World Bank unilaterally convened	Network of CSOs unilaterally convened	WB–GTONG jointly convened
Diversity of participants	CSOs	• CSOs • Government • Bank staff	CSOs	• CSOs • Government • Bank staff • Business
Participation structure	Two-day seminar	Separate meetings by sector	23 workshops around the country	Mix of participants in all forums
Regional focus	Process based in San Salvador	Process based in Bogota	Process spread around country	17 provincial pre-forums + 5 regional forums + national forum
Number of participants	50	50	500	4,000

Aires. Not only was the preparation time short – barely thirty days – but it coincided with a holiday period in Argentina, between 20 December 1999 and the end of January 2000.

Although the Bank recognized the potential difficulties attached to this time framework, it seemed to have no alternative. According to Myrna Alexander, in order to continue assisting Argentina, the Bank needed the CAS ready before the start of fiscal year 2001. In addition, as Alexander noted, the Bank needed the approval of the new Government which did not take office until 10 December. Alexander's concerns are echoed in general terms by Fowler, who stresses that "the Government is the final party that the Bank must be concerned with, both as a bureaucracy and as the political regime in power".[11] On the same lines, Bain and Gacitua suggest that consultations are best timed either at the beginning or in the middle of a government's term of office, in order to ensure that there is sufficient time to implement policy recommendations.[12] In the Argentinean case, the short time available for the preparation phase made the participation of several organizations difficult and created problems for the distribution of materials among participants. However, despite the short preparation time, the level of participation went beyond all expectations.

In the case of the national forum, the GTONG felt initially excluded from the preparation of the agenda, as the Bank-appointed facilitator had prepared it without its input. However, this situation was solved a few days before the event when the Bank shared the agenda and incorporated ideas from the GTONG.

The mass media played a key role in promoting the consultation, both in the provinces and in Buenos Aires. For the national event, the Bank hired a press agency to conduct public relations activities and ensure wide coverage of the event.

Selection and invitation of participants

The Bank and the GTONG jointly agreed on the types of organizations to invite to the regional forums. This selection included eight types of organizations: (i) community-based organizations; (ii) research centers; (iii) trade unions; (iv) religious groups; (v) the business community; (vi) universities; (vii) technical support organizations; and (viii) private foundations. In addition, the Bank invited municipal, provincial, and national government officials.

The Bank had initially planned to invite mainly private-sector organizations, the business community, and senior politicians to the national forum. However, it modified the participants list to include many representatives of civil society, including some who had participated in regional forums. Participation of the business community, government officials, political parties, and trade unions in the national forum was negligible.

Dissemination of information

As background papers for the CAS, the Bank produced twenty-five Economic and Sector Works (ESWs) that analyzed the Argentinean context in areas such as education, health, justice, and the financial system. These materials were distributed to participants in the consultation exercise via e-mail and computer diskettes. During the forums, the Bank also shared with all participants information about the projects that it finances in Argentina. While the mass media played an important role in disseminating the results of the consultation in some provinces, all materials produced and conclusions reached during the regional forums were posted on the Internet.[13] However, civil society actors pointed out that the Bank did not print out all the background materials for distribution and that many CSOs lacked access to computers and, in many cases, even electricity. Bank authorities had understood the distribution of background materials as the CSOs' responsibility, while CSOs felt it was the Bank's duty.

In addition, because of the short preparation time, many participants did not read the background materials in advance of the consultation meetings. This may have compromised the quality of the discussions, although the simple language and brevity of the papers made it relatively easy for participants to "catch up" during the consultation.

Resources

Organizing a massive consultation requires considerable human and material resources. The GTONG received a total of $55,000 to conduct the regional events, to cover participants' transportation costs, and to reproduce materials prepared by Bank staff. In addition, many CSOs raised additional funds to absorb the unexpected participation of hundreds of CSOs. The Bank devoted $100,000 towards direct costs related to the consultative process, including consultants' fees and the preparation of background materials. (This figure does not include permanent staff time allocated to the consultation.)

The cost of the consultation was a third of the total cost of preparing the CAS in Argentina. This figure is consistent with expectations. Clark and Dorschel write that "the Managing Director's Retrospective notes anecdotal evidence from discussions with Task Teams that estimates the figure for civil society consultations at approximately 30–40 percent of the total cost of the CAS exercise".[14] On the other hand, the amount was equivalent to only 0.00002 per cent of the Bank's portfolio in Argentina.

"Rules of the game"

The Bank and the GTONG jointly established "rules of the game" for the consultations that applied to both the Bank and the participants. This practice is consistent with expert advice. As Fowler has emphasized, "the Bank's role needs to be mutually agreed with stakeholders".[15]

In the case of Argentina, the CAS consultation was organized based on the following rules:

- *The process and its outcomes would be non-binding.* The Bank was not obliged to accept the recommendations proposed by the participants or to include them in the final CAS document. For its part, the GTONG was not obliged to accept the final CAS document. This rule was especially important for guaranteeing the autonomy of all actors involved and managing expectations.
- *If no government objection existed, the Bank would share the final CAS document with civil society.* This condition guaranteed the transparency of the process and demonstrated the Bank's openness to dialogue. However, government approval was necessary for disclosure.
- *Background papers would be starting points for discussion.* This meant that participants had to read the ESWs related to their field of interest. This approach was expected to generate more informed participation and more focused debates.

Organization and facilitation of the forums

It was agreed that there would be a distinct division of labor in the organization of the different forums. The Bank assumed full control over the organization of the national forum, while the GTONG had responsibility for organizing the regional forums. The GTONG used member CSOs as "focal organizations" that would run each regional forum. The GTONG selected a consultant to organize and facilitate the regional forums, while the Bank chose a consultant for the national forum. Each side chose a facilitator with whom they felt the relevant audience would feel most comfortable. The facilitator for the regional forums had experience working with international NGOs in Argentina and was therefore known to many CSOs. The Bank's chosen facilitator had close ties with the local establishment and therefore was expected to attract politicians and high-level functionaries.

Also in the hope of drawing eminent persons, the national forum was held in the Bolsa de Comercio, Argentina's Wall Street. However, many participants from civil society reacted negatively to organizing an event with CSOs in such a luxurious venue.

The role of the facilitators proved to be problematic in three ways. First, there was little coordination between the national and the regional facilitators, which made it difficult to link the two processes. Second, the facilitators were given little autonomy to resolve conflicts as they arose. Third, the selection of the facilitator for the national forum was not agreed in advance with the GTONG, which led that group to feel excluded from organizing the final event.

There was disagreement over the reasons for the existence of what turned out to be two quasi-independent processes. The Bank's Sub-Regional Director argued that the Bank assumed responsibility for the national forum in order to ensure the participation of high-level politicians and businesspeople, whose views were also essential for the design of the Bank's in-country strategy. Other observers added that the GTONG refused to organize the national event for fear of appearing to work too closely with the Bank. Michael Edwards, former Senior Civil Society Specialist at the Bank, has characterized this phenomenon as "too close for comfort".[16] However, GTONG members felt that the Bank did not trust them to organize a national event that was expected to attract well-known names and media attention.

Forum procedure

All forums in the Argentina CAS consultation followed the same procedure. At the start of each forum, government officials, if present, would provide opening remarks. Then, Bank staff, led by the Sub-Regional Director, presented general information about the Bank and key elements of its operations in the country. They also made clear their expectations of the process and the nature of their feedback. The coordinator of GTONG was also present to welcome participants and introduce the consultation.

After this general presentation, participants were instructed on the work methodology, namely, to convene in break-out groups by thematic areas. Each group was assisted by "volunteer facilitators", who usually worked for local CSOs and who had extensive experience regarding group dynamics. At the end of the day the groups returned to present their recommendations to the Bank. In some forums, participants presented formal documents that had been prepared in advance, either by their own organizations or as a result of pre-forum discussions in their provinces.

After listening to all presentations, Bank staff responded to the points raised by the participants and committed themselves to providing written feedback at the end of the process. Finally, before the close of the event, participants were asked to evaluate the meeting.

Follow-up activities

The regional facilitators each prepared a report on their respective events. These reports were then presented at the national forum. The national facilitator presented a summary of the regional discussions at the national forum. This resulted in the presentation of a coherent set of recommendations to Bank officials.

Although the Bank had committed itself to giving feedback to the GTONG, precise follow-up details were not planned ahead of time. This led to tensions during the evaluation meeting that took place after the consultation, as Bank staff and CSOs clashed on issues regarding the timing and the format of feedback.

Lessons learned

Both the Bank and civil society participants generally considered the Argentinean consultation a success. We can learn not only from the factors that contributed to this success, but also from some of the challenges that arose during the process. Some important lessons are listed below.

Specific and detailed "rules of the game" are essential inputs to participatory processes. These rules should give all actors a clear idea of their roles and responsibilities, so that they have an idea of what to expect from the process. Although the three basic rules agreed at the outset of the process helped to establish parameters for the Argentinean consultation, they were not expansive or detailed enough to preclude problems at each stage of the consultation, from preparation to evaluation and feedback. Table 8.2 shows problems that arose at different stages of the process, the sources of the conflict, and possible solutions. Virtually all of the problems could have been reduced, or avoided altogether, with better terms of reference.

In *The Practical Negotiator*, William Zartman and Maureen Berman present a deductive model by which, after defining certain general principles – the formula – the parties involved in a negotiation can start discussing the details of the agreement. According to the authors:

> Once parties are convinced that a mutually acceptable resolution of their disagreements is possible, they have two basic ways of arriving to an agreement. One is inductive – to put the agreement together piecemeal, building it primarily through mutual compromise or exchanged concessions on specific items. The other is deductive – to establish first the general principles, or formula, governing the issues susceptible of solution and then work out the implementing details.[17]

In the Argentinean case, the Bank and the GTONG seemed to arrive at a mutually agreed formula by which CSOs committed their participation to the consultative CAS and the Bank committed to share the results of the process (the final CAS document) if no government objection existed. In this sense, the parties defined a general formula for the agreement. However, the empirical evidence shows that the parties involved did not negotiate the details of the practical implementation of that formula. This explains why so many difficulties arose during the process. In the future, such processes would benefit from first establishing terms of reference (TOR) which present general principles that govern the issues, and then working out the details of the implementation of these principles.

Table 8.2 Problems, sources of conflict and possible solutions

Consultation phase	Problem	Sources of conflict	Possible solution
Preparation	Materials were not printed in time.	Lack of agreement about who was responsible for this.	Establishment of clear and mutually agreed TOR, delineating each actor's responsibilities.
	Insufficient time to read materials and ensure broad participation.	Lack of time, vacation season.	Mutual agreement on CAS timing from the start of the process.
	GTONG did not participate in planning the national forum.	Lack of mutual trust; delegation of tasks to different actors.	Establishment of clear, detailed and mutually agreed TOR for the whole process from beginning to end.
	CSS hampered facilitator involvement in conflict resolution.	Lack of delegation of authority to external experts.	Once TORs have been established, the CSS should let go.
Implementation	Bank staff disagreed with consultants about final report.	Lack of clear guidelines about style, format and content of report.	Establishing more specific TOR, including clear guidelines on length, tone and style.
	GTONG disagreed with the process of implementation of the national forum.	Lack of joint planning of the national forum resulted in lack of ownership.	Joint planning and ownership of the entire process.
	GTONG lacked resources for participation in national forum.	Poor planning of the national forum	Detailed joint planning and ownership of the entire process.
Follow-up	Disagreements between Bank staff and the GTONG on the format and process of the Bank's feedback.	Lack of specific agreement on feedback mechanism.	Clear and detailed TOR for all parties, including expected outputs.

A conflict resolution mechanism should be established and agreed upon by the participants at the start of the process. Even the establishment of a comprehensive set of "rules of the game" cannot anticipate all possible problems that may arise during the process. Therefore, a means by which to resolve problems as they surface is key for satisfactory progress of the consultation.

Preparation time is important, but short preparation time does not necessarily mean unsatisfactory results, as the quality of the final product may depend on other factors. Although the amount of time to prepare the forums in Argentina was less than ideal, CSOs responded quickly and effectively, and the consultation did produce useful results. This suggests that other factors may influence consultation success, such as, for example, the existence of articulated CSO networks, which can engage in information sharing to offset the challenges presented by time constraints.

CSOs can actively negotiate conditions for their own participation and influence the process. When the CSOs raised concerns about the participant list and the agenda of the national forum, Bank staff took note and incorporated the points into further design of the process.

The Bank's Civil Society Specialists can play an important role in articulating the interests of the different actors involved in the consultation process. The CSS are familiar with the concerns, strategies, and priorities of CSOs and government officials. This knowledge can facilitate a successful and productive consultative process.

Mistrust and collaboration can coexist. Despite some mistrust between the CSOs and the Bank, the process was conducted in a very collaborative manner. This should not preclude further efforts at building trust, however.

Disclosure of portfolio and other material can be an effective means of building trust. When the Bank gives civil society access to information concerning its operations in the country, it is perceived to be open, more transparent, and willing to collaborate.

The mass media can play an important role in convening the events and implementing the follow-up activities. The media can help convene consultation processes and provide transparency by publicizing events and their results. Therefore, organizers should consider including representatives from the media in the planning stage.

Actors with direct access to the decision-making process are not easily attracted to broad consultations convened by the Bank. For example, businesspeople, politicians, and trade unions based in Buenos Aires participated minimally in the national forum. Perhaps they did not see a need to attend the Bank-convened consultations, since they already have other channels of communication with the authorities. Yet, in keeping distance from the CAS consultation, these actors missed an opportunity to build consensus with other sectors of civil society.

Bank feedback, follow-up, and evaluation are constitutive parts of the consultation, and the strategies for conducting these phases of the exercise should be planned in advance. If participants do not see any consideration of the recommendations that emerged from the consultation, they may question whether their input was worthwhile and lose faith in the entire process. This is not to say that the Bank should incorporate everything it hears. However, the Bank should listen carefully, show that staff have considered all points raised, and provide reasons for its decisions. Although the Bank made commitments to provide feedback and follow-up, the actual details of how this would be done were not decided in advance. This led to tensions between the Bank and CSOs.

The most effective facilitators are those who have experience and knowledge of the participants with whom they are expected to work. Facilitators are more likely to be trusted if they are known to participants. Such trust facilitates the smooth progress of the consultation by creating an atmosphere in which all parties feel they can speak freely. Therefore, once credible and capable facilitators have been selected, the Bank should delegate them sufficient authority.

Consultations convened by the Bank can build CSOs' capacity and social capital. CSOs involved in the process learned how to present ideas to the Bank and how to establish new links with other social actors. These new skills and contacts will serve them well in the future.

The involvement of CSO networks in the organization of the consultations can be an effective means of achieving broad participation. The constituent members of the networks, as well as the links they have with CSOs outside the network, provide the Bank with an easy way of ensuring wide-ranging CSO participation.

An emerging model: avoiding representative chaos

The Argentinean example suggests a model predicated on the importance of a high level of *predictability* for the production of a good-quality product from a *heterogeneous* group of participants. A process can be defined as having a high level of predictability when participants have a realistic set of expectations, which reduces their uncertainty about possible negative outcomes. They then regard the process as fair and open and feel able to express themselves freely. A good-quality product is defined as one that is based on innovative approaches, varied perspectives and issues of relevance to civil society which are then presented in a meaningful way to the World Bank for consideration in the CAS preparation.

Experience has revealed a tension between working with a wide range of participants and producing a coherent set of recommendations for the Bank. Conducting participatory processes can be a messy business, especially when participation involves a wide range of stakeholders representing various – and sometimes divergent – perspectives and ideological positions. Bain and Gacitua state that "the pilots illustrate the heterogeneity of civil society organizations and the conflicts that exist between the government and civil society organizations, within civil society organizations, and between civil society organizations and the Bank".[18] The Argentinean case also shows that several problems arose while trying to conduct a consultative process with a wide range of participants.

According to common wisdom, working with a homogeneous group of people would produce a high level of consensus and a good-quality product but a low level of representation. In contrast, working with a highly heterogeneous group of participants would probably reach a high level of representation, but would present problems in achieving a good-quality product. As Fowler states, "widening stakeholder involvement makes the exercise less manageable and more difficult to focus around concrete goals".[19] The question, then, is how can a participatory process achieve both a high level of representation and a good-quality product?

Based on the literature reviewed and the collected empirical evidence, we have identified two variables that might permit the coexistence of a high level of representation and a good level of substantive production: the level of heterogeneity and the level of predictability. The level of heterogeneity, defined by the degree of diversity among participants, can be "low" or "high". The level of predictability – defined by a multiplicity of variables, such as clear rules of the game, mutual trust, and joint planning process – can also be "low" or "high". Therefore this model of analysis defines a typology with four possible outputs. Table 8.3 illustrates these four pure types.

Table 8.3 Possible participation outcomes based on predictability and heterogeneity

Possible outputs		*Level of heterogeneity*	
		Low	*High*
Level of predictability	*Low*	Non-representative chaos Representation: low Quality of product: low	Representative chaos Representation: high Quality of product: low
	High	Non-representative product Representation: low Quality of product: high	Representative product Representation: high Quality of product: high

On the one hand, as Table 8.3 shows, a highly heterogeneous group of participants who interact with clear rules of the game, who trust each other, and who have enough preparation time can produce a "representative product". Such an outcome results from a productive deliberative process and includes both agreements and well-established and understood disagreements. In contrast, a heterogeneous group working without clear rules and lacking mutual trust cannot produce a high-quality product and ends up generating "representative chaos".

On the other hand, a highly homogeneous group of participants (for example, all NGOs that deal with health issues) who operate with a high level of predictability can produce a high-quality product, but will lack a breadth of inputs, thereby resulting in a "non-representative product". In contrast, the same homogeneous group of participants working in a highly unpredictable environment tends to produce a non-representative and low-quality product, or "non-representative chaos".

It seems that a high-quality product can be achieved from a heterogeneous group of participants as long as the consultative process has a high level of predictability. By considering the factors listed below, consultation organizers can ensure both heterogeneity and predictability and therefore promote successful results.

Factors contributing to increased heterogeneity

* *Good knowledge of local civil society actors and organizations.* The involvement of local Civil Society Specialists and CSO networks can play a key role in producing a highly inclusive process.
* *Broad selection criteria of participants.* All sectors of civil society should be considered in the consultation, especially those without voice in existing channels of communication with policymakers.
* *Going beyond the capital city.* Regional and sub-regional consultations can provide

the Bank with local perspectives on priority issues and enrich the dialogue among civil society actors.

- *Government support of the initiative.* The views of municipal, provincial, and national government officials can bring new perspectives – often refreshingly realistic ones – to the debate.

Factors contributing to increased predictability

- *Pre-agreed, clear rules of the game, including clear terms of reference for all actors involved in the process.* When rules, roles, and responsibilities are clear and mutually agreed upon, participants have appropriate expectations, and surprises are less likely to occur. These rules should include details on the scope of the process, follow-up activities, selection and role of the facilitator, selection of participants, procedure, delegation of responsibilities, preparation and distribution of materials, information dissemination, and timing, among others.
- *Mutual trust and understanding among participants.* When individuals trust each other, they know what to expect from each other. A pre-existing and ongoing relationship between the Bank and civil society facilitates this common understanding.
- *An enabling political environment for participation.* When government officials are open and receptive to citizens' participation in the policymaking process, and freedom of speech and association are guaranteed, participants are more likely to believe that their contributions and recommendations will be taken seriously.
- *Enough preparation time and allocation of resources.* It is important to guarantee enough time for actors to prepare for participation, so that the participants know in advance the issues with which they will be dealing. This will make their contribution more useful.
- *Provision of materials in advance.* When participants receive materials prepared by the Bank or other institutions, they have a clear and common starting point. Participants can then accept, reject, or propose modifications to other parties' ideas based on the materials presented.
- *The presence of credible facilitators.* Facilitators can help the group to focus on the relevant issues and dispel tensions that emerge during debates. When participants can rely on the facilitators, they are confident that their opinions will be taken into account.

Conclusion

Organizing successful consultations is a priority for both the World Bank and civil society actors involved in the process. In the past, many of the Bank's consultative processes have experienced problems in achieving a representative and good-quality product. Many of these problems could have been avoided by implementing a detailed planning process, including clear rules of the game for all actors involved.

This chapter has emphasized the need to establish a high level of predictability, especially when working with a highly heterogeneous group of participants. According to the model presented above, when considering the factors for increasing predictability and heterogeneity in the preparation of the consultative process, the consultation will comprise a diverse range of participants with reasonable expectations of the consultative process itself and its results. This will free all actors to concentrate on providing the best input they can to the proceedings, confident that the effort will be worthwhile and that the end product will be of use and relevance to the authorities.

The output can indeed be helpful. In the case of the CAS consultation in Argentina, the World Bank's Sub-Regional Director firmly believes that the benefits exceeded its costs in two respects. First, the Bank has included in the CAS many dimensions proposed by civil society, such as the regionalization of policies and the implementation of a holistic approach to development through a combination of programs from different sectors. Second, the materials prepared for the forums can be used also for other activities in the country.

The fact that the CAS consultation in Argentina was conducted with a high level of predictability helped to yield this meaningful outcome. Moreover, the experience helped the Bank and CSOs to strengthen their relationship in Argentina and alerted the government and other political actors to the needs and opportunities of engaging with civil society.

Notes

1 The views expressed in this chapter are those of the authors and should not be attributed to the World Bank, its affiliated organizations, or its member governments. We thank Katherine Bain for her insightful comments.
2 See K. Bain and E. Gacitua, "Promoting a Participatory Country Assistance Strategy: Lessons Learned from Colombia, El Salvador, and Peru", in *Thinking Out Loud*, Washington, DC: World Bank, Civil Society Papers, 1999.
3 Cf. A. Fowler, *Striking a Balance: A Guide to Enhancing the Effectiveness of Non-Governmental Organizations in International Development*, London: Earthscan, 1997; R. Johnson and D. Redmond, *The Art of Empowerment*, London: Financial Times Professional Ltd, 1998; B. Kliksberg, *Seis Tesis No Convencionales Sobre Participación* [*Six Unconventional Theses About Participation*], Washington, DC: Inter-American Development Bank, 1998; R. Senderowitsch, "Participation and Retention in Nonprofit Organizations: The Myth of Show Me the Money", 1999, available at <http://www.icd.org.uy/mercosur/informes /2000/senderowitsch2.html>; A. Tannenbaum, *Control in Organizations*, New York: McGraw-Hill, 1968; A. Tannenbaum, B. Kavcic, M. Rosner, M. Vianello and G. Wieser, *Hierarchy in Organizations*, San Francisco: Jossey-Bass, 1974.
4 Interviewees included Myrna Alexander (World Bank Sub-Regional Director), Mark Hagerstrom (Sector Leader in charge of writing the CAS), and Marta Baima de Borri (Coordinator of the NGO Working Group).
5 A. Fowler, "Enhancing Participation in Country Operational Strategies", unpublished working paper, 1999, p. 4.
6 J.D. Clark and W. Dorschel, *Civil Society Participation in World Bank Country Assistance Strategies – Lessons Learned from Experience, FY97–98*, Washington, DC: World Bank, Social Development Papers, 1998.
7 See A. Thompson, *Público y Privado* [*Public and Private*], Buenos Aires: Losada, 1995.
8 For more details about the scope and size of the Argentinean civil society, see L. Salamon, *Global Civil Society*, Baltimore: Johns Hopkins University Press, 1999, pp. 373–92.

9 Bain and Gacitua, op. cit.
10 For a complete and detailed description of these consultations see Bain and Gacitua, op. cit; and J. Arboleda, *Participatory Country Assistance Strategy in Colombia: A Case Study*, Washington, DC: World Bank, Social Development Papers, 1999.
11 Fowler, op. cit, p. 35.
12 Bain and Gacitua, op. cit, p. 49.
13 See <http://www.worldbank.org/laccs>, Projects in Countries, Participatory CAS in Argentina.
14 Clark and Dorschel, op. cit, p. 6.
15 Fowler, op. cit, p. 44.
16 Cf. D. Hulme and M. Edwards (eds), *NGOs, States and Donors: Too Close for Comfort?*, Basingstoke: Macmillan, 1997.
17 W. Zartman and M. Berman, *The Practical Negotiator*, New Haven: Yale University Press, 1982, p. 89.
18 Bain and Gacitua, op. cit, p. 51.
19 Fowler, op. cit, p. 29.

9 The IMF and civil society

Striking a balance

Thomas C. Dawson and Gita Bhatt[1]

Summary

Introduction

As recently as 1995, some writers referred to the "eclipse" of civil society by government and market forces.[2] Yet in the last few years, and especially since the Seattle meeting of the World Trade Organization (WTO) in November 1999, newspaper headlines have been grabbed on several occasions by protesting civil society organizations (CSOs), especially nongovernmental organizations (NGOs). Their targets: the international financial institutions, the industrial country governments, and multinational corporations. Their actions: not only violent protests that naturally attract media attention, but also non-violent campaigns for such causes as debt reduction for poor countries. An astonishing revival, by any standards.

Until the mid-1990s, the International Monetary Fund (IMF or "the Fund") attracted only limited and sporadic attention from CSOs, most prominently in countries implementing adjustment policies with IMF support. However, civil society opposition to the Fund intensified in the latter half of the 1990s. The Asian financial crisis that erupted in mid-1997, and the IMF's perceived role in managing that crisis, added impetus to protests against the Fund. Developments in East Asia drew attention to the risks and costs of globalization, particularly the globalization of finance, and some saw the Fund as leading the process. This perception added fuel to the more familiar protests against the IMF's alleged role in imposing "austerity" on countries in difficulty – and especially on the poor in those countries.

A common theme for many of these campaigns has been the question of economic and social justice.[3] Many CSOs – and NGOs in particular – see themselves as representing the broad public interest and as having a role in ensuring that individuals participate directly in shaping the rules of the international economic system.

The IMF and the World Bank have often proved attractive CSO targets, for two main reasons. First, both are highly visible institutions that attract considerable attention and are seen as exceptionally powerful. Second, industrial countries are perceived as having significant influence on these institutions. The Bretton Woods institutions therefore give CSOs another lever against the governments of those countries.

At the same time, however, CSOs have frequently characterized the Fund as an unapproachable, secretive, undemocratic organization that is resistant to public opinion and participation. From the IMF's standpoint, it seems that CSOs often have little understanding of – and indeed much confusion about – the Fund's role and operations. Consequently, the IMF has, for the most part, had an uneasy relationship with civil society. More recently, however, there has been increasing recognition, on both sides, that IMF–CSO relations need not always be adversarial. In fact, several initiatives over the last few years have demonstrated that the Fund and civil society groups can relate more constructively.

IMF–civil society engagement raises several broad questions that this chapter seeks to address. First, which CSOs have been, and should be, party to engagement with the Fund? After all, CSOs are so diverse. They include business associations, policy research institutes, labor unions, religious groups, and NGOs. NGOs are particularly diverse: advocacy groups and service providers; national and international bodies; those based in "North" and those based in the "South"; community-based; religious-based; and so on. Many CSOs lean to the left politically, while others are conservative or neoliberal. Moreover, the groups with which the IMF should engage may vary widely from country to country.

Second, what questions should IMF–civil society engagement address? Broad issues have included debt relief, the distribution of the burdens of structural adjustment, poverty reduction, and globalization. Since these matters lie at the core of the Fund's work, many CSOs have called for reform of the institution.

Third, what are the limits to the IMF's engagement with civil society? The Fund is responsible to governments, which are, in most cases, accountable to their populations through reasonably well-defined democratic processes. In contrast, the constituencies and representativeness of many CSOs are often unclear.

This chapter examines the evolution of IMF–civil society relations and their effects on the Fund. It also seeks to address the tensions that underlie the relationship. Finally, the concluding section sets out some lessons that can be drawn.

The Fund's role in global finance

The IMF was established in 1944 to help restore world economic stability and growth in the aftermath of global depression and world war. The Fund was founded on simple, but enduring, principles: namely, that all countries share certain basic economic goals – including high levels of employment and income – and that these goals can be best achieved if countries maintain open payment systems and orderly exchange arrangements. Countries should avoid competitive exchange depreciations and work together through the IMF to make the international monetary system function more smoothly, including through financial assistance for countries undergoing balance of payments adjustment. The world economy has experienced a number of ups and downs in the intervening years, but the validity of this approach has stood the test of time. Indeed, the countries that adhered to it saw trade expand, national incomes rise, and employment grow, bringing the world a half-century of unparalleled prosperity.

Of course, the world economy has become more much complex than it was when the IMF first opened its doors. For one thing, the volume of private capital flows has grown exponentially. In addition, the system of pegged but adjustable exchange rates has been superseded by a variety of exchange rate arrangements. Meanwhile the membership of the Fund has expanded from some forty countries in 1947 to 183 today.

In the course of these developments, the IMF itself has had to evolve. During its first two decades, the Fund's role as a lender was episodic and minor. Subsequently, however, demands on the Fund began to expand.[4] Industrial countries had less need of IMF resources after the mid-1970s, but the Fund was successively faced with increased demands from various sources: countries hit by the debt crisis of the 1980s; low-income countries, mostly in Africa, needing structural adjustment; new members in Central and Eastern Europe and the former Soviet Union; and, most recently, middle-income countries suffering from sudden large outflows of capital. The IMF has been at the center of international efforts to manage and resolve these crises. Global economic and financial integration has made the Fund's mandate even more relevant today.

Yet, for all the changes in the world economy and at the IMF, some things have remained unchanged: notably, the emphasis on sound economic policies at the national level and effective monetary cooperation at the international level. What is often overlooked in discussions about the IMF is that it is not simply a source of financing or a mechanism for crisis management. The Fund's policy advice – known as "surveillance" – lies at the heart of all its work. Every IMF member country is obliged to consult annually with the Fund. At this time, the IMF staff prepare an in-depth analysis of the economy and policy advice for discussion by the representatives of all member countries on the Fund's Executive Board. In the process, the experience of individual countries is discussed and the lessons are disseminated throughout the membership. IMF surveillance plays an important role in promoting economic growth and financial stability.

The evolution of IMF–civil society relations

The recent history of civil society has mirrored recent changes in the world economy. Many CSOs are now organized on an international basis or have cross-border affiliations. Today, over 20,000 transnational NGO networks are active on the world stage.[5]

In some industrial countries, CSOs have become a significant political force, often endowed with considerable financial resources and technical skills. In the international arena, these Northern CSOs have formed alliances or networks with Southern CSOs.[6] It is increasingly difficult for governments to dismiss CSOs as having no political standing. For international financial institutions, they loom large at seminars, meetings, and protests.

Many CSOs have come to focus on issues of global finance. Some seek to inform their members and the public at large about what they consider to be the inequities of the prevailing system. Some aim to influence decision makers at national and international levels through the media. Others seek to influence or enforce specific policy changes. CSOs in these groups include advocacy NGOs such as Oxfam and Friends of the Earth in the international sphere; the Bretton Woods Project in Europe; the Latin American Association of Advocacy Organizations (ALOP) in Latin America; the Forum of African Voluntary Development Organizations (FAVDO) in Africa; faith-based groups such as International Cooperation for Development and Solidarity (CIDSE) and the Association of World Council of Churches related Development Organizations in Europe (APRODEV); and labor organizations such as the International Confederation of Free Trade Unions (ICFTU) and the Asian Labor Network on the IFIs. In addition, quite a few economic research institutions or politically linked think tanks critically follow the work of the Fund.

In the early 1980s, the Swiss Coalition of Development Organizations in Berne and various research institutes (including the Overseas Development Institute in London and the Overseas Development Council in Washington) expressed concerns about IMF prescriptions and, in particular, about the alleged harmful effects on the poor of IMF-supported adjustment programs. In the mid-1980s, political reactions, even riots, occurred in several program countries (e.g. Jamaica, Bolivia, Zambia) against World Bank- and IMF-supported structural adjustment policies. Large street demonstrations at the 1988 Annual Meetings in Berlin were an eye-opener for officials of the Fund and its member governments.

Starting from about 1989, CSOs – particularly US-based NGOs – began to look *systematically* into the operations of the IMF. Initially, Friends of the Earth–US and the Environmental Policy Institute, among others, began to approach the Fund, seeking information and answers to their concerns on what they alleged to be the adverse social and environmental impacts of conditionality[7] in IMF-supported programs.[8]

To press for changes at the Fund, these groups lobbied the United States Congress to withhold its support for a possible increase in IMF quotas unless specific steps were taken to ensure that social and environmental considerations were addressed in Fund-supported programs. Effective campaigning by these groups led the Congress to pass legislation seeking IMF reform.

As criticism of structural adjustment programs continued, together with public pressure (from about 1993) to relieve the multilateral debt burdens of the poorest

countries, the IMF's relations with civil society began to expand. The Asian financial crisis thrust the Fund into the public eye more than ever before. The adverse
social impact of the crisis increased the volume of an already loud civil society
voice at the international level, as well as in the afflicted countries themselves.
The IMF's approach to crisis management was called into question from all sides
of the political spectrum. Some critics even questioned the Fund's *raison d'être*. The
IMF came under pressure to address issues raised by CSOs and other critics on the
need to improve crisis prevention and resolution through reform of the international financial system and economic policy improvements in emerging market
countries.

The concerns of civil society groups *vis-à-vis* the Fund have thus evolved over the
years. Criticisms of IMF conditionality and alleged pains of the associated structural adjustment are long standing. Campaigns for debt reduction or outright debt
cancellation – and charges that the IMF is an obstacle to debt relief – have become
familiar since the mid-1990s. More recently, CSOs have attacked various aspects of
globalization, and the IMF as an agent partly responsible for driving that process.

Allies or adversaries?

The degree of opposition to the Fund and criticisms of it have varied widely
among CSOs. In this respect, three different groups can be distinguished.[9] First,
some CSOs concur with the broad objectives and policies of the IMF and accept
the validity of the methodology and framework used by the Fund in formulating
policy advice. These groups have little argument with the desirability, in general, of
an open international system of trade and exchange, disciplined macroeconomic
policies, and market-based structural policies. Disagreements between these CSOs
and the Fund tend to be limited, relating to policy priorities and sequencing.
Economic research institutes and other think tanks (e.g., the Institute for
International Economics and the Brookings Institution), business associations (e.g.,
the Bretton Woods Committee), and perhaps a majority of professional economists
can be counted among this group.

A second group of CSOs accepts the need for the IMF but seeks major reform
of the institution – both its policy directions and its operating procedures. The
majority of the CSOs with which the Fund engages belong to this group. They are
willing to interact constructively with the IMF, but criticize much of its work.

The reformers fall into at least two schools of thought on how the IMF should
be redirected. On the one hand, many labor, environmental, and religious groups
would like the Fund to extend its policy recommendations into areas such as social
protection, environmental policy, military expenditure, and gender issues. They call
on the Fund to enforce what they call "positive conditionality". On the other
hand, a second sub-group would prefer a more streamlined and focused IMF,
working in closer coordination with other international organizations. These
reformers include the Bretton Woods Project in the UK, Agir Ici in France, the
European Debt and Development Network (EURODAD), the Central and Eastern
European Bank Watch, and the Washington-based Development GAP.

A third group of CSOs can be called "abolitionists". They are much less interested in engagement with the Fund and rather seek its dissolution, or at least a significant reduction in its influence. These radical voices have come from various political corners: ultra-free market advocates, nationalists, environmentalists, feminists, and religious revivalists. Proponents on the left in this group tend to view IMF policies as reflecting the interests of banks and multinational corporations, particularly from the United States. Examples of abolitionists include the Fifty Years Is Enough Campaign, the Center for Economic and Policy Research, the Rain Forest Action Network, Global Exchange, Focus on the Global South, and the more recent Initiative Against Economic Globalization – Prague 2000 (INPEG).

The distinction between reformers and abolitionists sometimes blurs. Some groups have shown a mix of the two tendencies at different times (e.g., Friends of the Earth and the World Development Movement in the UK). Individual activists, too, have shifted their approach over time or between audiences.

The IMF's engagement with the first group of CSOs takes place in seminars and other meetings where the technical aspects of the Fund's work are discussed, and also in written correspondence. Various departments of the IMF regularly organize seminars, conferences, and forums with academics and representatives from think tanks. These groups have generally had ready access to the Fund staff.

It is difficult for the Fund to engage with the radicals, since there appears to be little common ground for debate. These groups pursue their objective of abolition in the court of public opinion and with governments.

The IMF engages constructively with its reformist critics in a variety of ways. Both the channels of contact and the actual interchanges with civil society groups have multiplied in recent years. Fund management has increased public activities, with more trips abroad, speeches, and press interviews. Management has held regular exchanges with representatives of Jubilee 2000, Caritas International, CIDSE and Results International, a Northern NGO that lobbies parliaments on issues of poverty and hunger. Likewise, members of the IMF's Executive Board have made themselves available for discussions with civil society groups. For example, in May 2000 the heads of Oxfam UK and US addressed both the IMF and the World Bank Boards on issues related to debt relief and poverty.

At staff level, operational and functional departments of the IMF have increasingly briefed NGOs on policy developments and consulted them on issues such as debt relief and poverty-reduction strategies. Both in Washington and in the field, the IMF and the World Bank have organized many meetings and workshops to discuss these matters and identify opportunities to work together.

The IMF has also organized numerous conferences and seminars with civil society participation. For instance, the Fund held high-level conferences on income distribution in 1995 and on economic policy and equity in 1998. Here senior policymakers, academics, religious leaders, and labor representatives from around the world discussed the issues faced by governments seeking to formulate and implement equitable policies. Similarly, two conferences were held in 1993 and 1995 on the links between macroeconomics and the environment. IMF staff have also participated regularly in seminars held by various civil society groups.

The Fund is also giving civil society liaison a higher profile at the country level. IMF resident representatives (that is, staff stationed in-country) have begun meeting with international and local NGOs to share information and discuss issues of mutual concern. IMF teams on official visits to member countries now routinely meet with trade unions. The results have varied, ranging from the establishment of in-depth dialogue to the unions' refusal to meet with the mission. Listening to labor unions' views on economic conditions has improved the IMF's understanding of how the labor market works. The Fund has also made conscious efforts to engage international labor leaders through the ICFTU, the World Confederation of Labor (WCL), and the International Labor Organization (ILO).

In addition to these formal meetings, the IMF's External Relations Department in 1996 initiated a biannual "Dear Friend" letter to keep civic groups informed about major developments. This letter, also translated into French and Spanish, now reaches more than a thousand NGOs and faith-based organizations in both the industrial and the developing world. The External Relations Department also conducts information missions to member countries that always include sessions with local NGOs. For example, a two-and-a-half-day seminar with NGO representatives was held in Yaoundé, Cameroon in January 1999. A seminar with civil society groups on social issues took place in Nigeria in September 1999. A seminar for NGOs in Zambia was held in April 2000. In March 2000, the Fund organized a workshop for US-based NGOs on financial programming. Additional IMF seminars and workshops with NGOs have taken place in France, the United Kingdom, Switzerland (for the Geneva 2000 summit), and the Nordic countries. The IMF has also held regional seminars for civil society representatives in Central and Eastern Europe (July 2000), East Asia (January 2001), and Africa (March 2001).

As a result of such interactions, many reformers in civil society now display greater understanding of the validity of the economic policy frameworks underlying Fund policy advice. Several propositions now command broad consensus among these CSOs: namely, that economic growth is necessary (though not sufficient) for poverty reduction; that macroeconomic discipline and market-oriented policies work best in generating sustained growth; and that financial assistance must include policy conditions. However, reformist circles remain concerned with the Fund's priorities, the sequencing of policy measures, and the speed of policy implementation. The nature of the disagreements is often due to differences in perception, interpretation, perspective, and framework.[10] These CSOs have exerted some influence on the IMF in the policy areas noted below.

Focal concerns of IMF–civil society engagement

Having established who in civil society is actively engaged in dialogue with the Fund, this chapter now turns to the specific issues addressed: structural adjustment, debt relief, and the regulation of global finance. The next section considers questions of institutional reform of the IMF itself.

Structural adjustment and the poor

Until the early 1980s, IMF-supported programs in low-income countries were relatively narrow in policy content and generally short in duration. These programs addressed balance of payments problems through the correction of fiscal imbalances (reducing inefficient public expenditure and raising tax revenues), curbs on credit growth and, in many cases, currency devaluations. Critics questioned the Fund's emphasis on budget deficits and demand compression. They argued that improved economic growth through supply-side reforms could contribute to balance of payments correction as well as higher living standards. They also charged the Fund with a lack of attention to income distribution.[11] Many also accused the Fund of ignoring the political realities that led governments to cut social expenditures while protecting more powerful interests. The disappointing growth performance of many developing countries in the early 1980s added to these concerns.

However, the IMF revised its approach after the Latin American debt crisis in 1982 and the subsequent African crisis. Drawing from lessons learned, Fund conditionality was expanded to include structural reforms. This shift reflected the fact that the difficulties of many developing countries were not simply manifestations of temporary fiscal imbalances, but rather a reflection of deeper problems that made it difficult to fix imbalances quickly. Economic stabilization thus required structural adjustment. The vehicles for deeper Fund involvement in the poorest countries were the concessional Structural Adjustment Facility (SAF), established in 1986, and the Enhanced Structural Adjustment Facility (ESAF), which replaced the SAF in 1987.

Even programs so broadened, however, often proved less than successful in achieving stability and growth, at least initially. Lack of commitment by the government authorities to program objectives and policies was an important ingredient of failure in some Fund-supported programs.[12] Adverse commodity price movements, natural disasters, and civil or cross-border conflicts also undermined various programs. To counter strong criticism that its adjustment policies hurt the poor, or that export promotion encouraged environmental destruction, the Fund sought to widen the scope of conditionality in its arrangements. To different degrees in different countries, the IMF pressed – often together with the World Bank – for improvements in the quality of public expenditure and for increased transparency and accountability in government and corporate affairs. Meanwhile, the short-term social costs of adjustment were to be addressed through adequate and affordable social safety nets.

This broadened scope of IMF policy concerns met with mixed reactions. Some observers applauded the Fund for tackling the structural problems and governance issues that, in many countries, stood in the way of healthy economic growth. But others charged that the IMF was intruding too far into the domestic affairs of sovereign states and thus weakening national ownership of economic policies.

Criticisms of the ESAF intensified in the mid- to late 1990s, particularly in the context of the Heavily Indebted Poor Countries (HIPC) Initiative. This program, adopted in 1996, conditioned debt relief on sustained adherence to ESAF-supported programs. Civil society critics perceived the conditionalities to be onerous, saw the time frame of debt alleviation as too long, and questioned the effectiveness of the approach to poverty reduction.[13]

Internal and external evaluations of the ESAF,[14] together with constructive suggestions from CSOs and other commentators, brought changes designed to ensure that Fund-supported programs in low-income countries would contribute more effectively to poverty reduction. To increase the effectiveness of programs, it was essential to strengthen country ownership: the programs must be designed by the governments themselves (albeit with advice and support from the international institutions), with civil society involvement.

Concurrently, the Fund and the Bank have attempted to develop a comprehensive and integrated approach to poverty reduction and growth that would answer the calls of their civil society and other critics. The result has been the proposal for country-owned and country-developed Poverty Reduction Strategy Papers (PRSPs). Since 1999, low-income countries applying for debt relief or new concessional loans from the Fund and the Bank are required to develop their own PRSP through a consultative process that involves wide and substantive participation by civil society, including the poor. In line with this thinking, the Fund converted ESAF into the Poverty Reduction and Growth Facility (PRGF) to support the implementation of countries' poverty reduction strategies: poverty reduction is now an explicit objective of IMF-supported adjustment programs for low-income countries.

Debt relief and poverty reduction

In 1993–94, EURODAD launched a campaign with its affiliates in sixteen countries to reduce the burden of multilateral debt in the South. Its campaign partners included Oxfam, the Debt and Development Coalition Ireland, the Nordic Network on Debt and Development, the Swiss Coalition, and the Bonn-based NGO, World Economy, Ecology and Development (WEED). The Jubilee 2000 campaign for debt cancellation, launched in 1996 and endorsed by prominent religious leaders, extended beyond Western Europe.

In the debate on debt issues, the IMF and the World Bank initially resisted rescheduling or reducing their own claims, citing legal impediments and the financial cost. However, as popular and parliamentary support for debt relief mounted, the shareholders of the Fund and the Bank relented, and the HIPC Initiative was launched. The resources required for debt reduction were found in the contributions from member countries and, for the Fund, in the increased value of the IMF's gold holdings. The HIPC Initiative was enhanced in 1999 with terms for broader, deeper, and faster debt relief linked to poverty reduction programs.

From the start, the HIPC process has benefited from consultations with civil society in all parts of the world. The Fund and the Bank have had more than 150 seminars, meetings, conferences, and other opportunities for dialogue with NGOs, schools, churches, journalists, the private sector, and the public at large on all aspects of the Initiative. The IMF and the World Bank have also invited the public to share their views on the HIPC Initiative, *inter alia* through the IMF website. Views have been sought both on technical aspects of the Initiative (e.g., definitions of debt sustainability, time frames, and links to policy reform) and on questions about the relationship between debt relief, social policies, and poverty reduction.

There is no doubt that pressure from civil society, especially through the Jubilee 2000 campaign, led the G7 governments, in particular, to agree to enhancements of the HIPC Initiative in 1999.[15] A number of CSOs produced detailed and insightful analyses of the HIPC Initiative and debt relief more broadly. This input was incorporated into the Joint IMF–World Bank Board proposals for enhancing the Initiative. However, criticism continues. Some argue that the Initiative is progressing too slowly, partly because of the way that it ties debt relief to programs of economic adjustment and reform. Another criticism is that the amount of debt relief is inadequate: Jubilee 2000 has called for total debt forgiveness.

The IMF continues to emphasize that debt relief alone cannot reduce poverty. It has to be accompanied by policies which ensure that the resources released through debt relief are not wasted, that the debt problem does not recur, and that the economy achieves growth and poverty reduction. The issues of structural adjustment, debt relief, and poverty reduction are inextricably interrelated.

Globalization and the regulation of global finance

A common view among many NGOs is that financial crises are less the fault of the countries involved than of the system that generates volatility in global finance. What shocked the world most about the Asian financial crisis was: (a) the sudden loss of confidence in economies that had been regarded as spectacular performers; (b) the consequent large-scale capital flight and dramatic erosion of international reserves; and (c) the depth of the output decline that followed. Policy weaknesses in the countries concerned became more apparent as the reasons for the Asian crisis were examined. The crisis made it clear that economies open to international financial flows must have strong financial institutions, as well as disciplined economic policies, if they are to avoid financial crises or limit their repercussions.

The Asian crisis is now behind us and the economies are recovering. However, access to foreign capital is critical to growth for developing economies, and many CSOs have expressed concern that other countries might become subject to similar crises if they are left at the "mercy" of volatile capital that globalization appears to encourage. The Fund is at the forefront of efforts to strengthen the international financial architecture, including through stronger domestic financial systems and upgraded Fund surveillance. For instance, the Fund and the World Bank are conducting Financial Sector Assessment Programs (FSAPs) in several countries every year and intend to provide technical assistance to address the identified vulnerabilities and risks. In addition, the Fund participates in many joint forums with regulators in the banking, securities, and insurance markets. Many CSOs have been keen to be consulted on these issues.

Time for a makeover: the question of institutional reform

In addition to advocating changes in policy, CSOs have also sought to alter the Fund's working methods and organization. There have been calls for greater transparency and accountability of the Fund and its operations, for democratizing the Fund through a reallocation of votes between member countries, and for improving its governance. In a number of ways, the IMF has changed in the directions proposed.

Impetus for these changes has come from within the Fund as well as through pressure from CSOs and other outside forces. The Fund is, after all, a dynamic institution that has evolved since its foundation in response to changes in the needs of its member countries and developments in the world economy. Hence, on questions of institutional reform, the IMF and CSOs have had some broadly similar objectives.

Country ownership

As indicated in the previous section, the scope of IMF policy conditionality has long been a point of contention, and the controversies have intensified in the wake of Fund involvement in recent crises. The debate has also moved beyond technical questions alone, with a good deal of new thinking on whether IMF conditionality undermines "ownership" of programs by the borrowing countries and thereby contributes to program failure.

In fact, the Fund has in recent years increasingly accepted the need for improved country ownership of a policy program. It is crucial to the sustainability and success of IMF-supported programs that they are widely understood, debated, and broadly supported by the people of the countries implementing them. In addition, the Fund is perhaps no longer as prepared as it once was to accept the role of scapegoat whom the borrowing government could blame for the country's hardships.

The new PRSP process offers one avenue to enhance country ownership. The PRSP is intended to reflect the outcomes of an open, participatory process involving government (including multiple ministries within the government), civil society, and relevant international institutions and donors. These discussions can give serious consideration to different designs and time paths for the implementation of an adjustment program. More recently, the Fund's Managing Director, Horst Köhler, has proposed streamlining and focusing IMF structural conditionality, both to reinforce country ownership of IMF-supported programs and to focus on the Fund's core responsibilities for monetary, fiscal, exchange rate and financial sector policies.[16] Of course, it will take some time before the benefits of greater ownership become apparent.

Transparency

A second major institutional criticism of the Fund has related to the limited transparency of its operations.[17] CSOs have demanded more transparency on the grounds that the IMF is an agent both for its member governments and for all people who are affected by its programs; therefore it is obliged to make information on its own processes and policies accessible to all concerned. Since the Fund is a central player in the management of the global economy, CSOs argue, it must also promote transparency as key to good governance. Indeed, CSOs claim that, without informed participation by all affected circles, policy decisions will overlook important inputs and will lack the legitimacy that only the public voice can bring.

Thanks in part to CSOs' demand for information, the IMF has in recent years vastly extended its publication policy so as to enhance its transparency. A high proportion of the Fund's official Executive Board documents are now made available on the IMF website. These include documents explaining Fund-supported programs, documents related to the periodic discussions that the IMF holds with each member country (the "Article IV consultations"), key documents on general Fund policy, reports of internal and external evaluations of Fund activities, detailed information on the IMF's financial accounts, and more. Executive summaries of Board policy decisions are usually made public through the columns of the *IMF Survey* as well as on the website. Most files in the Fund's archives that are over five years old have been declassified. In parallel, the IMF is also supporting member countries' efforts to adopt standards of good practice in several areas related to transparency: for example, in the development of data dissemination standards.

However, it must be recognized that the IMF cannot go public with all the content of its discussions with a member government. The Fund has to strike a balance between openness and the need to provide its members with candid and confidential advice.

Accountability

CSOs have sometimes accused the Fund of believing in the infallibility of its own prescriptions and of turning a deaf ear to other suggestions. External evaluation is an indispensable way to provide an organization with unbiased assessments of its activities. Between 1996 and 1999, the Fund commissioned three external evaluations by independent panels: on ESAF programs; on IMF surveillance activities; and on Fund research activities. Each of these evaluations was made public. The Fund also invited public responses to the ESAF evaluation.

A further step toward evaluation was taken in September 2000. After conducting several internal and external assessments and reviewing inputs from the NGO sector,[18] the Executive Board decided to establish an independent evaluation office (IEO). Operational from April 2001, this office is independent of IMF management, and its work program will be made public. It is presumed that most findings of the IEO's work will also be made public.

Governance of the IMF

Finally, civil society critics have urged that developing countries should gain a greater say in the decisions of international financial institutions. Consideration has been given to increasing the influence of developing countries in the IMF, by revisiting voting shares or possibly by changing the number of seats that developing countries occupy on the IMF Executive Board. In addition, new international forums have been created that give more representation to the developing countries. The Group of 20 (G20) stands out in this regard.

Forms of IMF–civil society engagement

Engagement implies a reciprocal relationship between two parties. The most basic form of interchange between the IMF and CSOs has been the *provision of information*, which is a prerequisite for all other types of engagement. Outreach efforts by staff in the External Relations Department of the Fund have provided large amounts of information on the activities of the IMF. Much of this information has been supplied in response to specific requests. These have stemmed, in part, from calls for transparency from various segments of civil society.

Conversely, CSOs have also kept the IMF informed of their activities and agendas. They have published their analyses of the Fund's programs and have disseminated (including to IMF staff) a wide variety of materials that espouse their concerns. Many CSOs also maintain websites where information about their activities can be accessed directly.

In specific contexts and instances, the IMF and CSOs have shared information. Both parties clearly benefit from exchange of information on issues of shared interest. CSOs can serve as conduits of "local knowledge", which may be valuable to the Fund in assessing the impact of the reform process. CSOs can also be useful intermediaries in explaining the short- and long-term effects of Fund-supported policies. Likewise, the IMF's perspective on country prospects and developments can broaden CSOs' understanding of the economic factors at play.

Very often, Fund staff and senior management have shared platforms with CSO representatives at seminars, workshops, and similar events. At the IMF/World Bank Annual Meetings of recent years, CSOs and the two institutions have participated in seminars and panel discussions. Debates have been lively, and occasionally acrimonious.

Issues like debt relief, structural adjustment, and poverty reduction have been the subject of *sustained discussion and dialogue*, rather than the occasional information sharing described above. While debates tended to be highly polarized just five years ago, the scale and quality of dialogue with some CSOs have improved, with mutual respect and a willingness to listen on both sides. This high-quality exchange has been evident in substantive discussions on debt relief and poverty reduction, where representatives of certain NGOs and religious groups have discussed the minutiae of debt reduction procedures with Fund staff. However, as discussed in the next section, the quality of dialogue has been uneven.

In a few cases, CSOs and the Fund have been allies in a tactical sense. For instance, the IMF and CSOs have worked towards the same end (though independently of each other) in garnering support in the US Congress to fund debt relief. Similarly, many NGOs have – like the Fund – repeatedly argued that markets in industrial countries should be more open to the exports of developing countries. In addition, both the IMF and many NGOs have called for increased aid and other development finance.

Limits to dialogue

As the preceding sections have indicated, contacts between the IMF and CSOs have become more frequent and the discussions more substantive. Even some of the Fund's harshest critics acknowledge that the institution has taken major steps to open up in the 1990s and that the Fund's outreach initiatives have entailed substantive dialogue.

However, the quality of dialogue has varied among interlocutors and situations. Many IMF staff have been frustrated with what they regard as unproductive discussions with some CSOs who simply lobby for a fixed set of outcomes. It is often felt that single-interest groups do not think about trade-offs in policy or consider the broad development issues that challenge the narrower causes they advocate.

Other Fund staff have noted that many groups seem only to criticize and do not suggest practicable alternatives. In other cases, where constructive dialogue appears to take place in private and campaigners acknowledge the positive shifts taking place within the Fund, in public the same individuals only criticize the institution.

Some other IMF staff have also been struck by how ill-informed many CSO criticisms of the Fund are, even at a basic level. Staff cite the inaccuracy of information that many CSOs disseminate. For instance, figures on debt relief or debt service relative to social spending have very often been wrong – and have remained unchanged even after the Fund has offered clarification of the figures.

On their part, many reformist CSOs, in both the North and the South, have been unhappy with what they see as a general reluctance in the IMF to consider seriously fundamental challenges to prevailing policy frameworks. They are frustrated by what they view as the IMF's "textbook" macroeconomic arguments that fail to address key social and political concerns. CSOs often view meetings with IMF resident representatives and senior staff as important, but they have often felt that Fund staff use these occasions to "correct" and "educate" CSOs, rather than to listen and learn from their alternative perspectives on IMF programs. These CSOs also suspect that such conversations have little impact on the Fund's policy recommendations.

The IMF has recognized the need to explain itself better and to reach out more to civil society, but it has also worried about the balance that it needs to strike in dealing with CSOs, and in particular NGOs. While Fund staff should consult with CSOs and listen to various views, in the end management has the responsibility to advise the borrowing government and the Executive Board on the policy measures that it thinks are most appropriate. IMF staff are acutely aware that their institution is governed by, and accountable to, its member governments. It is primarily through those member governments that the views of citizens – including as articulated through CSOs – should be expressed to the Fund.

Not surprisingly, the Fund's member countries have expressed, through the

Executive Board, widely different views on the merits of IMF–civil society inter-action. Government representatives have questioned the legitimacy of NGOs, especially those that are based in the North and have disproportionate influence in global forums. Whom do these organizations represent? While many Northern-based NGOs have established links with Southern NGOs or have taken individuals from the South on to their staff, most of them lack any direct experience in the South. This leads many governments in the South to raise the issue of legitimacy.

Board members have also raised questions about NGO transparency and accountability. Do some NGOs have dubious hidden allegiances: for example, through financing by particular groups, wealthy individual donors, or private busi-nesses? Do they have hidden agendas: for example, the protection of certain business interests from international competition? Many groups do not publish annual reports, do not disseminate their mission statements broadly, and do not reveal the sources of their funds. All too often, they are not clear about how they have arrived at the positions they take.

Labor unions, on the other hand, may have a better claim to legitimacy as part-ners in dialogue with the IMF. These bodies have a substantial dues-paying membership, and their officers are usually elected democratically. Partly as a con-sequence of this, the Fund has often been more comfortable engaging in discussion with labor organizations.

The biggest challenge facing more effective civil society engagement with the Fund is that there is no single coherent civil society position or agenda. The wide array of actors makes it very difficult for the IMF to assess the representativeness of the many groups that seek to engage with it. Many, while calling for democra-tization of the Fund and other international bodies, have done little to establish their own democratic credentials in terms of whom they represent and to whom they are accountable.

The Fund has grappled with this issue of NGO legitimacy and has considered the need to discriminate even more carefully in deciding which organizations to engage in an ongoing dialogue. One criterion for such selection could be the extent to which NGOs have operations on the ground in developing countries. Another possible criterion, suggested by some, would be to rely on codes of con-duct that lay out minimum standards for NGO integrity and performance, monitored largely through self-regulation.[19]

None of this is to deny the possibility or desirability of deeper IMF–civil society engagement. Indeed, Fund management has recognized the need for continuous contact with civil society groups within countries. The IMF recognizes the bene-fits that it can derive from constructive contacts with civil society groups. It appreciates what it can learn, especially from CSOs that are actively engaged in development work. But development of the relationships between the Fund and NGOs will depend on efforts and goodwill from both sides. As the IMF takes into account what it learns from dialogue with civil society, so too should civil society attempt to appreciate the work of the Fund, and the context in which that work is undertaken.

Lessons learned

Despite the short history of IMF–civil society relations, both sides have surely profited from the experience. There is no doubt that dialogue with CSOs has affected Fund policies. Perhaps the IMF's outreach with CSOs has also informed and affected their views. What are the main lessons that have emerged from this interaction? Six points may be highlighted.

First, dialogue is good, but informed dialogue is better. There is certainly scope for greater mutual trust and for a more open, two-way, critical and creative dialogue. The Fund has listened carefully to the concerns of civil society in the recent past and will continue to do so in the future. But the IMF's efforts should be reciprocated by greater effort on the part of civil society to understand the Fund – its objectives and its mandate. All parties – member country governments, the Fund, and civil society – must understand their respective constraints and opportunities.

Second, CSOs need to be more careful in inferring causal connections between the macroeconomic policies that the Fund recommends and undesirable microeconomic and distributive outcomes. For example, certain NGOs have made the preposterous claim that IMF-supported policies of fiscal responsibility have caused countless infant deaths in poor countries. Such emotive charges impede serious dialogue.

Third, many CSOs appear to seek engagement with the Fund in order to increase their credibility and standing with member governments. Perhaps direct engagement with their own governments would go a long way toward establishing the legitimacy of CSOs and increase their possibilities to engage with the IMF in policy discussions.

Fourth, active participation by CSOs in consultation with the governments of member countries on policies can make a substantial contribution to building ownership of policy programs. The PRSP process provides a major new opportunity for CSOs, member governments, and the Fund to work together in a truly consultative process. CSOs can play a key role in monitoring the PRSPs and ensuring that the negotiation and implementation of these strategies are broadly based and draw as much as possible on local knowledge.

Fifth, the Fund needs to take a more strategic approach to its engagement with civil society, in place of the somewhat ad hoc approach of the past. Already, a strategy is being developed to increase the involvement of IMF resident representatives in dialogue with civil society. The Fund plans to hold regular regional seminars for CSOs where specific country and regional issues can be discussed, while on a parallel track engaging with CSOs on broader policy issues. But flexibility remains essential, especially given that countries and contexts vary so much.

Finally, the IMF needs to address more actively and persuasively the widely held fears of globalization. The anti-globalization movement reflects some very real concerns: decision-taking in the interests of corporations rather than of people; poverty and inequality; environmental degradation; etc. In the areas for which it has some responsibility, the IMF needs to make its views and thinking on globalization – both the benefits and the risks – more accessible.

These lessons point to the need for changes in attitudes and culture on the part of both the IMF and civil society groups. Genuine partnership requires a willingness to listen to and understand different points of view. The Fund probably needs to work harder at being more open and flexible, at understanding the political and cultural constraints facing the economies of poor countries, and at listening to and learning from alternative views. Civil society, on the other hand, needs more of the discipline of greater objectivity and a greater understanding of economic realities and the nature of the IMF's mandate and role.

Many will be skeptical about the prospects for such changes. Yet, as John Ikenberry has noted, "there are junctures or 'breakpoints' when possibilities for major change are particularly great". At these moments, he continues, "the removal of obstacles of change occurs simultaneously with the presence of impulses to change".[20] Perhaps we are on the threshold of such a moment.

Notes

1 This chapter reflects the authors' views and not necessarily those of the IMF. The authors thank Graham Hacche, Prakash Loungani, and J.J. Polak for detailed and helpful comments on the draft.

2 Benjamin Barber, *Jihad vs. McWorld: How Globalism and Tribalism are Shaping the World* (New York: Ballantine Books, 1995).

3 Cf. Robert O'Brien, Anne Marie Goetz, Jan Aart Scholte and Marc Williams, *Contesting Global Governance: Multilateral Economic Institutions and Global Social Movements* (Cambridge: Cambridge University Press, 2000).

4 James Boughton, *The IMF and the Silent Revolution: Global Finance and Development in the 1980s* (Washington, DC: International Monetary Fund, 2000).

5 Michael Edwards, *NGO Rights and Responsibilities: A New Deal for Global Governance* (London: Foreign Policy Centre, 2000), p. 9.

6 John Clark, *Democratizing Development: The Role of Voluntary Agencies* (London: Earthscan, 1991); Michael Edwards and David Hulme (eds), *NGO Performance and Accountability: Beyond the Magic Bullet* (London: Earthscan, 1995).

7 The IMF lends to countries that have a balance of payments need under "adequate safeguards". These safeguards involve policy actions – so-called "conditionality" – that the borrowing country agrees to undertake to qualify for the loan. Policy conditions in an IMF-supported program are negotiated between the Fund and the borrowing country. They typically cover macroeconomic policies (i.e., monetary and fiscal policies), exchange rate policy, and a range of structural policies (e.g., financial sector policies, trade policy, reform of public enterprises, etc.).

8 Marijke Torfs and James Barnes, letter from Friends of the Earth–US to the IMF Managing Director (then Michel Camdessus), 21 March 1991.

9 Cf. Jan Aart Scholte, "The IMF Meets Civil Society", *Finance & Development*, Vol. 35, No. 3 (September 1998), pp. 42–5; Scholte, "'In the Foothills': Relations between the IMF and Civil Society", in Richard A. Higgott, Geoffrey R.D. Underhill and Andreas Bieler (eds), *Non-State Actors and Authority in the Global System* (London: Routledge, 2000), p. 261.

10 Ravi Kanbur, "Economic Policy, Distribution and Poverty: The Nature of Disagreements" (January 2000), available at http://www.people.cornell.edu/pages/sk145.

11 Morris Goldstein, "IMF Structural Programs" (paper presented for NBER Conference on Economic and Financial Crises in Emerging Market Economies, October 2000). Revised version (December 2000) is available at www.iie.com.

12 *The ESAF at Ten Years: Economic Adjustment and Reform in Low-Income Countries* (Washington, DC: IMF Occasional Paper No. 156, 1997).

13 *ESAF: Is It Working?* (Washington, DC: IMF Pamphlet, 1999).
14 Kwesi Botchwey, Paul Collier, Jan Willem Gunning and Koichi Hamada, *Report to the Group of Independent Persons Appointed to Conduct an Evaluation of Certain Aspects of the Enhanced Structural Adjustment Facility* (Washington, DC: International Monetary Fund, 1998).
15 http://www.oneworld.org/jubilee2000; www.j2000usa.org/j2000.
16 Horst Köhler, "Address to the Board of Governors of the Fund", Prague, 26 September 2000, at http://www.imf.org/external/np/speeches/2000/092600.htm.
17 "IMF Study Group Report: Transparency and Evaluation" (Washington, DC: Center of Concern, April 1998) [unpublished]; Ann M. Florini, "Does the Invisible Hand Need a Transparent Glove? The Politics of Transparency" (paper prepared for the Annual World Bank Conference on Development Economics, Washington, DC, April 1999).
18 Angela Wood and Carol Welch, *Policing the Policemen – The Case for an Independent Evaluation Mechanism of the IMF* (London/Washington, DC: Bretton Woods Project and Friends of the Earth–US, 1998).
19 Cf. Edwards, op. cit.
20 G. John Ikenberry, "The Political Origins of Bretton Woods", in Michael D. Bordo and Barry Eichengreen (eds), *A Retrospective on the Bretton Woods System: Lessons for International Monetary Reform* (Chicago, IL: University of Chicago Press, 1993), p. 177.

10 Civil society and the Financing for Development initiative at the United Nations

Barry Herman[1]

Summary

Introduction

At the end of 1997, the member states of the United Nations decided in the General Assembly to embark on an unprecedented process of official discussions about "Financing for Development" (FfD). The aim was to pr epare for a "high-level international intergovernmental consideration" of the subject that would take place "not later than the year 2001".[2] Just what this culminating meeting would try to accomplish was intentionally left vague. The meaning of "high level" was also left unspecified. Three years later, these issues remained unresolved, and the date for the meeting has been deferred to the first quarter of 2002.[3] Yet the prospect of FfD being an important international event became greater than ever. In March 2001, Mexico offered to host the meeting, which was officially designated "an international conference under the auspices of the United Nations, at the highest political level, including at the summit level".[4]

In assessing the role of civil society in the FfD process, this chapter first notes the circumstances that have encouraged governments to nurture the initiative. The second section examines the development of FfD to date, paying particular attention to the challenge of engaging the major multilateral economic institutions. The third section reviews the 55-year relationship of the UN with civil society organizations, as a prelude to the fourth section, which discusses civil society involvement in FfD. The conclusion suggests that active civil society engagement with FfD may help the initiative reach a unique outcome.

Promptings of the FfD initiative

FfD is an exploratory process of discussion of the member states of the United Nations about the aims, coherence and effectiveness of the host of policies and institutions relating to the financing of development. In particular, the initiative responds to the problem that existing specialized international forums and institutions have been ill-equipped to deal with broader systemic aspects of economic and financial policy.

The politics of international policy-making have become ever more complex, as globalization has removed any clear demarcation between domestic and international economic activity. International interventions in domestic economic and financial policy have burgeoned, notably in developing and transition countries. External finance is a key source of investment, and some of these inflows to developing and transition countries emanate from foreign governments and international organizations, which have always attached policy conditions to such funds. Even when a country lacks such official disbursements, the international community takes a close interest in domestic policies that affect financial movements.

This interest surged after the global financial disruptions of 1997–99. This experience showed that even small economies that integrate into global finance can become sources of systemic instability. International guidelines for policy are now deemed necessary to achieve both global stability and development. Adherence to more and more of these standards has been required to obtain funds from the major multilateral financial institutions.[5] Adoption of these policy standards is also said to raise the confidence of private financial markets and thus their willingness to place funds in a country.

Other important political developments with respect to the technicalities of global finance also unfolded as the 1990s drew to a close. Policy advice of the International Monetary Fund (IMF) to Asian countries hit by financial crisis in 1997–98 was widely criticized. The Fund responded with various reforms, but it still faced opposition from both the right and the left wings of the political spectrum in major countries. To address weaknesses in the "architecture" of global finance, the Group of Seven major industrialized countries (G7) in 1998 and 1999 established the Financial Stability Forum (FSF) and the Group of Twenty-Two (G22), later succeeded by the Group of Twenty (G20). While the IMF is a participant in these new bodies, it has also claimed the central mandate in "architecture" reform for itself.[6]

The debate about financial architecture reform spilled over into the UN in 2000, when it came time to set the FfD agenda. Certain major governments expressly opposed including items related to the financial architecture within the FfD remit, while some developing countries felt just as strongly that FfD should address these subjects. The compromise outcome was to include questions of the architecture on the FfD agenda, albeit with an implicit escape clause to drop them should too much controversy develop.[7]

Politics has also grown more prominent in policy making at the World Bank.

Management at the Bank struggled in the late 1990s to redirect the institution's lending programmes away from "structural adjustment" to "poverty reduction", in line *inter alia* with agreements reached at the 1995 United Nations Social Summit in Copenhagen. Success in this reorientation of the Bank required the cooperation of all other policy players, including the governments of aid-receiving countries, who were urged to engage civil society in their countries in dialogue about anti-poverty strategies.

Concurrently, the major suppliers of official development assistance (ODA) pledged to help developing countries reach a set of poverty reduction and development goals by 2015.[8] However, actual ODA plummeted more than a fifth in real terms between 1992 and 1997.[9] ODA volumes have recently begun a slow recovery, but aid ministers have faced difficulties building coalitions at home for increased ODA.

Another part of the emergent anti-poverty package of the late 1990s was to end foreign debt problems of many low-income countries. The principle of deep debt relief for those countries was accepted in 1996, with the adoption by the IMF and the World Bank of an initiative for Heavily Indebted Poor Countries (HIPCs). Yet creditor governments and multilateral institutions have yielded their claims very slowly. A significant part of the progress to date has resulted from increasingly effective mobilization by civil society organizations.

The politics of international development policy has also moved into the spotlight in regard to the World Trade Organization (WTO). Formed with high expectations in 1995, the WTO soon found itself deadlocked on several trade policy initiatives. The institution has moreover been scorned by much of global civil society as being anti-poor. Many observers have been sceptical that the developed countries would abide by important commitments (especially those phrased as "best efforts") to expand market access for developing countries in domestically sensitive areas such as agriculture and textiles.

Meanwhile, the Organization for Economic Cooperation and Development (OECD) attempted to define a common international set of policy standards towards foreign direct investment. The quest for this Multilateral Agreement on Investment collapsed in late 1998. Here, too, civil society denounced what was regarded as an unbalanced exercise in terms of the interests of multinational corporations *vis-à-vis* those of the host countries.

This, then, is the context in which the General Assembly has pursued the FfD process: global financial crisis; debates about the global financial architecture; new priorities for poverty reduction; and critical interrogation of the global trade and investment regimes. The FfD initiative aims to create an opening for the international community to think creatively about cooperation on financing of development in all its dimensions. The process has sought to engage "a broad range of stakeholders, including actors both within and outside the United Nations system".[10] Here, then, was an invitation to policy makers, policy thinkers and policy activists to use the UN as a forum for innovative deliberation on financial issues related to development. But could the UN serve that function?

The FfD process to date

Some delegates to the General Assembly who agreed in 1997 to launch the FfD process privately forecast that the discussions would quickly collapse in acrimonious disarray. After all, the history of "North–South dialogue" on international financial and trade issues at the United Nations since the 1970s had been nothing if not disappointing. The General Assembly has produced a succession of non-binding "international development strategies" (for the 1970s, 1980s and 1990s), plus an "Agenda for Development" adopted in June 1997. The General Assembly has also generated many resolutions on transfers of financial resources to developing countries, external debt crises, and so on. In addition, the United Nations Conference on Trade and Development (UNCTAD) has held ten sessions between 1964 and 2000, focusing on various policies to strengthen the international environment for development. During the 1990s the UN convened a succession of highly visible summits on economic, social and environmental issues. However, the expectations raised by each of these initiatives have usually been disappointed.

Indeed, governments that had been major donors to the UN's own technical assistance activities lost confidence in the 1990s and cut back their contributions, especially for the United Nations Development Programme (UNDP). The 1990s was a decade of seemingly perpetual reorganization of the Secretariat and the intergovernmental bodies that oversee its activities. Even sympathetic observers regarded the UN as congenitally inefficient and politicized. A hard-nosed analyst thus had to have strong doubts about the prospects of the FfD initiative.

Yet, as of this writing in March 2001, the FfD process remains very much alive and gathers increasing momentum. Neither Southern nor Northern governments in the General Assembly have allowed their fears to kill the process. On the contrary, some representatives have fostered a positive sentiment that has become infectious. Moreover, first the World Bank, then the WTO, and finally the IMF have decided to engage seriously with the FfD process. Various nongovernmental organizations (NGOs) have also become active. The probability has thus increased that the UN might actually spur a major new exercise on international economic and financial matters.

Building consensus

The FfD process has involved incremental confidence building. Following adoption of the December 1997 General Assembly resolution that mandated work on FfD, a set of exploratory meetings was held during the first half of 1998. These discussions began with a special session of the Assembly's Economic and Financial Committee (the "Second Committee"). In a striking departure from usual practice, a number of Permanent Representatives attended this meeting, including (an especially rare occurrence) from the United States. Participation of these senior ambassadors signalled that something unusual was happening. The meeting was a moment for frank exchanges on what could or could not be addressed under FfD. In fact, except for an insistence that FfD would not be "Bretton Woods II" – that is, a conference to negotiate a new global financial architecture – any and every subject was admitted for consideration.

The Second Committee asked the Secretariat to prepare a report on the prospective content of FfD for the autumn 1998 meeting of the Assembly. However, confidence among the delegations was at this stage so low that the Secretariat was instructed to present no more than a bare-bones synthesis of views in an "index report" of suggestions by "stakeholders". The Secretariat decided to gather such views through a survey designed to elicit suggestions on eight broad thematic areas that covered virtually everything that was conceivably relevant to FfD, namely:[11]

- mobilizing domestic resources for development;
- mobilizing international private financial flows for development;
- international financial cooperation for development;
- external debt;
- financing for development and trade;
- innovative sources of financing;
- governance of the international monetary, financial and trade system;
- interrelationships between major elements and other special topics.

At first, delegates were not willing to address each other directly, even informally, on the issues in the FfD process, owing to concerns that their remarks might be construed as stating a negotiating position. Instead, the Second Committee hosted a series of informal briefings organized by the Secretariat with various individuals from international organizations and the private sector. In addition, the Secretariat organized study sessions, where interested representatives met with Secretariat staff to consider policy issues in an informal seminar format. On one occasion or more Justin Zulu, the IMF Representative to the UN, joined these sessions in his personal capacity.

By the end of 1998, delegates were willing to go a step further. As envisaged in 1997, the Assembly created an "Ad Hoc Open-Ended Working Group on Financing for Development" to carry forward the discussions. Its primary task was to propose a specific work programme on FfD. Delegates now had to talk to each other, which they did, mainly in informal sessions built around the eight topic areas previously identified. At these meetings, held between 16–19 March and 5–8 April 1999, searching questions were raised about the nature of inter-governmental work at the UN and about the financial needs of development. Many governments participated at ambassadorial level, and some brought delegates from their capitals. The World Bank and the IMF sent high-level officials as well. The Working Group also hosted informal panel discussions with business and NGO representatives. Through these activities the Working Group created a sense that the UN could be reinvigorated as a forum on economic and financial issues.

The Working Group did not cover all the items in its remit. In particular, it did not set a substantive agenda for FfD. However, the Working Group did agree on the "scope" of the FfD exercise, which was regarded as a major achievement. It served as a "first cut" at defining the agenda itself. The Assembly was thus encouraged to take the next step by creating the formal FfD Preparatory Committee at the end of 1999. In early 2000, the "Prep Com", co-chaired by Ambassadors Jørgen Bøjer of Denmark and Asda Jayanama of Thailand, created an expanded Bureau of fifteen members that could act as a sort of executive committee of the Prep Com.

Like the Working Group before it, the Prep Com was concerned to avoid falling into the standard and ultimately frustrating negotiation practices of the General Assembly on development issues. Typically, the Assembly each year adopts long-winded compromise texts. These "policy" resolutions mainly reiterate wording previously accepted in UN or Bretton Woods forums. They have few, if any, concrete consequences. To avert such results, FfD meetings have whenever possible had an informal character, thus avoiding the need to negotiate a text on the outcome. When texts are required (e.g., reports of the Prep Com), every effort has been made to keep them as brief as possible, so reducing the amount of text that has to be negotiated.

Delegates have also made great efforts to avoid tabling position papers by one or another group of countries. Instead, a measure of North–South support has been sought from the moment that texts are introduced for negotiation, for example, in the form of joint texts of the Co-Chairs or of the Bureau. Sometimes, after a starting text has been introduced, the Co-Chairs have proposed that a respected delegate act as "facilitator" to try to move the draft text closer to consensus through a series of private meetings with individual representatives. In other instances, the facilitator's text is the first one circulated. Finally, the facilitator holds open, informal consultations about the proposed text. As that text already embodies changes requested by different countries, it is presented as a package. It can still be revised, but delegates know that new amendments might destroy a nascent agreement. With cajoling and commitment by all not to destroy the process, a consensus text emerges, albeit with some measure of drama and brinkmanship each time.

Employing this process – as well as no-holds-barred informal discussions that the Co-Chairs encourage in the Bureau of the Prep Com – delegates to the FfD process have developed a sense that they can work out their concerns together. This is not to say that delegates suddenly share common views. On the contrary, they differ deeply on many issues and do not always trust each other. However, their ability to reach consensus texts is a testament to the possibly important results for development that they realize might emerge from the FfD process. The ultimate goal, after all, is to produce a text at the culminating FfD meeting that embodies real commitments by each Member State.

With this objective in view, the Prep Com adopted a preliminary agenda in June 2000.[12] This gave the Secretariat its major substantive assignment: to develop, in conjunction with all relevant stakeholders, concrete proposals on the agenda items. In anticipation of this assignment, a staff was assembled in New York from different parts of the UN system, including the Department of Economic and Social Affairs (DESA), UNCTAD, UNDP and the World Bank. Housed in DESA, the staff has been headed by a well-regarded senior diplomat, Ambassador Oscar de

Rojas, formerly Venezuela's Deputy Permanent Representative to the UN and Chair of the Second Committee in 1997–98. The core FfD staff has been assisted by the regional commissions of the United Nations, the International Labour Organization, the IMF, the WTO, the OECD and the FSF. Individuals drawn from non-governmental and private bodies were also recruited to assist the deliberations.

By the end of 2000, this unique collaboration produced a report, issued under the name of the UN Secretary-General.[13] The report contained 87 formal proposals, plus many more recommendations embedded in the text. In effect, it attempted to address at least some of the concerns of all UN member states. The proposals related both to the implementation of existing commitments and to new measures on investment, ODA, trade and finance more generally. All in all, it was a rich policy feast.

In February 2001, the Prep Com began to consider the Secretary-General's report and other inputs into the FfD process. Underlining the importance of the meeting, the proceedings were opened by the President of the General Assembly, Harri Holkeri, along with the Secretary-General, Kofi Annan. A series of formal statements by governments and international organizations then set the stage for more than a week of intensive informal dialogue. Many national delegations were strengthened by officials sent especially for this purpose, including twenty-six from ministries of finance, central banks or representatives of the Executive Directors at the Bretton Woods institutions. Senior officials of the IMF, the World Bank and the WTO also participated in the discussions, as did representatives from several other international agencies and components of the United Nations Secretariat. At the end, the two Co-Chairs were able to identify many areas of convergence and issues for further discussion.[14]

The February meeting was thus a first effort to identify "which cows to milk" in the FfD process. Some delegations were concerned not to close the door prematurely to new proposals, especially as they had not yet heard from the High-Level Panel on Financing for Development, appointed in December 2000 by the Secretary-General and headed by Ernesto Zedillo, former President of Mexico. That panel's report was presented at the end of June 2001. Other additional inputs, including by the South Centre, were also still expected. Thus, while new ideas can possibly be added to the menu, the major challenge for future FfD meetings will be to narrow the focus and sharpen the proposals for adoption at the final meeting.

Involving other multilateral institutions

If FfD had ever been construed as a way for the UN to instruct or even give advice to other international organizations, the initiative would have died an immediate death. However, this has not been the intention. Rather, FfD has offered the UN as a forum for a broad consideration of financial issues bearing on development, with intimate participation of all major players, including in particular the multilateral financial and trade organizations.

Two things have been necessary to achieve this wide involvement. First, the other international institutions have had to see FfD as a serious initiative that was relatively free of the usual negotiating rigidities of the UN. As noted above, governments have made concerted attempts to demonstrate that the FfD process is promising in this regard. Second, the other multilateral agencies have had to see, if not an advantage, then at least no danger in drawing closer to the United Nations.

On the second point, FfD has built on a separate effort, legislated at the United Nations in 1996, to strengthen dialogue between the Bretton Woods institutions and the UN Economic and Social Council (ECOSOC).[15] This initiative introduced interaction at the intergovernmental level between ECOSOC and these institutions. As a first step, the Chairs of the Interim and Development Committees, the Groups of 10 and 24, a number of other ministers and senior officials, plus senior management of the Bank and Fund attended a special sitting of ECOSOC in April 1998. Further such meetings followed in April 1999, April 2000 and May 2001. In addition, a group of ECOSOC ambassadors visited the Executive Board of the World Bank in May 1998, and the President of the World Bank brought his Board to ECOSOC in February 1999. In May 1999 a group of ECOSOC ambassadors visited the Executive Board of the IMF, and a return visit was paid to New York five months later. A second round of meetings with the Bank and Fund Boards started in the spring of 2000.

These meetings began with considerable suspicion in some quarters and required a measure of diplomacy. As a senior UN Secretariat official has phrased it, the process began like neighbours somewhat awkwardly "talking over the back fence". However, with time the "comfort level" in the discussions rose.

Thanks to these contacts, the stage was partly prepared when the Bureau of the FfD Prep Com sought to arrange modalities for cooperation at an intergovernmental level with the IMF, the World Bank and the WTO. The Bank was immediately forthcoming, and in March 2000 the Bureau visited the Executive Board to elaborate the terms of Bank collaboration with FfD. Arrangements with the IMF advanced more slowly, which was not surprising given the retirement of one Managing Director and a protracted search for his successor at this time. Nevertheless, IMF staff participated in the substantive work programme of the FfD secretariat from the beginning, and an intergovernmental meeting between the FfD Bureau and the IMF Executive Board finally took place in February 2001. As for the WTO, in May 2000 the FfD Bureau met informally in Geneva with the General Council, the most senior body of that organization short of the biannual ministerial meetings. A few months later, the WTO established a channel for continued discussions with the Bureau through its Trade and Development Committee.

As noted earlier, other relevant international institutions also assisted in the preparation of the Secretary-General's report. Some of them, as well as the Bank and the Fund, participated in intergovernmental consultations at regional level, organized between August and December 2000 by the regional commissions of the UN Secretariat, UNCTAD, and the major regional development banks. The Prep Com had mandated these meetings as part of its effort to solicit views and suggestions from as many venues as possible.

Thus diplomats in New York have succeeded in involving all the major "institutional stakeholders" in the FfD process. Some have come warily and some enthusiastically, but all have been engaged in one way or another. This broad involvement has also encouraged significant participation in the FfD initiative by civil society.

The United Nations and civil society

Civil society organizations have been deeply involved with the United Nations from its earliest years. These associations have been a partner in the field during humanitarian emergencies and in development work. They have also sought to influence UN deliberations on issues ranging from conflict resolution to human rights and sustainable development. Civil society has had a role in several UN global conferences as a non-official channel for presenting ideas and concerns to the international community. Civil society can likewise play an important role in FfD.

Civil society organizations were present when the UN Charter was negotiated in San Francisco in 1945. Article 71 of the Charter explicitly allowed for their role in UN proceedings. However, the UN is an organization of states and states alone. As such, Member States determine the specifics of the UN's relationship with civil society.

UN parlance refers to civil society as "NGOs" (non-governmental organizations), where the designation "NGO" covers a broad canvas. In UN vocabulary, NGOs include more than the advocacy and service organizations that fall within the meaning of the term as it is used elsewhere in this book. For the UN, "NGOs" also encompass labour groups (like the International Confederation of Free Trade Unions), business associations (like the International Chamber of Commerce), and religious bodies (like Franciscans International). In this chapter, the term "NGO" carries its official UN meaning.

The UN Charter specifies that ECOSOC may consult with NGOs on matters within its competence. The Council has thus set and periodically revised the terms of such consultations. Some forty NGOs received "consultative status" with ECOSOC in the earliest years of the UN. By 1948 these NGOs found it useful to form their own organization, the Conference of Non-Governmental Organizations in Consultative Relationship with the United Nations (CONGO). This non-profit membership organization mobilizes NGOs for participation in some global forums or committees on specific issues, without itself taking positions. In the 1970s and 1980s, CONGO organized important parallel events alongside official UN meetings. By the 1990s, the more radical NGOs like Greenpeace did not become CONGO members, and today only about a third of the NGOs that have consultative status with ECOSOC are in CONGO.

In addition to consulting with NGOs on substantive matters, the UN has seen such entities as helpful partners in outreach about its work. Indeed, the General Assembly noted the potential importance of NGOs to the public information activities of the United Nations in a resolution adopted at its very first session.[16] With the memory of the failed League of Nations fresh in mind, the architects of the UN were concerned about the fragility of political support for a new institution with some radical ideas about preventing war, protecting human rights and fostering post-war employment and development. NGOs were a potentially important channel through which to build knowledge about and support for the UN at the grassroots level. In 1968 ECOSOC authorized a new, separate form of NGO affiliation with the Secretariat's Department of Public Information (DPI), aimed at fostering UN outreach activities.

By the 1970s NGOs – particularly those in developed countries – had become increasingly concerned about development policy issues. In part, this was follow-up activity for groups that had supported decolonization struggles. In addition, NGO attention to development issues reflected increased appreciation of North-South economic interdependence. A group of staff in DPI, UNDP and other offices saw a need to open UN channels of communication with such NGOs; thus they established the United Nations Non-Governmental Liaison Service (NGLS) in 1975 to meet this need.

Based in Geneva and New York, NGLS has provided information, advice, expertise and support to NGOs through publications and personal interaction with NGO representatives at UN centres. The service has been particularly active in relation to UN conferences. As of 1999, NGLS was supported by nineteen UN agencies, programmes, funds and departments, including the World Bank. In addition, NGLS has received support in recent years for specific activities from a number of governments and from the private United Nations Foundation.[17]

Today, almost 2,000 NGOs have "consultative status" with ECOSOC, while over 1,600 NGOs are associated with DPI. These numbers are likely to grow further, given the continuing stream of applications. Indeed, in January 2001, the ECOSOC Committee on Non-Governmental Organizations recommended the applications of fifty-two NGOs for consultative status, did not recommend six, closed the file on two, and deferred eighty-seven for consideration at a later date.[18]

There are three levels of NGO association with ECOSOC. First, NGOs in "general consultative status" are deemed to be concerned with most of the Council's activities and can request that the Committee on NGOs recommends items for the agenda of ECOSOC. Second, NGOs in "special consultative status" are given access to meetings in accordance with special competence in specific areas. Finally, NGOs with "roster status" are allowed to make occasional contributions to the Council, its subsidiary organizations, or other UN bodies. Frequently, NGOs that obtain consultative status with a specialized agency of the UN (e.g., the World Health Organization) will be accorded roster status in ECOSOC. However, roster NGOs can contribute to ECOSOC only by invitation.[19]

NGOs accredited to ECOSOC may consult with the UN Secretariat on matters of mutual concern, but some NGOs most value the opportunity to lobby government representatives on matters before the Council. In principle, NGOs can address the Council itself, although the request to speak has to be approved at that year's Organizational Session of the Council, which is held many months in advance of the working session. NGO participation is easier in some of the subsidiary bodies of ECOSOC. In particular, the Commission on Sustainable

Development has made regular provision for explicit, open dialogue between NGOs and government delegates. Other Commissions have also set aside times for government–NGO exchanges.

In general, NGOs are not invited to attend meetings of the General Assembly or its main standing committees. These gatherings are deemed to be the exclusive preserve of Member States. Many NGOs now seek to change this situation. They note that NGOs have already had consultative status and rights of participation in special sessions of the General Assembly (such as for the five-year review of the Beijing Conference on Women in 2000) as well as in some committees of the Assembly. Indeed, after several thousand NGO representatives participated in the Earth Summit in Rio de Janeiro in 1992, ECOSOC agreed to consider procedures to expand NGO access to intergovernmental negotiations. In 1996, as part of a broader review of UN–NGO relations, ECOSOC decided to establish uniform procedures for NGO participation in UN conferences and their preparatory processes.[20]

However, some governments have in recent years hardened their attitudes toward NGO involvement in UN proceedings. Delegates were unhappy, for example, when certain individuals carrying NGO credentials at UN meetings confronted particular government representatives about human rights in their countries. Representatives publicly expressed concern that the greater opening of the UN to NGOs posed possible physical danger as well as diplomatic embarrassment. Some delegations proposed that NGOs should be required to adhere to a "code of conduct". In addition, given the deluge of NGO representatives that are nowadays accredited to UN meetings, some delegations have called for limits on numbers. Others have voiced concern that some national NGOs reflect the views of their government rather than those of civil society in their country.

Nevertheless, although some representatives have recently voiced greater concern about NGOs, delegations on the whole remain committed to substantial NGO engagement in UN processes. Not only do NGOs often promote proposals with which many delegates feel personal sympathy, but NGO activism around a particular negotiation process also raises its visibility and hence its political importance. The general view of UN delegations toward NGOs is well captured by an NGO advocate who declares:

> While inclined to keep NGOs "in their place", [governments] are keenly aware that NGOs are valuable partners, sources of information, links to the public, sources of ideas and analysis. In short, NGOs are annoying but indispensable. So delegations are constantly closing the door, only to open it again still wider.[21]

NGOs and FfD

This book is testament to the range and depth of civil society activities regarding international financial issues in the 1990s. However, NGOs that are heavily involved with the UN have generally not worked extensively on financial issues. They have apparently expected the United Nations to set norms for social policy, gender equality, environmental sustainability and human rights, but not global financial reform. Moreover, virtually all UN efforts to get donor governments to implement commitments on development assistance have failed. Why, then, should NGOs put scarce resources into trying to influence policy on financial matters through the UN? Clearly, if engagement of NGOs in the FfD process was desired, it would be necessary to change NGO perceptions of the UN and build NGO confidence in FfD.

In fact, the FfD process has actively encouraged civil society participation in order to feed ideas and recommendations into the intergovernmental and inter-institutional discussions described earlier. The primary mechanisms to involve NGOs have been outreach, especially through the Internet, and face-to-face inter-actions between NGOs and delegations.

Outreach to NGOs in the FfD process began soon after the previously dis-cussed Second Committee meeting in March 1998. On 22 April, NGLS organized a briefing on FfD for NGOs by the Chair of the Second Committee and this author, as a representative of the Secretariat. There was considerable attendance and considerable interest, but also considerable confusion about this strange new negotiation process. Another outreach move at about this time, on the initiative of Harris Gleckman of the Secretariat, was to set up a web page for FfD, both to help delegates by posting their official statements and other useful information and to assist interested outsiders like NGOs.

NGOs again came into the FfD picture when the Secretariat undertook its survey of "stakeholders" for the previously mentioned "index report" that was sub-mitted to the General Assembly in autumn 1998. With the assistance of other UN departments, a list of official and non-official "stakeholders" was compiled. The emphasis with regard to non-official stakeholders was placed on "apex organiza-tions" (that is, organizations of organizations). Of the nearly 1,400 stakeholders approached in the survey, 878 were classified as either in the "business sector" or "civil society". A total of 55 responses were received from non-official entities, lower even than the overall response rate of 13.3 per cent. However, the survey was a very unusual inquiry that fed into a new and largely unknown political process.

The next FfD effort to engage with non-governmental actors came in 1999. The newly created Ad Hoc Open-Ended Working Group decided to incorporate non-state actors into its deliberations. With assistance from the Secretariat, the Working Group hosted two panel discussions at which business and NGO representatives could put forward contrasting views. The first panel, held in March 1999, paired speakers from Deutsche Bank and Lehman Brothers with speakers from the Centre of Concern and the Fifty Years is Enough Coalition. The second panel, convened the following month, brought together a senior venture capitalist from CIBC Oppenheimer, a professor of government at Harvard, and senior officials from the International Centre for Law in Development and the Centre for International Environmental Law.

Each panel was well attended by delegations and generated considerable sub-stantive discussion. However, these "informal" meetings were in practice quite formal in style. The speakers sat on the podium in a large, wood-panelled meeting room. Delegates who spoke from the floor were recognized as representatives of their countries and spoke in formal diplomatic style.

To complement this approach, the Working Group Co-Chairs sought a truly informal venue that would allow for greater give and take. For this, they organized a meeting in a smaller conference room with no podium and no panelling. This event was open to all accredited NGOs and country delegations and was held as an unstructured exchange of views. The room was filled to capacity. Nine NGOs made statements and drew comments from three country speakers. Most of the NGO contributors expressed concern about the slow progress in resolving the developing country debt situation, improving democracy in the international financial institutions, bringing about real "ownership" and participation in international programmes for developing countries, and ensuring that the FfD conference would take a holistic approach to the financing problem. Another informal exchange of this kind was repeated in April 1999, but there was little to add only one month later and that meeting was less successful.

By the middle of 1999, one could see that FfD had attracted the interest of some internationally active NGOs and that these bodies could interact with delegations in a serious and non-threatening manner on FfD issues. However, the level of engagement was still modest. The internationally active NGOs with interests in financial affairs were mainly based in Washington and European capitals and could come to New York only on special occasions. Indeed, the Washington-based NGOs appeared to regard New York as a largely peripheral forum. This would have to change if an adequately informed dialogue between UN delegates and NGOs on FfD were to take place.

The 2000 effort to engage civil society in FfD began with a well-attended briefing that DPI organized for its NGO community in New York. Participants included this author, Lori Heninger of the Quaker United Nations Office, and Mauricio Escanero, the Mexican Counsellor who had served as facilitator for the very difficult negotiations that created the FfD Prep Com. Although the Quakers had published a very useful pamphlet on FfD for the NGO community in late 1999,[22] most people attending the briefing were more curious than committed to participate in the process.

Meanwhile, interest in FfD began to grow outside New York among NGOs that lobby on HIPC debt and financial architecture reform. In late 1999, two mainly European NGO networks – Coopération Internationale pour le Développement et la Solidarité (CIDSE) and the European Network on Debt and Development (EURODAD) – requested speakers from the UN Secretariat to explain FfD. Some of these NGOs had learned about FfD through their involvement in preparations for the five-year review of the Copenhagen Social Summit. By the time the Social Summit review meeting closed at the end of June 2000 in Geneva, these and other NGOs had put a number of financial policy questions on to the global advocacy agenda. They were particularly concerned about the volatility of international finance and the damage that it can cause to people's livelihoods.

The Secretariat also attempted in early 2000 to contact civil society actors as part of the mandated outreach to "all relevant stakeholders" in order to get their views on how they should participate in the FfD process. Letters were sent to all the respondents to the 1998 survey, and e-mail announcements were sent to all others who had expressed an interest in FfD, principally through the Internet. Fifty-one responses were received to this inquiry, which compares with the fifty-five responses to the much larger, if less selective, survey in 1998. This time, however, more than 60 per cent of the responses came from NGO advocacy organizations, as against about a third in 1998.

The Secretariat drew on these responses in developing a proposal – adopted by the Prep Com and endorsed by the General Assembly – for three modalities of NGO participation in the ensuing stages of the FfD process.[23] The first modality involves formal NGO affiliation with the FfD process. This status accords the right to participate in FfD Prep Com meetings on the same basis that NGOs in consultative status participate in ECOSOC. (Subsequently the Co-Chairs have gone further and offered NGOs the opportunity to speak to a formal meeting of the Prep Com.) The Prep Com also said it would welcome initiatives that affiliated NGOs might take to organize public discussions on FfD for informative and analytical purposes and to which members of the Prep Com might be invited.

The second modality involves NGOs in face-to-face consultations. The Prep Com decided to hold hearings in New York with civil society in November 2000 and with the business and financial sector in December 2000. These events were envisaged as an opportunity for intensive discussion of a limited number of issues with selected NGO representatives and other stakeholders. Both sets of sessions attracted considerable attention. In fact, the two days of NGO hearings turned into a week of NGO-sponsored activities at the UN. Also, NGOs attending the business hearings posed some of the sharpest questions. The general atmosphere was one of frank appreciation of different viewpoints and sometimes a surprising meeting of minds of NGO, business and government participants. Also in the second modality, NGOs were invited to participate in the five regional consultations mentioned earlier.

The final modality for NGO inputs into the FfD process involves Internet-based consultations. In July 2000 the Secretariat distributed an information note and request for inputs to more than 10,000 addressees through various e-mail listservs.

Thus, at the time of writing (March 2001), NGOs appear to be responding in larger numbers to the FfD process. Their participation in informal dialogues at the February 2001 Prep Com meeting was welcomed. Their engagement in subsequent Prep Com meetings and in ad hoc inter-sessional consultations is expected as a matter of course. Some meetings are already being planned in which government, business and civil society representatives may sit together to sharpen possible FfD proposals. A certain momentum has thus emerged, and perhaps a certain space for new agreements has opened.

Conclusion

The UN has actively sought to engage civil society as a "relevant stakeholder" in the FfD process. Despite some rough edges in NGO relations with governments at the UN, civil society associations are considered valued partners. It is recognized however that, as one official who deals regularly with NGOs has put it, "NGOs have their own agendas, and one should not assume that your agenda is their agenda".

It is important that NGOs are actively engaged in FfD. Not only do they make substantive contributions, but they also serve as public monitors of governments. In particular, NGOs are concerned to ensure that the pledges that officials make in their capitals turn out, in fact, to be the position that the government espouses in international meetings. The watchdog function of NGOs thereby enhances transparency and accountability.

And FfD is worth the NGOs' time. The initiative marks the most intense effort ever to open communication between different international organizations regarding questions of finance. The process has already established a new degree of cooperation between the intergovernmental bodies that oversee the main institutions. It has also deepened cooperation between their respective secretariats and staffs.

Coupling the new modalities of official interaction with sustained NGO engagement will yield a dialogue unlike anything taking place in other international forums. If, as intended, leading policy makers are the main participants at the final "high-level event", FfD may forge a consensus that sets the agenda of policy reform for years to come.

FfD – and civil society participating in FfD – can thereby help to address what is perhaps the major political challenge of the new century: namely, the globalization of the world economy. This development is not an inevitable project. Globalization rests on a political foundation that can change. Strong international institutions that give effective voice to cries about injustice and policy failure can help push governments to confront the political as well as the technical weaknesses of currently prevailing approaches to globalization. This is where FfD is trying to go and where civil society can help it to reach.

Notes

1 This chapter has benefited from the comments of several people, especially Jan Aart Scholte and Barbara Adams, head of the New York Office of the Non-Governmental Liaison Service of the United Nations, who corrected several errors. All remaining errors are my own. Views expressed are those of the author and not necessarily of the United Nations.

2 General Assembly resolution 52/179, adopted by consensus on 18 December 1997. This and other official FfD materials can be found on the FfD web page: www.un.org/esa/ffd.

3 General Assembly resolution 55/213, adopted by consensus on 20 December 2000.

4 General Assembly resolution 55/245, adopted by consensus on 21 March 2001, paragraph 1.

5 See Devesh Kapur and Richard Webb, "Governance-related conditionalities of the international financial institutions", G24 Discussion Paper Series, No. 6 (August 2000), available at www.unctad.org/en/pub/pubframe.

6 Cf. "Statement by the Managing Director to the International Monetary and Financial Committee on progress in strengthening the architecture of the international financial system and reform of IMF", Washington, DC: IMF, 19 September 2000, available at www.imf.org/external/np/omd/2000/02/state.htm. See also Tony Porter, "The G-7,

the Financial Stability Forum, the G-20, and the politics of international financial regulation", Toronto: University of Toronto G8 Information Centre, 2000 – available at www.library.utoronto.ca/g7/g20/g20porter.

7 Cf. document A/55/28 of 10 January 2001, paragraph 44(e).

8 See *Shaping the 21st Century: the Contribution of Development Co-operation*, Paris: OECD, 1996, adopted by the Development Assistance Committee at the meeting of 6–7 May 1996 at the level of Development Co-operation Ministers and Heads of Aid Agencies.

9 Based on data of OECD, *Development Cooperation: 2000 Report*, Paris: OECD, 2001, annex tables.

10 General Assembly resolution 52/197, paragraph 4.

11 The survey results and the report can be found on the FfD web page.

12 See Annex to Committee Decision 1/1, contained in document A/55/28, paragraph 44 (also available on the FfD web site).

13 "Report of the Secretary-General to the Preparatory Committee for the High-Level, International, Intergovernmental Event on Financing for Development" (document A/AC.257/12).

14 "Joint statement of the Co-Chairmen at the conclusion of the Second Substantive Session of the Preparatory Committee on Financing for Development", 23 February 2001, available on the FfD web site (www.un.org/esa/ffd).

15 General Assembly resolution 50/227, adopted by consensus on 24 May 1996, Annex I, paragraph 88.

16 General Assembly resolution 13(I), adopted 13 February 1946.

17 Non-Governmental Liaison Service, *The NGLS Handbook*, New York and Geneva: NGLS, 2000 third edn, pp. 367–72.

18 "Report of the Committee on Non-Governmental Organizations on its Resumed 2000 Session (New York, 15–26 January 2001)", document E/2001/8 of 22 February 2001.

19 ECOSOC resolution 1996/31, adopted by consensus on 25 July 1996. See further "ECOSOC Concludes NGO Review", *NGLS Roundup*, November 1996.

20 ECOSOC resolution 1996/31, op. cit., Part VII.

21 James A. Paul, "NGO Access at the UN", New York: Global Policy Forum, July 1999, available at www. globalpolicy.org/ngos/analysis/jap-accs.htm.

22 Sarah Clark, Anna Rich and Lori Heninger, *Building a Common Future: United Nations Work on Financing for Development*, New York: Quaker United Nations Office, 1999.

23 General Assembly resolution 54/279, adopted by consensus on 15 June 2000, paragraph 2(e).

Part IV

Perspectives from civil society sectors

11 Trade unions and the promotion of socially sustainable global finance

Gemma Adaba[1]

Summary	
• Introduction	181
• The global economy – a summary statement of trade union concerns	182
• Trade unions in a globalizing world – a historical perspective	183
• Global finance – key challenges for trade unions	184
• Meeting the challenges of global finance – trade union strategies	189
• Two decades of trade union engagement – assessing the impacts	192
• Trade union strategies for the future	194
• Conclusion	196

Introduction

This chapter gives a historical overview of the engagement of the International Confederation of Free Trade Unions (ICFTU) within the global economy to effect changes for the benefit of its members, ordinary working men and women worldwide. The chapter documents the strategies that the ICFTU has adopted to influence the international financial institutions (IFIs), who have come to play an increasingly determining role in the economic policies of developing and transition countries. It describes the close involvement of associated trade union bodies on all six continents in these advocacy efforts.

The global economy holds a basic contradiction: financial markets that generate unprecedented wealth exist alongside extreme poverty for millions of the world's peoples. The prevailing free-market economic paradigm driving global financial market liberalization presents serious obstacles to change this situation. This paradigm negatively affects the real economy – including labour markets and conditions of work – and exacerbates poverty.

A shift is needed in the rules of global financial governance if significant improvements are to be made in achieving a critical objective for the future of the planet: shared prosperity and decent livelihoods for all. This chapter therefore makes a series of proposals for an alternative model of financial governance, one that puts people above markets and recognizes workers' rights to use their collective strength within trade unions to bring about a fairer distribution of wealth.

The global economy – a summary statement of trade union concerns

In our contemporary world, processes of globalization exert unprecedented influence on national economic policy-making. Countries that are able to attract foreign direct investment (FDI) and take advantage of the opportunities offered by the deregulation of trade and financial flows are becoming increasingly integrated into the global economy. At the same time, poor countries and poor people within rich and poor countries find themselves excluded from the much-touted "benefits of globalization".

Problems of poverty, marginalization and social dislocation result not from inadequate wealth creation in the global economy, but from a highly skewed distribution of that wealth and a lack of global rules to effect a fairer distribution. Concentrations of wealth in the world have reached staggering proportions. The assets of the 200 richest people amount to more than the combined annual income of 41 per cent of the world's people.[2] Meanwhile, 1 per cent of transnational corporations (TNCs) now account for over 50 per cent of all FDI.[3] The overwhelming majority of FDI is located in the developed countries and a handful of developing countries.

Despite the availability of large capital flows, many countries are unable to take advantage of market opportunities. They are unable to develop dynamic, higher-skilled, employment-generating sectors. They are susceptible to the vagaries of speculative financial capital movements. They cannot attract sufficient private capital flows. Furthermore, the operations of TNCs in host developing and transition countries often fail to establish links with related sectors that could build up the productive base of local industry.

Side by side with wealth creation, hundreds of millions of the world's people suffer poverty, deprivation, insecurity and disease. Moreover, statistics show a worsening of these disturbing social trends. The World Bank's *World Development Report* for 2000/2001 – on the theme of "attacking poverty" – asserts that the numbers of poor people have risen steadily in Sub-Saharan Africa, South Asia and Latin America over the past decade. In Central and Eastern Europe the ranks of the poor rose twenty-fold in the 1990s.[4] Today some 2.8 billion people in the world survive on less than \$2 a day, while 1.2 billion people live on less than \$1 a day.[5]

Given its emphasis on capital accumulation and capital-intensive production, the free-market model of globalization has created serious problems in labour markets. On the one hand, *laissez-faire* globalization has generated jobless growth in some sectors. On the other hand, where low-skilled workers are needed, their contribution is undervalued, and they are often forced to endure poor pay and working conditions. The situation is bleak for millions of men and women who find themselves unemployed, underemployed or in precarious employment. Global unemployment and underemployment now total one billion people.[6] Women bear a disproportionate burden of the social costs, in terms of high levels of unemployment, precarious or unremunerated work, and increasing poverty.

As a representative confederation of workers organized in trade unions worldwide, the ICFTU exists to promote the interests of its 156 million members: working men and women in national trade union centres in 148 countries and territories.[7] Not surprisingly, the ICFTU has been deeply concerned about the patent failure of the global economy to generate shared prosperity and well-being for all of the world's people. This global labour organization has long been one of the major bodies of civil society pressing for fundamental change in the global economy. Through representations in various international forums, the ICFTU has put forward proposals for alternatives to the dominant free-market economic model. The World Confederation of Labour (WCL), another international body of trade union organizations, has also been involved in advocacy on economic and social justice issues in relation to the global economy.[8]

Trade unions in a globalizing world – a historical perspective

The ICFTU has long focussed on the implications for labour of the growing interdependence of national economies.[9] Already in the early 1980s, trade union analyses drew attention to the social deficit inherent in the "investment-by-invitation" model of development. This approach frequently failed to stimulate domestic growth and employment and tended to erode human and trade union rights.[10] The ICFTU highlighted the economic leverage exercised by supranational corporations over states, their restrictive business practices, and their anti-union activities, including in export processing zones (EPZs), which employ a largely female, often exploited labour force.[11]

In this advocacy work the ICFTU cooperated closely with the International Trade Secretariats (ITS). These international federations link national unions that cover specific trades or sectors.[12] The ICFTU also collaborated with the Trade Union Advisory Council (TUAC) to the Organization for Economic Cooperation and Development (OECD).

The various trade union bodies coordinated efforts to promote ethical behaviour and fair labour practices in TNCs through intergovernmental standards. These efforts have been instrumental in getting agreement on the OECD Guidelines on Multinational Enterprises, first adopted in 1976, and the Tripartite Declaration of Principles Concerning Multinational Enterprises and Social Policy, adopted by the International Labour Organization (ILO) in 1977. During this period, the ICFTU and the ITS also worked intensely in support of United Nations work for the adoption of a code of conduct on TNCs, but these efforts failed owing to fierce opposition from business interests.

In addition to FDI, capital flows to developing countries at this time took the form of commercial loans and bilateral credits. In the 1980s a mixture of internal and external factors (including poor financial management, oil shocks and unfavourable terms of trade) provoked a debt crisis around these borrowings. Responses to this crisis gave new prominence to the International Monetary Fund (IMF) and the World Bank in multilateral lending with conditionality. The IFIs came to dominate the international development environment. The conditionality arrangements tied to their structural adjustment loans exercised considerable leverage over national economic policies.

The "shock treatment" of IMF stabilization measures to reign in deficit spending and reduce inflation had painful effects on the real economy. Workers and their families bore the brunt of this pain. They suffered sharp rises in the prices of essential consumer goods (with cuts in subsidies), layoffs of public-sector workers, wage freezes and cuts, and the deterioration of education and health services.

The ICFTU had to respond to its affiliated organizations all over the developing world who were grappling with these pains. The question of structural adjustment became a priority item for the ICFTU's Economic and Social Committee around 1982, when this body held a series of expert group meetings with the Bank and the Fund. A major theme of the ICFTU's lobbying efforts during the 1980s was the need for debt relief as a precondition for economic recovery in developing countries.[13] For example, a 1986 ICFTU Latin America regional conference adopted a strategy to put greater pressure on the IMF and the World Bank to produce enduring solutions to the debt crisis affecting the region.[14]

A common thread in ICFTU policy proposals of the 1980s was the call for alternatives to prevailing models of development, whether in relation to trade, FDI or finance.[15] This was a plea for the incorporation of a social dimension into international economic policy. According to the ICFTU, people and the satisfaction of their basic needs should be placed at the centre of the development paradigm. This approach would recognize the rights of workers to organize, bargain collectively and be consulted on economic policy issues. The policy process should include consultative mechanisms for dialogue between social partners and governments regarding national and sectoral reforms. Workers have a legitimate voice in decision-making that affects their lives, and this right to be heard should be exercised through their freely chosen organizations.

Global finance – key challenges for trade unions

The increasing globalization of finance has continued to be a challenge for trade unions in recent years. Consequently, it has remained a priority area of ICFTU advocacy work.[16] More and more developing countries have come within the framework of stabilization and structural adjustment policies of the IMF and the World Bank. Alternative policy options have not been available to these countries. The IMF "stamp of approval" on macroeconomic policies has been a precondition to obtain concessional loans from the World Bank and the regional development banks. Adherence to IMF prescriptions has also determined a country's credit rating and thus its access to bilateral and commercial loans.

To meet these challenges the ICFTU has developed a strategy of critical, constructive engagement with the IFIs, promoting a series of alternative policy proposals. These recommendations have addressed the content of stabilization and structural adjustment programmes as well as the processes and institutional frameworks needed for effective policies. The main concerns for the ICFTU have related to the social dimension of structural adjustment, labour market deregulation, and the social costs of global financial crises.

The social dimension of structural adjustment

During the so-called "first generation" of structural adjustment programmes, IMF prescriptions operated within a narrow framework of tight monetary and fiscal policy. According to the Fund, countries needed to "get their macroeconomic fundamentals right" as a precondition for restored growth. This meant reducing current account deficits through cuts in public expenditure, usually in the fields of education and health. Public-sector reform packages were put in place in many countries, involving cuts in staff and the imposition of user fees for health services and education. Structural adjustment programmes redefined the role of government. The state was said to have been too overbearing in development. Governments needed to assume a minimalist role and allow the private sector and free markets to generate economic growth.

As for workers, structural adjustment programmes required that wages be kept in check in order to maintain low inflation. Collective bargaining was discouraged and, by extension, so were the activities of trade unions. In the orthodox economic literature that inspired IFI policies, unions were often characterized as self-interested, rent-seeking groups whose operations led to over-regulation, distorted product markets, and reduced efficiency.[17]

The IFIs have assumed that the negative social effects of structural adjustment programmes would be short-term. The pains would go away without specific countervailing measures to protect vulnerable groups and essential social sectors or to ensure equitable distribution of the ensuing economic growth. On the contrary, targeted measures would distort the virtuous functioning of the market.

However, as much research has demonstrated, structural adjustment programmes have had persistent contractive effects.[18] They have not only failed to stimulate significant economic growth and employment, but they have also actually exacerbated levels of poverty. African economies have continued to show low or negative growth, with widespread poverty, while Latin American economies, despite growth, have shown huge and increasing disparities between rich and poor.

The ICFTU has since the 1980s continually highlighted the negative social consequences of the policy prescriptions of the IFIs. For example, it condemned the sudden cuts in subsidies on basic consumer items in many African countries during the 1980s.[19] According to the ICFTU, austerity measures need to be eased, even if this means accommodating less than optimal inflation rates and continuing subsidies on essential consumer goods.

For the ICFTU, structural adjustment programmes should not be an end in themselves, but a means to secure well-being for a country's people. If this important objective is not met – even in the short term – then policies need to be rethought. It is not enough to get the macroeconomic fundamentals right. This effort needs to be balanced by policies that get the social fundamentals right.[20]

The ICFTU has argued for a significant social dimension to be incorporated fully into structural adjustment programmes, not merely introduced as an "add-on" in piecemeal fashion. The ICFTU has insisted that social stability is important and that social conflict – resulting from a popular sense of deprivation and exclusion – is a threat to economic stability and growth. The ICFTU has further argued that, even where structural adjustment produces growth, it will not be sustainable if mechanisms are not found to share the prosperity among ordinary citizens.

More specifically, the ICFTU has consistently argued that sound industrial relations are a key component of the social dimension of structural adjustment policies.[21] In this regard, the global financial institutions should observe core labour standards. These principles are enshrined in several ILO conventions and declarations,[22] including:

- the Forced Labour Convention, 1930 (No. 29);
- the Freedom of Association and Protection of the Right to Organise Convention, 1948 (No. 87);
- the Right to Organise and Collective Bargaining Convention, 1949 (No. 98);
- the Equal Remuneration Convention, 1951 (No. 100);
- the Abolition of Forced Labour Convention, 1957 (No. 105);
- the Discrimination (Employment and Occupation) Convention, 1958 (No. 111);
- the Minimum Age Convention, 1973 (No. 138).

In 1998, the ILO brought these core standards together in a Declaration on Fundamental Principles and Rights at Work. A further ILO convention, No. 182, covering Worst Forms of Child Labour, was adopted in 1999.

Observance of core labour standards introduces an important, rights-based approach to structural adjustment programmes. It provides one of the best guarantees of good governance, transparency and accountability, since unions are a well-organized group with a legitimate voice, representative of the interests and aspirations of workers.

Labour market reforms

Once IMF-style macroeconomic policies were firmly in place, the IFIs turned to the privatization of state-owned enterprises and the associated restructuring of labour markets. Privatization was added to the list of conditionalities for countries to qualify for structural adjustment loans. The multilateral development banks introduced privatization programmes in many Latin American and African countries, in sectors including telecommunications, electricity, transport (particularly railways) and, sometimes, water. After the end of the Cold War, the World Bank also promoted much privatization in Central and Eastern Europe as well as in the countries of the former Soviet Union.

These privatization programmes have had mixed results. Some have brought efficiency and productivity gains, but at tremendous social costs in retrenchment and unemployment. No adequate mechanisms were put in place to ensure labour adjustment. In other instances, the private sector has lacked the institutional capacity to manage operations efficiently and overcome the problems of loss-making public enterprises.

Privatization programmes have taken the IFIs into the area of labour market reforms. The World Bank in particular has highlighted the need to remove "labour market rigidities". Chief among these obstacles are "strong unions" and their alleged rent-seeking behaviour, as well as collective bargaining rights and job security provisions guaranteed in labour codes.

Hence, on the advice of the World Bank, many governments have revised labour codes as part of their privatization programmes. Various forms of labour market deregulation have been promoted, including the breakup of enterprises into production and service units, the outsourcing of some operations, and short-term contracts for workers. The Bank has made no efforts to uphold collective bargaining agreements from the pre-reform era. Severance pay arrangements have often been inadequate or nonexistent and have lacked harmonization across sectors.

In most instances, trade unions have not been consulted on these changes. Often the Bank has tried to distance the unions from any negotiations on the future of workers affected by privatization and labour market reforms. Indeed, during the early days of IFI involvement, contacts between unions and the multilateral financial institutions were quite limited.

The international trade union movement has raised serious concerns about labour market deregulation policies promoted by the World Bank. Among other things, the ICFTU has objected that the Bank has bypassed the ILO, despite the latter's mandate and vast experience on issues of labour markets. The ICFTU has called for increased cooperation between the World Bank and the ILO on all labour adjustment issues.

Financial crises: multilateral debt and systemic breakdowns

After years of sustained lobbying on the part of the ICFTU and civil society more generally, debt relief finally registered on the radar screen of the IFIs around the mid-1990s. It became clear that the onerous debt-servicing obligations of heavily indebted poor countries (the so-called HIPCs) were unsustainable. Debt – including multilateral debt – was a major impediment to achieving economic growth. In 1996 the IMF and the World Bank therefore launched a joint initiative aimed at relieving the debt burdens of forty-one HIPCs. In 1999 the Group of Seven (G7) Summit in Cologne approved arrangements to get faster and deeper debt relief through so-called "enhanced HIPC" terms. However, at the time of this writing (late 2000), the ICFTU and other civil society organizations were heavily criticizing delays in implementing the Cologne decisions.[23]

In addition to debt relief, the ICFTU has been concerned with global finance in relation to the systemic crisis of the late 1990s. The crisis began in Asia with currency devaluations and massive outflows of short-term capital from Thailand in July 1997. The problems spread rapidly to Indonesia, Korea, Malaysia and the Philippines. Further contagion effects subsequently extended the crisis to Russia and Brazil. With hindsight it was clear that the huge flows of short-term credits and portfolio investment released on the emerging-market economies of South East Asia had been unsustainable from the outset. Financial sectors were unprepared, lacking adequate mechanisms of accountability, transparency and prudential regulation.

ICFTU analyses have also shown serious weaknesses in existing global financial governance in relation to the crisis. Neither the IMF's early-warning surveillance mechanisms nor the Basle Committee's supervisory system were able to prevent or stem the financial crisis of 1997–98. Contrary to orthodox presumptions about the fairness of the market as a regulator, contagion effects spread the crisis to economies with strong financial sectors and good macroeconomic policies.

Of serious concern to the ICFTU was the fact that ordinary workers often bore the costs of mistakes by imprudent lenders and borrowers and misguided governance institutions.[24] In 1998 all of the affected countries in Asia recorded substantial increases in unemployment and underemployment, significant declines in real earnings, and considerable rises in poverty.[25] These harms were concentrated in sectors of the economy linked to international trade and financial flows. The crisis reversed many gains in living standards made by the South East Asian countries over the years. ILO studies have shown that vulnerable groups such as women, children and migrant workers were among the worst affected. Women bore much of the burden of keeping families together and caring for the elderly on reduced household incomes.[26]

Some recent signs point encouragingly to a resumption of economic growth in some South East Asian countries. However, the social sector always lags behind the economic and financial sectors. Nor is there an automatic link between economic growth and a positive distribution of the gains. Gaps will persist unless strong, targeted social sector programmes are put in place. In effect, millions continue to live in poverty and lack social protections. This will continue to be a major concern for the ICFTU.

In sum, then, the ICFTU has engaged with global finance principally in relation to (a) the social dimension of structural adjustment policies; (b) labour market reforms associated with privatization programmes; and (c) the employment and other social consequences of debt and other financial crises. Across these issues, the ICFTU has urged the integration of a systematic social dimension into the policies of the IFIs, based on principles of equity, equality, accountability, transparency, observance of core labour standards, and the promotion of sound industrial relations practices. The latter includes mechanisms for trade union participation in policy-making at national and international levels.

Meeting the challenges of global finance – trade union strategies

In meeting the challenges described above, the ICFTU has developed a variety of strategies. It has lobbied at the global, regional and national levels. The ICFTU has also given particular attention to building the institutional capacity of its members to deal with issues of global finance.

Before addressing these points in detail, it is appropriate to give a brief outline of relevant policy-making processes of the ICFTU. The principal statutory body is the ICFTU Congress, which meets every four years to determine general policy directions and priority work areas. Around a thousand trade union leaders from affiliated organizations all over the world attend. Since the late 1980s successive Congresses have mandated the ICFTU to promote changes in the functioning of global finance through changes in institutional arrangements and rules of governance.

The ICFTU has responded to this mandate by providing analyses of global economic developments and their social impacts. Drawing on this work, the ICFTU's 33-member Economic and Social Committee formulates policies for endorsement by the 65-member Executive Board. The Board includes representatives from all regions, from the Women's and Youth Committees, from the ITS, and from the TUAC. The Economic and Social Committee and the ICFTU Executive Board each meet once a year. Their policy positions are rooted in the aspirations of workers for sustainable livelihoods in secure working and living environments, with opportunities to share in the benefits of globalization through decent wages.

Lobbying at the global level

The ICFTU lobbies on issues of global finance at different levels of governance. At the global level it has often targeted the G7 governments, given their dominant role in international policy-making and their majority shareholder status within the IFIs. Prior to or coinciding with the annual G7 Summits, the ICFTU and the TUAC have organized high-level trade union meetings with the president or the prime minister of the host country. Since the late 1980s the ICFTU and the TUAC have published a joint statement covering the main issues under discussion at the Summit. The media attention which these events attract has given trade unions strategic opportunities to advance key elements of their platform, such as the need for a social infrastructure (including strong employment policies, social insurance, and the observance of core labour standards) to underpin global financial governance.

To take a specific context, labour organizations made concerted efforts to influence the G7 response to the systemic crisis that started in Asia in 1997. Trade union delegations met the G7 Ministers of Labour and Finance in London in February 1998. They thereby influenced the G7 response, which explicitly recognized the role of labour standards and social policy in achieving a successful recovery from the crisis.

In addition to the G7, the ICFTU has often lobbied the Bretton Woods institutions. Since the early 1990s the Confederation has presented a Statement to the Spring and Annual Meetings of the IMF and the World Bank.[27] These declarations provide a channel for the voice of workers to be heard. They also give the ICFTU an opportunity to take positions on topical agenda items being debated at the Bank/Fund meetings and to address these issues at side events such as press briefings and seminars. The ICFTU closely coordinates lobbying efforts at national and international levels. Thus its affiliated organizations draw on the ICFTU Statement to make representations to their finance ministers and central bank governors ahead of the Spring and Annual Meetings.

Together with the ITS and the TUAC, the ICFTU has also held consultative meetings with the World Bank in its preparations of the annual *World Development Report*, especially when this document has had special implications for labour. Thus consultations were held on the 1995 report, with its theme of "workers in an integrating world" and the 1997 report, on "the state in a changing world".[28] Trade unions were reasonably satisfied that their concerns were heard and influenced the content of these publications. Similarly, trade unions had opportunities to make inputs to the 2000/2001 *World Development Report* on poverty.[29] In the age of new information technology, these consultations took the form of electronic discussions.

In 1996 one of the ITS, the International Federation of Building and Wood Workers (IFBWW), started lobbying the World Bank to incorporate core labour standards into its procurement guidelines and standard bidding documents. These rules and procedures constitute the Bank's framework for contracting business with the private sector. Results of these efforts have so far been encouraging but inconclusive.

Finally at the global level, the ICFTU has in cooperation with the ITS initiated an annual consultative meeting with the Executive Directors and top-level management of the IMF and the World Bank on key policy issues of global finance and development. These meetings began in 1999. In addition, the ICFTU and ITS have together organized meetings with relevant departments of the World Bank to discuss their programmes of privatization and sectoral reform, including the impacts on labour. Such discussions have addressed public-sector reform, privatization of energy and water industries, and reform in the transport and maritime sectors.

Lobbying at the regional level

The ICFTU has three regional organizations. ICFTU/AFRO covers Africa. ICFTU/APRO is the Asia and Pacific Regional Organization. ICFTU/ORIT is the Spanish acronym for the Inter-American Regional Organization of Workers.

The ICFTU/ITS office in Washington, DC has arranged meetings for ICFTU/AFRO and ICFTU/APRO with the IMF and the World Bank. The office has also facilitated dialogue between ICFTU/ORIT and the Inter-American Development Bank (IDB). These Washington-based events have given regional trade union leaders opportunities to present their concerns to senior IFI staff involved in specific countries.

The meetings between the IFIs and Asian trade union leaders took place in the aftermath of the Asian financial crisis. The ICFTU and ICFTU/APRO lobbied for changed policies at various institutions, including the G7, the Bretton Woods agencies and the Asian Development Bank (ADB). ICFTU/APRO presented detailed proposals to the IFIs, based on the conclusions of a regional conference that was held to explore responses to the crisis.[30]

For its part, the IDB has participated in ORIT's efforts at capacity building on structural adjustment questions. This regional bank has for some years funded a training programme for trade union leaders, basing it in selected universities in the Caribbean and Latin America. The IDB has also agreed to trade union proposals to establish a joint task force to define and pursue areas of work in relation to economic reforms and labour adjustment.

In West Africa, ICFTU/AFRO mounted an important initiative following the devaluation of the CFA franc in January 1994. The regional body convened a conference on the trade union response to the devaluation and developed a common action programme for the affected countries. This strategy emphasized trade union rights, payment of salary arrears, maintenance of purchasing power, and subsidies for basic needs. A conference in Chad (a CFA zone country) later in 1994 resulted in a social pact between the government and the unions, with commitments on the part of government to make concerted efforts to introduce programmes that would mitigate the hardships engendered by the devaluation.

Lobbying at country level

The ICFTU has encouraged its affiliated organizations to seek consultations at country level with resident or visiting missions of the IMF and the World Bank on issues related to macroeconomic policies, structural adjustment, and the Bank's Country Assistance Strategy (CAS). More recently, the ICFTU has informed its affiliated organizations in developing countries about the new framework agreements – the Poverty Reduction Strategy Papers (PRSPs) – that will link debt relief and targeted assistance to poverty reduction programmes supported by the IFIs. The ICFTU has urged its national affiliates to approach both their governments and the World Bank on the status of the PRSPs and to get involved in the policy formulation process at the initial stage.

The ICFTU has also focused attention at country level on some of the difficult issues of the post-communist transformation in Central and Eastern Europe and the former Soviet Republics. In particular, the ICFTU supported a campaign in early 1997 by the Russian trade union federations on the non-payment of wages. In April 1997 the ICFTU General Secretary led a delegation of Russian trade union leaders to the World Bank to press for the allocation of compensatory mechanisms within the loan portfolio, in order to guarantee the payment of wage arrears. In Bulgaria the ICFTU worked with its national affiliate in 1997 to respond to the IMF's proposals for a currency board to stabilize the volatile exchange rate.

Capacity building

In all of this lobbying – at global, regional and national levels – the ICFTU has faced challenges of limited capacity. Few trade unionists have been familiar either with the concepts and operational implications of structural adjustment policies or with the institutional workings of the IFIs. The ICFTU has felt that capacity building in this area is critically important. Trade union leaders need to be equipped to be credible advocates for workers.

With this objective in mind, the ICFTU has since 1992 engaged in a major programme of national and regional conferences and seminars on macroeconomic policies and structural adjustment issues. Typically, government officials from relevant ministries as well as IMF and World Bank staff involved in country programmes are invited to participate. The IFIs have an opportunity to present basic concepts of structural adjustment and ongoing programmes to union leaders, and trade unionists have an opportunity to voice their concerns to Bank and Fund officials. Government positions and concerns are also expressed at these meetings, thereby creating a tripartite dialogue. Through these seminars, union leaders have become better equipped to deal with structural adjustment policies. They have thus been able to advance the social dialogue on difficult reforms, an opportunity that was otherwise rather rare.

Over the years, many such seminars have been held in Africa, Asia, Latin America, and Central and Eastern Europe. These events have typically received good media coverage, thereby raising public awareness and facilitating public scrutiny of the issues. In some instances, government representatives and the IFIs publicly recognized the need for social dialogue and committed themselves to sustain it. This was notably the case in Romania and Zambia after their 1992 conferences on structural adjustment. A conference organized in Ghana in 1993 resulted in the formation of a special trade union task force to work with the government on targeted programmes for poverty eradication.

Research coming from the national and regional seminars organized by the ICFTU has, in turn, fed into and enriched debates at the Economic and Social Committee, serving as inputs for the formulation of the ICFTU's global policies. For example, research on gross sectoral disparities in wage trends in Africa was used to press the case for comprehensive labour market information systems (LMIS) in the context of labour market reforms.[31]

Two decades of trade union engagement – assessing the impacts

Thus far we have seen that the international trade union movement has addressed issues of global finance since the early 1980s. The ICFTU, the ITS and other labour organizations have highlighted concerns about social aspects of structural adjustment programmes, labour market reforms, and global financial crises. Unions have pursued these problems at global, regional and national levels. It is now important to assess what impacts these activities have had.

Trade union efforts to sustain a dialogue with the IFIs proved difficult in the early days of first-generation structural adjustment programmes, when economic orthodoxy was strongly entrenched in these institutions. IFI transactions with client governments were highly confidential, and the notion of stakeholder participation was alien to the development paradigm.

However, persistence and a proactive approach on the part of unions have helped to advance the notion that dialogue with labour organizations is important to the reform process. Over the years, the IFIs have moved slowly in the direction of greater openness, transparency, and responsiveness to change. In recent years, they have used information technology expertly to increase their transparency and the availability of documentation.

The climate of dialogue has also improved. For example, the IMF took the lead in 1995 to propose and sponsor a seminar for trade union leaders in Central and Eastern Europe. This allowed trade union leaders to exchange views with IMF and World Bank staff on critical issues related to ongoing reforms, including privatization. The Fund sponsored a similar meeting in 1996 for the Southern African Trade Union Coordinating Council (SATUCC).

During the financial crisis of the late 1990s, heightened involvement of the IFIs with trade union organizations in South East Asia helped in finding solutions to some of the social problems that workers faced. Following ICFTU discussions with the Managing Director of the IMF in 1998, the Fund supported trade union proposals for a tripartite crisis committee (of labour, business and government) to work out a national compact in Korea. Similar dialogue in Indonesia eased the repression of trade union leaders in that country and eventually led to the official recognition of previously outlawed unions.

Trade unions have also made progress on other fronts relating to the social dimensions of global finance. For example, pressures from unions and other civil society organizations led to the joint IMF/World Bank HIPC Initiative in 1996 and its subsequent enhancement in 1999. Recent initiatives to put poverty reduction at the centre of IMF/World Bank policy further testify to a new-found willingness to change. The IFIs have become highly conscious of the greater public scrutiny they are under following street protests during the Spring and Annual Meetings of 2000.

ICFTU and ITS efforts to get the IMF and the World Bank to address core labour standards have borne some – albeit limited – fruit. A milestone was reached when the 1995 *World Development Report* recognized unions as important actors and included a discussion of core labour standards.[32] Nevertheless, the Bank has continued to show great reluctance to accommodate core labour standards, in particular freedom of association and the right to collective bargaining. Some Bank economists have argued that incorporating these standards cannot be justified according to the economic efficiency criteria that guide the institution. On the other hand, the Bank has acknowledged that child labour, forced labour and discrimination in employment can lead to market inefficiencies; hence it can incorporate these core standards into its work. The Social Protection Department of the Bank has begun a programme of work on child labour, and the

International Finance Corporation (IFC) and the Multilateral Investment Guarantee Agency (MIGA) have incorporated the prohibition of child labour and forced labour into their business contracts.[33] Disappointingly, the Bank's opposition to promoting the core ILO conventions on freedom of association and collective bargaining as universal standards has persisted. The latest *World Development Report* again invokes the efficiency argument and concludes that "empirical evidence on the benefits of unionization and collective bargaining [to economic growth] is generally quite mixed".[34]

Trade union strategies for the future

Although, as just demonstrated, the international trade union movement has made some progress in respect of global finance, major challenges remain. IFI consultations with unions are still ad hoc rather than a systematic process. The onus remains on unions to maintain a highly proactive approach in order to get consulted. In terms of substantive issues, trade unions face important future challenges: (a) to incorporate a social dimension into the global financial architecture; and (b) to effect a shift in fundamental policy paradigms.

A social dimension for the new global financial architecture

Important new elements have been brought to the global financial architecture in the aftermath of the systemic crisis of the late 1990s. The IMF has improved the Special Data Dissemination Standard. It has developed a Code of Good Practices on Fiscal Transparency, a Code of Good Practices on Transparency in Monetary and Financial Policies, and Financial Sector Assessment Programs. Still, the IMF must coordinate more closely with other financial standard-setting bodies like the Bank for International Settlements (BIS), the International Organization of Securities Commissions (IOSCO) and the International Accounting Standards Committee (IASC).

Even with such closer coordination, however, serious gaps in the global financial architecture would persist. The social dimension has still not been integrated, and economic orthodoxy prevents the governance institutions from moving in the right direction on critical points such as capital controls, the mobilization of resources for development, and supervision of special financial markets such as hedge funds and offshore centres.

The ICFTU seeks to reverse these social deficits. It has proposed a framework of guiding principles that integrate economic, financial and social policy, as overseen by a proposed International Commission on International Financial Market regulation (ICFTU 1998). This Commission would coordinate the standard-setting functions of various governance bodies, as well as the regulatory and surveillance functions of the IMF. It would set the agenda and priorities for a bold programme of work on critical and contentious issues involved in the prevention of systemic risk.

With respect to social policy, trade unions will urge that the IFIs seek increased cooperation with the United Nations and its relevant specialized agencies, with a view to pooling relative strengths and profiting from best practice. Key in this regard is the forthcoming UN Conference on Financing for Development (FfD), which aims to mobilize financial resources for poverty eradication and sustainable development. The FfD should promote increased cooperation between the IMF, the World Bank, the World Trade Organization (WTO), and the UN and its specialized agencies, working within the framework of the Economic and Social Council (ECOSOC).

Towards a fundamental paradigm shift

Change in the global financial architecture must go hand in hand with change in the underlying paradigm. So long as the IFIs remain within the existing *laissez-faire* approach, they will not produce lasting solutions for poverty eradication and shared economic growth. The ICFTU must therefore argue for a fundamental paradigm shift.

Preventing systemic crises and restoring long-term growth will require a fundamental reconstruction of the way governments, through the network of international financial institutions and organizations, regulate and manage the global market. A fundamental shift in the prevailing economic paradigm is a prerequisite to these architectural changes.

Cornerstones for this alternative paradigm include:

- macroeconomic policies oriented toward expansionary, demand-led growth, employment promotion, poverty eradication, shared prosperity, social stability, gender equity, and respect for core labour standards;
- growth of employment as a means of combating poverty, as envisioned in the ILO Global Programme on Decent Work;
- government rights to control foreign capital flows in the interest of macroeconomic stability;
- government rights to determine the pace and sequencing of capital account liberalization;
- strengthened financial sectors and supervisory systems;
- binding international standards for the prudential regulation of financial markets;
- core labour standards as enshrined in the ILO Declaration on Fundamental Principles and Rights at Work and its follow-up;
- collective bargaining as an important mechanism to ensure positive distributional effects from growth and productivity gains;
- international taxation of foreign exchange transactions;
- achievement of the target of 0.7 per cent of GNP towards official development assistance (ODA);
- deeper, wider, faster debt relief for the heavily indebted poor countries, with freed-up resources targeted to poverty reduction and the provision of social services;

- mechanisms for the orderly resolution of financial crises, with the costs of adjustment distributed equitably between borrowers and lenders and with social safety nets to protect vulnerable groups;
- consultative mechanisms to facilitate dialogue between IFIs and civil society organizations on financial and economic policies and their social dimensions.

Conclusion

Together with the ITS and the TUAC, the ICFTU intends to sustain and deepen its dialogue with the IFIs at global, regional and country levels, seeking strategic opportunities such as the Spring and Annual Meetings to further its advocacy efforts. The trade unions will move to high-profile campaigns that target priority issues such as poverty reduction through employment-generating growth and the promotion of workers' rights through core labour standards. Advocacy will aim to have these standards incorporated systematically into policy frameworks and operational instruments, such as the CAS, the PRSPs, and the Procurement Guidelines of the World Bank.

Underlying the ICFTU's proposals is the conviction that, unless a fundamental shift is made from the existing policy framework, economic disparities between and within countries will persist and worsen. Economic and social crises will continue to emerge in one country after another. The solution must lie in doing things differently, guided by a paradigm shift in which the processes of globalization and financial market liberalization are embedded in an alternative framework of principles and rules, as outlined above. Within this framework, all institutional actors – and not least the IFIs – need to be made accountable for their role in ensuring that globalization brings about sustainable economic and social development with equity. Such a framework would eliminate the dichotomy and the contradictions between the financial sector and the real economy. It would connect and integrate financial and economic policy with social policy. It would recognize the well-being of people rather than the health of market indicators as the central objective of development.

So unions are important actors in global financial governance. They add an important layer of checks and balances against misguided economic and financial policies and the mismanagement of domestic or global finance. Far from distorting markets, unions assist in removing information failures in the market by providing timely and relevant inputs from their members. Through collective bargaining, unions help to ensure that the benefits of globalization are spread among workers. Involving unions up-front in the consultative process on IFI policies provides a way to ensure popular support for much-needed reforms that are politically difficult to implement. Involving unions keeps employment firmly on the social agenda as a means of eradicating poverty and attaining the goal of providing decent livelihoods for all.

Notes

1 This chapter has benefited from helpful comments and suggestions made by James Howard, Director, Employment and International Labour Standards, ICFTU, Brussels. I am also grateful for research support provided by Peter Bakvis of the ICFTU/ITS Washington Office and Fons Vannieuwenhuyse of the ICFTU Brussels headquarters.

2 UNDP, *Human Development Report 1999*, New York: Oxford University Press, 1999, p. 37.

3 UNCTAD, *World Investment Report 2000: Cross-Border Mergers and Acquisitions and Development*, New York: United Nations, 2000.

4 World Bank, *World Development Report 2000/2001: Attacking Poverty*, New York: Oxford University Press, 2001, p. 3.

5 Ibid.

6 ILO, *World Employment Report 1998–99: Employability in the Global Economy: How Training Matters*, Geneva: International Labour Office, 1998; press release ILO98/33.

7 http://www.icftu.org.

8 http://www.cmt-wcl.org.

9 Cf. ICFTU, *World Economic Review: The Reality of Interdependence*, Brussels: ICFTU, 1984.

10 ICFTU Statement to the Third Conference of the United Nations Industrial Development Organization, New Delhi, January 1980.

11 "Export Processing Zones", *Trade Unions and Transnationals Information Bulletin*, Special Issue No. 3, March 1983.

12 The International Trade Secretariats include Public Services International (PSI), Education International (EI), the International Transport Workers' Federation (ITF), the Union Network International (UNI, the Federation of Professional, Technical, Commercial, Clerical Communications, Banking Workers), the International Metal Workers' Federation (IMF), the International Textile, Garment and Leather Workers' Federation (ITGLWF), the International Federation of Chemical, Energy, Mine and General Workers' Unions (ICEM), the International Union of Food, Agricultural, Hotel, Restaurant, Catering, Tobacco and Allied Workers' Associations (IUF), the International Federation of Journalists (IFJ), and the International Federation of Building and Wood Workers (IFBWW).

13 ICFTU, *World Economic Review: The Reality of Interdependence*.

14 ICFTU/ORIT, "First the People and then the Debt", Statement of the Conference on Debt and Development, Buenos Aires, 1986.

15 ICFTU, *Report on Activities, Financial Reports 1979–1982*, presented to the Thirteenth World Congress of the ICFTU, Oslo, June 1983; ICFTU, *Report on Activities, Financial Reports 1983–1986*, presented to the Fourteenth World Congress of the ICFTU, Melbourne, March 1988; ICFTU, *Report on Activities, Financial Reports 1987–1990*, presented to the Fifteenth World Congress of the ICFTU, Caracas, March 1992.

16 Cf. ICFTU, *Report on Activities, Financial Reports 1991–1994*, presented to the Sixteenth World Congress of the ICFTU, Brussels, June 1996; ICFTU, *Report on Activities, Financial Reports 1995–1998*, presented to the Seventeenth World Congress of the ICFTU, Durban, South Africa, April 2000.

17 S.A. Herzenberg *et al.*, "Introduction to Labor Standards and Development in the Global Economy", papers presented at the Symposium on Labor Standards and Development – Washington, DC: US Department of Labor and Bureau of International Labor Affairs, December 1990; K.M. Murphy, A. Schleifer and R.W. Vishy, "Why Is Rent-Seeking so Costly to Growth?", *American Economic Review, Papers and Proceedings*, Vol. 83, No. 2 (1993), pp. 409–14.

18 A. Khan, *Structural Adjustment and Income Distribution: Issues and Experiences*, Geneva: ILO, 1993; E. Buffie, "The Long-Run Consequences of Short-Run Stabilization Policy", in S. Horton, R. Kanbur and D. Mazumdar (eds), *Labour Markets in an Era of Adjustment*, Washington, DC: World Bank, EDI Development Studies, 1994; R. van der Hoeven,

"Implications of Macroeconomic Policies for Equity and Poverty", in *Globalization and Liberalization: Effects of International Economic Relations on Poverty*, New York and Geneva: UNCTAD/ECDC/PA/4/Rev.1, Interagency Thematic Contribution to the International Year for the Eradication of Poverty, 1996.

19 ICFTU, background paper and conclusions of a conference on The African Worker and the World Economic Crisis, Dakar, 1984.

20 ICFTU, "Preparing for Geneva 2000: Achieving Social Development for All in a Globalizing World", Statement to the Preparatory Committee for the Special Session of the UN General Assembly on Implementation of the World Summit for Social Development and Further Initiatives, New York, April 2000; ICFTU, "Globalising Social Justice – The Challenge for Geneva 2000", Statement to the Special Session of the UN General Assembly: "The World Summit for Social Development and Beyond: Achieving Social Development for All in a Globalising World", Geneva, June 2000.

21 Bernie Russell, *Fighting for Workers' Human Rights in the Global Economy*, Brussels: ICFTU, 1997.

22 See http://www.ilo.org.

23 ICFTU/TUAC/ITS, "Achieving Poverty Reduction, Debt Relief, Social Protection and International Financial Stability", Statement to the Annual Meetings of the IMF and the World Bank, Prague, September 2000.

24 ICFTU/TUAC, "International Trade Union Statement on the Global Economic Crisis", Brussels and Paris, December 1998.

25 ILO Tripartite Meeting, Recommendations of the ILO's High-Level Tripartite Meeting on Social Responses to the Financial Crisis in East and South East Asian Countries. Bangkok, April 1998; ILO, *Unemployment and Underemployment*, Jakarta: ILO Office Research Paper, 1999.

26 ICFTU–APRO, Statement on the Financial and Economic Crisis by Women and Young Workers of South-East and East Asia, Bangkok, July 1998; ICFTU–APRO, Statement of the Regional Workshop on Social Safety Nets conducted by the ICFTU–APRO with the ILO and the Japanese Institute of Labour (JIL), Manila, July 1998; "Perspectives – Social Aspects of the Follow-up to the Asian Financial Crisis", *International Labour Review*, Vol. 138, No. 2 (1999).

27 Cf. ICFTU, "Globalisation on Trial", Statement to the Annual Meetings of the IMF and the World Bank, Washington, DC, October 1998; ICFTU/TUAC/ITS, "Securing the Conditions for Reducing Poverty and Achieving Sustainable Growth", Statement to the Spring Meetings of the International Monetary Fund and the World Bank, Washington, DC, April 2000; ICFTU/TUAC/ITS, "Achieving Poverty Reduction, Debt Relief, Social Protection and International Financial Stability", 2000.

28 World Bank, *World Development Report 1995: Workers in an Integrating World*, New York: Oxford University Press, 1995; World Bank, *World Development Report 1997: The State in a Changing World*, New York: Oxford University Press, 1997.

29 *World Development Report 2000/2001*.

30 ICFTU/APRO.

31 ICFTU, *Report on Activities, Financial Reports 1995–1998*, Brussels: ICFTU, 2000.

32 *World Development Report 1995*, ch. 11.

33 IFC, "Harmful Child and Forced Labor", IFC Policy Statement, March 1998.

34 *World Development Report 2000/2001*, p. 74.

12 Business associations and global financial governance

James C. Orr

Summary

• Introduction	199
• History: the emergence of global finance as a business issue	200
• A survey of business associations	202
• What do business associations seek?	205
• Strategies and tactics	207
• What impact can business associations have?	209
• A look to the future	210

Introduction

Business associations were the first civil society groups to interact with national governments and multilateral institutions on global financial governance issues. Decisions of global institutions occasionally had a direct financial impact on banks, exporters and foreign investors. For decades after World War II, businesses and their associations were the most active civil society organizations in attempting to influence global financial governance. In recent years, competition has emerged from every quarter of civil society, as other groups increasingly see their interests affected and begin efforts of their own to influence decisions.

This chapter's discussion of business association engagement with global financial institutions has six parts. The first section below presents a historical review of business associations' efforts to influence global financial governance, noting variations across different regions and industries. The second section surveys some of the more prominent Northern business associations that have targeted efforts toward influencing global financial governance. The third section examines the aims of business associations. While most are admittedly rooted in commercial self-interest, there are notable exceptions, particularly in Europe, where a sense of social responsibility plays a strong role. The fourth part of the chapter considers the strategies and tactics used by business associations that have proven most effective in engaging governments and institutions. The fifth section examines cases of successful influence, while the concluding section looks to the future.

The democratization of global financial governance has ended business' monopoly on civil society influence in this area. Global institutions and governments are increasingly encumbering businesses to maximize benefits for other stakeholders. Meanwhile, public fears of globalization and a widespread tendency to blame multilateral institutions and corporate greed for the world's ills have put business associations very much on the defensive.

It should be noted that, owing to limits of the author's experience, this study focuses almost entirely on Northern business associations. This is not to minimize the efforts of business associations of the South and the East, which have become increasingly active on global financial questions, although they have yet to attain the same level of influence as their Northern counterparts.

History: the emergence of global finance as a business issue

The architecture and rules of global financial governance were created with the interests of business in mind, or so most businesses and their associations have always presumed. At the end of World War II, multilateral structures were created to promote international financial stability, limit disruptive swings in exchange rates and ensure smooth payments across borders. Governments were the architects of the new arrangements, but companies, banks and investors were the principal beneficiaries.

For four decades, business executives watched global financial governance from the sidelines. They were largely content to allow governments to make all decisions and run the global financial institutions as they thought best. Indeed, the province of global financial governance seemed quite remote even to the most internationally active banks and exporters. Business associations paid little attention to global financial regimes, particularly when compared to their very active involvement in governance of domestic financial systems.

For their part, global financial institutions and governments knew very well what business wanted and needed. In fact, official and commercial interests were closely aligned. Over the years, something of a revolving door has existed, allowing executives to migrate between private banks and the national and multilateral agencies. For example, three of the last four presidents of the World Bank were heads of commercial banks in their prior positions. Likewise, top officials at the German Bundesbank and the US Treasury moved to their current government jobs from senior positions in private banks, the World Bank or the International Monetary Fund (IMF). This revolving door has facilitated government's understanding of business interests and needs in global finance.

Industry concern with global financial governance issues has grown at an accelerated pace in recent years. Around the world, companies face a more competitive business environment. Business has slowly awoken to a new reality characterized by intense global competition, greater dependence on faraway markets, and new vulnerability to financial crises wherever they occur. For example, bankers claim that the Asian financial crisis of 1997–98 resulted in millions, if not billions, of dollars in investment losses and lost export opportunities.[1]

With the globalization of financial markets, private capital has increasingly overtaken official funds in most sectors in all but the poorest countries. In the 1990s it is estimated that private investors placed $1,700 billion in major emerging-market economies, as compared to $320 billion from all official sources.[2] As a major source of much-needed capital, industry sees an important role for itself in shaping the future structure of the global financial system. If private capital is to replace official funds more broadly, new incentives must be provided to motivate private investors and lenders.

In this new situation, multilateral institutions will need to concentrate on leveling the playing field for private investors, establishing and enforcing rules, and managing crises. They will have to focus their own limited capital on marginal countries and sectors, either to encourage the private sector to provide resources or to inject social investments into regions where private capital will not go.

Competition has sharpened in the policy realm, too. Labor, environmental and anti-poverty groups have entered the debate and now vie with business to set the rules for global finance. New battle lines are being drawn over the terms under which multilateral resources are dispersed, as non-business stakeholders increasingly lay claim to a seat at the table. Business has not welcomed the growing number of initiatives from other civil society groups directed toward global financial governance, largely because they have come at the expense of business. As the provider of capital, goods and employment, business considers itself to be the predominant stakeholder in the global financial system.

Companies feel increasingly beleaguered as they are forced to fight to protect and maintain the system that has generally worked to their benefit. Governments have failed to make the case that globalization brings more benefit than harm, so businesses see that they must take on this challenge themselves. The recent backlash against globalization and radical proposals advanced by groups on the political fringes have forced business to divert more time and resources to defending multilateral agencies and to competing with other groups for influence *vis-à-vis* governments and global institutions. For instance, at the 1999 Seattle meeting of the World Trade Organization (WTO), little business effort was directed toward achieving specific trade objectives. Instead, for the first time, business representatives had to engage in public debate with other members of civil society to defend the institution of the WTO and the importance of trade liberalization to society as a whole.

Meanwhile, governments and multilateral institutions are tightening the rules governing the conduct of global financial business. Many critics charge that the current system allows investors to privatize their gains and socialize their losses. Evidence of moral hazard in the Asian financial crisis countries led global institutions to propose new restrictions on the free flow of capital.

New rules are also being considered to force private capital providers to share in the cost of financial bailouts. For example, efforts are afoot to force bondholders to restructure through strict application of the Paris Club principle of "comparable treatment". Other proposals would require countries to include "collective action" clauses in their international bond covenants (as distinct from the voluntary inclusion of such clauses). Further suggestions would permit IMF lending to countries that are in arrears to private creditors and would allow the Fund temporarily to block litigation by investors seeking immediate payment.

A survey of business associations

Over the last two decades or so, business associations have become much more active in regard to global financial governance. New groups have sprouted, taking a variety of forms. Approaches and interest levels have varied between regions. Different sectors of industry have also exhibited differing levels of involvement. Some experiences illustrate this diversity.

Different countries, different approaches

In the United States it was not until the late 1970s that business associations first exhibited significant interest in global governance issues. Congress, which for years had approved funding for multilateral financial and development institutions without protest, began to balk at enacting this legislation. Sometimes this resistance came at the urging of civil society groups such as environmental and human rights organizations that wanted the global institutions to move in new directions. There was marked erosion in the long US tradition of bipartisan support for the Bretton Woods institutions. Lawmakers discovered that funding legislation could be held hostage for concessions from the White House on other issues. Moreover, this legislation could be loaded up with extraneous provisions that could not otherwise have been enacted.

Internationally active firms grew concerned that Congress might break US commitments to multilateral institutions, endangering American commercial interests in the process. These companies voiced support to Congress for funding measures and against restrictive policy conditions. Initially they worked through large existing trade groups, including the National Association of Manufacturers, the American Bankers Association, and the United States Chamber of Commerce.[3] In addition, they sometimes formed temporary alliances such as the Ad Hoc Coalition of IMF Supporters, created in 1983 to lobby Congress for the passage of IMF legislation. Ultimately these same businesses backed the creation of new organizations with a specific brief to track issues of global financial governance.

The Bretton Woods Committee (BWC) was one such organization. Established in 1984, the BWC conducts civic and congressional education and makes policy recommendations to multilateral institutions and government leaders. Two former US Secretaries of the Treasury helped to create the BWC, in part to enlarge and focus corporate lobbying efforts on funding legislation for the IMF and the World Bank. Today, the BWC has about 600 members, including former US cabinet members, former lawmakers, and business and civic leaders across the country. Over the years, the BWC has been very influential in persuading Congress to enact politically unpopular funding measures for the World Bank and the IMF. More recently, the BWC has encouraged the global financial institutions to grant debt relief to the world's poorest countries. The BWC has also published reports designed to encourage the multilateral institutions to consider other new options.[4]

The Institute of International Finance (IIF), established in 1983, serves as a global trade group for internationally active financial institutions from around the world. The Institute was the creation of thirty-eight internationally active commercial banks who met at Ditchley Park, UK, during the Latin American debt crisis to search for ways to protect their interests in borrowing countries. The mission of the IIF later broadened to include attempts to influence the policy directions of the IMF and the World Bank. The IIF monitors developments in emerging-market economies and advocates the interests of its members at the multilateral institutions.[5] Based in Washington, the IIF today represents over 300 banks and other financial institutions from fifty countries.[6]

Japan followed a different path. In 1983, Japan's Ministry of Finance, the Bank of Japan and leading financial service companies established the Japan Center for International Finance (JCIF), an industry advisory group dedicated to research on global financial issues. At its inception, the JCIF was designed as a Japanese version of the largely American-dominated IIF. In addition to monitoring international financial developments for its members, the JCIF holds biannual policy consultations with the managements of the IMF and the World Bank.

In the wake of sharp drops in export earnings related to exchange rate swings in the late 1980s, leaders of Japan's powerful business organization, the Keidanren, pressed the Japanese government to establish a system of fixed (or more fixed) exchange rates. Keidanren members also funded research efforts in Japan and overseas, joined international study commissions on exchange rate issues, and published papers that urged governments to back a new regime of fixed or semi-fixed exchange rates.

In 1995, Japan's leading international bank, the Bank of Tokyo (now the Bank of Tokyo–Mitsubishi) funded and staffed a new think tank, called the Institute for International Monetary Affairs, for research on global financial issues. The Institute publishes papers focused on Japan's role in the international financial system and international financial stability.[7]

In contrast, Europe's business associations have been less active on global financial governance. Perhaps European preoccupations over the last decade with regional economic and financial integration have sapped the energy needed to track global financial interests closely. The broad-based International Chamber of Commerce, headquartered in Paris, has maintained a watching brief on global financial issues on behalf of its thousands of European and international business members.[8]

Business associations also exist outside the Group of Seven (G7) countries. Most countries of Africa, Asia, Latin America and Europe have national bankers associations that represent the interests of the local commercial financial community *vis-à-vis* the government and international financial institutions on issues related to international markets and global financial governance. Often, local manufacturing or farmers lobbies will engage the multilateral development banks and the IMF where possible. This process has been accelerated by new requirements on the international institutions to consult civil society groups more widely on policies and programs.

Foreign chambers of commerce (e.g. American Chambers of Commerce abroad) can also sometimes influence the policy debates concerning global finance. This proved especially true recently in Russia, where associations of foreign corporations pressed the IMF to require fairer tax treatment and the legal enforcement of contracts by the Russian government.[9] Indeed, the international financial institutions sometimes feel more comfortable consulting associations of transborder companies than local business lobbies.

Different industries, different approaches

Not surprisingly, many of the interventions into global financial governance have come from business associations that represent the financial sector. The growing participation of international banks in cross-border finance puts them at the front line when financial crises erupt and institutions like the IMF swing into action. During the Latin American debt crisis in the early 1980s, the entire community of companies with financial exposure in the region totaled only about thirty international banks. They found themselves drawn into protracted rescheduling negotiations with borrowers and frequently competed with official institutions for repayment of loans.

Banks learned through this experience that major governments and the IMF had the potential to exert tremendous influence on the policies of borrowing governments. The G7 and the Fund could direct countries to meet payment obligations, or they could demand that private lenders make more concessions. Banks and their trade associations battled to convince governments and the IMF to withhold funding where necessary to ensure that countries bargained in good faith with commercial creditors. Ironically, lobbying by bank representatives sometimes proved counterproductive, particularly after allegations that IMF funds served to bail out commercial banks.

The approach of small banks presents an interesting contrast. Engaged in a perpetual battle for survival against their larger cousins, small banks typically show little sympathy for the problems of big banks. One trade group of small banks in the United States, the Independent Bankers Association of America (IBAA), periodically lobbied Congress to withdraw special protection for big banks making what the IBAA termed "risky overseas loans". The IBAA sought to put an end to the so-called "too-big-to-fail" doctrine. Mostly to spite big banks, it also tried to block favorable accounting treatment for overdue loans owed by developing countries and to block IMF funding legislation.[10]

Given the nature of their members' business, manufacturers associations have had a more tenuous connection to global financial issues. They have generally been content to allow banks to provide leadership. Big banks, in particular, have provided the bulk of the financing required for public and Congressional education efforts to build support for the global financial institutions. In 1983, when Congress temporarily balked at enacting legislation to increase the IMF quota, commercial banks feared a dry-up of IMF funds for Latin America's recovery. Large American banks contacted their major manufacturing customers and asked for their help in lobbying Congress; however, only a few manufacturers answered the call. One such company was the aircraft manufacturer Boeing. Its treasurer calculated that the firm was trying to market aircraft in more than thirty countries where the IMF had or was negotiating programs; so Boeing joined banks in active lobbying for the increase in IMF funding.

Agricultural business associations came late to debates about global financial governance, but they have had a powerful impact on the legislative outcome in the United States. Faced with declining farm exports following the financial collapse of a succession of Asian economies in 1997–98, farm groups identified IMF lending as an important means to refinance demand. They joined in coalitions with financial companies and manufacturers to persuade Congress to support IMF funding. Their strong influence over farm state legislators became a decisive element in the 1998 battle to win Congressional appropriations for the IMF.

Finally, protectionist industry associations have been wary of global financial institutions. They argue that the World Bank and other multilateral lenders finance new industries in developing countries that end up taking market share from traditional producers. In recent legislative battles, representatives from the steel, textile, and electronics industries pressed Congress to condition US support for the IMF and multilateral development institutions in ways that were designed to protect their commercial interests. For example, in 1998 the US Treasury had to convince Congress to reject legislative riders that would make US funding for the IMF contingent upon Korea's adoption of the trade liberalization that was sought by impacted American industries.

What do business associations seek?

Business has various objectives in respect of global financial governance. The primary objective for some is to preserve a system where the marketplace imposes discipline. Others see the need to move more towards a rules-based system. Still others want to tilt the system to favor their own commercial interests. A few put a high premium on achieving equity for other stakeholders and good governance standards.

Among the first-order objectives of business is *stability*. Industry believes that optimal levels of long-term lending and investment only occur when governmental and regulatory risks are reduced to a minimum. These voices insist that uncertainty over profit repatriation rights or threatened penalties in the wake of financial crises will limit investor interest and no doubt raise the cost of funds for borrowers.

The business community has strong support for actions to grant *prompt and effective relief* to countries that encounter financial disruption. Business also supports *effective development lending programs* aimed at poor countries and weak sectors. Both financial rescues and development assistance serve to build or restore buying power.

Banks and investors also want *unencumbered entry and exit* from foreign markets, so that they can follow changing opportunities. Even in the face of strong evidence that multilateral agencies bailed out private investors in Asia, business maintains strong opposition to any form of forced private-sector participation in the resolution of future financial crises.

Stable exchange rates are a very high business priority, particularly for exporters of manufactured and agricultural goods. There is strong support in Japan and elsewhere in Asia to return to an exchange rate system with more fixity, given the stability in export markets that such a system might provide.

International businesses have led the fight for *greater data disclosure*, both by borrowing countries and by the global institutions themselves. Mexico's failure to fully disclose its debt levels and reserve position helped to precipitate the Mexican financial collapse of the early 1980s that cost foreign banks dearly. Korea's concealment of the level of impaired reserves also hastened that country's costly collapse in 1997. Disclosure has worked very well in the domestic context as a stabilizing force and an enforcement mechanism. The United States' highly efficient and effective financial regulatory system is based on public disclosure, providing markets with the information needed to impose real discipline and police the system. The importance of increased disclosure and transparency has been a recurrent theme in recent multilateral efforts to shore up and harmonize financial regulatory regimes. At the Okinawa G8 Summit in 2000, heads of state expressed their support for more disclosure and greater transparency by borrowers, lenders and multilateral institutions. Similar urgings were directed at banking centers that compete for funds by safeguarding the identity of account holders, and at countries that serve as tax havens.

US companies have also been active in urging governments and multilateral financial institutions to *end corruption*. Corruption breeds market distortions, inefficiencies and inequities. US firms face tough domestic laws, passed in 1977, which prohibit the payment of bribes to foreign officials. They have long sought to impose similar standards on others, and OECD guidelines now support this direction.[11] Business has also backed programmatic lending by multilateral development banks that seeks to end corruption in borrowing countries. Some have even argued that multilateral loans should be withheld from countries where corruption remains rampant.[12] Many companies have supported the anti-corruption efforts of Transparency International, a nongovernmental organization (NGO) launched in 1993.[13]

Furthermore, industry wants global institutions to *enforce compliance* with accepted norms and rules of behavior in international commerce and finance. For example, smaller Korean companies and foreign competitors alike urged the IMF to stop the Korean government from favoring the *chaebol* (large industrial conglomerates) over other domestic and foreign companies. Similarly, US and other foreign investors in Russia have pressed the IMF to withhold funds from that country until the government adopts a tax collection system that does not discriminate against foreign investors.

The private sector would like to see *greater reliance on self-regulation* by business. When faced with the prospect of new regulations, business always asks to be allowed to regulate itself. In some cases, self-regulatory efforts have worked well and have maximized public welfare. In other instances, however, self-regulatory efforts have proven ineffective, and government bodies have had to superimpose their rules on reluctant industries.

For instance, when sovereign lenders comprised thirty international banks, self-discipline worked well. The bank advisory committee system they devised (the so-called "London Club") cajoled most of the firms concerned to accept financial haircuts and provide new funds. However, in today's emerging-markets crises, foreign creditors can number into the thousands, ranging from the largest commercial and investment banks down to individual investors whose retirement accounts are invested in emerging-market bonds. The likelihood of an effective self-regulatory mechanism arising out of this mass of competing and conflicting interests is relatively remote.

A catalog of business aims would not be complete without a discussion of corporate citizenship and commitments to *social and environmental responsibility.* Almost every major multinational corporation in the United States and Europe devotes a significant share of the corporate philanthropy budget to the promotion of domestic and international well-being. In the area of global financial governance, this takes several forms. Some public education groups, like the Bretton Woods Committee in the United States, are supported entirely by philanthropic contributions from individual companies whose motivation is a sense of social responsibility to promote international welfare. These companies expect and get little or nothing in return.

In Europe, where a progressive corporate culture is more common, international firms have led the way by committing substantial budget resources and executives' time to development initiatives and efforts to produce greater equity in poor countries. US companies have been slower to move in this direction, perhaps because their stockholders are more demanding and have their eye on the bottom line. However, there are exceptions. For example, Ben and Jerry's Ice Cream devotes 7.5 per cent of its pre-tax profits to philanthropic activities designed to improve the quality of life in local communities and abroad. The firm has a loyal public, based in part on its commitment to social responsibility. Likewise, grants from the founder of Microsoft, Bill Gates, are currently funding poverty-reduction planning in some heavily indebted poor countries that wish to qualify for debt forgiveness initiatives. Though critics may argue that these efforts are sometimes undertaken for public relations advantage, there are many more expressions of good corporate citizenship that go completely unheralded.

Strategies and tactics

Business associations select different targets and employ varied tactics to influence global financial governance. Associations educate, lobby, and even make threats in order to win policy concessions. They work both openly and quietly behind the scenes. They work alone and, on occasion, in coalition with other civil society groups such as NGOs and research institutes.

Business groups most typically target governments. Associations issue reports calling for changes in national policy. They meet with officials of finance and development ministries charged with regulating international finance and development policy. Ministry officials weigh these requests, balancing interests, and transmit instructions to their representatives within the multilateral institutions. Sometimes ministry officials take the initiative themselves systematically to gather views from the main private-sector actors in advance of international discussion of issues. For instance, a US Treasury undersecretary may call together the executives of associations representing financial sector companies to learn their views on the workability of proposals to slow capital flight in countries facing financial upheaval. More typically, however, the initiative comes from the business associations. Their meetings with government regulators generally happen out of public sight, although that need not imply any sinister intent or outcome. In the case of the United States, Treasury officials with responsibility for global financial governance spend a significant portion of their time meeting with civil society organizations of every kind to explain policy, seek guidance and win support for their initiatives. These meetings have been critical to building interest group support, which in turn enables the Treasury to convince a skeptical Congress to enact unpopular legislation.

Business associations also work directly with lawmakers, at least in the United States. They testify in support of, or in opposition to, proposals at Congressional hearings. They suggest amendments to legislative language to skirt problems or increase benefits. And they lobby members of Congress to support legislation. Lobbying occurs through visits with lawmakers, letters, phone calls, newspaper advertisements, etc. Whether or not lawmakers act on this advice is likely to be a function of the business group's political or financial importance to individual legislators.

Annual passage of foreign assistance funding is always a tenuous proposition in the US Congress. Without active lobbying from business associations and their members, or at least tacit support, it is unlikely that these measures could ever emerge from committee consideration. Again, interests need to be balanced. Other activist civil society organizations, often including development NGOs and environmental groups, must also concur in the direction of the foreign assistance legislation or it cannot be enacted. In the past, opposition to IMF conditionality, World Bank neglect of the environment, and funding shortfalls for debt reduction of Heavily Indebted Poor Countries (HIPCs) have forced lawmakers to regroup and change legislation to win broader civil society support.

Business associations occasionally direct their efforts at the international financial institutions themselves. For instance, the Institute of International Finance every year issues an open letter to the heads of the IMF, the World Bank, and the G7 finance ministers, listing its concerns related to international financial regulation and the actions of these bodies. This letter gets wide publication and always provokes debate within policy circles.

Some international companies also engage the multilateral institutions directly, rather than through a business association. For example, a large international energy supplier unsuccessfully lobbied the World Bank to provide a guarantee to cover a private energy development project that sponsors believed needed official backing to win support among private lenders. After the World Bank declined, the company tried to pressure it to change its decision by lobbying Congressional conservatives to cut the Bank's funding, arguing that the institution was inattentive to private-sector needs.

In another instance, one of the world's leading financial companies found itself often competing in certain emerging markets with the International Finance Corporation (IFC), the private-sector arm of the World Bank. This financial company warned the IFC that if it continued to waste taxpayer funds performing services that private investment banks would do for the same fee, then executives of the firm would tell Congress that a cut in funding was in order. Whether or not this protest was the prompting, the IFC soon tightened its policy to prevent competition with private firms.

Occasionally, business associations cooperate with other civil society organizations to win changes in global financial governance. In the United States, church and poverty groups led the lobbying effort to persuade Congress to fund US obligations to HIPC debt reduction, but failed to find the support they needed. This prompted activists to seek allies in the business community. They collaborated with business representatives on a letter expressing business community support that ultimately attracted signatures from many internationally active firms. Now funding for HIPC debt reduction appears to have broader support in Congress.

However, collaboration between business associations and other CSOs is still rare. More typically, business associations seek to counteract the pressures of some other civil society actors whose aims are inimical to their own. As noted previously, business associations directed considerable time and money to putting out their own message at the 1999 Seattle WTO meeting, when confronted with outspoken advocacy groups who blamed corporations for many of the world's ills.

What impact can business associations have?

Business associations have brought much to debates on global financial governance. Banks and investors are the main suppliers of capital to finance growth and development. They thus have an inherent interest in finding ways to solve problems that limit cross-border financial transactions. Banks have pioneered new financial innovations and techniques that can be harnessed to help multilateral financial institutions increase their effectiveness. Finally, corporations have an ability to self-regulate that may be preferable to government regulation in some instances.

Up to now, the impact of business associations on global financial governance has been limited and is hard to characterize. Most efforts have focused on civic and Congressional education. In the United States, educational efforts by companies have helped to persuade Congress to enact politically difficult legislation like IMF funding measures, resources for debt relief, etc. However, broader efforts to increase public support for foreign assistance have failed to make significant headway. The surprisingly harsh backlash against globalization and the broad array of charges laid at the feet of multilateral institutions indicate the enormity of the educational task ahead.

Business associations can claim a few successful efforts to change the behavior of global financial institutions. The decision by the IFC to avoid transactions where private sector lenders were prepared to manage the deal is one good example. Business associations have also been influential in pushing the World Bank to move toward greater reliance on financial guarantees as compared to direct loans. Guarantees have the advantage of allowing the World Bank to stretch its resources further while relying on more experienced judgments of market participants about the viability of projects. Unfortunately, World Bank requirements that host country governments provide offsetting guarantees and that guarantees to the private firm must count against the Bank's lending limit to that country have served to limit the use of guarantees up until now.

Other industry interventions with the global financial institutions have met with failure. For example, over the years, bankers groups have made forceful arguments that the IMF should not lend to countries that are in arrears with respect to their commercial debt. Historically, the IMF respected the position of commercial bankers and pressed governments to resolve their differences with commercial lenders as a precondition for IMF support. However, in some cases, when the Fund felt that commercial lenders were at fault, it threatened to lend – and in a few instances actually did lend – into arrears. This issue continues to divide banking associations from the IMF. In September 1999, executives of the Institute of International Finance complained that actions and statements by IMF and other officials were designed to force banks to provide new financing or rescheduling in Ecuador, Pakistan, Romania and Ukraine.

Some might argue that business has had deleterious effects on global financial governance. Business associations have clearly resisted efforts by other civil society groups to democratize multilateral institutions, sometimes in tacit collusion with the institutions themselves. For years, the IMF and the World Bank paid no more than lip service to new mandates that required the involvement of civil society groups. However, from the late 1980s, the World Bank and later the IMF began more sincere efforts to involve other stakeholders.

For some, important equity issues are posed by the fact that "control" of finance remains in the hands of business. A strong anti-industry, anti-profit, anti-creditor bias underlies a substantial amount of the opposition to multilateral organizations on the streets of Seattle, Washington and Prague. Lenders have faced such prejudices since Biblical times. Manufacturers have faced them since the dawn of the industrial revolution. Control is unlikely to change.

A look to the future

Over the years, business associations have helped to shape policies in global financial governance and make it more efficient. With all their weaknesses and with the stark economic inequities that remain in much of the world, the multilateral financial institutions have nevertheless helped to lead the world to a period of unprecedented growth and increasing prosperity. Much more needs to be done, of course, and the system remains very much stacked in favor of business, which retains more influence than other stakeholders. Yet, if current trends continue, business will gradually lose this advantage. In the meantime, it is well to consider that there need not be a contradiction between, on the one hand, principles of profit maximization and free trade and finance flows and, on the other, increasing the welfare of people and countries at the bottom of the economic ladder.

Business associations are awakening to the fact that the future of global financial institutions can no longer be taken for granted. Other politically influential stakeholders are demanding their rightful place at the table. Multilateral institutions are addressing long-ignored problems like moral hazard. Street activists and some governments are openly calling for restrictions on capital that were once considered taboo.

The Seattle WTO demonstrations were an epiphany for business. The demonstrators rejected the notion that everyone benefits from globalization. Governments were overwhelmed and unable to make the case effectively for globalization. The US President undercut his own position and the chances for progress by publicly empathizing with protestors. When Bill Clinton hinted that he might block imports from countries that ignored workers' rights, and developing countries saw that they might have more to lose than gain, the WTO talks collapsed. Business was caught flat-footed and was powerless to change the outcome.

In the aftermath of Seattle, business has concluded that it must both engage the critics and conduct much closer oversight of the institutions that govern the international financial system. It is likely that new business organizations and mechanisms will be needed. Some may involve cooperative efforts between business, labor, environmentalists, human rights advocates, and others. Democracy in global financial governance will increase as a result, but business associations will serve to moderate the pace of change and attempt to control its direction and minimize its disruptive impact.

Notes

1 *Report of the Working Group on Financial Crises in Emerging Market Economies*, Washington, DC: Institute of International Finance, 1999.
2 *Capital Flows to Emerging Market Economies*, Washington, DC: Institute of International Finance, 2000.
3 "Fact Sheets Supporting IMF Quota Legislation", unpublished papers of the United States Chamber of Commerce, 1999.
4 See www.brettonwoods.org; *Bretton Woods: Looking to the Future, Report of the Bretton Woods Commission*, Washington, DC: Bretton Woods Committee, 1994; *Private Sector Financing for the IMF: Now Part of an Optimal Funding Mix*, Washington, DC: Bretton Woods Committee, 1999.
5 *Capital Flows to Emerging Market Economies*.
6 http://www.iif.com.
7 *In Search of a Stable Currency System in the 21st Century*, Tokyo: Institute of International Monetary Affairs, 2000. See also http://www.iima.or.jp.

8   http://www.iccwbo.org/.
9   For information on such organizations see the websites of the American Chamber of Commerce in Russia (http://www.amcham.ru/) and the US–Russia Business Council (http://www.usrbc.org/).
10 http://www.ia-usa.org/k0032.htm.
11 *Convention on Combating Bribery of Foreign Public Officials in International Business Transactions*, Paris: Organization for Economic Cooperation and Development, 1997.
12 *Bretton Woods: Looking to the Future.*
13 Frederik Galtung, "A Global Network to Curb Corruption: The Experience of Transparency International", in Ann M. Florini (ed.), *The Third Force: The Rise of Transnational Civil Society*, Washington, DC: Carnegie Endowment for International Peace, 2000, pp. 17–47.

13 The environmental movement and global finance

Andrea Durbin and Carol Welch

Summary	
• Introduction	213
• A history of engagement	215
• Accomplishments	221
• Challenges for the future	223
• Conclusion	226

Introduction

While global financial issues may seem tangential to environmental problems, the past twenty years have taught environmental organizations that the global economy has enormous implications for environmental protection. Environmentalists have long understood the impact that international financial institutions (IFIs) like the World Bank and the International Monetary Fund (IMF) have on the protection of natural resources and biodiversity. But recent events, such as the Asian financial crisis in the late 1990s, have clearly shown that financial volatility can also negatively affect the environment. Environmentalists have learned that, in order effectively to safeguard biodiversity and ecosystems, they must also develop a keen grasp of financial phenomena like currency speculation, capital controls and short-term investments in bonds and equities. The Asian financial crisis unleashed a vigorous debate about how the global economy is run, and how the global financial architecture – or rules governing the global financial system – affects people and the environment. As a result, civil society groups, including environmental groups, have a growing awareness that addressing global economic and financial issues is crucial for achieving sustainable development.

Instability in the financial sector makes it very difficult to develop and adhere to sustainable development plans. Financial volatility, as evidenced in Asia as well as Latin America and Russia, also leads to serious economic and social stress. This threatens environmental protection measures by diminishing the relative importance and capacity of government environmental programs, and by increasing the number of poor people who depend on increasingly stressed natural resources to maintain a basic livelihood. For example, the Asian financial crisis in 1997 led the Thai government to abandon the national sustainable development plan that it had just launched. Indonesia and Russia, two countries with vast tracts of forests and unique biodiversity, implemented plans to increase exports of forest products after the financial crisis struck those countries in 1998. The demands of meeting creditor obligations and getting national accounts in order after financial crises were major factors driving these decisions.[1]

Environmentalists are still learning the links between finance and the environment and are developing increasingly sophisticated environmental protection efforts that analyze and address global economic issues. The environmental community has a longer history of targeting individual financial institutions such as the World Bank, the IMF and regional development banks like the Asian Development Bank or the Inter-American Development Bank. Environmentalists are now also working to reform private financial institutions and the overall global financial architecture.

The World Bank and the IMF have historically played an important role in setting the stage for private investment. Their structural adjustment loans promote policies that favor private-sector interests and produce severe human and environmental costs.[2] Similarly, project loans from the World Bank have resulted in environmental degradation when they have underwritten large dams, roads through forests, or oil extraction.[3] Owing to these impacts, and because the IFIs are government-owned agencies, environmental groups have targeted the World Bank and the IMF for almost twenty years.

However, the dynamics of the global economy are changing. Private capital flows may now have an even larger impact on sustainable development than the IFIs. Private financial flows from the industrialized countries to the developing world have dramatically increased during the past decade, from \$42 billion in 1990 to a peak of \$256 billion in 1997.[4] This change in the global economy has forced the environmental movement to confront the challenge of influencing private capital flows directly, as well as through official actors like the World Bank and the IMF.

The first part of this chapter charts a history of how the environmental community has tackled global economic and financial issues. The story begins in the early 1980s with the start of the campaign to reform the World Bank. In the late 1980s, environmental advocacy efforts expanded to target the IMF, whose economic policy loans can encourage unsustainable development. Since the mid-1990s environmental NGOs in the United States and then Europe have begun to pursue campaigns on the private financial sector as well.

The second part of the chapter analyzes the impacts that the environmental movement has had on global finance, including why some of these successes occurred and what lessons can be learned for the future. The third part lays out some of the new challenges that the ever-changing global economy presents for environmentalists. The chapter concludes with recommendations for mechanisms that would allow both civil society and governments to discuss the environmental and social impacts of global finance.

A history of engagement

The global environmental movement has multiplied and strengthened in the last twenty years.[5] Many pressing environmental problems know no boundaries, such as forest and biodiversity losses, depletion of the ozone layer, global climate change and pollution of transboundary waters. In response, national environmental organizations have increasingly cooperated with each other, building a global environmental movement. An example is Friends of the Earth International. Founded in 1971 with groups in four countries, it now operates in sixty-eight countries around the world.[6]

Environmental organizations address diverse issues, ranging from species protection to land conservation, from toxic pollution to investment in mass transportation. Many environmental organizations work to reform financial and economic systems, which they see as the underlying causes of environmental degradation. These groups include Friends of the Earth International, the Environmental Defense Fund (US), Urgewald (Germany), the World Wildlife Fund, and the Center for International Environmental Law (US).

In terms of goals, environmental groups aim to make IFIs more transparent and democratic. These institutions should support environmental sustainability, recognizing and mitigating the negative environmental aspects of global financial activities. Global financial regulations should promote more stability, equity and fairness. More recently, environmental groups have shifted their attention to the introduction of environmental management systems and standards into the private-sector side of financial investment. The ultimate goal of all these efforts is to establish global economic and financial rules and practices that promote environmentally sustainable development around the world.

The Bretton Woods institutions

Environmental groups were first drawn to global financial issues in the early 1980s, when stories about deforestation in the Amazon became front-page news. The destruction caused by slash-and-burn agriculture presented a global crisis. Environmentalists were shocked to learn that the World Bank was actually underwriting this problem through a controversial road project in Brazil called Polonoroeste. The Bank was financing the construction of BR–364, a national highway that would connect the populous southern central region of Brazil with the more remote, rainforested region in the northwest. The objective was to encourage migration to the rainforested areas. These areas were home to more than forty indigenous groups, many of whom had had no previous contact with the outside world. Polonoroeste led to more migration than originally anticipated – nearly half a million people between 1981 and 1986.[7] The result was increased degradation of one of the world's greatest forest areas.

Large dam projects such as India's Sardar Sarovar Dam (Narmada) also mobilized international resistance by environmentalists, led by Southern NGOs such as the Narmada Bachao Andolan movement.[8] These campaigns helped paint a

picture for the public in the United States and Europe about the impacts of World
Bank-financed projects in the developing world. In 1983, three environmental
NGOs working in Washington, DC – Friends of the Earth, the Sierra Club and the
National Wildlife Federation – came together on these issues. They lobbied the US
Treasury Department and the US Congress to secure environmental reforms of
the Bank. The campaign launch coincided with two days of Congressional over-
sight hearings. Environmental groups in other countries, including Germany,
Sweden, the Netherlands and Australia, also established campaigns on the World
Bank and began to lobby their government officials. For the first time, the
Executive Board of the World Bank began to hear from NGOs about environ-
mental and social problems associated with proposed projects.

Since the early 1980s, environmental groups and other NGOs have worked to
make the World Bank more democratic, transparent and inclusive of civil society.
These institutional reforms are crucial to change the nature of the Bank's development assistance. The network of NGOs that monitor World Bank-financed
projects has spread across the globe since 1983 and has spawned parallel networks
that monitor the regional development banks. For example, the Asian NGO
Working Group tracks the Asian Development Bank, and Red-Bancos tracks the
Inter-American Development Bank. When the World Bank or a regional development bank considers financing a controversial project with serious environmental
impacts, these networks can be activated quickly to lobby Executive Directors
from donor and borrowing governments alike.

Environmental groups have also scrutinized the World Bank's sister institution, the IMF, for its failure to address the environmental impact of its loans.
Different from the World Bank, the IMF addresses macroeconomic issues, including stabilization of currencies and balance-of-payment problems of its 183
member states. The IMF also lends money to many of its poorer member countries and helps catalyze larger financing packages with other actors. These
structural adjustment loans are designed to alter a government's economic policies
by measures such as reducing spending and consumption and encouraging more
liberalization of trade, investment and finance. Such policies often harm the environment and the poor.[9]

NGOs began to pay attention to the IMF largely as a result of changes in the
global economy, particularly the onset of the debt crisis in developing countries.
Mexico's external debt default in 1982 and the ensuing debt crisis highlighted the
problem of debt in poor countries for NGOs. It also provided a highly visible
example of how global financial issues and policies can harm the poor and the
environment through measures like drastic reductions in social service expenditures
and increased exports of natural resource-based products.[10] The debt crisis also
expanded the activities of the IMF and the World Bank. They stepped in with
loans on more favorable (concessional) terms, but demanded strict debt repayment
schedules and dramatic changes in countries' economies, including budget cuts,
devaluation, and liberalization of international trade, investment, and eventually
finance. NGOs began more closely to monitor the IMF after it obtained a structural adjustment facility in 1986.

Since then, environmental groups like Friends of the Earth have struggled to change the institutional culture of the IMF so that civil society would have a voice in its economic policy prescriptions. This practice would reduce the negative consequences of Fund-sponsored economic reforms. In 1989, the US Congress for the first time passed IMF reform legislation. It required the US Executive Director at the Fund to promote transparency and accountability measures, including public access to information about IMF loans and the creation of an independent appraisal unit. US environmental groups like Friends of the Earth, the Sierra Club and the Environmental Defense Fund lobbied members of Congress to demand important reforms of the IMF. The passage of this legislation, together with subsequent reform clauses in 1992 and 1994, helped to shape the US government's position within the IMF and notified the Fund that it was being watched and would face greater challenges if it continued to block reform efforts.

The debt crisis

While the environmental community has pioneered and dominated the debate about World Bank reform, faith-based groups have led the effort to address problems with structural adjustment lending. These religious actors include the Maryknoll and Columban orders as well as social justice networks and offices of Catholic and Protestant churches. The environmental community has played an important complementary role in questioning the economic model that guides structural adjustment, particularly the viability of a growth strategy based on unsustainable exploitation and export of natural resources.

Some environmental organizations have also explored innovative financing schemes as a way to resolve debt problems while simultaneously protecting the environment. Conservation organizations like the World Wildlife Fund, the Nature Conservancy, and Conservation International have advocated "debt-for-nature swaps" as a way to mobilize financial resources for environmental protection. The US government embraced the concept in 1991 when it passed the Enterprise for the Americas Initiative, which provided debt relief for Latin American states that agreed to use the financial resources to set aside land for conservation purposes. Conservation organizations continue to promote debt-for-nature swaps, both on a governmental level and with their own funds.

Emerging market crises

The financial crises of the 1990s, beginning in Mexico in 1994 and continuing in Asia in 1997–98, deepened NGO concerns about a deregulated global economy. The crises provided vivid examples of how unfettered financial flows can profoundly affect societies and the environment. Unemployment rates went up, families lost their savings, and forests were burned to make way for export crops. For example, the Thai government cut its environmental budget by 40 per cent and had to slash its pollution control budget by 80 per cent.[11] The Indonesian government had to suspend all environmental programs in Jakarta – one of the world's most polluted cities – because of crisis-induced budget cuts.[12] The social and environmental ramifications of the financial crisis impressed upon NGOs the importance of advocating global economic rules that regulate financial flows and reduce volatile short-term capital flows.

After the Asian financial crisis, some environment and development organizations entered a new debate on the global financial architecture. The financial crisis made it undeniably clear to NGOs and others how finance and the rules (or lack thereof) governing financial flows can deeply affect communities' well-being. The financial crisis brought new attention to the global financial system and also exposed cracks in the so-called "Washington Consensus", the dominant view of free-market economic development.

In response, many NGOs have taken crash courses to learn about global financial flows. In the US and in the UK, informal working groups of economic justice, faith-based, environmental, and social justice groups have met to discuss various proposals related to new rules for the financial system. Organizations such as the International Forum on Globalization have developed alternative proposals to govern global finance and unveiled them at events in parallel to official meetings.[13] Still other NGOs such as Oxfam, the European Network on Debt and Development, and Friends of the Earth have met with Group of Seven (G7) governments and with the IMF to make recommendations about ways that global economic rules can be altered to provide more protection and stability. Many of these same groups, as well as Southern NGOs such as Focus on the Global South, also provided input into the Group of Twenty-Two (G22) working papers that were commissioned following the Asian financial crisis.[14] NGOs also criticized the conditions attached to the IMF's bailout agreements for individual countries during the financial crisis. For example, the Environmental Defense Fund critiqued many of the conditions in the Indonesian and Brazilian rescue packages, including incentives to increase natural resource extraction.[15] The debate over financial liberalization and capital flows is one of the newest areas for NGO activism.

Private finance

Environmental groups have begun to examine not only the rules of global finance, but also the actors that play according to and benefit from those rules.[16] In recognition of the growing importance of private investors and capital markets in determining the development paths of emerging market economies, NGOs have undertaken relatively new efforts aimed at educating private financiers and holding them accountable for the role that they play in (un)sustainable development.

According to the Institute of International Finance, private capital flows to the emerging markets of the developing world reached $153 billion in 2000, working their way back up after the financial crisis of 1998, which set private investment in the emerging markets plummeting to $139.1 billion, after reaching a peak of $269.4 billion in 1997.[17] While the IMF and bilateral creditors have offered major bailout packages to certain large emerging-market countries to cope with financial crises, the proportion of private relative to official flows to the developing world has generally increased. Private finance accounted for under 50 per cent of total capital flows to emerging markets in the early 1990s and rose to over 90 per cent by the end of the decade.[18] While private capital flows among the Northern countries are higher, the rise in North–South movements is of particular concern, since many of these countries lack social safety nets to help people cope with crisis, and since banking and financial regulatory standards are not as developed as in many Northern countries. Meanwhile, the amount of official development assistance has reached an all-time low. The result is that private capital and private actors wield more influence on development and the potential for achieving sustainable development than in the past.

Environmental groups face formidable challenges in shifting their advocacy focus to include private financial actors and private capital flows. Compared with public financial institutions, NGOs have fewer hooks and leverage points for trying to make private capital flows more sustainable. Private investors and companies do not have the poverty alleviation or sustainable development missions of the World Bank or the IMF. No binding international rules hold private companies accountable to communities or require them to protect the environment. Most private commercial banks and Wall Street investors do not evaluate new or existing investments for their environmental or social impacts.

In 1995, Friends of the Earth launched a program devoted to influencing private capital flows and harnessing the power and influence of financiers to promote more responsible corporate behavior. Today, other NGOs such as the National Wildlife Federation (US), EuroNatur (Germany), and the Rainforest Action Network (US) have also developed programs on private finance.[19] Many other NGOs utilize private financial advocacy tools to complement corporate or project campaigns. Such strategies include: (a) shareholder activism; (b) education of investors and financial analysts; (c) dialogues with private banks; and (d) public pressure campaigns.

Shareholder activism has been pioneered by investor groups such as the Interfaith Center for Corporate Responsibility (US), the Coalition for Environmentally Responsible Economies (US), and "socially responsible investors".[20] Shareholder activism strives to foster corporate change by relying on shareholders' power and access to company management. In the United States and most industrialized countries, shareholders have the right to introduce proposals that are voted upon by all investors. In well-governed companies, shareholders can work with management to improve corporate social performance. In the past few years, socially responsible investors, religious institutional investors and labor pension funds have been developing closer relationships with public-interest groups, and many are seeking to complement NGO efforts on issues such as sweatshops and genetically engineered agricultural products. These alliances are increasingly linking investors with social movements and allow concerned shareholders to act in solidarity with NGOs while improving shareholder value through sound management and good governance.

NGOs have also been working with other members of the financial community, such as investment analysts and credit-rating agencies, to translate social and environmental concerns into financial language. Some NGOs have offered financiers environmental, social and political data on companies or projects, in an attempt to provide a complete picture of investment risk. For example, activists working to halt the Three Gorges Dam in China have targeted underwriters and potential buyers of bonds to educate them on the technical and financial risks associated with the project. Similarly, NGOs such as the Rocky Mountain Institute and the World Resources Institute have worked directly with companies to capture the financial benefits of so-called "eco-efficiency". Bolstering these investor and company education efforts is a growing body of research that demonstrates the link between social and financial corporate performance,[21] as well as the competitive returns afforded by socially responsible mutual funds.[22] In these ways, NGOs have begun to persuade the private sector that social and environmental initiatives can provide financial benefit as well as meet society's growing expectations for responsible corporate behavior.

In addition, a handful of environmental organizations have worked with major investment banks as a way of leveraging environmental change. For example, Milieudefensie, a Netherlands-based NGO, has worked with ABN–AMRO Bank to develop environmental management systems as well as environmental and social guidelines to govern credit, investment and/or underwriting transactions. In some cases, NGOs are promoting the hard-won social and environmental policies of the World Bank as models for the private financial sector. Complementing this NGO activity is the Financial Services Initiative of the United Nations Environment Programme (UNEP), which has advanced environmental awareness and best practices among investment banks worldwide.[23] The UNEP initiative has urged financial institutions to sign a set of sustainability principles. It also encouraged insurance companies to lobby in support of the Kyoto Protocol in December 1997.

Finally, activists have applied pressure tactics that are common among corporate accountability and World Bank campaigns to financial services companies. These initiatives include paid newspaper advertisements, letter-writing efforts and even credit card boycotts to highlight financiers' support of environmentally and socially egregious companies and projects. Milieudefensie was able to access ABN–AMRO management by circulating a petition to 5,000 of its customers. The petition prompted the bank not only to demand an independent social and environmental audit from a controversial client, but also to consider new environmental mining guidelines. The International Rivers Network has sponsored a boycott of the Morgan Stanley Dean Witter Discover credit card, calling for a halt to that company's financing of the Three Gorges Dam and urging it to adopt environmental and social policies governing its transactions generally.

While environmental NGO advocacy in the private financial arena is relatively new, it has reflected and adapted many of the lessons, strategies, and demands from the World Bank and IMF campaigns. Many NGO demands on the private financial sector are similar to those pressed on the World Bank, the IMF, and corporations generally: that is, information disclosure, public participation, and integration of environmental and social concerns into core business operations.

Accomplishments

Over the past decade, environmental and other NGOs have clearly become more influential players in global finance. Even the mainstream press, including *The Economist* and the *Financial Times*, has acknowledged that NGOs and civil society in general have an important contribution to make in global economic matters. The effectiveness of the environmental community's efforts can be seen in some of the achievements that have been accomplished over the years.

The efforts of environmental groups to reform the World Bank resulted in the creation of an Environmental Department in 1989, the hiring of environmental specialists, and the creation of new environmental policies starting in 1991, including measures on environmental assessment, forests and energy. The World Bank has also established a new and unique accountability mechanism. The independent Inspection Panel, launched in 1994, provides local people affected by World Bank-financed projects with a mechanism to seek redress if they have suffered harm. The Inspection Panel sets a new model for accountability at international institutions by recognizing the rights of those most directly affected.[24] Similarly, the World Bank is more open and transparent today than it was a decade ago, with a substantial information disclosure policy in place.

Beyond the impact on the structure and organizational culture of the World Bank, environmental NGOs have also affected certain projects. These groups stopped the Bank from financing some projects, such as the Narmada Dam in India in 1994 and the Arun III Dam in Nepal in 1995.[25] Environmental NGOs have also provided inputs that led to substantive improvements in projects, such as with the Chad–Cameroon Oil Pipeline Project in Western Africa, which the World Bank approved in 2000.

However, environmental organizations have not yet achieved their fundamental goal: to redirect the entire loan portfolio of the World Bank toward environmentally and socially sustainable development. Too many projects financed by the Bank still cause deforestation, exacerbate environmental pollution, and threaten the global climate.

Furthermore, environmental groups have begun successfully to replicate these new policies in bilateral financial institutions, such as export credit agencies (ECAs). The government-owned ECAs support private-sector investment in the developing world, but until the last five years none of these bodies had environmental standards or procedures. Thanks to the efforts of the environmental movement, these agencies in the United States now have new policies in place. ECAs in other countries, including Canada, the UK, Australia and Germany, are in the process of setting standards. Environmental groups have even put this issue to the G7 Summit, where ministers in 1997 called on the OECD to establish international environmental standards for ECAs.[26]

Change at the IMF has come more slowly, but is becoming more evident. For example, in April 2000 the Fund finally agreed to establish an independent evaluation unit. The IMF is also more transparent than it was ten years ago and is starting to pay attention to the role of civil society. Environmental and development

NGOs are still pressing the IMF to seek inputs from civil society when it prepares loans and develops advice for a country. Civil society participation is incorporated in the Poverty Reduction Strategy Papers (PRSPs) that the Fund launched together with the World Bank in 1999.

It took long to convince the IMF that its policy prescriptions can have a negative impact on the poor and that it should take poverty concerns into account. This argument was not won until the Asian financial crisis highlighted the negative impact of IMF policies on the poor. At the same time, the first-ever external review of the IMF structural adjustment facility drew attention to social issues.[27]

While the IMF has finally admitted that its programs can adversely impact the poor, it has yet significantly to accept that they also impact the environment. The IMF has held two seminars, one in 1993 and one in 1995, on links between macro-economics and the environment.[28] It also has one staff person who has gathered and disseminated information on environmental issues as they are seen to relate to the IMF's work. However, the IMF has not employed systematic analytical tools in its loan programs to account for environmental impacts and concerns. Environmental groups thus continue to face an uphill battle to reform the institution.

The debt cancellation movement, particularly the Jubilee 2000 campaign, is one of the most notable successes of NGO campaigning on global finance. Efforts to cancel the debts of poor indebted countries started in the 1980s and brought some limited results. However, the impact increased after 1996, when the World Bank and the IMF announced plans to participate with creditor governments in a single debt relief program, the Heavily Indebted Poor Countries (HIPC) Initiative. NGOs criticized the policy as offering too little debt relief with too many conditions attached. Rejection of this much-vaunted scheme helped to unite diverse NGOs from around the world in a single, focused call for debt cancellation by the year 2000. The international Jubilee 2000 movement is largely faith-based, but also includes support from key environmental groups, including Friends of the Earth branches around the world. Environmental organizations have also promoted the concept of "ecological debt": the understanding that Northern countries have benefited from natural resources in the South for years and therefore a debt exists from the North to the South.[29]

There are many reasons why the Jubilee 2000 Campaign for debt relief has made an impact. Its message is a simple one that has widespread appeal. Since debt impacts so many sectors, including health, education, labor, and the environment, many organizations and constituents have supported the call for relief. For the environmental community, the campaign has provided an opportunity to highlight the links between high debt burdens and environmental degradation, such as unsustainable levels of logging, fishing and mining in order to service debts. Channeling the various links to the overarching issue of debt has brought different constituencies together and created a large, focused, and powerful political force that has forced new commitments and action on the problem of debt.

In the new field of private finance advocacy, NGO achievements have been modest but promising. Investment banks previously considered environmental responsibility to be an obligation for the resource extraction and manufacturing sectors, but now they increasingly recognize their own role and responsibility in sustainability.[30] In general, European financial institutions such as Union Bank of Switzerland have taken the lead in establishing environmental management systems and developing and disclosing environmental policies. Banks in the United States have generally been less attuned to environmental issues. Nevertheless, major investment houses like Citigroup, Merrill Lynch and Morgan Stanley Dean Witter have assembled high-level teams to examine how environmental issues could be integrated into core business areas. These groups have included heads of global investment banking, heads of credit policy, general counsels and other senior staff. Major banks like BankAmerica have responded to NGO calls for transparency by developing annual reports on environmental performance. Although these measures move in the right direction, NGOs will continue to judge banks' commitment to corporate responsibility by the environmental impacts of their portfolios, and very little progress has been made in this respect.

Another sign of progress is that the financial rewards and public expectations of responsible corporate performance have started to manifest themselves through small savers and the financial community itself. The popularity of socially responsible investment (SRI) is increasing dramatically worldwide. In the United States, one out of every eight dollars under professional management is invested with some kind of non-financial screen or activism component, and SRI represents the fastest-growing type of investment generally.[31] New financial research providers such as Innovest Strategic Value Advisors have been created to supply investors with corporate environmental information. In the UK, a recent law requires all private-sector pension funds to disclose what, if any, ethical policy they follow.[32] This measure reflects growing concern among pension fund beneficiaries about the ethical impact of their managed investments.

Finally, NGOs have demonstrated their ability to influence capital markets. A handful of US investment banks, credit-rating agencies and financial analysts have proactively consulted with NGOs to obtain information on controversial companies, projects, and issues, a sign that Wall Street has started to recognize the value of environmental performance. In late 1999 and early 2000 a broad alliance of labor unions, environmentalists, human rights groups and others mounted a successful campaign against the initial public offering (IPO) on the New York Stock Exchange of PetroChina, a Chinese state-controlled oil company. Through intense investor education, press work, and an innovative "alternative road show" hosted by the American union federation AFL–CIO, public-interest organizations exposed the financial risks associated with PetroChina and urged investors to boycott the IPO. Once expected to raise $10 billion, the offering ultimately brought in only $2.89 billion. Although NGOs exerted significance in this case, it will remain the exception rather than the rule until capital markets develop ways to integrate, analyze and reward or punish corporate social behavior.

Challenges for the future

The growth of global financial flows presents a major future challenge for environmental groups and other NGOs that are concerned about global justice and sustainable societies. Until recently, environmental groups and other NGOs have focused their advocacy efforts largely on official multilateral institutions and the governments that are shareholders in these institutions. The reasons to focus on bodies like the World Bank and the IMF were simple. Official finance accounted for the larger portion of capital movements to developing countries. Official agencies had (and have) a catalytic role in mobilizing other financial flows. And the IFIs are accountable to governments and, therefore, to citizens.

Yet the impact of financial flows on the environment is complex. In some cases, capital movements to countries or sectors with lax environmental regulations may result in environmental pollution or unsustainable use of natural resources. In other cases, investment flows can bring environmentally advanced technologies to the developing world. This complex relationship can make it more difficult to develop solutions for guiding private capital flows toward sustainability.

Another challenge is to address the problems associated with short-term, more volatile financial flows. It is widely supposed that these flows (as opposed to long-term investments in, say, the timber or oil industries) have little connection with the environment. Yet the links exist and can profoundly affect environmental quality and the future for sustainable development. In the Asian crisis, when investors pulled out billions of dollars in short-term investments, the economies of the region were put under enormous pressure and made drastic changes in response. Currency values crashed, central bank reserves dwindled, interest rates soared, and government spending came under intense pressure. The financial crisis put millions of people in poverty and heightened pressures on the environment. The Asian crisis has brought better understanding of the connections between volatile financial flows, poverty and environmental degradation. However, a significant gulf persists between recognition of the problem and the implementation of effective corrective responses.

The growing but still modest numbers of NGOs that seek to reform global finance face further challenges owing to the nature of the private financial community itself. Capital markets are huge and decentralized, and current and pending investments are largely confidential. These conditions present formidable challenges for NGO research, analysis, and advocacy. The drive for profit, competition, fiduciary responsibility and a focus on short-term earnings often thwart NGO efforts to prioritize investments in sustainability. Likewise, critical social investments in electricity and health care for the poor may be foregone in favor of more lucrative opportunities. In these circumstances, NGOs have debated whether the financial system can resolve the tension between investments that provide capital and investments that promote labor, community, and sustainability.

Despite these challenges, civil society has many opportunities for advocacy and innovation in global finance, *inter alia* in the debate on the global financial architecture. The dynamics of this debate are similar to those regarding debt cancellation. Prior to the global movement for debt cancellation, finance ministries in the rich countries refused to acknowledge the depths of the debt crisis and the human suffering that it caused. Solutions were piecemeal approaches that barely dented the debt burdens suffered by poor countries. Similarly, official discussions on the global financial architecture have thus far been modest in scope, and current proposals are unlikely to solve the problem of volatile capital. NGO interventions may push the debate forward.

The success of advocacy efforts and constituency building on global financial issues will depend on how well environmentalists and other civil society groups engage, educate, and motivate grassroots supporters and activists. NGOs must present financial flows in a straightforward conceptual framework. Project campaigning at the World Bank has been successful in part because the "victim" can be readily seen and understood: a river being dammed; local people being forcibly removed; a forest being cleared. Seeing a clear victim motivates people to take action.

However, global finance does not always have clear victims. Moreover, financial flows can be both positive and negative, depending on their size, stability and purpose. This complexity makes it difficult for advocacy groups to present financial issues in a clear, understandable, and engaging way. This challenge is one of the most important tasks for the future.

In regard to the capital markets, NGOs must continue to press the private sector to integrate environmental and social issues into financial analysis and decisions. NGOs can help to ensure that the ethical values of small savers are reflected in the decisions of their money managers.

Environmentalists and civil society in general must seize the opportunity of the debate on the global financial architecture. Deliberations about financial rules should be more transparent, with detailed accounts of IFI activities in this area. Likewise, the G7 and the Group of Twenty (G20) must be more transparent about their discussions. They should release background papers for meetings, hold consultations and briefings, and disseminate more detail about their deliberations. Governments should also consider the establishment of advisory bodies that could be comprised of NGOs, the private sector and academics to gain greater breadth of perspectives in the policy-making process.

In addition, developing countries need to have a greater seat at the table to assess financial flows and regulations. This discussion has been dominated by the so-called "systemically significant" countries. For example, South Africa has been the only African country in the G22 and the G20. Debates about the international financial architecture should occur in a transparent, credible forum that is inclusive of all countries.

This power imbalance between North and South must be rectified if financial flows that promote sound economic development, poverty alleviation, and environmental sustainability are to be encouraged. For instance, the IMF and the World Bank must have a more democratic governing structure that weighs the interests of borrowing countries equally with those of creditor countries. As a more inclusive body, the United Nations should have a greater role in debates about global financial architecture. Some of its agencies, such as UNCTAD, have also developed reasoned critiques of the existing financial architecture and proposed alternatives. Currently, the UN is attempting to establish a forum, through its Financing for Development initiative, that would allow all interested parties to participate.

Conclusion

Events of the last decade have shown that there are substantial connections between global finance and environmental protection. The challenge of the next decade is to develop ways to balance financial and economic policies with environmental stewardship. This challenge faces the IMF, the multilateral development banks, private financial institutions, and the overall global financial architecture.

The forum where these discussions take place is important. The forthcoming UN Financing for Development Conference provides the right kind of venue. It has an appropriate agenda, addressing finance, the role of the IFIs, debt, investment, and trade rules. The meeting is also geared toward participatory dialogue, offering opportunities for involvement to all countries. If the political will is there, governments can use the meeting to seek solutions and respond to some of the criticisms and concerns about unregulated globalization.

Environmental groups like Friends of the Earth want governments to use this meeting to launch new negotiations for a binding corporate code of conduct that would be a prerequisite for any future agreement on investment liberalization. The Financing for Development initiative should also promote new rules to reduce short-term capital flows and new mechanisms to hold the private sector accountable for damages in the event of a financial crisis. Financing for Development can contribute to a greener approach to globalization and the construction of sustainable societies.

Notes

1 "Preparing for the Landing of Chinese Lumberjacks," *Vladivostok*, 26 February 1999; Bruce Gilley, "Sticker Shock", *Far Eastern Economic Review*, 14 January 1999.
2 Cf. Wilfrido Cruz and Robert Repetto, *The Environmental Effects of Stabilization and Structural Adjustment Programs: The Philippines Case*, Washington, DC: World Resources Institute, 1992; David Reed (ed.), *Structural Adjustment and the Environment*, Boulder, CO: Westview, 1992; Reed (ed.), *Structural Adjustment, the Environment and Sustainable Development*, London: Earthscan, 1996; J.J. Kessler *et al.*, *Structural Adjustment and Natural Resources: The Life Support System under Pressure*, Amsterdam/Gland: AIDEnvironment/WWF–International, 1996.
3 Cf. Bruce Rich, *Mortgaging the Earth: The World Bank, Environmental Impoverishment, and the Crisis of Development*, Boston: Beacon Press, 1994.
4 World Bank figures cited in Hilary French, "Capital Flows and the Environment", *Foreign Policy in Focus*, Vol. 3, No. 22, August 1998.
5 Cf. Thomas Princen and Mattias Finger (eds), *Environmental NGOs in World Politics: Linking the Global and the Local*, London: Routledge, 1994; Ken Conca *et al.* (eds), *Green Planet Blues: Environmental Politics from Stockholm to Rio*, Boulder, CO: Westview, 1995; Paul Wapner, *Environmental Activism and World Civic Politics*, New York: State University of New York Press, 1996.
6 <http://www.foei.org>.
7 Rich, op. cit. p. 27.
8 Jai Sen, "A World to Win – But Whose World Is It, Anyway? Civil Society and the World Bank, The View from the 'Front': Case Studies", in John W. Foster with Anita Anand (eds), *Whose World Is It Anyway? Civil Society, the United Nations and the Multilateral Future*, Ottawa: United Nations Association in Canada, 1999, pp. 337–89.

9 Cf. literature cited in note 2.

10 Cf. Susan George, *A Fate Worse than Debt: The World Financial Crisis and the Poor*, New York: Grove Weidenfeld, 1990; and Bade Onimode (ed.), *The IMF, the World Bank, and the African Debt: The Social and Political Impact*, London: Zed Books, 1989, 2 vols.

11 "The IMF: Selling the Environment Short", unpublished report, Friends of the Earth, March 2000, p. 7.

12 Ibid, p. 8.

13 "Alternatives to Globalization", preliminary report, available at <www.ifg.org/pubs>.

14 The G22 papers can be found at <http://www.ustreas.gov/press/releases/docs/g22-wg1.htm>; <http://www.ustreas.gov/press/releases/docs/g22–wg2.htm>; and http://www.ustreas.gov/press/releases/docs/g22-wg3.htm.

15 See <http://www.environmentaldefense.org/programs/International/>.

16 John Ganzi, Frances Seymour and Sandy Buffett, with Navroz K. Dubash, *Leverage for the Environment: A Guide to the Private Financial Services Industry*, Washington, DC: World Resources Institute, 1998.

17 Institute of International Finance, *Capital Flows to Emerging Market Economies*, January 2001.

18 World Bank, *Global Development Finance*, Vol. 1, 1997, p. 3; and Institute of International Finance, *Capital Flows to Emerging Market Economies*.

19 See, for example, <http://www.nwf.org/finance> and <http://www.floodwallstreet.org>.

20 See, for example, <http://www.iccr.org>; <http://www.ceres.org>; and <http://www.socialfunds.com>.

21 See, for example, <http://www.sristudies.org>

22 "Fund Performance Update: Socially Responsible Funds Continue to Get Top Marks in 2000", news release by the Social Investment Forum, 26 July 2000.

23 See <http://www.unep.ch/etu/fi/index.htm>.

24 "A Citizen's Guide to the World Bank Inspection Panel, Second Edition", Center for International Environmental Law, available at <http://www.ciel.org/ifi>.

25 Sen, op cit.

26 Communiqué of the G8 Heads, Denver Summit, June 1997.

27 *External Evaluation of the ESAF: Report by a Group of Independent Experts*, Washington, DC: International Monetary Fund, 1998.

28 The proceedings from the 1995 seminar were published in Ved Gandhi (ed.), *Macroeconomics and the Environment*, Washington, DC: International Monetary Fund, 1996.

29 See, for example, J. Martinez-Alier, "Ecological Debt vs. External Debt", unpublished paper available from the author at the Universitat Autonoma de Barcelona.

30 Cf. Jan Jaap Bouma, Marcel Jeucken and Leon Klinkers (eds), *Sustainable Banking: The Greening of Finance*, Sheffield: Greenleaf/Deloitte & Touche, 2001.

31 *1999 Report on Socially Responsible Investing Trends in the United States*, Social Investment Forum, 1999.

32 1995 Pensions Act, section 35.

14 Global finance and gender

Irene van Staveren[1]

Summary

• Introduction	228
• What is the gender problem in global finance?	229
• The women's movement and global finance	236
• Conclusions and proposals	241

Introduction

This chapter analyzes gender dimensions of global finance that underlie the involvement of the women's movement with financial markets and financial policies. These gender dimensions occur at all levels: the micro level (including the intra-household level); the meso level (industry, banking, government institutions, taxation); and the macro level (nationally as well as globally).

With globalization, the micro, meso and macro levels of finance have become more and more interrelated. For example, credits to developing countries from the International Monetary Fund (IMF) and the World Bank add to the domestic supply of money, leading to increased government consumption and investment and/or reduced foreign-exchange shortages. Bilateral development co-operation and World Bank lending often support domestic credit institutions and programs in developing countries. In this way the 8–10 million households that borrow from micro-credit programs are indirectly dependent on global sources of finance.[2] Meanwhile, remittances from migrant workers form a substantial source of foreign exchange in countries like the Philippines and Bangladesh.

Adopting this understanding of global finance as a tightly woven web of macro, meso and micro conditions, this chapter examines how global finance influences, and is influenced by, the differentiated economic positions of women and men. Such gender analysis of finance is a new field of study. Therefore, my contribution here should be taken as only preliminary. It does not claim to cover all possible intersections between finance and gender.

Within this limitation, the chapter discusses four gender biases of global finance:

(1) the under-representation of women in financial decision-making; (2) increased gender gaps in the economic positions of women and men; (3) the gender-based instability of financial markets; and (4) inefficient resource allocation in financial markets due to gender discrimination. The chapter then describes the globalization of the women's movement and its attention to problems of global finance. Finally, the chapter presents some policy recommendations for a more gender-balanced global financial system and suggests what role the women's movement can play in changing the orientation of financial markets and governance.

What is the gender problem in global finance?

As seen throughout this book, civil society has protested against negative effects of global finance in terms of democratic deficits, inequities, instabilities and inefficiencies. The women's movement has added particular concerns about the gender biases that have generally made these negative impacts worse for women relative to men. Gender biases in markets and governance tend to grow as the scale of markets and economic policies increases. For example, although the globalization of finance has reduced many barriers to obtain credit and to invest, female entrepreneurs remain marginalized in many respects.

Very little research has been done on the gendered effects of global finance; therefore conclusions about the gendered effects of global finance should be taken with necessary caution. Only a few studies have addressed the gendered impacts of globalization in general.[3] Other investigations have focused on the gendered impacts of global trade, particularly in cash crops and in manufacturing goods.[4] However, these studies have paid only marginal and largely implicit attention to finance.

A recent special issue of *World Development* includes three articles that deal with gender and global finance.[5] A special issue of *Feminist Economics* on globalization also contains an article on global finance and gender.[6] Each of these studies indicates that, on the whole, the gender effects of global finance are not very positive. Data, case studies, and theoretical analysis together suggest four types of relationships between gender and global finance: namely, that women are under-represented in global finance; that global finance increases gender gaps; that prevailing gender structures encourage instability in global financial markets; and that gender discrimination leads to inefficient resource allocations in global financial markets. The following pages elaborate on each of these four points in turn.

Undemocratic: under-representation of women

Women are hardly represented among the main decision-makers in financial markets and institutions. This tends to marginalize women's issues in policy processes regarding government lending, investment rules, and private-sector financial activities. The Boards of the World Bank and the IMF are strongly dominated by men. In the World Bank, less than 10 per cent of the Executive Directors and senior officers are female.[7] The World Trade Organization is an almost exclusively male forum. Likewise, G7 decision-making can hardly be regarded as democratic (see Birdsall in this volume) and certainly not as gender balanced. In the private sector, corporate decisions on finance are taken in boardrooms that are largely male domains.

The consequences of these decisions are borne by both women and men as producers, consumers, borrowers, employees, taxpayers, users of public services, and home and community-care providers. However, research indicates that, on the whole, the negative effects on women are greater than on men.

For example, austerity measures connected with IMF/World Bank-supported structural adjustment programs (SAPs) tend to fall more heavily on women. In most households, women are responsible for maintaining consumption levels, a task that becomes more difficult with SAP measures like cost-recovery fees for health care and education, increased import prices for food and medicine after a currency devaluation, and the abolition of subsidies on basic goods and services.[8] Both the reduction and the privatization of public services affect women more than men, given women's lower incomes and attributed responsibilities in the household.[9] Finally, SAPs tend to substitute public services with home-provided services that often fall on the shoulders of women, such as the provision of health care, child care, education, and public utilities like energy, transport, and drinking water.[10]

Decisions on tax policy can also have gendered effects, although conclusive evidence is not yet available, as only a few studies have been done on this subject.[11] For example, in some developing countries like Nigeria, men have tax deductions for their children, even though the mother is responsible for most child-related expenditures. In addition, government revenue in developing countries often relies on value-added tax (VAT) rather than income tax. Since men generally earn higher incomes than women, income tax affects men more than it does women. However, men also have a higher capacity to pay, and tax allowances, tax evasion, and income from the informal sector can mean that little income tax is actually paid. In contrast to income tax, VAT cannot easily be circumvented. In countries where women are responsible for household consumption, women's incomes are taxed relatively more through VAT. Also, VAT affects men and women to the same degree, ignoring the differences in purchasing power that favor men.

Thus, macroeconomic policies and public finance have gender-biased impacts. Men dominate decision-making in global finance, but women experience the greatest negative effects of these decisions.[12] A more equal representation of men and women in the boards of international financial institutions, national financial bodies, and financial corporations would make policy more democratic from a gender perspective. Greater gender equality in decision-making on financial governance would better represent the interests of both men and women. This could prevent the large opportunity costs that women currently experience in global finance.

However, gender inequalities and interests are not necessarily the same for elite women and poor women. So, representation of women on the boards of financial institutions is a necessary but not sufficient condition for gender-aware decision-making. Policy formulation should also take account of the views of poor women as stakeholders in the realm of finance, for example, by consulting women's NGOs and women's credit institutions. Only then would more gender-balanced decision-making begin to impact positively on the distribution of effects of financial policies on men and women.

Inequitable: increased gender gaps

The globalization of finance has brought some advantages for women. First, it has increased competition, and hence the supply of credit, for diversified target groups. Through this process women have gained more access to credit, although not equally in the formal and informal sectors. Second, in some countries it has become easier for women to access foreign-exchange markets, for example, to receive remittances from partners or relatives abroad, or to send funds home to family. Third, the much-expanded financial sector in the contemporary economy has substantially increased opportunities for women's waged employment (albeit for the most part in lower-paid and less-protected jobs).[13]

However, these gains for women need to be balanced against losses. Like other markets, financial markets are characterized by segmentation, involving distortions and transaction costs.[14] Some authors even argue that financial markets suffer from deeper imperfections than other markets, in particular from asymmetric information, agency problems, and adverse selection.[15] Most texts on distortions in financial markets completely ignore the gender dimension. In one exceptional case, Sally Baden has distinguished a variety of gender-based distortions in credit markets.[16] These distortions are reflected in transaction costs on the supply side (credit institutions) as well as on the demand side (individual female borrowers as compared with male borrowers). These transaction costs limit the net gains from financial transactions for women and make financial services less accessible and more expensive for women (see Table 14.1, adapted from Baden).

These distortions are irrational. They are based on a gender ideology that assumes women to be less capable of economic success than men. Take, for example, the prejudice that "women are less able to make investments profitable". Just as gender biases in labor markets (masculine and feminine sectors and jobs) and land markets (absent or limited land property rights for women) disadvantage women, so too gender segmentation of financial markets creates disadvantages for women.

Apart from transaction costs, some gender distortions lead to costs that are part of the service itself, like administration costs rather than transaction costs that occur outside the exchange. Since women have less property and lower earnings, and since they are usually responsible for household livelihood, women tend to save smaller amounts as well as to save and borrow less regularly than men. Women, therefore, need greater flexibility in saving and credit. However, credit institutions are not always prepared to provide this flexibility because of the corresponding administration costs.

The effects mentioned above take place in formal credit markets as well as in informal borrowing, in small institutions as well as in large commercial banks,

Table 14.1 Gender-based distortions in financial markets

Type of gender-based distortion	Transaction costs for credit institution	Transaction costs for female borrowers
Information constraint	Women are perceived as risky, not creditworthy enough; information gathering might go through male intermediaries.	Women have lower literacy rates and are less mobile, which results in lower access to financial market information.
Negotiation constraint	Women have less experience in taking formal credit, therefore requiring more time from bank personnel.	Women may need husband's permission; have higher opportunity costs to travel to a bank; women may face discriminatory attitude by bank personnel.
Monitoring constraint	Women's economic activities may be more difficult to monitor, since they are often in different and smaller-scale sectors than men's activities that are financed through credit.	Women may find it difficult to control their loans in the household when other family members (particularly men) find it in their right to exercise control over this money.
Enforcement constraint	Women often lack formal property rights, which makes it difficult for creditors to claim collateral when a loan is not repaid.	Women may be more susceptible to pressure, intimidation, or violence from creditors or their agents.

and in credit as well as in saving. How do gender-based distortions in financial markets arise? The answer lies in the gendered institutions that operate in an economy.[17] In financial markets, the following three main structures of constraint can be identified: gender inequality in property rights; gender segmentation of financial markets; and discriminatory norms in financial markets.

Gender inequality in property rights

The almost universal norm of the male as breadwinner and head of household has benefited men's property rights.[18] Women's property rights are often assumed to be secured via the (male) household head. In some countries, inheritance laws allocate less property to female heirs than male heirs. Even when women have financial resources of their own, they often find it difficult to acquire property because of discriminatory rules and practices in, for example, the land market. In the case of joint property, women need the permission of their husbands to use these assets as collateral for obtaining credit, whereas men generally do not require such permission from their wives. Women's limited possession of property and their constrained property rights limit their access to financial markets.

The norm of male breadwinner and male household head also constrains women's control over financial resources within the household. When men regard all resources in the household as their possession, women may lose control over loans that they have taken in their own names or savings that they have accumulated from their own earnings. Men may use women's loans without repayment or use women's savings without paying interest or even paying back the amount. As a result, credit and saving may not improve women's financial situation and in some cases may even worsen it. Such results can depress demand for credit by women and also discourage savings by women.

Gender segmentation of financial markets

Financial markets exhibit gender segmentations. For instance, women tend to demand smaller loans than men. Most female creditors lend to women rather than to men. Most women borrowers obtain their credit from institutions that have special programs for women, or informally within women's groups.

Owing to the gendered transaction costs described in Table 14.1, credit institutions select borrowers on the basis of their gender. This restricts female borrowers to limited sources of credit, which drives up interest rates for women. Excess demand for credit induces lending institutions to use quantity rationing, rather than price rationing, to allocate capital.[19] This practice marginalizes women and women's activities (like home-based production) in their portfolios.[20] Thus women tend to borrow against higher interest rates and find it difficult to borrow for the type of activities that they prioritize.

Gender segmentation is also evident in regard to savings. Banks prefer savings accounts that are not very flexible in terms of the amount and regularity of deposits and withdrawals. However, women generally want such flexibility, because of their attributed responsibility for regular household provisioning. As a result, female savers tend to generate higher administration costs and are less attractive clients for financial institutions.

Discriminatory norms in financial markets

Although credit institutions tend to regard women as risky borrowers, the reality is different. In fact, women tend to have high repayment rates. Credit programs that lend exclusively or mainly to women show repayment levels of around 97 per cent, which is higher than many repayment rates of men.[21]

Credit institutions also often assume that women borrow for consumption without capacities to repay. Yet when women borrow for consumption purposes they are often addressing short-term liquidity problems that are solved by long-run cash flows that assure repayment.[22] Moreover, what seem to be consumer goods may, in fact, be capital investments that improve women's productivity in the care economy (think, for example, of refrigerators or washing machines).

Gendered institutions impact on financial markets at the macro level: through the savings rate, interest rate, and investments. Baden concludes that globalization of financial markets through liberalization has not substantially raised savings rates in developing countries. Gender discriminations of the kind described above have arguably made it still more difficult to build effective and efficient financial markets. Gender inequality contributes to low savings rates, low investment rates, and distorted interest rates.

Unstable: gender-based instability in financial markets

Gendered aspects of global finance extend beyond problems of democracy and equity to issues of stability as well. Ilene Grabel has identified five interrelated sources of risk that together generate global financial instability: currency risk, capital flight risk, fragility risk, contagion risk and sovereignty risk.[23]

Financial instability can never be abolished completely. Uncertainty is inherent in economic processes.[24] However, this does not mean that nothing can be done against excess instability. We can question the adequacy of the present institutional framework of national and international financial markets and reconsider the current practice of the IMF and the G7 as a continuous fire-fighting brigade.

From a gender perspective, such reconsideration is all the more urgent owing to the particularly adverse consequences of recent financial crises on women. As noted earlier, the austerity measures connected with SAPs tend to hit women doubly hard. In the prevailing gender division of labor, women are usually responsible for household food security, family health care, and the supply of household energy and safe drinking water. Thus cuts in government budgets concerning food subsidies, agricultural inputs, health services, and sanitation hurt women more than men. In addition, cuts in educational budgets do not help to reduce the school enrollment gap between boys and girls.[25]

A shift of the burden of financial risk to those who are not responsible for it is costly and unfair. This shift has a significant gender dimension. The generation of excessive financial risk is almost exclusively a male activity. Men are the main decision-makers in finance, men undertake the larger financial transactions, and men are the main speculators. Yet the persons who carry the consequences of global financial crises – especially in the care economy – are predominantly women. Research is incomplete, but various case studies suggest that women in the developing world experience significant increases in unpaid labor time during economic crises.[26]

So the (mainly female) care economy compensates for (mainly male) rent-seeking in financial markets. Regarding the Asian crisis, for example, Diane Elson and Nilufer Catagay remark: "Creditors were in effect 'bailed out' while poor women acted as unpaid provisioners of last resort."[27] This phenomenon is highly invisible and largely undocumented. Moreover, the shift of production and savings from the monetized to the care economy is hard to measure and often implicit. Case studies of such substitution effects indicate that women are sometimes required to give up their savings, including jewelry. They become more vulnerable to male violence at home and can even be drawn into paid and forced sex services.[28] For example, after the onset of the Asian crisis in 1997 the Korean government urged women to "Get Your Husband Energized",[29] even though 86 per cent of job losses in the banking and financial services sector were women's jobs.[30]

The buffer function of the care economy for financial market instability should not be overstretched. The resultant burden of extra work on women can generate a spiraling sequence of negative externalities that adversely affect real and financial markets. Such negative externalities include unattended small children, with consequent psychological and health risks. Human capital formation of children may decrease, particularly among girls who are required to do unpaid labor for the household. The quality of health care and hygiene declines when the family substitutes for private or public services. Such negative externalities are not only inequitable – disadvantaging women and the poor – but also inefficient, as the discussion below will show.

There are signs that the buffer function of the care economy in time of financial crisis is overshooting. Resources in the care economy are exhausted, with consequent reductions in the quality of care.[31] In addition, the recovery of the monetized economy from a financial crisis can be paralyzed. When non-monetized savings (through greater unpaid labor) increase more than investment, the monetized economy will suffer from a lack of effective demand.[32] When government services are cut too much, the quality of health care, education, and other services will suffer, with negative consequences for the level of human capital in the labor force, which will impact negatively on a country's productivity.[33] Finally, when a financial crisis leads women to shift resources from the market to the care economy – for example, through subsistence food production – market demand, and hence market production, will not be enough for recovery from that crisis.

In sum, then, while the care economy can function as a buffer against financial instability, a better institutional framework for financial markets and financial governance is needed to prevent crises and the associated risk of over-burdening the care economy.

Inefficient resource allocation in financial markets due to discrimination

In the experience of the Grameen Bank in Bangladesh, loans to women yield substantially higher household consumption than loans to men. In the case of women, it takes an average of $0.91 lent to generate $1 of household consumption, as compared with $1.48 for men.[34] The Grameen experience shows that lending to women is not less profitable than lending to men – on the contrary. Moreover, female repayment rates are higher. In 1991, 15.3 per cent of male borrowers from the Grameen Bank missed repayments, compared with only 1.3 per cent of female borrowers.[35] A similar record is found in lending to women elsewhere.[36]

Cost–benefit ratios of investing in women are even higher in respect of formal investment. A World Bank report entitled *Gender, Growth, and Poverty Reduction* estimates losses in real output that result from gender biases in investment. In Burkina Faso, for example, a transfer of resources (like fertilizer and labor) from men's to women's plots of land within the same household could increase agricultural output by 10 to 20 per cent.[37] Research in Tanzania indicates that reducing time burdens of women in the care economy could increase household cash incomes for smallholder coffee and banana growers by 10 per cent, labor productivity by 15 per cent and capital productivity by 44 per cent.[38]

Regression analysis over the period 1960–1992, with GDP growth as the dependent variable and education and employment among the independent variables, indicates that Sub-Saharan Africa has suffered considerable efficiency losses from gender biases in investment. If Sub-Saharan Africa had matched East Asia's growth of educational attainment for women, annual per capita GDP growth would have been about 0.5 percentage points higher.[39] In addition, if Sub-Saharan Africa had matched East Asia's growth rates in female-sector employment, annual per capita GDP growth would have increased by more than 0.3 percentage points.[40] So, together, gender biases in investment in education and in employment have reduced annual per capita GDP growth in Sub-Saharan Africa by 0.8 percentage points. Since per capita annual GDP growth in the region was only 0.7 per cent over the years 1960–1990, less gender inequality in investments could have doubled annual per capita economic growth during this period. As a consequence, Sub-Saharan Africa's GDP per capita could have been 30 per cent higher than it actually was in 1992.[41]

It is likely that similarly productive gains would also result from a correction of gender disparities in respect of other assets. For example, research on micro-credit in Bangladesh concludes that loans to women generally yield higher marginal returns than loans to men.[42] Given present gender inequalities in the allocation of credit and the law of diminishing returns, this outcome is not surprising. However, gender equality in access to resources will only translate into productive gains, women's increased well-being and economic growth when these resources receive a market price, which is not the case when discrimination operates. As Stephanie Seguino has shown, wage discrimination persists in spite of increased levels of female human capital.[43]

The women's movement and global finance

Just like finance, the women's movement has reached unprecedented levels of global integration at the end of the twentieth century. High points in this integration have been the four United Nations Conferences on Women, held at Mexico City (1975), Copenhagen (1980), Nairobi (1985) and Beijing (1995). The NGO Forums accompanying these meetings have been major occasions for women from across the world to exchange information and share views.

The Platform for Action agreed upon by 189 governments at the Beijing Conference has become an anchor for the global women's movement. Women's associations refer widely to this document to justify their actions, to ground their research, to monitor policies, and to assess progress in the status of women worldwide.

The Beijing Platform for Action has played a central role for at least four reasons. First, with some 30,000 participants, Beijing raised enormous expectations, much higher than the preceding three UN conferences. Second, the Beijing Platform for Action incorporated a wide range of subjects, including controversial matters like inheritance and sexuality. Third, the proposals agreed at Beijing are of an unprecedentedly high standard, not least because of wide NGO participation and NGO pressure. Finally, the Beijing Conference came at a time when gender issues left the margins of national and international policy-making, so that even male-biased institutions like the World Bank made efforts to understand gender issues.[44]

Along with other issues, the Beijing Platform for Action pays considerable attention to the economic position of women.[45] It makes special mention of the disadvantaged position of women in the labor market, of women's unpaid contributions to the economy, and of women's limited access to resources. The document gives no explicit attention to financial markets, but it does refer to the need for gender equality in access to credit and financial decision-making.

For example, paragraph 166 of the Beijing Platform for Action urges governments *inter alia* to facilitate women's "equal access to and control over . . . credit". Paragraph 167 presses governments, central banks, national development banks, and private banking institutions to "increase the participation of women . . . to include women in their leadership, planning and decision making . . . to better meet the credit and other financial needs of the micro-, small-, and medium-scale enterprises of women". Paragraph 169 demands that international funding agencies "review, where necessary reformulate, and implement policies, programs and projects, to ensure that a higher proportion of resources reach women in rural and remote areas". Paragraph 176 urges the financial sector as well as NGOs to "invest capital and develop investment portfolios to finance women's business enterprises [and to] support credit networks and innovative ventures, including traditional savings schemes". Finally, paragraph 177 defines actions to be taken "by the private sector, including transnational and national corporations [to]: (a) adopt policies and establish mechanisms to grant contracts on a non-discriminatory basis; (b) recruit women for leadership, decision making and management and provide training programs, all on an equal basis with men; (c) observe national labor, environment, consumer, health, and safety laws, particularly those that affect women".

Between the first and fourth UN Conferences on Women, several important international networks were set up to engage with issues of gender equality. One prominent example is Development Alternatives with Women for a New Era (DAWN), launched in 1985 as a Southern women's network. Two years later, DAWN published a widely read pamphlet on the negative impacts of economic crises and structural adjustment on women in developing countries.[46] The pamphlet not only addressed financial institutions like the World Bank and the IMF, but also challenged North-based women's organizations to rethink their perspectives, in particular that their focus should not be poor women in the South so much as powerful financial institutions in the North. Next to DAWN, another transnational Southern initiative on structural adjustment is the African Women's Economic Policy Network (AWEPON).[47]

In the North, the US-based Women's Environmental and Development Organization (WEDO), created in 1990, has contributed extensive work on the IMF, the World Bank, the GATT/WTO and transnational corporations. WEDO argues that progress on women's rights and equality is compromised by economic globalization and that, "on balance, women are still the shock absorbers for structural change".[48]

In Europe, the network Women In Development Europe (WIDE) has since 1993 linked national platforms from an increasing number of European countries. WIDE has focused its lobbying activities on European Union (EU) institutions like the European Commission and the European Parliament. WIDE's training programs on financial issues are discussed further below.

During the 1990s various alliances developed between North- and South-based women's NGOs, helped by new global communications technology such as fax, e-mail and the Internet.[49] One such network is the Women's Global Alliance for Economic Justice, founded in 1992. Its current membership includes, in addition to DAWN, WEDO and WIDE, the US-based network Alternative Women In Development (Alt-WID), the Women In Development network of the Society for International Development (SID-WID), the Canadian Research Institute for the Advancement of Women (CRIAW), the Canada-based National Action Committee (NAC), the US-based Center for Women's Global Leadership, and the lobby group European Solidarity towards Equal Participation of People (EUROSTEP).

Local, national, regional and global women's associations have addressed issues of finance in four main ways: information and training; advocacy; provision of credit; and gender audits. These four activities are discussed in turn below.

Information and training

Women's NGOs have issued numerous leaflets, brochures, and reports over the past decade on women and structural adjustment programs, economic reform, credit and other issues of finance. In addition, several women's organizations have developed economics training courses for women at the grassroots level to enable them to discuss costs and benefits for women of particular economic trends and policies. In the area of finance more particularly, economic literacy courses have addressed questions of structural adjustment lending, capital markets, micro-credit and public finance, including the idea of gender audits, or gender-aware government budgets.

To take a specific example, WIDE has developed an economic literacy course for women living in Europe and concerned with women elsewhere in the world. *Women in the Market: A Manual for Popular Economic Literacy* was first published in 1998 and is being continuously revised in the light of experiences in training sessions.[50] The course is targeted at the hundreds of members of national WIDE platforms in Europe. It aims to assist women to assess the responsibility of Europe, the EU and global economic institutions for intended and unintended negative consequences on the poor, and poor women in particular. The manual also seeks to facilitate networking within WIDE and with partners in the South.[51]

Several training sessions, lasting from between half a day to three days, have been organized in European countries including Austria, Belgium, Denmark,

Finland, and the Netherlands. Financial topics covered have included government budgets, different definitions of money, and monetary policy. In addition to the training manual, WIDE has also distributed background readers on specific economic themes, one of them concerning money, financial markets, and instability.[52]

The WIDE course uses popular techniques. It starts by having participants map their own economic situation (e.g. in terms of job, income, expenditures, savings, credit, unpaid labor, and distribution of resources over dependants). Then participants reflect on these circumstances and those of people related to them, both near and distant. Role play is used to help participants analyze economic issues from different points of view. Finally, the participants together develop ideas for concrete action.

Advocacy

Much advocacy on global finance by women's associations has targeted the general neoliberal framework of mainstream contemporary macroeconomic policy, including many of the arguments elaborated earlier in this chapter. In addition, some actions have focused on particular institutions and policies of global finance.

One important initiative in this regard is "Women's Eyes on the World Bank", launched at the Beijing Conference. This "global campaign to transform the Bank to meet women's needs" aims: to increase participation of grassroots women in Bank activities; to institutionalize a gender perspective in Bank projects and programs; to increase Bank investment in women's health services, education, agriculture, land ownership, employment, and financial services; and to increase the number and racial diversity of women in senior management positions at the Bank. The campaign has achieved some success. For example, the Latin American chapter has secured agreement from senior World Bank officials to develop solid gender analyses of the design and implementation of projects, including those related to financial services.[53]

Another advocacy forum, initiated by the United Nations, is called "Women Watch – The UN Internet Gateway on the Advancement and Empowerment of Women". Its website and electronic discussion groups offer information and a discussion platform for women's NGOs, feminist researchers and other interested individuals to monitor the implementation of the Beijing Platform for Action. Among other things, Women Watch has sponsored moderated online dialogs for the Beijing+5 review in 2000. One of these dialogs, called "End Women's Economic Inequality", handled economic and financial issues.[54]

Provision of credit

In line with the Beijing recommendations, an increasing number of grassroots women's organizations are supplying credit to women. In an analysis of thirty-four micro-credit programs with large numbers of poor clients, the Microcredit Summit Campaign found that, on average, 76 per cent of the borrowers were women. Some programs like Working Women's Forum (India), the National Anti-Poverty

Organization (Nigeria), and ACLEDA (Colombia) had over 95 per cent women clients.[55]

One of the first international civil society organizations to extend credit lending to women was Women's World Banking (WWB). Established after the first UN Conference on Women, WWB now operates in over forty countries. In its 1996 report, WWB ambitiously claims that it is "the only women-led global network that aims to open the world's financial system to low income women".[56] Today, WWB affiliates are providing credits, savings facilities and business development services to about ten million women.[57] Since poor women often lack traditional collateral, creative alternatives are accepted such as jewels, tools, or personal and group guarantees. WWB has also developed new services such as loan guarantee programs, guidance to business support networks, and development of coalitions of micro-finance organizations to influence financial systems to benefit poor women. Yet, a large gap still exists between the supply of and the demand for credit. An estimated 500 million female micro-entrepreneurs require financial services, while WWB currently reaches only ten million.

Many other women's organizations have emerged at the national level to support credit for women. The Indian Self-Employed Women's Association (SEWA) is probably the best known example. It even runs its own bank.

Gender audits

A fourth activity of women's associations *vis-à-vis* global finance concerns the promotion of gender audits. Ethical auditing is a new device for monitoring the behavior of firms and governments. Whereas audits have traditionally evaluated the financial condition and behavior of an organization, ethical audits address social and environmental issues. Social audits can include a specific gender focus.

For example, gender audits of public finance check government revenue and expenditure item by item. Such audits were first undertaken in South Africa in 1996, quickly followed by Australia, Canada, the UK and Tanzania.[58] Over time, emphasis has shifted from general statements on overall budgets toward more detailed analysis of particular budgets such as health care or infrastructure.

Gender audits of public finances have also become more sophisticated. Not only do they assess the tax burden on men and women and the distribution of expenditures between men and women, but they also pay increasing attention to the relationship between, on the one hand, gender biases in public expenditures and, on the other, production, productivity, consumption, savings, investment, incomes, labor supply, and welfare.[59] Gender audits reveal the allocation inefficiencies in government budgets caused by gender discrimination.[60] By asking questions about the equity and efficiency outcomes of government budgets on women and men, gender audits force a re-evaluation of the long-held assumption that government budgets and economic policies generally are "gender neutral" in their impact.[61]

Some activists in the women's movement have called for gender audits (albeit not always using this terminology) to be carried out in respect of public financial institutions. For example, a participant in the online dialog organized by the UN's Women Watch initiative has suggested that multilateral development banks should be required to subject their projects to gender quality assessments. Meanwhile, Gita Sen has proposed a strategy to mainstream gender in finance ministries, calling for an assessment of financial policies in terms of the differential impact on the well-being of women and men, impacts on the care economy, and effects on gender power relations.[62]

Conclusions and proposals

Before proceeding to specific conclusions, I want to address the suggestion heard in some feminist circles that women should completely withdraw from global finance and stick to small-scale local finance. The idea of "de-globalizing" finance may seem appealing. In this scenario, local communities and women would generate their own sources of finance, free from outside public or private sources of credit.

However, this approach is not adequate. First, the majority of micro-finance programs cannot survive without outside support.[63] Credit programs specifically targeted at women also rely on outside funding. For example, Women's World Banking generates investment income and supports loan guarantees from a capital fund of $25 million created by donors in Asia, Europe and the USA.[64] Likewise, the Grameen Bank has achieved its positive rate of return only with foreign donor funds.[65]

Second, micro-credit programs are not necessarily free from gender biases. Small is not inherently beautiful. In research on the Grameen Bank and three other micro-credit programs in Bangladesh, Anne Marie Goetz and Rina Sen Gupta found that only 37 per cent of women borrowers retained control over their loans. In other cases, male relatives took over significant control.[66] Even Grameen Bank, which performed best, saw more than a third of its female borrowers lacking sufficient control of their loans. Clearly, access to credit is not the only challenge for women, but also control over loans.[67]

Thus, whether international, national or local – and whether public or private – finance apparently cannot escape the gender biases that are deeply embedded in economic processes. The solution is not to limit financial streams to one sphere (like the local) or one sector (like official channels). Hence, my policy suggestions do not seek to abolish one or the other arena of finance, but rather seek to reform financial institutions at every level and in every sector. The following five proposals may help to implement the Beijing Platform for Action as it relates to finance. The suggestions are aimed at both policy-makers in official institutions and activists in the women's movement.

First, financial institutions need to develop into transparent organizations that can stand the scrutiny of "good governance" criteria, including those of democratic representation. Financial governance agencies (national as well as international) can further this objective by increasing the numbers of women among their directors and senior staff. The women's movement can promote this goal by undertaking gender audits of these institutions, calling them to account for shortfalls of good governance from a gender perspective.

Second, measures are needed to reduce gender-based distortions in financial markets. Progress can be made at various levels, including through the law (inheritance and property rights), land reform programs and raising public awareness. In order to reduce gender distortions within financial institutions, international development agencies and donor governments could require a gender audit of the portfolios of development banks when they support regional development banks and national and local credit programs in developing countries. Gender audits would help to ensure women's benefits from credit. In order to reduce gender distortions outside institutions but operating largely invisibly in financial markets, governments have a responsibility to take away the sources of these distortions, just like they have done with, for example, anti-trust laws.

Third, action should be taken to break the monopoly of the IMF on international policy advice. As shown earlier, this situation has supported male rent-seeking in global finance. As Aslanbeigui and Summerfield argue:

> Feminists, women's organisations, and NGOs that represent the needs of women . . . should participate in the debate concerning reform of the IFIs. Otherwise they will miss a unique opportunity to help construct a gender-conscious international financial architecture.[68]

A greater number of information providers and policy advisers would allow more views and interests to be represented: those of men and women, businesses and labor, higher classes and the poor alike.

Fourth, loans by the World Bank and the regional development banks should be reconsidered in favor of grants for human development, including in particular its gender aspects. In making this shift the banks could well use the Gender and Development Index (GDI) and the Gender Empowerment Measure (GEM) of UNDP. The GDI incorporates gender inequalities into the Human Development Index (HDI). The GEM measures women's decision-making power in the economy and politics. UNIFEM has also developed indicators of women's progress.[69] A shift from loans to grants would acknowledge the global public goods status of education and health care and prevent a shift of the burden of excessive risk to the care economy. Moreover, reduction of the gender gap in education would increase the marginal returns of investment in human capital.

Fifth, micro-credit programs for women should shift attention from increased *access to* loans to increased *control over* loans. For example, forward linkages by credit institutions – such as favorable contracts with agricultural input providers – would reduce the liquidity of women's credit and hence men's opportunities to appropriate it for their interests. It would also be advisable to register collateral in women's names. Female borrowers could be further empowered through the formation of women's groups that collectively control their members' resources. Greater women's control of loans would promote more effective and efficient use of credit by and for women.

In conclusion, the activities of the women's movement in the field of global finance would probably become more effective with a shift of focus from the micro to the macro level. Finance is increasingly a globalized phenomenon, and the gender problems to which it gives rise need to be addressed with more than training or women's credit programs. Therefore, the women's movement might consider a shift towards the sorts of issues mentioned above, like the financing of human development with loans or grants, the IMF monopoly on financial policy advice, and gender audits of influential financial institutions.

Notes

1 I am grateful for the helpful comments and suggestions received from members of the Women In Development Europe network, particularly Brigitte Holzner and Christa Wichterich, from other participants in the Civil Society and Global Finance Project, and from Aloy Soppe. Remaining errors are exclusively my own responsibility.

2 Jonathan Morduch, "The Microfinance Promise," *Journal of Economic Literature*, Vol. 37, No. 4, 1999, p. 1,569.

3 Eleonore Kofman and Gillian Youngs (eds), *Globalization: Theory and Practice*, London: Pinter, 1996, part 3; Lourdes Beneria, "Globalization, Gender, and the Davos Man", *Feminist Economics*, 1999, Vol. 5, No. 3, pp. 61–83; V. Spike Peterson and Anne Sisson Runyan, *Global Gender Issues*, Boulder: Westview, second edition, 1999; Christa Wichterich, "The Globalized Woman. Reports from the Future of Inequality," unpublished; translated from *Die Globalisierte Frau: Berichte aus den Zukunft der Ungleichkeit*, Hamburg: Rowolt, 1999; Lourdes Beneria, Maria Floro, Caren Gowan and Martha MacDonald (eds), Special Issue on "Globalization", *Feminist Economics*, Vol. 6, No. 3, 2000; Marianne Marchand and Anne Sisson Runyan (eds), *Gender and Global Restructuring: Sightings, Sites and Resistances*, London: Routledge, 2000.

4 Maria Floro, "Women, Work and Agricultural Commercialisation in the Philippines", in Nancy Folbre, Barbara Bergmann, Bina Agarwal and Maria Floro (eds), *Women's Work in the World Economy*, New York: New York University Press, 1992, pp. 3–40; Susan Joekes and A. Weston, *Women and the New Trade Agenda*, New York: UNIFEM, 1994; United Nations, *World Survey on the Role of Women in Development: Globalization, Gender, and Work*, New York: United Nations, 1999; WIDE, "Gender, Trade and Rights: Moving Forward", Brussels: WIDE, 1999; Marzia Fontana and Adrian Wood, "Modeling the Effects of Trade on Women, at Work and at Home", *World Development*, Vol. 28, No. 7, 2000, pp. 1,173–90; David Kucera and William Milberg, "Gender Segregation and Gender Bias in Manufacturing Trade Expansion: Revisiting the 'Wood Asymmetry'", *World Development*, Vol. 28, No. 7, 2000, pp. 1,191–210.

5 Ajit Singh and Ann Zammit, "International Capital Flows: Identifying the Gender Dimension", *World Development*, Vol. 28, No. 7, 2000, pp. 1,249–68; Maria Floro and Gary Dymski, "Financial Crisis, Gender, and Power: an Analytical Framework", *World Development*, Vol. 28, No. 7, 2000, pp. 1,269–83; Joseph Lim, "The Effects of the East Asian Crisis on the Employment of Women and Men: The Philippine Case", *World Development*, Vol. 28, No. 7, 2000, pp. 1,285–306.

6 Nahid Aslanbeigui and Gale Summerfield, "The Asian Crisis, Gender, and the International Financial Architecture", *Feminist Economics*, Vol. 6, No. 3, 2000, pp. 81–103.

7 World Bank, *Annual Report 1999*; and <http://www.worldbank.org/html/extdr/about/orgcharts/officers/>.

8 UNDP, *Human Development Report 1995*, New York: Oxford University Press, 1995.

9 UNICEF, *The Invisible Adjustment: Poor Women and the Economic Crisis*, Santiago: UNICEF, the Americas and the Caribbean Regional Office, 1989.

10 Diane Elson, "Sector Programme Support," 1998, a collection of papers published by the Graduate School of Social Sciences, Genecon Unit, Manchester: University of Manchester (for OECD/DAC–WID).

11 Janet Stotsky, "Gender Bias in Tax Systems", IMF Working Papers, Washington DC: IMF, 1996; Edward McCaffery, *Taxing Women*, Chicago: University of Chicago Press, 1997.

12 Caren Grown, Diane Elson and Nilüfer Çagatay, "Introduction", *World Development*, Vol. 28, No. 7, 2000, pp. 1,145–56. Introduction to a Special Issue on "Growth, Trade, Finance, and Gender Inequality".

13 L. McDowell and G. Court, "Gender Divisions of Labor in the Post-Fordist Economy: The Maintenance of Occupational Sex Segregation in the Financial Services Sector", *Environment and Planning A*, Vol. 26, No. 9, September 1994, pp. 1,397–1,418.

14 Pan Yotopoulos and Sagrario Floro, "Income Distribution, Transaction Costs and Market Fragmentation in Informal Credit Markets", *Cambridge Journal of Economics*, No. 16, 1992, pp. 303–326.

15 Singh and Zammit, op. cit. p. 1,255.

16 Sally Baden, "Gender Issues in Financial Liberalization and Financial Sector Reform", paper prepared for EU (DG VIII) and OECD/DAC–WID, Sussex: Bridge, 1996.

17 Nancy Folbre, *Who Pays for the Kids? Gender and the Structures of Constraint*, London: Routledge, 1994.

18 Francine Blau, Marianne Ferber, and Anne Winkler, *The Economics of Women, Men and Work*, Upper Saddle River: Prentice-Hall, third edition, 1992; Naila Kabeer, *Reversed Realities: Gender Hierarchies in Development Thought*, London: Verso, 1994; Bina Agarwal, *A Field of One's Own: Gender and Land Rights in South Asia*, Cambridge: Cambridge University Press, 1994.

19 Yotopoulos and Floro, op. cit. p. 304.

20 Baden, op. cit.

21 Women's World Banking, 1996, <http://www.womensworldbanking.org>.

22 Baden, op. cit.

23 Ilene Grabel, "Identifying Risks, Preventing Crisis: Lessons from the Asian Crisis", *Journal of Economic Issues*, Vol. 34, No. 2, 2000, pp. 377–83.

24 Frank Knight, *Risk, Uncertainty and Profit*, Chicago: University of Chicago Press, 1921.

25 Elson, "Sector Programme Support".

26 Caroline Moser, "The Impact of Recession and Adjustment Policies at the Micro Level: Low Income Women and Their Households in Guayaquil, Ecuador", in UNICEF, *The Invisible Adjustment: Poor Women and the Economic Crisis*, second revised edition, Santiago: UNICEF, 1989, pp. 137–66; Isabella Bakker (ed.), *The Strategic Silence: Gender and Economic Policy*, London: Zed Books, 1994; Pamela Sparr (ed.), *Mortgaging Women's Lives: Feminist Critiques of Structural Adjustment*, London: Zed Books, 1994; Diane Elson, "Male Bias in Macroeconomics: The Case of Structural Adjustment", in Elson (ed.), *Male Bias in the Development Process*, Manchester: University of Manchester Press, 1995, pp. 164–90; UNDP, *Human Development Report 1999*, New York: Oxford University Press, 1999; UNIFEM, *Progress of the World's Women 2000*, New York: UNIFEM, 2000.

27 Diane Elson and Nilüfer Çagatay, "The Social Context of Macroeconomic Policies", *World Development*, Vol. 28, No. 7, 2000, p. 1,355.

28 Thanh-Dam Truong, "The Underbelly of the Tiger: Gender and the Demystification of the Asian Miracle", *Review of International Political Economy*, Vol. 6, No. 2, 1999, pp. 133–65.

29 Singh and Zimmit, op. cit. p. 1,260.

30 World Bank, *East Asia: The Road to Recovery*, Washington DC: World Bank, 1998.

31 Moser, op. cit.; Ruth Pearson, "Global Change and Insecurity: Are Women the Problem or the Solution?" in Isa Baud and Ines Smyth (eds), *Searching for Security: Women's Responses to Economic Transformations*, London: Routledge, 1997, pp. 10–23.

32 Korkut Ertürk and Nilüfer Çatagaty, "Macroeconomic Consequences of Cyclical and Secular Changes in Feminization: A Experiment at Gendered Macromodeling," *World Development*, Vol. 23, No. 11, 1995, pp. 1,969–77.

33 Elson, "Sector Programme Support".

34 Morduch, op. cit., p. 1593.

35 Ibid., p. 1583.

36 Women's World Banking.

37 World Bank, *Gender, Growth, and Poverty Reduction. Special Program of Assistance for Africa, 1998 Status Report on Poverty in Sub-Saharan Africa*, Technical Paper No. 428, Washington DC: World Bank, 1999, p. 10.

38 Ibid., p. 20.

39 Ibid., p. 15.

40 Ibid., p. 16.

41 Ibid., p. 17.

42 Mark Pitt and Shahidur Khandker, "The Impact of Group-Based Credit Programs on Poor Households in Bangladesh: Does the Gender of Participants Matter?" *Journal of Political Economy*, Vol. 106, No. 5, 1998, pp. 958–96.

43 Stephanie Seguino, "Gender Inequality and Economic Growth: A Cross-Country Analysis," *World Development*, Vol. 28, No. 7, 2000, pp. 1,211–30.

44 World Bank, *Enhancing Women's Participation in Economic Development*, World Bank Policy Paper, Washington, DC: World Bank, 1994; World Bank, *Toward Gender Equality: The Role of Public Policy*, Development in Practice Series, Washington, DC: World Bank, 1995; World Bank, *Advancing Gender Equality: From Concept to Action*, Washington, DC: World Bank, 1995.

45 UN, *Platform for Action and the Beijing Declaration*, New York: United Nations, 1996.

46 Gita Sen and Caren Grown, *Development, Crises, and Alternative Visions: Third World Women's Perspectives*, New York: Monthly Review Press, 1987.

47 AWEPON, *Women Standing Up to Adjustment in Africa: A Report of the African Women's Economic Policy Network*, Washington, DC: The Development GAP, 1996.

48 "Global Survey Finds Progress on Women's Rights and Equality Compromised by Economic Globalization", WEDO Press Release, March 1998, at <http://www.wedo.org/monitor/mapping/htm>.

49 Geertje Lycklama à Nijeholt, Virginia Vargas and Saskia Wieringa (eds), *Women's Movements and Public Policy in Europe, Latin America, and the Carribean*, New York: Garland, 1998, p. 33.

50 WIDE, "Women in the Market. A Manual for Popular Economic Literacy", Brussels: WIDE, 1998.

51 Ibid., p. 5.

52 Irene van Staveren, *Robinson Crusoe and Silas Marner, or Two Stories on the Gendered Monetary Economy*, Brussels: WIDE, 1998.

53 See <http://www.wedo.org/news/Sept97/womens.htm>.

54 See <http://www.sdnhq.undp.org/ww/women-economy/msg02630.html>.

55 See <http://www.soc.titech.ac.jp/icm/wind/summit.html>.

56 See <http://www.soc.titech.ac.jp/icm/wind/wwb-report.html>.

57 Funding Partners Meeting, 15–16 June 2000 in Zürich.

58 Rhonda Sharp and Ray Broomhill, "Women and Government Budgets", *Australian Journal of Social Issues*, Vol. 23, No. 1, 1990, pp. 2–14; Debbie Budlender and Rhonda Sharp with Kerri Allen, "How to Do a Gender-Sensitive Budget Analysis", *Contemporary Research and Practice*, Canberra/London: Australian Agency for International Development/Commonwealth Secretariat, 1998; Susan Himmelweit, "Care and the Budgetary Process", paper presented at the "Out of the Margin 2" – Conference on Feminist Economics, University of Amsterdam, 2–5 June 1998; Fatma Kiongosya and Christine Warioba, "Report of the Review of the Budget Guidelines by the Planning Commission and Ministry of Finance with a Gender Perspective", Dar es Salaam: Tanzania Gender Networking Programme (TNGP), 1998.

59 Rhonda Sharp, "Women's Budgets", in *The Elgar Companion to Feminist Economics*, New York: Edward Elgar, 1999.

60 Mayra Buvinic, Catherine Gwin and Lisa Bates, *Investing in Women: Progress and Prospects for the World Bank*, Washington, DC: ODC/ICRW, Policy Essay No. 19, 1996.

61 Diane Elson, "Integrating Gender Issues into Public Expenditure: Six Tools", 1997, paper by the Genecon Unit, University of Manchester, Graduate School of Social Sciences; Sharp, op. cit.

62 Gita Sen, "Gender Mainstreaming in Finance Ministries", *World Development*, Vol. 28, No. 7, 2000, pp. 1,379–90.

63 Morduch, op. cit.

64 See <http://www.soc.titech.ac.jp/icm/wind/wwb-report.html>. The figure dates from December 1995.

65 Ibid.

66 Anne Marie Goetz and Rina Sen Gupta, "Who Takes the Credit? Gender, Power, and Control Over Loan Use in Rural Credit Programs in Bangladesh", *World Development*, Vol. 24, No. 1, 1996, p. 49.

67 See also Linda Mayoux, "From Access to Women's Empowerment: Ways Forward in Micro-Finance", speech given at the Annual GOOD Conference, 13–15 September 1999, St. Albans, "Gender Orientation On Development".

68 Aslanbeigui and Summerfield, op. cit., p. 99.

69 UNIFEM 2000.

Part V

Looking ahead

15 What next?

Civil society's prospects in a world of global finance

Alison Van Rooy

Summary	
• Introduction	249
• Why bother? Growing civil society attention to the IFIs	250
• Issues for the future	253
• Future scenarios	259
• Conclusion	261

Introduction

Why should we devote so much attention, in this book and in the debates that this book examines, to civil society and global finance? After all, civil society organizations (CSOs) are mobilizing locally and globally around a vast number of issues and institutions. Global finance is but one concern on a much larger agenda.

The answer is that international financial institutions (IFIs) are crucially important for human development in the world; so it matters deeply how they are governed. Of all the areas of global finance covered in this book, the IFIs have gained most CSO attention. For a very long time, IFI decisions were not part of a larger public conversation about political intent and impact. Today, CSOs are playing an important role in making IFI activities more transparent. Taking up that role is easier said than done, of course.

This chapter begins with a rapid history of CSO motivations in addressing the IFIs and then examines some of the issues that face this work now and in the future. What issues are shaping today's campaigns? How are CSOs mobilizing, and with whom? How will dynamics within the various movements – and within the IFIs – affect future strategies? As in all areas of human endeavor, civil society mobilization is contested, political, and full of contradictions over its own governance and accountability. The story is more complex than good guys versus bad guys.

Musing on these fast-moving currents, the conclusion of the chapter suggests three broad possible courses for the future. In the first scenario, trends now underway would move CSO attention away from targeting finance, just when its impacts are being felt. In the second scenario, the hope of real CSO influence would dissolve when IFIs undertake only a wimpish shift of vocabulary rather than substantive policy change. In the third (optimistic) scenario, CSO mobilization on IFIs would produce crucial new mechanisms of global accountability. The last scenario presents new challenges for global governance: who should decide what that world will look like?

Why bother? Growing civil society attention to the IFIs

This chapter begins with a story about changes in the numbers, skills, motivations, and activities of globalized civil society organizations *vis-à-vis* the IFIs. Why are civil society organizations bothering with the IFIs in the first place?

More CSOs, more capability

Part of the answer lies in the major growth of CSOs worldwide. While the numbers are notoriously impressionistic, data does indicate a remarkable swell in organizational enthusiasm at the international level. Figure 15.1 shows some 38,000 registered nongovernmental organizations (NGOs) working in more than one country as of 1996, double the number of a decade earlier. Tallies of national and local CSOs involve still more guesswork. Anheier and Salamon estimate that 800 registered CSOs operate in Ghana, 11,000 in Thailand, more than 17,500 in Egypt, and at least 2 million in India.[1]

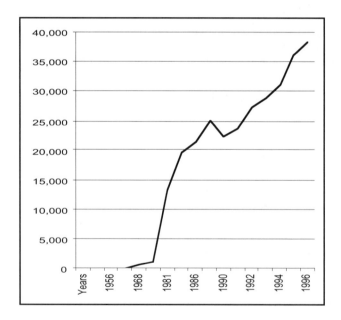

Figure 15.1 Numbers of international nongovernmental organizations.

Source: Union of International Associations (<www.uia.org>)

It is easier to count the CSOs that rally around specific meetings and intergovernmental bodies. The United Nations conferences of the 1990s attracted especially large civil society crowds. The standard-setting 1992 Earth Summit in Rio de Janeiro involved 1,200 associations and an estimated 15,000 people at the parallel NGO Forum. In 1993 around 7,000 participants from 800 NGOs attended the UN Human Rights Conference in Vienna. The 1995 UN Social Summit in Copenhagen saw 4,500 people at the parallel event. The 1996 Habitat meeting in Istanbul hosted 8,000 people from 2,400 NGOs.[2]

CSOs have also flocked to global economic institutions. Since 1973 the World Bank has involved NGOs in 752 of its projects. Today some 37 per cent of Bank projects have NGO inputs.[3] The International Monetary Fund (IMF) has a mailing list of around 1,000 NGOs.[4] The November 1999 demonstrations at the World Trade Organization (WTO) meetings in Seattle attracted more than 700 organizations and between 40,000 and 60,000 men and women, the biggest rattling of swords in recent history.

Over the past fifteen years, in large part because of the debt burden and opposition to structural adjustment, many CSOs have turned their attention to the IFIs. John Clark argues in this volume that the World Bank, by its very institutional makeup, has been particularly amenable to civil society campaigns. The Bank is seen as aloof and arrogant, but is still relatively accessible. It appears monolithic, yet many friends of CSOs work on the inside. It is a global force, but has individual projects that can be scrutinized locally. Its financing decisions are secret, but its funds have to be authorized by democratic governments. Some CSO interest has also arisen regarding the regional multilateral development banks (MDBs), accusing them of similar sins.[5]

Although the IMF lacks several of these characteristics of the World Bank, it has recently also become a target of concerted civil society advocacy efforts. On a small scale, CSO activism regarding the IMF dates back to the early 1980s.[6] However, the Fund has risen on the CSO agenda especially since the late 1990s, after its perceived mishandling of the Asian financial crisis and its proposed greater social policy role through the Poverty Reduction Strategy Papers (PRSPs).

To address the financial areas of global organization, CSOs have had to develop different kinds of knowledge, including macroeconomic theory, debt restructuring options, terms of trade debates, and monetary policy. The Jubilee 2000 campaign to cancel the external debts of poor countries is a powerful example where non-economists have skillfully tackled a question of international finance. Increased economic literacy across global civil society is evident from the lengthening list of prominent CSOs that work on international finance.

Civil society interest in multilateral financial institutions is also reflected in the growing commitments of grantmaking organizations to take a closer look at the IFIs. The Charles Mott Foundation has supported research in this area for some time, including the Rethinking Bretton Woods Project of the Center of Concern in Washington, DC. The Ford Foundation is now sponsoring work on IFI reform. The Swedish Ministry of Foreign Affairs is looking at the MDBs.

In sum, growing numbers of CSOs have growing capacities to address questions of global finance. *Potentially*, civil society associations could gain a more influential position in global finance. The next section considers why they would seek that influence.

Increased public scrutiny of "globalization"

We are witnessing the solidification of a political ogre in "globalization". The term has acquired a powerful discursive role. It encapsulates (and repackages) concerns over wealth and poverty, sovereignty and social justice, cultural identity, and corporate whims. Although some have dismissed such fears as "globophobia",[7] globalization has come under greater critical public scrutiny.

An example from Canada well illustrates this trend. In 1999, already before the Seattle demonstrations, the Canadian Council for International Cooperation held public deliberations on globalization, centred on a three-hour forum with 350 people in different parts of the country.[8] What did the participants think about globalization?

- They were concerned about the current course of globalization and wanted change.
- They wanted to strengthen local communities in the face of globalization, but not isolationism.
- They acknowledged the value of global competition as a stimulus to innovation and excellence, but worried that the current playing field is not level.
- They expressed strong desires for more education about globalization and its impacts, including better consumer information.
- They did not accept that government is "powerless" to act in the face of globalization.
- They felt that government is not listening to the people on questions of globalization and that more citizen participation is needed.
- They wanted broader accountability regarding globalization, involving corporations as well as governments and individuals.
- They worried about the environmental impacts of the current pattern of globalization.
- They supported the idea of a "fairer" global economy, but were confused and sceptical about how this goal could be achieved.

Such views hardly amount to "globophobia". They reflect long-standing social, environmental and ethical concerns – and reasonable ones at that. Indeed, few participants in the Battle of Seattle came to fuss over negotiating points on the WTO agenda. Most protestors were involved because they identified the WTO (rightly or wrongly) as a primary agent of harmful globalization. Later demonstrators turned on the World Economic Forum (WEF), the IMF and the World Bank for similar reasons.

For instance, note the following fragment from publicity material for a protest in Boston against biotechnology in March 2000:

We are riding a wave that began in Seattle and will continue to rise as we move toward the demonstration against the IMF and the World Bank on April 16 in Washington D.C. This is the beginning of a new movement that will move beyond the realm of reform, protest, and alternatives . . . This is the beginning of a revolutionary movement to create a new society built out of a new logic that breaks from the system of domination and exploitation, the logic of the state and capital, the logic of sexism and racism that brought us to the current crisis in democracy. We will build our movement and a new society out of a humanistic logic based on principles of solidarity, democracy, and cooperation.[9]

This momentum is still felt across activist communities in North America and beyond.[10] For example, a flyer for the General Assembly of the Organization of American States (OAS) at Windsor, Ontario in June 2000 read: "Missed Seattle? Come to Windsor!"

Therefore, when looking to the future of mobilization around international finance, it is crucial to understand both the mobilizing force of "globalization" as a rallying call and the real and reasonable concerns that this idea encapsulates. It is too easy to dismiss the theatre of opposition as fringe antics. If bodies like the IMF, the World Bank, the WEF and the WTO – widely perceived to be the motors of globalization – fail to give these protests serious attention, they will continue to be in for a rough ride.

Issues for the future

Thus far, this chapter has argued that a growing number of capable organizations are increasingly rallying around globalization targets, including in particular the IFIs. Well, what next? At least seven issues for the future are worth mentioning.

Washington Consensus: repaired or unraveled?

The principles and methods by which international finance is promoted and regulated are no longer (if they ever were entirely) taken for granted in Washington. A short story of the fall of the so-called "Washington Consensus" would attribute some credit to CSOs. However, it would give much more attention to the viscerally felt crises in Asia, Russia, and Brazil, and the *cris de cœur* brought on by the inadequacy of IFI tools in dealing with them.[11]

The modified consensus now in place accepts that the state must be strengthened, not belittled, in the search for market liberalization. This is hardly a radical change of direction, of course, but the practical repercussions are important. The revised debate talks of strengthening central state institutions, heightening supervision of deregulated and privatized agencies, bolstering judicial systems, and targeting social spending to vulnerable circles via local governments, NGOs and other agencies.

The evidence of a modified consensus shows up most dramatically in the World Bank. It is visible in the Bank's retroactive efforts to "fix" structural adjustment in the Structural Adjustment Program Review Initiative (SAPRI), in its proactive efforts with the PRSPs, in its recent "Voices of the Poor" exercise,[12] and in its national consultation strategies (like the ones recounted in this book by Senderowitsch and Cesilini). Of course, the story is not uncomplicated. Further jarring of old norms came with the departure of the Bank's Chief Economist, Joseph Stiglitz, over differences of orthodoxy. In June 2000 Cornell Professor Ravi Kanbur resigned over the Bank's heavy-handed efforts to change the ideological stamp on the *World Development Report* that he was assembling.

Yet, the overall picture at the World Bank shows greater openness to non-governmental voices, whether or not the effort is ornamental. When new initiatives are added to older mechanisms – including the Inspection Panel and the NGO Liaison Committee – it is evident that the Bank aims to avoid future problems (in both policy and public relations) by extending greater engagement with CSOs.

Other "architects of globalization" like the IMF, the WTO and proponents of the Free Trade Area of the Americas (FTAA) may not be far behind the World Bank. Moves to increase access to documentation, to meet with CSOs, to appoint staff for CSO "liaison", and to supply funding for participation are all on the rise.[13] These measures have not come without controversy, of course. For example, debate on the FTAA has produced a pretty flimsy "engagement" mechanism that did not extend beyond permission for CSOs to submit written comments. Nevertheless, the number and variety of mechanisms are growing, as are the expectations that officials ought to use them.

In short, tremors in the Washington Consensus about the direction of economic reform have encouraged a more open stance to CSOs on the part of the IFIs. CSOs have gained an officially accepted role in development practice and – in small doses – in development policy commentary. However, this repair – or unraveling – of the Washington Consensus will not lessen CSO enthusiasm. In all likelihood, the doors that are slowly opening will be pried open still further. The question is whether meaningful policy change will follow.

UN reform, crisis and the IFIs

The perpetual project of UN reform also has an influence on how and why CSOs engage with the IFIs. Many global CSOs identify with the normative ethos of the UN system, often contrasting the high-minded views presented in UNDP's *Human Development Report* with the sins of the Bretton Woods institutions. On the one hand, the crisis in the UN system (lack of faith in its effectiveness and subsequent underfunding by member governments) endangers a core CSO ally. On the other hand, the UN may be diverting CSO attention. All those conferences and Prep Coms may, at the end of the day, be of negligible importance to the struggle for social and economic justice.

Certainly there is much around the UN to keep CSOs busy. Recent years have seen a tour of the "Plus-Five" follow-up meetings to the Rio, Vienna, Beijing, Copenhagen, and other conferences. Efforts to generate new ideas around Financing for Development are currently underway (see Herman in this volume).

Opposition to the Global Compact between the UN and the business world is growing in many CSO quarters.[14] Stop-and-start CSO enthusiasms continue for a permanent people's assembly at the UN.[15] Then there is ongoing work around the Economic and Social Council (ECOSOC) and the Security Council, the unending financial crisis (will the US ever pay its dues?), and reform of UNDP.

The sheer scale of UN-related activities may pose a problem, diverting – and exhausting – CSOs. Efforts at the United Nations may keep CSOs from deepening their work on the IFIs. Alternatively, global civil society may abandon the UN and look for greener pastures in Washington or Geneva.

Tackling global markets

Yet another issue for CSO mobilization is the changing international financial market. How capital moves through the global trade and speculative financial system – and how it may be regulated – is a topic of keen concern. The Tobin tax has been the hottest point in this debate.[16] Many activists have argued that the Tobin tax proposal could dampen volatility and subsidize development work (part of the Financing for Development package).

However, other conversations – on foreign direct investment, hedge funds, and capital controls – are also underway. Many CSOs hope to promote the role of public agencies (national as well as international) in stemming destabilizing private flows. For example, could the IMF, or some other public body, have prevented or slowed the Asian crisis? Many CSOs have argued that the Fund should not have proscribed national capital controls of the sort implemented in Malaysia. Yet, when one considers the very small resources that the Bank and Fund have at their disposal in comparison with total world financial flows, are CSOs right to focus on these two institutions?

Some CSO initiatives *vis-à-vis* global financial markets have targeted the private side of the equation. In comparison with campaigns around retailers (like Nike and Gap) and mining companies (like Talisman, Alcan, and de Beers), mobilization around corporate investors and speculators has remained modest. However, a very small but growing movement for ethical and environmentally responsible investment has developed, particularly around the pension funds of ethically charged organizations such as unions. Although this activity is less vivid than the pictures of street protest, it may ultimately have greater influence.

Partnerships: the North–South divide(s)

Another key issue for the future – highlighted once again at Seattle – is the nature of the relationship between Northern and Southern CSOs engaged in advocacy around the IFIs. Who, between the North and the South, determines the focus of efforts? Who sets the strategy? Who is physically present? Who pays? Of course, these strains are part of more general difficulties among CSOs working on global finance over strategy (what should we do and why?), coordination (who should do it?), and focus (what should we target?).[17]

The Battle of Seattle provoked some Southern mutterings about American labor protectionism.[18] The struggle over the World Bank Arun Dam project in Nepal saw North–South disagreements over the reason for opposition. The Narmada Dam campaign experienced rifts within and outside India about the strategy for the campaign.[19]

In recent years, this debate has also extended to North–South–East relationships. Nodari Simonia (in this volume) notes the rise of "entrepreneurial" NGOs (including mafioso) that have set themselves up in Russia to profit from the wash of international money. Similar stories abound throughout Central and Eastern Europe. East–West NGO partnerships remain relatively new and untested.

We will continue to see conflicts and compromises in civil society "partnerships" between North and South. It can be no other way, given disparities in culture (including organizational culture), language, experience, and funding. As we witness a slow realignment of power and influence among (already heterogeneous) organizations, different strategies and tactics around the IFIs may emerge. Possible changes may include more shareholder activism and short-term strategic alliances between civic and corporate actors (on capital controls, for example). Another new direction might see civil society engage in more active lobbying of domestic parliaments and bureaucracies on issues of global finance.

Labor activism and international trade regimes

Another significant trend for the future is growing CSO concern about international trade and trade agreements. This issue may come to overshadow campaigns on the IFIs. Such a change in emphasis would bring other kinds of CSOs to the international table, affecting the future of all.

Many of the prominent civil society organizations now focused on the Bank and the Fund (and increasingly the WTO) are umbrella social activist groups, with or without a membership structure. These kinds of actors will likely recede in prominence as attention shifts from Washington to Geneva. At the same time, international labor confederations will gain a much higher profile. The union presence is already formidable in some areas, of course. An AFL–CIO poll conducted several years ago found that two-thirds of its national membership was already engaged in global activity. An even higher percentage said that unions needed to do more in this area.[20]

Certainly, the big CSO players in globalization debates in Canada these days are the coalitions built around labor and cultural industries (including publishing) during campaigns on the Canada–US Free Trade Agreement, the North America Free Trade Area (NAFTA), and now the FTAA.[21] These labor networks are independently funded, much more membership-based, and better linked into the concerns of a domestic constituency. The trade campaigns have also pulled together some of the most interesting experiments in cross-border solidarity, including Common Frontiers and the Hemispheric Social Alliance. One activist writes that Seattle was "significant in part in establishing the importance of trade and investment issues and of the organizations that administer them and in highlighting as seldom if ever before the weight of civil society organizations as a factor in decision-making".[22]

The question is whether growing activism around global trade may eventually displace CSO attention to the IFIs and global finance. My suspicion is that Seattle was a powerful marker in a movement, one which (rightly or wrongly) identified trade reform as both core to global justice and more malleable to the popular will than finance.

The legitimacy backlash: "who are these people anyway?"

Greater roles (and/or greater visibility) of some civil society organizations has raised the ante in the legitimacy stakes. Peter Spiro goes so far as to call NGOs the "new global potentates". He argues:

> Armed with the leverage of large memberships, and knowing that those members are likely to be a docile herd, NGO leaders have emerged as a class of modern day, nonterritorial potentates, a position rather like that commanded by medieval bishops.[23]

Spiro is typical of commentators who overstate the role of CSOs in global affairs. On similar lines, Jessica Mathews has described NGOs "pushing around" even the strongest governments.[24] *Newsweek* has even claimed that, "once relegated to the do-good fringes of traditional diplomacy, NGOs have moved front and center on the world stage . . . there is a basic re-sorting of power from nation-states to non-governmental entities".[25]

However great or exaggerated their power, CSOs are being called to account for their activities and the origin of their "voice". Indeed, CSOs themselves are also interrogating their legitimacy, generating various voluntary codes of conduct for ethical behavior and fundraising.[26] Others seek legitimacy through formal, national accreditation. Meanwhile, the International Committee on Fundraising Control is addressing the challenge of accountability in thirteen countries.[27]

The drive for accountability has provoked discussion of what, more precisely, "civil society" entails. What organizations and people and values are implied? Who counts? What are the criteria for belonging? The North–South Institute has put its two cents' worth into this effort,[28] but many others have also contributed to the debate.

This discussion of criteria has important implications for the relationship between CSOs and the IFIs. First, it has consequences for consultation mechanisms. Who should be invited? To what? With access to what information? How often? Who should pay? That process threatens, at a minimum, endless months in committee.[29]

Once CSOs have secured their right to speak, there are a number of grounds on which they can claim legitimacy for their work.[30] These grounds include:

- practice-to-policy: CSOs offer practical expertise through demonstration (providing models of good practice), experience (offering insights drawn from on-the-ground involvement) and representation (where CSOs claim to speak on behalf of those who will be affected);

- working through the grassroots: by acting with, and working to strengthen, grassroots organizations, CSOs adhere to and strengthen democratic principles and practice;
- representing their members: some CSOs have a large membership base with a formal or informal role in governance;
- value-based campaigns: CSOs promote a particular value which is widely recognized within society and/or enshrined in international law;
- knowledge and research: CSOs can act as experts on a particular issue and seek to change policy through input to committees and advice to policymakers
- alliances and networks: individual CSOs can legitimize their involvement in a campaign by being part of an alliance or network which contains other members who gain their legitimacy through one of the other routes.

These debates about the legitimacy of CSOs are important, but there is a danger that they distract attention from a serious conversation about the legitimacy of other actors. What about the legitimacy of the IFIs, particular governments, and major corporations? Who, at the end of the day, is worthier than whom? The authors of this book have repeatedly debated this topic. On the one hand, some have asked, "Why should Executive Directors at the IFIs – as representatives of democracies – deal with *non*-representative groups?" In contrast, others have argued that the IFIs suffer from a major failure of public control – that is, they do not work well as democratic organs. For me, the rebuttal is the more interesting part of the conversation: how could the legitimacy of intergovernmental organizations themselves be improved? At the global level, riven with anarchy, *Realpolitik* and closed-door negotiations, that is a tall order.

Ethical energy

A final issue for the future of CSO attention to the IFIs relates to the motivating energy. The force behind campaigns to date has largely lain in sustained ethical outrage. Many (but not all) NGO staff are poorly paid. Their organizations are financially vulnerable. The campaigns are long and difficult. The steam to move forward must come from somewhere. Cynics could list the privileges of prestige and travel, but these benefits are pretty thin for most activists. How far can moral energy take the campaign? Conference fatigue has already taken a considerable toll on those following the UN circuit.[31] Seattle, Washington, and Prague have given the movement a much-needed boost.

One possible outcome, if the current tide of activism ebbs, is a shift of focus away from the IFIs. CSOs may come to regard the IFIs as less relevant in comparison with other players (see John Clark's points about the Bank in this volume). Or CSOs may conclude that the IFIs have reformed themselves. Energy expended on IFI campaigns could be recouped by grouping around new, more "strategic" targets. The WTO is an obvious example, as is the WEF.

The short story is that energy and time are the most important resources for any CSO engagement of globalization. Certainly funding, information technology, and increasingly sophisticated knowledge of world systems are factors in the success of international activism; yet ethical energy is the motor that puts those tools to work. If new targets are a pull factor, burnout may be a significant push factor away from the world of the IFIs. I do not see it today, in 2001, but ask again in 2003.

Future scenarios

Given the activities and trends described above, what possibilities face the future of IFI–civil society relationships? At least three scenarios present themselves: change of target; change of discourse; and change of institutional mechanisms.

Change of target

There are mixed assessments within the CSO world about the success of their work so far. John Foster, a Canadian activist, complains about recent efforts by international organizations to engage civil society organizations:

> While there have been some openings, a few important victories, as well as some curtsies from the powerful, generally speaking civil society organizations and NGO networks have not succeeded in bridging the moat of a well-defended and constantly reinforced castle.[32]

A first scenario, already mentioned, would see CSOs shift their attention away from the IFIs towards, in particular, issues of trade and the WTO. Alternatively, CSO campaigns on global finance might shift to more specific subjects: for example, around debt, following on Jubilee 2000; or the Bank for International Settlements; or the role of export credit agencies in development; or the policies and investment practices of international mutual fund managers.

For hardliners within the IFIs, such a change of target might bring a sigh of relief. For those inside the MDBs and the Fund who are struggling to open their organizations to new views and new voices, such a development would be a real blow.

Change of discourse

A second scenario would see a rush by the IFIs to reformed vocabulary rather than any substantive change. Rhetorical alterations in policy papers, speeches, and even organizational charts (as "Civil Society Liaison Officers" are put on the payroll) are likely to continue, but without much change in policy direction or behavior. Some critics are casting questioning eyes over the new Poverty Reduction Strategy Papers for just this reason.

It is also possible that discourse moves little. Debates may get stalemated over sovereignty, as states like Malaysia or Brazil try to limit CSO participation on global finance. Or progress may stall over issues of legitimacy, including disputes over CSO representativeness and accountability. This scenario would bring a dogged continuation of the status quo until CSO players are worn out.

Change of institutional mechanisms

A third possible scenario would see the institutionalization of some measure of CSO "oversight" over intergovernmental activities. CSOs have already had real decision-making roles in local government (such as with counterpart fund management in Peru). CSOs have also entered a few corporate governance arrangements, such as Placer Dome's NGO reference committee, which has tried to help the mining company deal with questions of ecological sustainability. And CSOs have gained some role in international treaty making, such as input from ActionAid during the Earth Summit.[33]

As for multilateral agencies, we can today see multiple nascent mechanisms for CSO oversight (with a small "o"). For example, the OAS has its Inter-American Strategy for Participation, and the World Bank involves CSOs in its Inspection Panel procedures. The UN Commission on Sustainable Development has introduced an interesting permanent mechanism for engaging CSO views on environment and development.[34] However, none of these mechanisms come close to a monitoring or enforcing role.

Of course, CSOs already have some measure of informal oversight over the IFIs. Indeed, that is an implicit premise of this whole volume of essays. But what would a more formal system of CSO oversight look like?

The proposed UN Peoples' Assembly offers one possibility. Andrew Strauss and Richard Falk write that:

> [T]he very existence of a citizen-controlled international assembly would both reinforce democratic practices within countries and undermine author-itarian rules. . . . Naive? Idealistic? Premature? That is what critics would say. But if wealthy cosmopolitans such as Turner and Soros could agree on the benefits of providing seed money, it could happen.[35]

I am skeptical about this possibility, less because of financing problems and more because of difficulties in identifying "peoples" and how they should be represented.

There is more on offer for CSOs in the proposal to modify the UN's relationships with the Bank, the Fund, and the WTO. These changes would see the General Assembly (through its Economic and Social Council) wield more meaningful oversight over the Bank and the Fund (technically UN agencies, but long departed from the family home) and take the WTO under its wing as well. Since the UN has relatively stronger mechanisms for CSO involvement, civil society could by these means gain a stronger role *vis-à-vis* the IFIs.

Conclusion

This last possibility – that we could create new mechanisms for the governance of international finance – poses its own challenges. This chapter has offered several answers to the question "what next?" and suggests that CSOs are interested in – and increasingly equipped to serve – an oversight role, despite and because of a host of other forces that shape their work and partnerships. In concluding, we can look even further forward: what would a CSO oversight role in the IFIs mean, much more broadly, for democracy itself?

The whole of this volume, of course, deals with democracy (among other things) without often calling it by name. The core question – who decides, and how – applies to finance as much as to any other policy realm. In its origins, democracy was a way of making decisions that involved small groups. Today, democracy needs to be refashioned to encompass countries of multiple millions. The issues are terribly complex. Again, who decides, and how?

The rise of social mobilization around the institutions of global governance thus provides an added spur to rethinking – and improving – democracy. Today's democracy stretches the link between the governed and the governors a long way. The distance from the citizen to what is done and said in global organizations on our behalf is large indeed. When decisions about global finance fall outside intergovernmental circles, that distance is greater still. This simple point bears repeating: even for citizens of strong democracies, it is incredibly difficult to participate directly in the decisions of global governance that deeply affect our lives.

This is the core dilemma of global governance. Our global system is anarchical: self-regulating without overarching authority. It is not chaotic, but operates through negotiated and imperfect cooperation among unequals. This system of global governance includes the big names such as the UN, NATO, the World Bank, the IMF, and the WTO. It also includes multiple other entities – both inside and outside government – that regulate air traffic, seas, climate change conventions, and accounting standards.

If we were poorer democrats, these concerns probably would not matter. If we were disinterested in politics, then it would not matter what happened in Geneva or Washington or Seattle or Prague. CSO mobilization is often (though not always) a vibrant manifestation of democratic concern. Political disengagement is the more serious threat. The good news is that there are lots of men and women – educated, active, hooked up – who are looking at ways to supplement (not usurp or replace) the imperfect democracies we have built. Improving the global governance of finance may thus be a step on the road to improving global democracy.

Notes

1 Helmut Anheier and Lester Salamon, *The Nonprofit Sector in the Developing World: A Comparative Analysis*, Manchester: Manchester University Press, 1998.
2 Anita Anand, "Global Meeting Place: United Nations' World Conferences and Civil Society", in John W. Foster with Anita Anand (eds), *Whose World Is It Anyway? Civil*

Society, the United Nations and the Multilateral Future, Ottawa: United Nations Association in Canada, 1999, pp. 90, 92, 96, 101.

3 See <http://wbln0018.worldbank.org/essd/essd.nsf/NGOs/home>, "Frequently Asked Questions".

4 See <http://www.imf.org/external/np/tr/2000/TR000613.htm>.

5 North–South Institute, "Series on the Multilateral Development Banks": *The African Development Bank*, by E. Philip English and Harris M. Mule; *The Asian Development Bank*, by Nihal Kappagoda; *The Caribbean Development Bank*, by Chandra Hardy; *The Inter-American Development Bank*, by Diana Tussie; *Titans or Behemoths?* by Roy Culpeper, all published by Boulder: Lynne Rienner, 1995 and later; Gabriel Casaburi and Diana Tussie, "Governance and the New Lending Strategies of the Multilateral Development Banks: Some Research Questions", Working Paper 1, Buenos Aires: FLACSO, no date.

6 Jan Aart Scholte, "The International Monetary Fund and Civil Society: An Underdeveloped Dialogue", unpublished report, August 1998.

7 Sylvia Ostry, "Globalization – What Does It Mean?" *Globalization and Its Discontents*, Report of The Annual Policy Conference of The Group of 78, Cantley, Quebec, October 1999, pp. 14–21.

8 CCIC, *Choices in Common, Communities in Common: Canadians Deliberate about Globalization*, Final Report, September 1999.

9 See <http://www.biodev.org/index2.htm>.

10 The momentum has already been the subject of an international conference on "Protesting 'Globalisation': Prospects for Transnational Solidarity", held under the auspices of the Research Committee on Social Movements and Collective Action of the International Sociological Association, 10–11 December 1999.

11 Robin Broad and John Cavanagh, "The Death of the Washington Consensus?", *World Policy Journal*, Vol. 16, No. 3, Fall 1999, pp. 79–88.

12 Deepa Narayan, Robert Chambers, Meera Shah, and Patti Petesch, "Global Synthesis: Consultations with the Poor", Washington: World Bank, September 1999 (discussion paper).

13 Robert O'Brien, Anne Marie Goetz, Jan Aart Scholte and Marc Williams, *Contesting Global Governance: Multilateral Economic Institutions and Global Social Movements*, Cambridge: Cambridge University Press, 2000; Gabrielle Marceau and Peter N. Pedersen, "Is the WTO Open and Transparent? A Discussion of the Relationship of the WTO with Non-governmental Organisations and Civil Society's Claims for More Transparency and Public Participation", *Journal of World Trade*, Vol. 33, No. 1, February 1999, pp. 5–49; Jan Aart Scholte with Robert O'Brien and Marc Williams, "The WTO and Civil Society", *Journal of World Trade*, Vol. 33, No. 1, February 1999, pp. 107–24; Jan Aart Scholte, "'In the Foothills': Relations between the IMF and Civil Society", in R. Higgott *et al.* (eds), *Non-State Actors and Authority in the Global System*, London: Routledge, 2000, pp. 256–73; Yasmine Shamsie, *Engaging with Civil Society: Lessons from the OAS, FTAA, and Summits of the Americas*, Ottawa: The North–South Institute, 2000, available at <http://www.nsi-ins.ca/ensi/research/voices/index.htm>.

14 Georg Kell and John Gerard Ruggie, "Global Markets and Social Legitimacy: The Case of the Global Compact", paper presented at a conference on "Governing the Public Domain beyond the Era of the Washington Consensus? Redrawing the Line Between the State and the Market", York University, 4–6 November 1999.

15 Andrew Strauss and Richard Falk, "All that Dough: Conditions are Just Right for Global Democratization", *The Philadelphia Inquirer*, 12 October 1997, p. E6.

16 Rodney Schmidt, *A Feasible Foreign Exchange Transactions Tax*, Ottawa: The North–South Institute, 1999, available at <http://www.nsiins.ca/ensi/publications/resrep.html>.

17 Lisa Jordan and Peter van Tuijl, "Political Responsibility in NGO Advocacy: Exploring Emerging Shapes of Global Democracy", paper for NOVIB, April 1998, published at <www.oneworld.org/euforic/novib/novib1.htm>.

18 Countered in Jay Mazur, "Labor's New Internationalism", *Foreign Affairs*, Vol. 79, No. 1, January/February 2000, pp. 79–93.

19 See Foster with Anand, *Whose World Is It Anyway?*; Paul Nelson, "Heroism and Ambiguity: NGO Advocacy in International Policy", *Development in Practice*, Vol. 10, Nos. 3 and 4, August 2000, pp. 478–90; John D. Clark, "Ethical Globalization: The Dilemmas and Challenges of Internationalizing Civil Society", in M. Edwards and J. Gaventa, eds, *Global Citizen Action*, Boulder: Rienner, 2001, pp. 17–28; Jordan and Van Tuijl, "Political Responsibility in NGO Advocacy".

20 Mazur, "Labor's New Internationalism".

21 John W. Foster, "Confronting the Global Economic Constitution", in Alison Van Rooy (ed.), *Civil Society and Global Change: The Canadian Development Report 1999*, Ottawa: The North–South Institute, 1999.

22 John W. Foster, "The Quest for an 'Enabling Environment': Civil Society Engagement in International Decision-Making", UNRISD Copenhagen +5, Background paper, Unpublished, 2000, p. 24.

23 Peter J. Spiro, "New Global Potentates: Nongovernmental Organizations and the 'Unregulated' Marketplace", *Cardozo Law Review*, Vol. 18, December 1996, p. 963.

24 Jessica Mathews, "Power Shift", *Foreign Affairs*, Vol. 76, No. 1, January/February 1997, pp. 50–66.

25 Cited in Jordan and Van Tuijl, "Political Responsibility in NGO Advocacy", p. 22.

26 Tatsuro Kunugi and Martha Schweitz (eds), *Codes of Conduct for Partnership in Governance: Texts and Commentaries*, Provisional version presented to the "World Civil Society Conference: Building Global Governance Partnerships", 7–11 December 1999, Montreal, Tokyo: United Nations University; Michael Edwards, *NGO Rights and Responsibilities: A New Deal for Global Governance*, London: Foreign Policy Centre, 2000.

27 See <www.icfo.org>; John Beishon, "Keeping Tabs on Multinational NGOs", *Alliance*, Vol. 4, No. 3, September 1999, pp. 11–13.

28 Alison Van Rooy (ed.), *Civil Society and the Aid Industry*, London: Earthscan, 1998.

29 This is the topic of a large research project now underway at the North–South Institute called *Voices: The Rise of Nongovernmental Voices in Multilateral Organizations*. More information is available at <http://www.nsi-ins.ca/ensi/research/voices/index.htm>.

30 The following points are drawn from Jennifer Chapman and Thomas Fisher, "The Effectiveness of NGO Campaigning: Lessons from Practice", *Development in Practice*, Vol. 10, No. 2, May 2000, pp. 151–65.

31 Michael Edwards, "Does the Doormat Influence the Boot? Critical Thoughts on UK NGOs and International Advocacy", *Development in Practice*, Vol. 3, No. 3, October 1993, pp. 163–75; and Chapman and Fisher, "Effectiveness of NGO Campaigning".

32 Foster, "Quest for an 'Enabling Environment' ", p. 1.

33 Alison Van Rooy, "The Frontiers of Influence: NGO Lobbying at the 1974 World Food Conference, the 1992 Earth Summit and Beyond", *World Development*, Vol. 25, No. 1, January 1997, pp. 93–114.

34 Megan Howell, "The NGO Steering Committee and Multi-Stakeholder Participation at the UN Commission on Sustainable Development", *Civil Society Engaging Multilateral Institutions: At the Crossroads*, Montreal: Montreal International Forum, Vol. 1, No. 1, Fall 1999.

35 Strauss and Falk, "All that Dough".

16 Global finance

Representation failure and the role of civil society

Nancy Birdsall[1]

Summary

•	Introduction	264
•	Global financial governance: market failures plus imperfect democracy	265
•	Civil society and global finance: the record so far	273
•	A future role for civil society in global finance	279
•	A concluding note	282

Introduction

Finance has become newly global in the last decade – in the form of flows that are faster, larger, more volatile, and increasingly and dangerously correlated across the world. So too civil society, with its increasing scale and influence and its protestations about the global economy; indeed, in many quarters civil society activities are seen as another sign of the diminished powers of the nation-state.[2] Finance and civil society both epitomize globalization: connections that are not only international, consisting primarily of relations among sovereign states, but also "global", consisting of economic, political and social links among many different overlapping groups and agents – apparently quite independent of twentieth-century-style inter-state "international" relations.

This book poses two questions linking global finance and civil society. The first question asks what, if anything, civil society has contributed to make global finance more effective, equitable and democratic. The second, normative question asks what the role of civil society should be.

In this chapter I try to answer these two questions. My responses are necessarily tentative and incomplete, given the novelty of the issues. My answers also – probably far too much – reflect my own experience (many years working inside global financial institutions) and prejudices.

My answer to the normative question is optimistic. Civil society groups, despite their imperfections, can contribute to making highly imperfect global financial markets more effective and fair. They can do so in two principal ways. First, they can address the inherent and intractable representation failures in the official institutions of global finance. They can press to make these public institutions more representative and thus at least somewhat more "democratic". Second, civil society groups can create and disseminate more information about how private financial markets work, thereby exposing for wider public scrutiny such remediable problems as money laundering, tax havens and inadequate regulation of hedge funds.

However, my answer to the positive question is less comforting. To date, civil society groups have had limited impact on global financial markets. To increase their impact, civil society actors must broaden their focus beyond specific issues and institutions – such as the environment and the World Bank – to other institutions and to the shortcomings of private financial markets. At the same time, civil society groups also need to narrow their focus, putting more emphasis on the fundamental problem of the poor representation of poor countries and poor people in global finance – what might be called the democratic deficit in global financial governance.

Global financial governance: market failures plus imperfect democracy

Global financial markets are riddled with problems. What economists refer to as "market failures" make even local financial markets unstable and ineffective. Market failures arise because, in a world of imperfect information, lenders and investors cannot perfectly assess the creditworthiness of borrowers. They thus rely on imperfect analysis of risk, on reputation, and on collateral or other types of guarantees. One effect of these poor substitutes for perfect information is that many creditworthy borrowers simply cannot borrow. For instance, a successful but still poor micro-entrepreneur is often unable to borrow to expand her business. In addition, financial markets are inherently vulnerable to bandwagon and herd behavior. For example, a panic-driven bank run can leave everyone involved (depositors, bank shareholders, borrowers, and even taxpayers, who end up footing the bill if government intervenes) worse off.

Global financial markets are as fragile as local markets. Instability in the global market is more dangerous because there is no exempt corner of stability to come to the rescue. Information across borders is less easily assessed. Government measures that can have critical effects on financial markets (monetary, exchange rate, and fiscal policies) are hard to predict and difficult to monitor. Although the International Monetary Fund (IMF) may help to counter herd-driven panics, global financial markets have no real lender of last resort (comparable to the central bank function of the Federal Reserve in the United States, for example). Nor is a world bankruptcy procedure available to distribute the losses.

In the last fifty years, the international community has developed many official institutions of what might be called "global financial governance". Some agencies were designed specifically to address the inherent problems of imperfect markets. The IMF was originally designed to minimize the costs of financial uncertainty at the global level – disruptive to trade, for example – and to minimize the domestic costs for countries adjusting to balance of payment problems in a fixed exchange rate system. Beginning with the debt crisis in Latin America in the early 1980s, and then during the 1990s when financial crises that threatened global financial stability erupted in East Asia, Russia and Brazil, the IMF has taken on some of the characteristics of a lender of last resort. The IMF also played that role in Mexico in 1994–95, but it is less obvious that global financial stability was at risk in that case. The World Bank was created to provide a mechanism for transferring investment to capital-poor countries that otherwise might be or appear to be insufficiently creditworthy.

Today many other international institutions also play some role, implicit or explicit, in the governance of global finance. The United Nations has many agencies involved in the transfer of resources to relatively poor countries. The Bank for International Settlements (BIS) and the Basle Committee bring together national central banks. The G7, the G20, and the G77 are clubs of states that among other things discuss and try to coordinate national monetary and fiscal policies. The World Trade Organization (WTO) and the dozens of regional and bilateral trade groups, as well as the many multilateral banks at the regional and sub-regional level – all of these bodies play roles in global financial governance.

In short, there is no lack of official international institutions that deal directly or indirectly with global finance. But the system of global financial governance is not particularly effective or equitable. (It could be argued that "effective" governance should embrace issues of fairness as well as problems of efficiency and stability and not treat equity as an extra. Here I adhere to the more common, but perhaps wrongheaded, definition of "effective".) In the 1990s, financial crises in Mexico (1994–95), East Asia (1997–98), Russia (1998), and Brazil (1999) grabbed headlines, as did the near-crisis of a hedge fund, Long Term Capital Management (1998). The threat to global financial stability and the high economic and social costs to affected societies brought home – even to insiders – the reality that the global financial system is far from *effective*.[3] Though systematic analyses are hard to come by, the evidence also suggests that markets are far from *equitable* in the distribution of the costs of global financial crises. For example, it appears that workers suffer real wage losses that persist over time in countries subject to crises.[4] In addition, countries with more open capital markets are more likely to have greater wage gaps between skilled and unskilled workers, at least for some time.[5] The immediate costs of local banking crises are often absorbed by governments, who in the medium term pass on at least some of the costs to taxpayers. Given that tax systems in many developing countries are relatively regressive, tax-financed bailouts usually constitute an unfair transfer from poor taxpayers to generally wealthier bank shareholders and debtors – as Keynes put it, from taxpayers to rentiers.[6]

Moreover, the institutions, rules and norms that make up global financial governance are far from *democratic*. Dahl has argued that international organizations of any type are by their nature undemocratic, whatever their rules regarding decision-making.[7] Citizens cannot effectively exercise much control over key decisions made by their official representatives in international settings. Foreign affairs are seldom the dominant issue for voters in selecting representatives in a system of democratic representation, and information about foreign affairs (and even more so about global financial issues) is not easily accessible. This is true even in mature, functioning democracies and all the more so in countries where democracy has shallow roots.

A critical representation failure in global financial governance is the lack of accountability of the system to relatively poor countries and to the poor within those countries. In the UN General Assembly, the decision-making system of one-country-one-vote may seem to represent poorer countries. However, that approach fails to align voting power with financial responsibility, so it is virtually irrelevant in matters of global finance. In the World Bank, voting power is aligned with ownership shares. At its founding, when ownership shares were closely related to financial contributions, this formula made sense. Today, however, some major shareholders, especially the United States, exercise influence that is out of proportion to their costs. As Kapur puts it, for a country like the United States the marginal cost of influence at the Bank today is zero.[8] In criticizing the policies of the IMF in dealing with the Asian financial crisis, Stiglitz has argued that the Fund is not accountable to the countries most likely to bear the costs of its decisions – namely, the dependent developing countries.[9] By implication, the IMF and the World Bank are also not accountable in these countries to the poor and working-class populations, who generally bear a substantial portion of the burden of policy decisions that these institutions encourage or even impose on government leaders.

To this democratic deficit at the international level must be added the problem of poor representation within countries and its effects on their positions within the international financial institutions (IFIs). Many developing countries are hardly fully democratic, and their representatives at the international institutions that affect global finance are therefore not particularly accountable to their own citizens. Of course, many representatives act professionally in trying to promote their citizens' interests. However, with gaps of accountability they and their governments may end up making different tradeoffs than they otherwise would.

To be sure, the democratic deficit in suprastate institutions is not limited to developing countries. For example, a troublesome democratic deficit arguably operates in respect of the European Union and the European Central Bank.[10] However, the deficit operates with a double whammy in the case of the IMF and the World Bank. Not only are the people most affected by those agencies often poorly represented in their own governments, but their governments are also poorly represented in the international institutions.

In an odd twist, many developing countries, especially those that are representative democracies, view their own civil society with some suspicion. They resent the efforts of the international financial bureaucracies to have direct – even if only informal – contact with those groups. Government officials typically argue that they are the true representatives of their populations through which all IFI contacts with local groups should be channeled. Only a few years ago, the borrowing members of the Inter-American Development Bank (IDB) resisted management's proposals to budget for "outreach" efforts to civil society groups in borrowing countries. The proposal was included in an original version of a staff task force report on the IDB's Country Offices, but was subsequently omitted from the budget for the proposed program. A more explicit and ambitious program of outreach has gone forward in the country-based offices of the World Bank. Borrowers have less voting power in the World Bank than in the IDB, and their reaction to the World Bank policy was therefore more muted.

Despite the objections of some developing country officials, the IMF and the World Bank have recently formalized the inclusion of civil society groups in the preparation by countries of so-called "Poverty Reduction Strategy Papers" (PRSPs). In an effort to ensure greater ownership of reforms, and more consensus among citizens on their country's poverty reduction strategy, the Fund and the Bank will monitor the extent to which those strategies were developed in a participatory way, including open discussion with civil society groups. It may not be a coincidence that PRSP consultations are being implemented primarily in the poorer countries that are most dependent on the international institutions for concessional finance.

The democratic deficit within the two best-known IFIs, the IMF and the World Bank, almost surely reduces their effectiveness. Indeed, recent efforts to ensure more ownership have largely been aimed at recovering effectiveness. For example, a report of the Bank's independent evaluation office found that only 62.5 per cent of projects were "satisfactory" in 1991, down from 85 per cent in 1980.[11]

Other examples also illustrate the problems. On the environment, for instance, the Bank only slowly recognized the ecological costs of some of the projects it financed.[12] That recognition came primarily as a result of outside pressure led by environmental nongovernmental organizations (NGOs). A second example concerns participation in project areas like irrigation, urban housing and rural development. Here, the Bank only recognized benefits of direct accountability to local participants in the last two decades, implying that Bank-sponsored projects were for many years less effective than they might have been.[13] In a third area, IMF and World Bank stabilization and adjustment programs, the evidence of ineffectiveness in producing more growth and less poverty is more controversial. However, both institutions have recognized that the conventional approach to conditionality in those programs may not have worked well, making the policies less effective than they might have been.[14]

The democratic deficit also helps explain the IFIs' historic emphasis on economic growth and stability over equity. Of course, the World Bank has explicitly aimed to reduce poverty, at least since the presidency of McNamara in the late 1960s. During the 1990s the Bank has considerably increased its emphasis on social issues and raised its lending for health, education and other programs most likely to reach the poor. However, these efforts are relatively recent and have resulted in part from outside pressures.

Even with its long-standing focus on poverty reduction, the Bank was silent on income distribution and redistributive issues until the fall of the Berlin Wall made concern about equality as well as poverty more acceptable in mainstream economic and political circles.[15] The lack of attention to distribution meant that legitimate efforts to increase stability and growth via stabilization and adjustment programs (with benefits for all, including the poor) seldom included provisions – implicit or explicit – to unravel subsidies that benefited the rich. Nor did the programs seek to alter tax systems or spending priorities in the interests of equity.

As for the IMF, only in the last few years – and under outside pressure – has it given attention to the unintended ill-effects on the poor of its medium-term stabilization programs. Likewise, the Fund only belatedly recognized the unintended harms of its efforts (most notably in East Asia in 1998) to reduce capital flight with high interest rates and reduced fiscal deficits.

Moreover, the democratic deficit in the IFIs is only the tip of the iceberg of imperfect representation in the larger world of global finance. In the 1990s, official net transfers across borders became smaller and much less relevant than private transfers for some developing countries (see Figures 16.1 and 16.2). During this decade, the net transfers of the IMF and the four main multilateral banks represented only about 10 per cent of all financial transfers to developing countries.

It is true that most private financial transfers have concentrated in around a dozen of the larger and mostly middle-income developing countries and that official transfers, even when relatively small, can matter, because they signal to the private sector that recipient countries have sound economic programs and therefore catalyze private flows. And of course some countries – e.g. in Africa – depend almost entirely on official transfers (see Figure 16.3). On the other hand, it is also true that private inflows have been much more important than official inflows for some small countries, including Chile, Costa Rica, El Salvador, Latvia, Poland and Thailand. Private flows have also mattered immensely for several low-income countries like India, Indonesia and China (see Figure 16.4).

Of course, private flows are determined by market forces that are by their nature "undemocratic" and "unfair". In a perfectly competitive market, with an equal initial distribution of assets, private capital flows could be "fair", but neither of these two other-worldly conditions obtains. To the extent that private flows are regulated, the public objective is to minimize instability and to reduce the costs to legitimate participants of fraud, corruption, money laundering and so on. These are all legitimate objectives, but they do not necessarily make financial markets more democratic or more equitable. Institutions such as the Basle Committee, the International Accounting Standards Committee, and the Financial Stability Forum are focussed on making global finance more stable and efficient within an inherently imperfect market, not on making it more fair.

The hard reality is that global financial markets are imperfect. The IFIs are fundamentally unrepresentative and undemocratic. The private associations, norms, and practices that along with the official institutions constitute the "system" of global finance are not particularly concerned with equity or democracy.

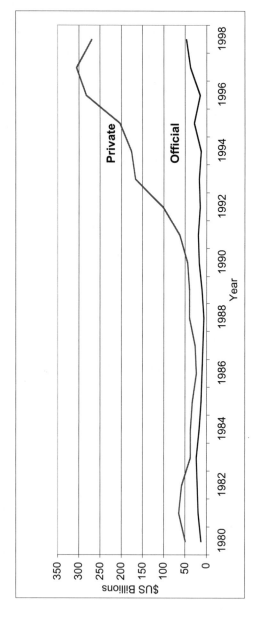

Figure 16.1 Total net official and private capital flows: developing countries.*

Source: World Bank, *World Development Indicators*, 2000.

Note

* Developing countries include the following regions: East Asia and Pacific, Eastern Europe and Central Asia, Latin America and Caribbean, Middle East and North Africa, South Asia, and Sub-Saharan Africa.

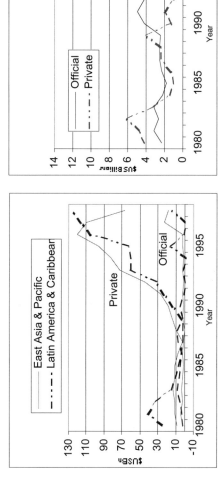

Figure 16.2 Official and private flows: East Asia and Pacific, Latin America and Caribbean.

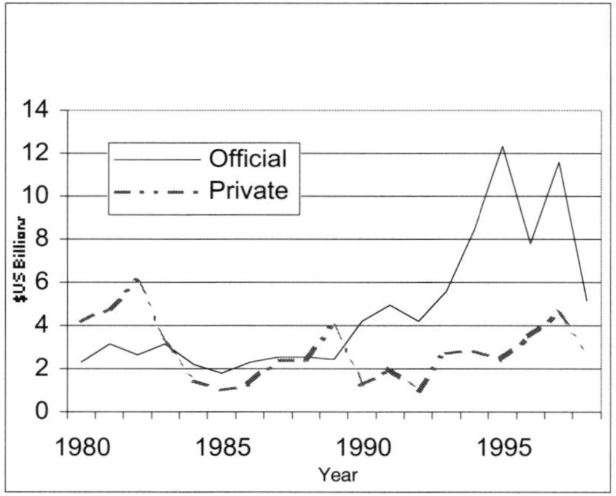

Figure 16.3 Official and private flows: Sub-Saharan Africa (not including South Africa).

Source: World Bank, *World Development Indicators,* 2000.

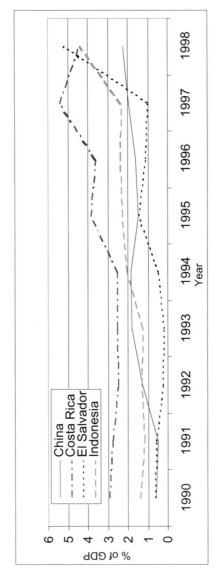

Figure 16.4 Gross private capital flows (percentage of GDP, PPP).

Source: World Bank, *World Development Indicators*, 2000.

Civil society and global finance: the record so far

The editors of this book define civil society organizations (CSOs) as "voluntary" (i.e. not-for-profit) groups that make deliberate attempts to shape governance, that is "to mould the rules of social and political life". For the purposes of my discussion I further narrow the definition to groups that are "disinterested" in their own welfare; that is, they define their objectives (at least in principle) as advancing the larger welfare of a global society. I therefore exclude, for example, unions and non-profit associations of businesses, which exist fundamentally to advance the interests of specific groups. (In practice, of course, the distinction is not always clear-cut, as many labor and business associations at least claim to promote the public interest.)

In the preceding chapter, Van Rooy describes a notable increase in the number of non-profit organizations concerned with international issues. The number of CSOs working in more than one country has doubled in the last decade, to a current total of about 38,000 registered associations. Increases have been particularly rapid in CSOs that work on "global" issues such as human rights, women's rights, the environment and development. For a decade and more, many of these groups have focussed attention heavily on the World Bank. Clark (in this volume) notes that the World Bank in particular has made a fine target for CSOs, because many Bank staff are fundamentally friendly to the broad social objectives of CSOs and because the Bank's powerful shareholders are themselves democratic and thus can be effectively lobbied. More recently, CSOs have also turned their attention to the IMF, in large part because the Fund holds the debt of many of the world's poorest countries and has been the central player in structural adjustment as well as in stabilization programs in those countries. The Jubilee 2000 coalition is the most visible example of this increased interest in the Fund. The last several years have also seen the rise of more generalized concern about "globalization" and the emergence of the WTO as a new rallying point for civil society mobilization. Demonstrations at the Seattle meeting of the WTO in November–December 1999 and the IMF/World Bank meetings in Washington in April 2000 and Prague in September 2000 reflected not only the specific interest of some CSOs in undermining trade agreements or attacking specific policies of the institutions. The protests also reflected a larger inchoate set of public worries about globalization: for example, that it favors the privileged over the working majority; and corporate interests over social justice, local cultural identity, and environmental protection.

Civil society groups from the "North" – the world's richer economies and in particular the United States – dominated in Seattle, Washington, and Prague. Civic groups from the "South" – the developing countries – were much less represented, probably because geography made their participation difficult. Commentators from developing countries, including President Zedillo of Mexico, complained with some justification that the dominance of US civil society was unrepresentative and that its apparent opposition to greater global economic integration meant that the activists were prepared to impose underdevelopment on the South.[16] Civil society groups in the South are less likely to condemn free trade, the central issue in Seattle, seeing trade as a good vehicle for more jobs and faster development.

Northern CSOs chose the meetings of the WTO and the IMF/World Bank largely for visibility and symbolic reasons. In fact, civil society campaigners who are most concerned with the activities of these institutions exert day-to-day pressure for change not at mass demonstrations, but through the governments of their own countries. This strategy makes sense, since those governments have the controlling share of decision-making power. A focus on national authorities has been especially apparent in the United States, where CSOs have been particularly effective in lobbying the Congress for reform of multilateral institutions. CSOs have also targeted some European governments. For example, environmental groups in Germany pushed their government to the forefront of efforts to have the World Bank manage programs to protect the Amazon forests. In short, civil society groups in the United States, and to some extent in Europe, are most effective when they push their own democratic governments to take certain positions within the institutions. This is not to say that management and staff in the international institutions are powerless – only that ultimately they are more like bricklayers than architects in the global financial system.

In contrast, civil society associations in the South have found it both more difficult and less effective to lobby their own governments. Instead, the multilateral institutions themselves are often the best – and sometimes the only – available targets for direct lobbying. In most developing countries the rule of law and norms of transparency and public accountability are weak. Hence it is usually easier to influence the relevant international agency than the government on issues such as the environmental impact of a World Bank-financed project, or the content of trade agreements with respect to local labor standards, or the allocation of losses among corporate firms, workers, and consumers following a financial crisis.

As noted above, many democratic governments in the South still reject the very existence of CSOs and their advocacy role. CSOs are often – and often correctly – viewed as vehicles for the political opposition or for resistance to necessary economic reforms. In nondemocratic countries of the South, CSOs have even less space for advocacy or lobbying of their own governments. Indeed, as Figure 16.5 suggests, an effective civil society depends on a strong and democratic state. An effective advocacy role for civil society is as likely to reflect as to contribute to better representation of citizens in politics generally.

For all these reasons, CSOs in many developing countries find international institutions like the World Bank a more accessible target of lobbying efforts than their own governments. In a kind of boomerang effect, civil society groups in the South often collaborate with groups in the North to press the IFIs to adopt policies that the Southern groups want. In other words, they try to change policies and practices in their own countries through international agencies. For example, civil society groups in developing countries that cannot get redress from their own governments use the independent Inspection Panel of the World Bank, set up at the behest primarily of the United States in response to Northern civil society pressure. Some Southern groups even end up lobbying Northern governments in order to change policies that they cannot easily affect locally. For example, the heads of NGOs in Uganda and India have testified about the World Bank and the IMF before US Congressional committees.

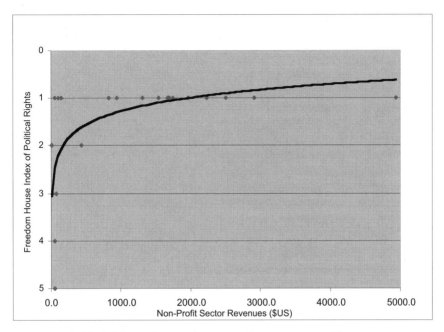

Figure 16.5 Political rights and per-capita non-profit sector revenues.*†

Sources: Johns Hopkins Comparative Non-Profit Sector Project; Freedom House.

Notes
* A regression of the log of per-capita non-profit revenue against political rights gives a statistically significant result (95% level). (Similar results are obtained if GDP, rather than population, is used to standardize non-profit sector revenues.)
† Figure prepared by Brian Deese.

The above graph looks at the relationship between civil society participation and democratic "strength" across countries. Civil society activity is represented (imperfectly, for sure) by per-capita non-profit sector revenue, and democratic strength is measured by Freedom House's political rights variable that ranges from 1 (most open and democratic), to 7 (least open and democratic). Data on non-profits are only available for twenty-two countries: thirteen from the North, four from Eastern Europe, and five from Latin America. The absence of data and research into levels of civil society participation in many less democratic states is itself a signal of civil society's weaknesses in these areas.

The regression line indicates that there is an association between the democratic strength of a country and the level of activity of its civil society. Countries with low Freedom House scores (high levels of openness and democratic freedoms) tend to have non-profit sectors with higher revenues, and presumably more activity. In non-democratic societies – without traditional lobbying channels and forums for outsider input – the environment may be less conducive to CSO activity.

An additional obstacle that civil society in the South faces with respect to global finance is its weakness on technical and analytical issues, and the relative dearth of local independent policy research. Policy think tanks in the South are at best small and poorly funded. In many Southern countries they do not exist at all. In some cases – as in China and much of Latin America – they are largely dependent on government. As a result, advocacy groups in the South are largely reliant on analysis done elsewhere, including by citizens of the developing countries who reside in the North.

Using different tactics, then, civil society organizations in both the North and the South have ultimately focused most of their advocacy regarding global finance on the two principal IFIs: the World Bank and, more recently, the IMF. Lobbying on the World Bank has played a salutary role in increasing the Bank's attention to the environment, to problems of women, indigenous groups and minority ethnic groups, and to the potentially negative social impacts of Bank-financed projects and adjustment programs. CSO pressure has played some role in pushing the Bank to formulate formal policies and procedures on participation of groups affected by resettlement and infrastructure projects. Likewise, CSO advocacy has helped to introduce environmental assessments of all Bank-financed projects and gender assessments to gauge the impact of Bank projects on women. Civil society pressure has also complemented the efforts of the major shareholders to make the World Bank more transparent: with earlier open consultation of stakeholders; and with greater public disclosure of project and policy documents. The recently increased focus of CSOs on the IMF – though to date not as successful as campaigns on the World Bank – has pushed the Fund toward more transparency about its deliberations and decisions.

So, with their watchdog function on certain issues in certain institutions, CSOs have made these fundamentally undemocratic IFIs somewhat more accountable and thus (one hopes) more effective, at least on some issues. Since disinterested CSOs have put considerable focus on the plight of the poor and minority groups in developing countries, they have also pushed these official institutions toward more concern with social equity. CSOs have provided a weak but important substitute for the lack of effective representation of poor people in poor countries in the deliberations and decisions of the IFIs.

However, only a few CSOs have focussed on making the IFIs more representative or more democratic. It could be argued that a more representative system of governance – by making these institutions more accountable to the groups whose lives they affect most – is the real key to their long-run effectiveness and fairness.

The official institutions are unrepresentative in two respects: *vis-à-vis* states and *vis-à-vis* citizens. In terms of state representation, the IFIs accord limited power to the developing countries. Table 16.1 shows the allocation of ownership shares and thus formal voting power among countries. The table also indicates the distribution of seats on the Executive Boards of the major IFIs. In the two global institutions and the European Bank for Reconstruction and Development (EBRD), formal decision-making power is concentrated with the high-income non-borrowing member states. A complete review of the voting rules and quota and other systems would in general show even greater concentration of power and control of decisions. In the regional banks, the ownership shares shown for borrowers exaggerate their power, since these banks borrow only against the capital of the non-borrowers; thus their operations are still fundamentally dependent on the non-borrowers. On the other hand, because most day-to-day decisions at the board level are made by consensus, the voice of borrowers is more important.

Table 16.1 Ownership shares and Executive Board seat distribution of major IFIs

	Voting share				Seats[a]			
	US	Other G7	Other Non-borrowers	Developing country borrowers	US	Other G7	Other non-borrowers	Developing country borrowers
IMF	17.33	30.33	19.35	33.05	1	6	6	11
World Bank	16.95	27.37	17.53	38.15	1	6	7	10
Inter-American Development Bank	30.5	14.53	4.53	50.44	1	3	1	9
Asian Development Bank	13.09	26.67	8.69	51.55	1	4	1	6
European Bank for Reconstruction and Development	10.28	47.29[b]	30.26	12.17	1	6	12[a]	4
African Development Bank	6.2	26.9	16.9	50.0	1	4	1	12

Notes

a In a few cases, both non-borrowers and borrowers are represented in one chair – e.g. the case of the Netherlands and Armenia in the World Bank. We have categorized these instances as non-borrower chairs.

b Includes a representative of the European Investment Bank and a representative of the European Commission.

In terms of citizen representation, populations of the developing countries – who as taxpayers guarantee the repayment of IFI loans – often lack adequate systems of representation. Developing country citizens have little influence in their own governments' decisions to borrow or in the implementation of IFI-financed projects and policies. Ensuring that global financial transfers are more democratic is an objective that the major development-driven CSOs in the North have neglected, at least in comparison to their concern with issues such as the environment, labor standards, and poverty reduction. The CSOs have tended to focus on specific issues much more than on giving people in the borrowing countries political tools to drive the IFI agendas. Although there has been recent increased CSO emphasis on participation of developing country populations, it has been confined to the poorest countries and focussed strongly on the Heavily Indebted Poor Country (HIPC) Initiative for debt relief.

In fact, there is a certain irony in one outcome of this history. Pressure of civil society in the North, especially in the United States, actually augments US influence in the international institutions. The governments – not to speak of the peoples – of the South end up having even less say in the decisions of the IFIs, while the views of powerful CSOs in the North figure strongly. Notable examples of this dynamic are the Narmada River hydroelectric project in India and the resettlement project in western China (near Tibet). In both cases, governments withdrew their requests for World Bank loans to support these projects following long periods of opposition from CSOs that were (at least initially) mainly based in the North.[17]

There is one new area of focus among civil society groups that provides an opportunity for better linkage of the goal of development with the objective of representation. This is the emergent view that ideas, policies and practices that are imported into the developing countries via international loans cannot substitute for local political will. The implication is that citizen participation in the development of the economic reform agendas supported by the IMF and the World Bank is key to the viability and sustainability of the policies.[18] Both internal and external evaluations have concluded that IFI conditionality has often not worked, especially in Africa, in the absence of local ownership of reform programs, grounded in greater citizen participation. The Bank and the Fund now seek to ensure that borrowing governments "own" the programs and that local citizens and local civil society groups participate in the decision-making process. In this new approach, the country itself takes full responsibility for formulating its "own" strategy for development, in the form of the previously mentioned Poverty Reduction Strategy Paper. Staff of the IFIs will assess the extent to which the country's strategy reflects adequate "ownership" via adequate "participation" of its citizens.

This form of participation can be beneficial to the extent that it makes governments in the South more accountable to their own citizens. However, the approach is also full of dangers and difficulties. Inasmuch as loans become conditional upon participation, the IFIs may, ironically, end up being more intrusive. They are, after all, now making judgments not only about economic policy, but about political practice as well.[19] However, constructive involvement by legitimate local civil society groups – both in the countries themselves and in the North – could determine whether the approach ultimately compounds the problem or addresses it by truly creating more representation of the people affected by global financial programs. Indeed, civil society groups can help official institutions to determine what constitutes "participation": how to define legitimate representation; how to set appropriate standards for local transparency; etc. Both local and outside civil society groups can play a role in this regard. Civil society in the North can sponsor independent analysis and provide technical and financial support for in-country groups.

What about the world of global finance beyond the IFIs? Civil society groups have maintained a near-singular focus on the official bodies, as evident even in the structure and content of this book. Yet, in terms of the impact of global finance on peoples' lives, the public agencies in many cases play a small role compared to the private markets. For example, in terms of the value of outstanding loans, the World Bank went from being the world's fourth largest bank in 1960 to its sixty-second largest in 1997 (or thirty-fourth if the concessional window, IDA, is included).[20] The dominance of financial markets was obvious in Mexico, East Asia, Brazil and Argentina in the 1990s.

However, civil society groups concerned with the effects of global markets on equity and democracy have contributed little to the search for a new and better "international financial architecture". CSOs have said little about the effect of tax havens and offshore banking on tax competition; about the potential benefits of forced collective action clauses in sovereign bond issues; about the responsibility of international banks and credit-rating agencies for inadequate risk analysis;

about the absence of leverage restrictions on hedge funds; and so on. All of these questions are relevant to the effectiveness and equity of global financial markets. Commercial financial flows affect people in developing countries indirectly – but far more than World Bank and IMF transfers – through large impacts on economic security as well as the distribution of economic gains and losses.[21]

A few recent and notable exceptions to the absence of civil society work on global financial markets suggest the potential for the future. One initiative is the use of stockholder activism to press for more responsible investment.[22] CSOs have also proposed taxes on international financial transactions (along the lines of the Tobin tax) and have made recommendations for global coordination to reduce the deleterious impact of tax havens on the ability of governments to raise revenue.[23]

The relative neglect of these larger issues may have arisen because the IMF and the World Bank provide easy targets. Perhaps CSOs also concluded that the global market is hopelessly undemocratic and impenetrable. Yet there are earlier examples of apparent success in areas related to global finance – for example, in effective civil society pressure to reduce investment in apartheid South Africa. In any case, problems affecting private flows deserve far more attention from CSOs.

In summary, civil society efforts to influence global finance have been highly concentrated on a few issues and a few official institutions. Attention to the market itself and to the many official and private institutions engaged in some form of organization or regulation of market-driven activities has been limited. Moreover, with regard to the World Bank and the IMF, CSO concern has been focussed on specific issues rather than on the fundamental problem of representation failure and the resulting lack of accountability of the institutions to the poorer countries of the world and to the poor within those countries.

A future role for civil society in global finance

What disinterested global civil society fundamentally wants is more and better (that is, more fair, democratic and effective) governance of the global economic and financial system. On the one hand, the more visible global institutions have come to symbolize – in part correctly – the unrepresentative power of corporate and financial interests in the global economic system. The IFIs make good punching bags for decrying the worst aspects of that system. On the other hand, these institutions are still among the best-available vehicles for managing globalization in the interests of fairness and democracy as well as effectiveness. In that sense, civil society needs them: the IMF, the World Bank, and the WTO, as well as a host of other agencies, including the regional development banks, the BIS, UN agencies and so on.

Consider the analogy with the emergence of the social contract at the national level. To mitigate the worst injustices and inequities that unfettered markets generate, Western capitalist societies all rely on their governments to manage some form of social contract. Over time, as the Western economies became richer and more globally integrated, their governments spent more on publicly financed social programs.[24] At the global level, there is no world government with which global civil society can forge a comparable social contract. Nor are societies ever likely to agree to a global government, at least with the structure and procedures familiar to us in the nation-state. A global government would make the problems of representation even more problematic. So states have muddled through with a potpourri of international institutions. In this messy system of global financial governance, civil society has implicitly treated the IFIs as the best-available vehicles for managing a global social contract.

A future role for civil society in global finance would ideally be built on a more explicit vision by CSOs of the global financial institutions as part of the solution rather than as part of the problem. It is better to live with the IFIs – to push them to become more equitable and democratic – than to live without them. Such a perspective would apply not only to the IMF and the World Bank, but also to the myriad of other institutions that affect the global financial market, such as the G7, the WTO and clubs of central bankers.

With this forward-looking perspective, civil society groups would ideally pay more explicit attention to the fundamental representation failures that mar virtually all of the official institutions that deal with global finance. These representation failures make the institutions less effective and less focused on equity issues than they would otherwise be. These democratic deficits also mean that public institutions are likely to represent less the public interest at the truly global level and more the national interests of the more powerful states and private financial and corporate interests.

Effectiveness and greater emphasis on equity ultimately depend on a better alignment of power with financial responsibility and political accountability, both in the IFIs and in the larger set of public institutions that manage globalization. That alignment requires both greater representation of borrowing countries in the institutions and more democratic representation of their peoples – as taxpayers, consumers, and workers as well as financiers and managers.

Civil society groups in the North appear to view lobbying for better representation of developing countries in the IFIs as a nearly hopeless objective.[25] However, several signs of progress at the official level suggest that openings for change do exist. Political pressure on the major shareholders from disinterested civil society could make a difference. For example, the US has over the years reduced its capital shares in the World Bank and the IDB, usually to minimize new financial commitments. This has made it possible for Japan and (in the case of the IDB) European members to acquire or increase their shares. Today large borrowing states such as Brazil, India and China would no doubt also be prepared to raise their quotas. Indeed, models for multilateral banks that are largely or completely owned by the borrowers do exist. The Andean Development Corporation and the Development Bank of Southern Africa are wholly owned by their borrowers, as are the European Investment Bank and the Nordic Investment Bank.

In addition, recent difficulties in appointing new heads of the WTO and the IMF have generated considerable discussion of the shortcomings of the model under which the advanced economies manage and "own" the leadership positions. In its recent report on IMF reform, the Overseas Development Council, a Washington-based think tank, criticized the effective veto that the United States holds on some Fund decisions.[26] In the case of the WTO, the growing relevance of the developing countries in world trade was relevant to the selection of a Thai citizen as a future head of the organization. In other settings, too, the advanced economies are increasingly anxious to bring the major developing countries into the decision-making process. Thus the recently created Group of Twenty (G20) includes Brazil, China, India, Mexico and others to discuss and move toward a new international financial architecture. To be sure, G7 dominance of global economic governance persists, but these moves also reflect growing sensitivity to the costs of representation failures in an interdependent global system.

True, civil society groups that work with and represent the poor in developing countries probably do not regard additional seats for developing country governments at the official tables of global finance as a high priority. They see – often justifiably – current governments as promoting the interests of local élites rather than those of the poor. However, improved representation of poor countries at the global level would eventually, with deepening democracy, contribute to better representation of the interests of the poor.

The challenge of improving representation within developing countries is a more complicated task for the long run. Here, too, civil society groups could make a difference. There is ample room for advocacy, analysis, and lobbying to make national governments of the South more accountable to their citizens. In particular, civil society groups in the North could encourage efforts to reduce tensions between governments in the South and local CSOs. Northern partners could support training, financial accountability and transparency of CSOs in the South, as well as the development of adequate fiscal and regulatory arrangements for civil society in developing countries. In addition, civil society in the North could help strengthen independent research and policy institutions in developing countries, thereby reducing the near-monopoly of the IMF and the World Bank on economic policy advice in many poor countries.

For the future, then, CSOs should focus more on the issue of representation in the IFIs; and CSOs in the North should work closely with partner CSOs within developing countries to strengthen the latter's technical capacity and to support their efforts in building democracy. In the short run, this approach might seem to limit the capacity of CSOs to push the IFIs on specific issues. In the long run, however, progress on representation questions is probably necessary to make these institutions accountable – and thus more effective and more fair.

Finally, as emphasized earlier, global finance involves much more than public institutions. Particularly for the objective of advancing equity, civil society groups could fruitfully give more attention to how private markets work. Multiple issues and proposals could be addressed. Mandatory collective action clauses in sovereign bond issues might ensure that private creditors (as opposed to local taxpayers) share more of the losses when countries cannot meet their debt obligations. Risk analysis of banks and credit agencies could be more responsible. Derivatives markets that create risks for non-beneficiaries could be better regulated. Greater transparency in international banking, including disclosure of large foreign transfers, would reduce money laundering and discourage outflows of capital from ill-gotten gains.[27] Multilateral agreement on taxing of multinationals on a unitary basis, with mechanisms to allocate revenues internationally, could raise billions of dollars for developing countries.[28] These issues are ripe for benign and creative pressure for reform from disinterested civil society groups. On these issues, civil society can be effective not because it represents electorates, but because it provides a perspective that otherwise goes unheard.

A concluding note

Global economic and financial governance is by its nature imperfect. Global financial markets are imperfect, and many people who are deeply affected by this system are voiceless within it: they lack representation. Although civil society groups are not inherently democratic or representative, many are truly disinterested in the best sense of the word. Indeed, civil society is in some ways better able to think and act globally than official multilateral institutions and private-market associations. For the time being, we can therefore see civil society's watchdog role over the institutions of global finance – public and private – as a legitimate shoring up of what would otherwise be minimal accountability of these institutions to the poor in poor countries. In the long run, however, the global commonwealth will be better served when the disinterested perspective of global civil society has a greater impact on making private markets more transparent and when the public institutions are themselves more representative of all the global public. This will be achieved both when the governments of developing countries are better represented and when those governments better represent the interests of all their citizens.

Notes

1 I am grateful for comments on an earlier draft from John Clark, Brian Deese, Ann Florini, Timothy Kessler, Jan Aart Scholte and Alison Van Rooy, and to Brian Deese for superb research help.
2 Ann Florini and P.J. Simmons, "What the World Needs Now?", in Ann Florini (ed.), *The Third Force: The Rise of Transnational Civil Society*, Toyko and Washington, DC: The Japan Center for International Exchange and the Carnegie Endowment for International Peace, 2000, pp. 2–13.
3 Cf. Council on Foreign Relations, "Safeguarding Prosperity in a Global Financial System: The Future International Financial Architecture", report of an Independent Task Force, 1999; Robert Rubin, "International Financial Architecture", speech given at Johns Hopkins Paul H. Nitze School of Advanced International Studies (SAIS), 21 April 1999; and Barry Eichengreen, *Toward a New International Financial Architecture: A Practical Post-Asia Agenda*, Washington, DC: Institute for International Economics, 1999.
4 Ishac Diwan, "Labor Shares and Financial Crises", unpublished draft paper for the World Bank, 1999.
5 Jere Behrman, Nancy Birdsall and Miguel Szekely, "Economic Reform and Wage Differentials in Latin America", *Inter-American Development Bank Working Paper Series*, No. 435, October 2000.
6 Quoted in Nancy Birdsall, "Managing Inequality in the Developing World", *Current History*, Vol. 98, No. 631, November 1999, pp. 376–81.
7 Robert Dahl, *On Democracy*, New Haven: Yale University Press, 1998.

8 Devesh Kapur, "From Shareholder to Stakeholder: The Changing Anatomy of Governance of the World Bank", Harvard mimeo, 2000.
9 Joseph Stiglitz, "The Insider", *The New Republic*, Vol. 222, No. 16, April 2000, pp. 56–60.
10 Sheri Berman and Kathleen McNamara, "Bank on Democracy," *Foreign Affairs*, Vol. 78, No. 2, March–April 1999, pp. 2–9.
11 Will Wapenhans, "Effective Implementation: Key to Development Impact. Report of the World Bank's Portfolio Management Task Force", Washington, DC: World Bank, 1992.
12 Robert Wade, "Greening the Bank: The Struggle over the Environment, 1970–1995", in Devesh Kapur, John P. Lewis and Richard Webb (eds), *The World Bank: Its First Half Century*, Washington, DC: Brookings Institution, 1997, pp. 611–734; Jonathan A. Fox and L. David Brown (eds), *The Struggle for Accountability: The World Bank, NGOs, and Grassroots Movements*, Cambridge, MA: MIT Press, 1998; Robert O'Brien, Anne Marie Goetz, Jan Aart Scholte and Marc Williams, *Contesting Global Governance*, Cambridge: Cambridge University Press, 2000.
13 On the benefits of greater participation to returns on project investments, see Deepa Narayan, "The Contribution of People's Participation: 121 Rural Water Supply Projects", World Bank, "Workshop on Participatory Development", 1994; Jonathan Isham, Deepa Narayan and Lant Pritchett, "Does Participation Improve Performance? Establishing Causality with Subjective Data", World Bank, 1995; and Bernardo Kliksberg, "Six Unconventional Theories About Participation", *International Review of Administrative Sciences*, Vol. 66, No. 1, March 2000, pp. 61–74.
14 Tony Killick, Ramani Gunatilaka and Ana Marr, *Aid and the Political Economy of Policy Change*, London: Routledge, 1998; Paul Collier, "Consensus-Building, Knowledge and Conditionality", paper presented at the World Bank Annual Conference on Development Economics, April 2000; Joseph Stiglitz, "More Instruments and Broader Goals: Moving towards the Post-Washington Consensus", United Nations University, WIDER Annual Lectures 2, January 1998; Nancy Birdsall, Stijn Claessens and Ishac Diwan, "Will HIPC Matter? The Debt Game and Donor Behavior in Africa", Carnegie Endowment Economic Reform Project Discussion Paper No. 2, March 2001.
15 Nancy Birdsall and Juan Luis Londoño, "Asset Inequality Matters: An Assessment of the World Bank's Approach to Poverty Reduction", *American Economic Review Papers and Proceedings*, Vol. 81, No. 2, May 1997, pp. 32–7.
16 Ernesto Zedillo, "Globaphobia", *Worldlink*, March/April, 2000, available at <http://www.worldlink.co.uk>.
17 Kapur, op. cit.
18 *Report of the Group of Independent Persons Appointed to Conduct an Evaluation of Certain Aspects of the Enhanced Structural Adjustment Facility*, Washington, DC: International Monetary Fund, 1998.
19 Devesh Kapur and Richard Webb, "Governance-Related Conditionalities of the IFIs", G24 Discussion Paper No. 6, August 2000.
20 Kapur, op. cit.
21 Nora Lustig, *Shielding the Poor: Social Protection in the Developing World*, Washington, DC: Brookings Institution Press, 2000.
22 Sophia Tickell and Jenny Kimmis, "UK Pensions and Pro-Poor Investment", unpublished paper, Oxfam, 2000.
23 Oxfam, "Tax Havens, Releasing the Hidden Billions for Poverty Eradication", 2000.
24 Dani Rodrik, "Why Do More Open Economies Have Bigger Governments?", *Journal of Political Economy*, Vol. 106, No. 5, October 1998, pp. 997–1032.
25 Based on personal interviews with a handful of Washington-based CSO representatives.
26 Overseas Development Council, *The Future Role of the IMF in Development*, ODC Task Force Report, April 2000.
27 Cf. Nancy Birdsall and Devesh Kapur, "Clearing Muddy Waters", *Financial Times*, 13 September 1999, p. 14.
28 Oxfam, op. cit.

Index